PLEASE RETU

GEORGE HOLMAN
TRIANGLE
65-13TH AVE

1923
F.H. HOLMAN
17-15th Ave

Manuf. of Hydraulic Cements.

Prof. Bleininger

*Bull. #3 Series 4
Ohio Geol. Survey.*

STRESSES IN STRUCTURES

BY

A. H. HELLER, C.E.
Late Professor of Structural Engineering
Ohio State University

REVISED BY

CLYDE T. MORRIS
Member American Society Civil Engineers
Professor of Structural Engineering
Ohio State University

THIRD EDITION

NEW YORK
JOHN WILEY & SONS, Inc.
London: CHAPMAN & HALL, Limited
1916

COPYRIGHT, 1905,
BY
ALBERT H. HELLER

COPYRIGHT, 1907, 1916,
BY
C. C. HELLER

PRESS OF
BRAUNWORTH & CO.
BOOKBINDERS AND PRINTERS
BROOKLYN, N. Y.

PREFACE.

The object sought to be attained in this book was not the making of an exhaustive scientific treatise on stresses, but to supply in one a text-book suited to the usual limited time which can be given to the subject, and a book of reference for the student in his future practical work, and for the practical engineer whose time is too much taken up to get with advantage from elaborate treatises, a working theory for whatever problem he may have in hand.

This may seem a difficult object to attain in one book. The method in which this object is accomplished is the only claim for originality which the author makes. The points which have been kept in mind are:

1st. A nomenclature to correspond as nearly as possible to general practice in this country, and arranged alphabetically in a table to which reference can be made for the meaning of any letter in a formula wherever found.

2nd. An avoidance of lengthy explanations of demonstrations with a multiplicity of letters and references to figures. The figures are made to speak for themselves as much as possible.

3rd. While elementary proofs are avoided, there will be few things which the engineer, who has not studied Analytical Mechanics and Strength of Materials, will have to take on faith. Indeed, there is much which for the college student will be review, but is put in on account of its fundamental importance.

4th. Not all the matter is intended for class room work, but some only for reference by the student should he have use for it in his future career as an engineer. On the other hand, many things should be amplified and taken up more in detail in connection with the problems which the student solves. The method adopted by the author is to take up a lesson first in the form of a lecture combined with questions, of which the student makes notes. These notes are studied and reviewed at the next meeting of the class. Solutions of problems are required to be kept in neat form in a separate book for future reference.

5th. Numerous references are given so that more extended treatments of different subjects may be readily found by the engineer when occasion requires.

As a book of reference, it is hoped that it will enable the engineer to put more time than usual upon questions of design, which generally receive too little attention both from the standpoint of economy and strength. A. H. HELLER.

The above preface was written by Prof. Heller shortly before his death, which occurred February 20th, 1906.

He had intended to cover, in his book, the common forms of statically indeterminate structures, as well as the three hinged arch and cantilever bridges, as will be seen by repeated references to succeeding chapters which are not included in this book.

We believe that the fourteen chapters here presented, covering as they do the stresses in all the forms of simple trusses, will be of benefit to the profession as a reference book and to schools as a text book. The manuscript for this book was used by Prof. Heller in his classes in typewritten form, and is believed to be comparatively free from errors. We will be glad to have any typographical or other errors brought to our attention.
Columbus, Oct. 9, 1906. C. T. MORRIS.

THE writer has used this book as a text in his classes for the past nine years, and has found that in many places the concise forms of Prof. Heller's statements in the manuscript which he left, and which was published without material alteration in the last edition, were not easily understood by the beginner, and it has been the aim in this edition to expand the explanations and to give numerical examples to illustrate the methods where experience has shown this to be necessary.

There has been little change made in the first four chapters. In this edition, Chapter V includes both Chapters V and VI

PREFACE.

of the old edition, as it was thought there was not a logical reason for dividing the chapter. An explanation of Bow's notation is added and several of the graphical solutions have been redrawn using this notation. A new article on the derrick is also added.

There has been little alteration in old chapters VII, VIII, IX and X, except in the chapter numbers.

Old Chapter XI has been expanded into two chapters, Chapter X on Roof Trusses, and Chapter XI on Bridge Trusses.

In Chapter XII, on Stresses from Uniform Load, solutions have been added for the deck Pratt, sub-divided Warren, Whipple and Pettit trusses, and skew bridges.

In Chapter XIII a complete solution of the stresses in a Pratt truss railroad bridge from wheel loads is added and a moment table is given for Cooper's loading.

In Chapter XIV a more complete explanation is given of the solution of the stresses in bridges with curved track.

Many of the figures have been redrawn and a large number of new ones added.

CLYDE T. MORRIS.

COLUMBUS, O.,
   March, 1916.

Acknowledgment is due from the Publishers to Mr. C. T. Morris, Professor of Structural Engineering, Ohio State University, for the valuable work done by him in the preparation for the press of Professor Heller's manuscript.

TABLE OF CONTENTS.

		Page
Chapter I. *Stresses and Deformations within the Elastic Limits*		1
Art. 1.	Object of the Study of Stresses	1
" 2.	Kinds of Structures	1
" 3.	Forces Acting on Structures	2
" 4.	Kinds of Loads	2
" 5.	Manner of Application of Loads	3
" 6.	Materials of Construction	4
" 7.	Elasticity and Stress	4
" 8.	Elastic Limits	5
" 9.	Deformations	6
" 10.	Unit Stresses	6
" 11.	Modulus of Elasticity	6
" 12.	Kinds of Stress	9
" 13.	Distribution of Stress	10
" 14.	Tensile and Compressive Stresses	12
" 15.	Shearing Stresses	12
" 16.	Shears	13
" 17.	How Shearing Stresses Occur	14
" 18.	Shear Modulus	15
" 19.	Work Done in Deforming a Body. Resilience	16
Chapter II. *Stresses and Deformations Beyond the Elastic Limit*		22
Art. 20.	Non-elastic Stress and Deformation	22
" 21.	Stress-deformation Diagrams	22
" 22.	Ductility and Plasticity	23
" 23.	Ultimate Strength	24
" 24.	Factor of Safety	26
" 25.	Peculiar Properties of Iron and Steel in Non-elastic State	28
" 26.	Shifting of the Elastic Limit	28

TABLE OF CONTENTS.

			Page
Art.	27.	Hardening Effects of Non-elastic Deformation	30
"	28.	Fatigue of Iron and Steel	30

Chapter III. *The Laws of Equilibrium and their Application* 35

Art.	29.	The Problem	35
"	30.	Properties and Relations of Forces	35
"	31.	Two Forces in Equilibrium	37
"	32.	Three Forces in Equilibrium	38
"	33.	Four Forces in Equilibrium	39
"	34.	Any Number of Forces in Equilibrium	40
"	35.	Force Polygon	41
"	36.	Location of Resultant	42
"	37.	The String Polygon	42
"	38.	Properties of the String Polygon	43
"	39.	The Laws of Equilibrium	44
"	40.	Methods of Application of the Equations of Equilibrium	45
"	41.	Which Equations of Equilibrium to use	47
"	42.	Statically Indeterminate Cases	49
"	43.	Comparison of Graphic and Algebraic Methods	50
"	44.	Rules to be Observed in the Use of the Graphic Methods	51

Chapter IV. *Application of the Laws of Equilibrium to the Structure as a Whole. Reactions* 55

Art.	45.	Reactions	55
"	46.	Reactions for a Single Force	55
"	47.	Reactions for any Number of Loads	60
"	48.	Reactions for Uniform Loads	63

Chapter V. *Application of the Laws of Equilibrium to a Part of a Structure. Stresses* 67

Art.	49.	Stresses	67
"	50.	Stresses in the Simplest Form of Truss. Stress Diagrams	67
"	51.	Stresses in a Crane	70

TABLE OF CONTENTS.

		Page
Art. 52.	Stresses in an Unsymmetrical Truss Unsymmetrically Loaded.	71
" 53.	Bow's Notation.	72
" 54.	Stresses in a Roof Truss for Wind Load.	73
" 55.	Stresses in a Cantilever Truss.	74
" 56.	Stresses in a Compound Fink Roof Truss for Vertical Loads.	75
" 57.	Stresses in Solid Beams.	76
" 58.	Stresses in Trusses. Algebraic Solution.	77
" 59.	Stresses in a Truss with Parallel Chords.	79
" 60.	Graphical Solution by Sections. Culman's Method.	80
" 61.	Graphical Solution. The Method of Sections by Moments.	81
" 62.	Stresses in Derricks.	84
" 63.	The String Polygon as a Moment Diagram.	87
" 64.	The Graphic Method of Sections for Uniform Loads.	87
" 65.	Moment Areas.	88
Chapter VI.	*Stresses in Beams and Girders.*	91
Art. 66.	Classification of Beams.	91
" 67.	General Consideration of Stresses in Solid Beams.	92
" 68.	Bending Stresses in Solid Beams. Theory of Flexure.	92
" 69.	Bending Stresses and Moments of Resistance for a Beam of Rectangular Cross Section.	96
" 70.	Moment of Resistance for a Beam of Any Cross Section.	96
" 71.	Location of the Neutral Axis.	99
" 72.	Moments of Inertia.	101
" 73.	Oblique Loading.	103
" 74.	Relation between the Bending Moment and the Shear at Any Cross Section of a Beam.	107
" 75.	Shearing Stresses in a Solid Beam.	108
" 76.	Resultant of Bending and Shearing Stresses. Principal Stresses in Beams.	112
" 77.	Lines of Principal Stress.	116

TABLE OF CONTENTS.

Page

Art. 78. Working Stresses for Cases of Compound Stress.............................. 117
" 79. Stresses in Girders........................ 118
" 80. Beams Stressed beyond the Elastic Limit..... 121

Chapter VII. *Deflection of Beams and Girders*............. 127

Art. 81. Equation of the Elastic Line................. 127
" 82. Deflection of a Cantilever Beam for a Load at its End............................. 129
" 83. Deflection of a Beam Supported at its Ends and Uniformly Loaded................... 130
" 84. Deflection of a Beam Supported at its Ends and Carrying a Single Load at Any Point.. 131
" 85. Deflection of a Beam Carrying a Number of Loads................................. 132
" 86. Deflection of a Beam or Girder having a Variable Cross Section........................ 133
" 87. Deflection of a Beam Due to Shear.......... 135
" 88. Resilience of Beams...................... 137
" 89. Points of Contrary Flexure................. 140

Chapter VIII. *Special Cases of Beams and Girders Loaded and Supported in Different Ways*....................... 144

Art. 90. Explanation of Table..................... 144
" 91. Shear and Moment Diagrams.............. 154
" 92. Shears and Moments in Cantilever Beams... 154
" 93. Shears and Moments in a Beam Supported at Both Ends............................ 155
" 94. Combinations of Concentrated and Uniform Loads on Cantilever Beams and Beams Supported at the Ends.................. 156
" 95. Bending Moments and Shears for Beams having Fixed Ends...................... 157
" 96. Bending Moments and Shears for Continuous Beams................................. 158
" 97. General Equations for Continuous Beams.... 160
" 98. Practical Uses of Continuous Beams........ 163
" 99. Live Loads on Beams..................... 164
" 100. Two Concentrated Moving Loads a Fixed Distance Apart........................ 164

TABLE OF CONTENTS.

		Page
Art. 101.	Any Number of Concentrated Moving Loads, Fixed Distances Apart	165
" 102.	A Continuous Uniform Moving Load	166
" 103.	Combination of Uniform Live and Uniform Dead Load	167
" 104.	Maximum Live Load Shears in a Continuous Beam of Two Spans	167
" 105.	Maximum Live Load Shears in a Continuous Beam of Three Spans	169
" 106.	Maximum Live Load Moment in a Continuous Beam of Two Spans	169
" 107.	Maximum Live Load Moment in a Continuous Beam of Three Spans	170

Chapter IX.	*Stresses in Blocks and Columns*	175
Art. 108.	Concentric Loads on Blocks	175
" 109.	Eccentric Loads on Blocks	175
" 110.	Columns Eccentrically Loaded	179
" 111.	Columns Concentrically Loaded	182
" 112.	End Conditions	184
" 113.	Column Formulas	189
" 114.	Columns in Towers	190
" 115.	Combination of Buckling and Bending	197

Chapter X.	*Roof Trusses*	206
Art. 116.	Roof Construction	206
" 117.	Truss Elements	206
" 118.	Types of Roof Trusses	207
" 119.	Stresses in Roof Trusses	209

Chapter XI.	*Bridge Trusses*	214
Art. 120.	Construction	214
" 121.	Classification of Trusses	217
" 122.	Bridge Trusses now out of Date	218
" 123.	Modern Bridge Trusses	222
" 124.	Special Types of Bridge Trusses	227

Chapter XII.	*Stresses in Simple Bridge Trusses for Uniform Loads*	233
Art. 125.	Dead Loads for Bridges	233
" 126.	Live Loads	234

TABLE OF CONTENTS.

		Page
Art. 127.	General Considerations Regarding Stresses in Simple Trusses..................	235
" 128.	Position of Live Load for Maximum Chord Stresses..........................	239
" 129.	Position of Live Load for Maximum Web Stresses............................	241
" 130.	Stresses in a Pratt Truss by Coefficients.....	246
" 131.	Stresses in a Simple Warren Truss..........	251
" 132.	Stresses in a Sub-divided Warren Truss.....	253
" 133.	Stresses in a Half Hip Truss................	255
" 134.	Stresses in a Whipple Truss................	256
" 135.	Stress Coefficients for a Double Intersection Warren Truss............................	257
" 136.	Stresses in a Baltimore Truss..............	260
" 137.	Stresses in a Camel Back Truss............	268
" 138.	Stresses in a Pettit Truss..................	277
" 139.	Skew Bridges.............................	281

Chapter XIII. Stresses in Railway Bridges from Wheel Loads 285

Art. 140.	Kinds of Stress	285
" 141.	Loading.................................	285
" 142.	Equivalent Loadings......................	286
" 143.	Preliminary Considerations in the Calculation of Stresses from Wheel Loads............	287
" 144.	Position of Load for Maximum Moment at Any Point of a Truss or Girder...........	289
" 145.	Maximum Moment in a Deck Plate Girder...	291
" 146.	Limits of Span for which a Particular Series of Wheel Loads will Give a Maximum Moment..............................	292
" 147.	Position of Load for Maximum Web Stresses in a Truss.............................	293
" 148.	Particular Cases of the Application of the Criterion for Maximum Web Stresses.....	294
" 149.	Maximum Shear in a Pratt Truss..........	294
" 150.	Fields of Shear in a Truss.................	295
" 151.	Position of Load for Maximum Shear in a Girder or Beam.......................	295

TABLE OF CONTENTS.   xiii

			Page
Art.	152.	Maximum Floor Beam Concentration and Stress in the Hip Vertical	296
"	153.	Stresses in a Pratt Truss for Wheel Loads.	297
"	154.	Maximum Stresses in Trusses with Sub-Panels	305
"	155.	Calculation of Moments and Shears by Wheel Loads	306
"	156.	Equivalent Uniform Loads	311
"	157.	Graphical Methods	312

Chapter XIV.	Stresses in Bridges from Horizontal Forces	316
Art. 158.	Wind Loads	316
" 159.	Lateral Systems	317
" 160.	Deck Plate Girder Lateral Systems	317
" 161.	Through Plate Girder and Pony Truss Lateral Systems	318
" 162.	Deck Bridge Lateral Systems	318
" 163.	Through Bridge Lateral Systems	321
" 164.	Portal Bracing	322
" 165.	General Case of Portal with Columns Fixed at Both Ends	324
" 166.	General Case of Portal with Posts Fixed at Top and Partially Fixed at the Bottom	329
" 167.	General Case of Portal with Columns Partially Fixed at Both Ends	332
" 168.	Particular Cases of Stresses in Portal Bracing	334
" 169.	Case No. 1, Simple X Bracing	335
" 170.	Case No. 2, Plate Girder Portal	342
" 171.	Case No. 3, Latticed Portal	344
" 172.	Case No. 4, Knee Braced Portal	345
" 173.	Case No. 5, Latticed Portal for Shallow Trusses	347
" 174.	Case No. 6, Plate Girder Portal, Knee Braced	348
" 175.	Plate Girder Portal for Shallow Trusses	350
" 176.	Stresses in Railway Bridges having Curved Track	350

NOTATION.

The same letter is sometimes used to denote entirely different quantities which can not possibly be mistaken for each other.

Sub-scripts and super-scripts denote particular values or values referred to particular axes, origins, or points.

In general, capital letters denote totals, small letters denote units and distances, and Greek letters denote angles.

Max. and min. written as sub-scripts denote maximum and minimum values.

$A = $ total area of cross section (square inches).
$A_f = $ net area of *one* flange (square inches).
$A_w = $ gross area of the cross section of the web $=$ th.
$a = $ distance shown in the figure.
$b = $ width of a rectangular cross section.
  $= $ width center to center of supports.
  $= $ distance shown in the figure.
$C = $ centrifugal force per pound.
C_1, C_2, C', etc. $= $ constants of integration.
$c = $ distance shown in figure.
$D = $ total direct stress in posts with portal attached.
D_1, D_2, D_3, etc. $= $ stresses in diagonal members.
$D_c = $ degree of curve of track.
D. L. $= $ dead load or dead load stress.
$d = $ distance from the neutral axis to a parallel axis.
  $= $ depth between centers of gravity of the flanges of a girder.
  $= $ depth between centers of chords of trusses.
  $= $ differential when written in connection with and preceding a variable.
$dA = $ an infinitesimal element of area.
$E = $ modulus of elasticity in tension or compression (pounds per square inch).
  $= $ equilibrant of two or more forces.
$E_s = $ modulus of elasticity in shear or shear modulus (pounds per square inch).

NOTATION.

e = eccentricity of the center of gravity of a train with regard to the center line of the bridge.
  = distance shown in the figure.
H = horizontal reaction.
  = $4 + 8n + n^2$.
h = height of a rectangular cross section.
  = depth of the web of a girder.
I = moment of inertia of an area about its neutral axis.
I_Q = moment of inertia of an area about an axis QQ parallel to the neutral axis.
I_v = moment of inertia about the principal axis VV.
I_z = moment of inertia about the principal axis ZZ.
k = in continuous beams, a fraction less than unity which multiplied by the span length gives the distance of a load from a support.
k_0 = that value of k which corresponds with x_0.
k_1 = distance center to center of bearings, on the pin, at the top of the post.
k_2 = distance center to center of bearings, on the pin, at the bottom of the post.
L = total length.
L_1, L_2, L_3, etc. = stresses in lower chord members.
$L. L.$ = live load or live load stress.
l_1, l_2, etc. = partial lengths of L.
M = moment at any point or bending moment (foot pounds or inch pounds).
M_1, M_2, M_a, etc. = moment at points 1, 2, a, etc.
M_R = moment of resistance of a beam.
M_s = statical moment of an area.
M_x = moment at a distance x from the origin = M.
m = ratio of longitudinal to transverse deformation = reciprocal of Poisson's ratio.
N = number of panels.
n = a factor less than unity which multiplied by l gives the span length nl.
P = concentrated load or force or panel load.
P_1, P_2, P_3, etc. = concentrated loads from left to right.
P_i = instantaneously applied load.
p = panel length.
q = proportion of dead load at unloaded chord.

NOTATION.

$R =$ reaction.
   $=$ resultant of two or more forces or loads.
R_1, R_2, etc. $=$ reactions beginning at the left.
       $=$ rays in a force polygon.
$r =$ radius of gyration.
  $=$ radius of a circle.
$S =$ total shear or total shearing stress on a section.
$S_x =$ total shear at a distance x from the origin $= S$ (pounds).
$s =$ unit stress (pounds per square inch).
$s_1 =$ unit stress in the extreme upper fiber of a beam's cross section.
$s_2 =$ unit stress in the extreme lower fiber of a beam's cross section.
$s_c =$ unit stress in compression.
$s_s =$ unit stress in shear.
$s_t =$ unit stress in tension.
$s_w =$ working unit stress.
$s_u =$ ultimate strength in bending or modulus of rupture in cross-breaking.
$t =$ thickness of web plate (inches).
U_1, U_2, etc. $=$ stresses in upper chord members.
$V =$ vertical reaction due to horizontal forces.
V_1, V_2, etc. $=$ stresses in vertical members.
       $=$ vertical components of inclined reactions.
$v =$ vertical distance perpendicular to the neutral axis.
  $=$ coördinate parallel to the principal axis VV.
$v_1 =$ distance of the extreme upper fiber of a beam's cross section from the neutral axis.
$v_2 =$ distance of the extreme lower fiber of a beam's cross section from the neutral axis.
$W =$ total uniform load.
$w =$ uniform load per unit of length (pounds per foot).
  $=$ distance shown in figure.
$x =$ horizontal coördinate or distance lengthwise of a beam.
$x_0 =$ distance of point of zero moment from the origin.
$y =$ vertical coördinate or deflection of the elastic line.
$y_i =$ deflection due to an instantaneously applied load.
$y_{max} =$ maximum deflection of the elastic line.
$z =$ coördinate parallel to the principal axis ZZ.
$\alpha =$ angle shown in Fig.
$\beta =$ angle shown in Fig.

NOTATION.

δ = unit deformation in line of stress for tension or compression (inches per inch).

δ_s = unit deformation due to shear (inches per inch) = angle produced, in circular measure.

δL = total deformation in length L (inches).

θ = angle shown in the Fig. and usually measured from the vertical. Also see Eq. (49), page 173.

π = 3.1416.

Σ = "the sum of" = summation of all terms similar to that following this sign.

$\int$ = sign of integration and denotes the summation of all the infinitesimal values of the following variable.

ϕ = angle shown in the Fig.

∞ = infinity.

CHAPTER I.

STRESSES AND DEFORMATIONS WITHIN THE ELASTIC LIMITS.

1. Object of the Study of Stresses. In order that an engineer may be able to design structures to resist forces—to carry loads—he must know how forces are transmitted, and the properties of the materials of construction for transmitting them. The subject consists of two distinct parts:

1. The stresses must be calculated; this part is based upon that branch of mechanics called *statics*, which treats of the equilibrium of forces.

2. The amount and distribution of material in a structure must be determined so as to resist the stresses safely and economically; this part is based upon the *strength of materials* as determined by experiments.

In what follows, only so much of the second part of the subject will be considered as is necessary to bring out the practical applications of the first part.

2. Kinds of Structures. The kinds of structures to be considered are beams, girders and trusses, singly and in combinations forming railway and highway bridges, roofs, buildings, cranes, etc.

A beam, in general, is a single piece or a combination of pieces of material which carries loads in cross bending between or beyond supports.

An engineer's definition of a *simple beam* is one consisting of a single piece, as a stick of timber or an I beam, but in building construction an architect's definition is any member which *directly* carries external loads in cross bending.

The engineer's definition of *a girder* is a beam which is built up of a number of pieces rigidly held together, while the architect terms *a girder* any member in cross bending, which carries the ends of other beams, whether it be composed of one or many pieces. Several forms of girders are shown in Fig. 1.

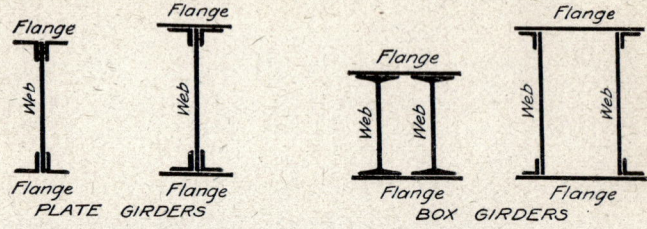

Fig. 1.

A *plate girder* is a girder having one web—a single plate.

A *box girder* is a girder having two or more webs.

The flanges are usually made of angles or of angles and plates.

A TRUSS[1] is a beam composed of a number of *members* connected together, by pins or rivets, so as to form a stable structure, the stresses in the members being tensile and compressive, and the loads being applied at the joints.[2] See Fig. 2 for the names of the different members of a truss and Chapter XI for different kinds of trusses.

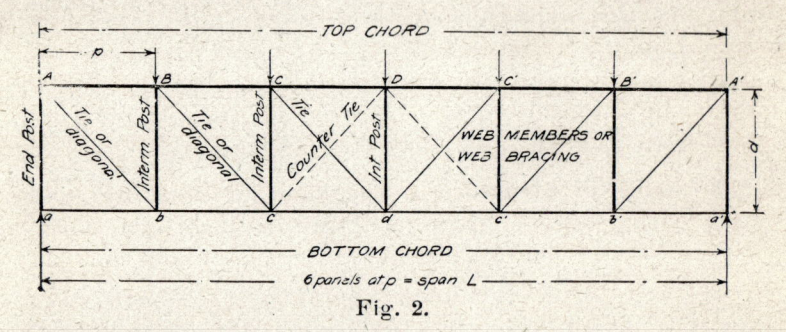

Fig. 2.

3. Forces Acting on Structures. When structures are in service there are *external* and *internal* forces acting. The external forces are the *loads* and the *reactions*. The *reactions* are caused by the loads and are the forces acting at the supports to hold the structure in equilibrium.

---

[1] The term girder is sometimes used in place of truss, especially for continuous or lattice trusses.

[2] Occasionally, a truss carries loads which are not applied at the joints and some of the members must also act as beams.

The *internal forces* produced by the loads are called *stresses*. The stresses are the internal resistances offered by the material to the deformations caused by the loads.

4. Kinds of Loads. The *dead load* consists of the weight of the structure itself, together with such accessories as are permanently fixed in position.

A LIVE LOAD is a moving load, or one that moves over the structure, and may have any practical points of application. It is assumed that a railway train moves over a bridge on the track and a horse on the roadway. Pedestrians, vehicles, the wind blowing against a moving train, and traveling cranes are examples of live loads[1].

A CONCENTRATED LOAD is one that is treated as being applied at a single point or along a line, such as a wheel load. Practically, every load is applied over an area although this area may be very small.

A DISTRIBUTED LOAD is a continuous load applied over an area and is usually *uniformly distributed*. A structure's own weight is usually taken as uniformly distributed, and live loads are often *assumed* to be uniformly distributed. The pressure of water against a dam, or of earth against a retaining wall, are examples of *non-uniformly distributed* loads.

5. Manner of Application of Loads. Loads are applied gradually, more or less suddenly or with *impact*.

A dead load, like the structure's own weight or the weight of snow, is usually gradually applied but not necessarily so.

Theoretically the effect of an instantaneously applied load, if it is not applied with a blow, is double that of a gradually applied load (19), but the effect of a suddenly applied load is usually much less, unless it is applied with a blow.

A LIVE LOAD may be gradually applied, but is usually applied more or less suddenly and with some impact. The weight of a railway train is applied to a bridge more or less suddenly, depending on its speed; it is also applied with impact on account of some of the moving parts of the engine being unbalanced, on account of "flat wheels," "low joints," etc. The striking of a horse's hoofs upon the floor of a bridge, and the jolting of a vehicle due to inequalities of the floor, are examples of impact.

---

[1]The definitions of dead and live loads here given do not correspond with those given in mechanics but with the usage of engineers.

All loads, (dead or live), which are not gradually applied, produce *vibrations* which gradually disappear if the loads come to rest on the structure. In other words, the distortions of the structure are momentarily greater than for the same *static loads* and these are evidences of stresses, exceeding the *static stresses,* which may be called *vibratory stresses.*

If the *impulses* causing vibration are applied at intervals corresponding in a certain way with the time of vibration of the structure, the effect will be *cumulative,* and the stresses may be very great. Practically, there is more or less interference[1].

Vibratory stresses are usually the result of a number of different causes, and it is important that the construction be of such a character as to keep them within proper limits; allowance is usually made for them in a more or less arbitrary manner under the name of *impact stresses.*

IMPACT STRESSES usually include all stresses in excess of those due to the same loads gradually applied. *The total equivalent static stress is, then, equal to the sum of the dead load, live load, and impact stresses.* In getting stresses, all loads are treated as being gradually applied, producing static stresses. To make allowance for impact, a certain percentage of the live load stress is added, depending upon the directness with which the live load stress is imparted. The impact stress is greater for a short span than for a long one[2].

6. Materials of Construction. The ordinary materials of construction are stone, brick, concrete, timber, cast iron, cast steel, wrought iron, and steel. Steel is the material most largely used for structures in which the engineer has most to do with stresses.

These materials have various properties to a greater or lesser degree, such as density, hardness, brittleness, ductility, elasticity, strength, etc. The most important of these are strength, elasticity and ductility.

7. Elasticity and Stress. The materials of construction are more or less elastic, that is, they undergo changes of form under the action of forces. Let Fig. 3 represent a bar held rigidly at

---

[1] For a full account of measurements of vibrations of railway bridges and their causes, see a paper by Professor F. E. Turneaure in the Trans. Am. Soc. C. E. Vol. 41, p. 411, and a paper by Professor S. W. Robinson in the Trans. Am. Soc. C. E. Vol. 16, p. 42.

[2] See the bridge specifications of the Am. Ry. Engineering and Maintenance of Way Assoc.

Art. 8. ELASTIC LIMITS. 5

its upper end; if a weight W be suspended from it, it will stretch; at the same time a resistance is developed in it which increases, as the bar becomes deformed, until it balances, or holds in equilibrium, the external forces acting on the bar and the deformation ceases.

A STRESS is the internal resistance developed in a body by forces deforming it. A stress may be imagined to be carried from molecule to molecule as the links of a chain transmit a force by acting in *opposite directions* upon each other, so that, at *any* imaginary cross section as pq, Fig. 3, the internal forces are acting in opposite directions and away from the section. In this way, the effect of the weight W is transmitted through the bar to its support at the top, producing a stress at every cross section equal to W. *It is plain that, at the ends of the bar, the stresses will have opposite directions, just as the external forces have opposite directions.*

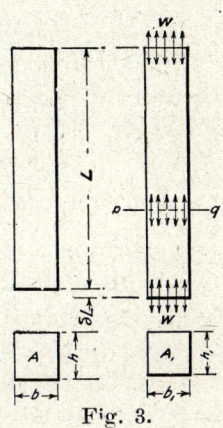

Fig. 3.

In Fig. 4 the directions of action of the external forces and stresses are reversed —the bar is in *compression;* the bar of Fig. 3 is in *tension.*

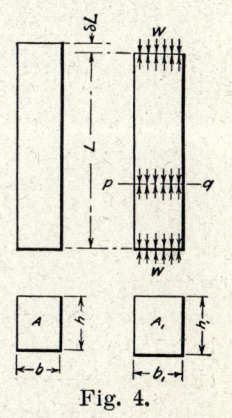

8. Elastic Limits. If, from the bars of Figs. 3 and 4, the loads be removed, they will return to their original dimensions or shape, provided the stresses have not exceeded a certain limit called the *elastic limit.* It has been found by experiments, that for steel *stresses and deformations are directly proportional to each other within a certain limit called the limit of proportionality.*

Fig. 4.

(HOOKE'S LAW). Practically, these two limits are the same, although the true elastic limit is below the limit of proportionality (21).

When the stress has exceeded the elastic limit, some of the deformation is permanent and the body is said to have *taken a set.*

The elastic limit of any material depends upon its grade and quality, and is much more sharply defined in wrought iron and steel than in other materials of construction. Cast iron and timber, for example, can scarcely be said to have elastic limits, but, practically, certain values may be assigned within which the permanent deformations are negligible.

9. Deformations.[1] Besides the longitudinal deformations in the bars of Figs. 3 and 4, there are also transverse deformations; the area of the cross section is contracted in tension and expanded in compression, so that in one case A_1 is less, and in the other case A_1 is greater than A. *Within the elastic limits the deformations are proportional to the stress, and depend upon its intensity.*

The relation between the longitudinal and transverse deformations has not been well determined for most materials, but for metals the *transverse deformation* is usually taken from $\frac{1}{5}$ to $\frac{1}{4}$ (*Poisson's Ratio*) as much per inch as the longitudinal; this ratio may be taken as 0.3 for iron and steel.

10. Unit Stresses. If the forces W are applied uniformly over the ends of a bar, the stress at any cross section will be uniformly distributed, and the unit stress will be the stress per unit of area.

$$s = \frac{W}{A_1} = \frac{W}{A} \text{ (nearly)} \qquad (1)$$

Within the elastic limit, deformations are so small that A and A_1 are practically equal and, in any case, it is usually the stress per unit of *original* area that is wanted.

WORKING STRESSES for structures are the unit stresses used in their design (24), and are taken well within the elastic limits. If the elastic limits were exceeded in any part of a structure, it would not return to its original shape, and might finally become unfit for the purpose for which it was intended; there might also be a dangerous redistribution of stresses. We are, therefore, chiefly concerned with stresses within the elastic limits.

11. Modulus of Elasticity. *According to Hooke's Law, deformations and stresses within the elastic limits, for any one kind of stress, are proportional to each other.* For example, if a bar of steel having an elastic limit of 40000 lbs. per square inch be subjected to a pull of 10000 lbs., producing an elongation of 0.01 in.,

---

[1] The term *strain* is used by most writers to denote the deformation accompanying stress, but since engineers commonly use strain to denote stress, the term is here avoided.

Art. 11.   MODULUS OF ELASTICITY.   7

a pull of 20000 lbs. will produce an elongation of 0.02 in., of 25000 lbs., 0.025 in., etc. The constant ratio of stress to deformation is a physical constant, usually represented by E, and is called the *modulus* (measure) *of elasticity*; for tension and compression, it is the same and is called *Young's Modulus*. In the form of an equation.
$$\delta = \frac{s}{E} \text{ or } E\delta = s \qquad (2)$$

For steel E is about 29000000 when δ is in inches and s in pounds per square inch, that is, the *longitudinal deformation per lineal inch is* $\frac{1}{29000000}$ *part of an inch for every pound stress per square inch of cross section*[2].

Referring to a steel bar as shown in Fig. 3, if $W = 60000$ lbs., $b = 2$ in., $h = 3$ in., $L = 290$ in., we have $A = 6$ sq. in., $s = 10000$ lbs., per sq. in.; $\delta = \frac{10000}{29000000} = \frac{1}{2900}$ in.; $\delta L = \frac{290}{2900} = 0.1$ in.; $b_1 = 2 - \frac{2 \times 0.3}{2900}$ and $h_1 = 3 - \frac{3 \times 0.3}{2900}$. It is evident that A_1 will be but slightly smaller than A.

The modulus of elasticity is a measure of the stiffness of a material. Since $\delta = \frac{s}{E}$, for the same unit stress, *the deformation will be least for the material having the greatest modulus of elasticity*. Steel and iron are stiffer than timber. Stiffness is important in structures subjected to impact stresses.

There is naturally considerable variation in the value of a physical constant, particularly for some materials; the following values of Young's Modulus may be taken as general values.

YOUNG'S MODULI OF ELASTICITY.[3]

White oak and long-leaf pine 1000000 to 2000000.
Wrought iron 26000000 to 30000000.
Steel 27000000 to 31000000 (includes all grades).
Cast iron 12000000 to 15000000 (increases with strength).

---

[1]This equation is easily remembered; it can not be $Es = \delta$ because this would give an absurdly large deformation.

[2]Some writers use the term coefficient of elasticity in place of modulus of elasticity, but in order to have the coefficient in the form usually given to physical constants, it would have to be the reciprocal of the modulus. For steel, the coefficient of elasticity would be $\frac{1}{29000000} = 0.0000000345$. Comparing this with the coefficient for thermal expansion, the total change in length due to a change of temperature of t degrees equals 0.00000665 Lt and the total change in length due to a change of stress of s pounds per square inch equals 0.0000000345 Ls.

[3]For further data with regard to the modulous of elasticity, see Johnson's *Materials of Construction*, Burr's *Elasticity and Resistance of the Materials of Engineering*, Goodman's *Mechanics Applied to Engineering*, and Ewing's *Strength of Materials*.

In members composed of two different materials, if the deformations are equal, from Hooke's law the unit stresses in the materials will be directly proportional to their moduli of elasticity. This gives us a means of estimating the stresses in the two materials of a reinforced concrete member due to shrinkage in setting or to temperature changes.

Suppose a bar of steel one inch square were embedded in the center of a concrete member 6 in. square, and the whole subjected to a fall in temperature of 40° Fahr. If the coefficient of expansion of the steel is .0000065, and of the concrete .0000055, the drop in temperature will cause tension in the steel and compression in the concrete, the bond between the two being assumed to be perfect.

If the two materials could contract independently, the steel would contract $40 \times .0000065 = .00026$ in. per inch of length, and the concrete would contract $40 \times .0000055 = .00022$ in. per inch; but the combination being firmly bonded, will contract some amount between these two values, causing tension in the steel and compression in the concrete. As equilibrium exists in the member the total tension in the steel must equal the total compression in the concrete, or

$$s_s A_s = s_c A_c, \quad \text{from which} \quad s_s = 35 s_c. \quad \ldots \quad (a)$$

The total deformation in each material will be the algebraic sum of the deformations due to temperature and to stress, and these total deformations must be equal, as the bond is not broken.

Let δ_{st} = deformation of steel due to temperature;

δ_{ss} = deformation of steel due to stress;

δ_{ct} = deformation of concrete due to temperature;

δ_{cs} = deformation of concrete due to stress;

$E_s = 30{,}000{,}000$;

$E_c = 2{,}000{,}000$.

Then $\delta_{st} - \delta_{ss} = \delta_{ct} + \delta_{cs}$, or

$$.00026 - \frac{s_s}{30000000} = .00022 + \frac{s_c}{2000000} \quad \ldots \ldots \ldots (b)$$

Solving equations (*a*) and (*b*) we get

$$s_s = 840 \text{ lbs. per sq. in.}$$

$$s_c = \frac{840}{35} = 24 \text{ lbs. per sq. in.}$$

12. Kinds of Stress. The fundamental idea of a stress is that of *two equal, opposite forces* acting in any direction on the opposite sides of a plane section, taken in any direction, through any point of a body at which the stress is desired. It is usually desired to find that section for which the intensity of stress is a maximum, since this is the stress to which the working unit stresses are applied to determine the required area of the section.

It may be shown that, in general, there are three stresses, of *tension* or *compression*, acting at *right angles to each other*, which are called *principal stresses;* these simple principal stresses occur in any body under stress no matter how produced. Since we usually have to deal with forces assumed to act in a plane, we consider only two principal stresses; *the intensity of stress in the direction of one of these is greater, and of the other is less, than in any other direction.*[1] In the case of simple tension, Fig. 5, the maximum principal stress is equal to P acting on the section CD. On *any* inclined section, AB, there will be a normal component N (tension) and a tangential component S, called a SHEARING STRESS. If the material is homogeneous (isotropic), CD is the critical section; but if it were timber, for example, with the grain running in the direction AB, the critical section would be AB.

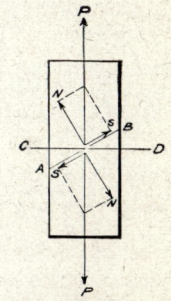

Fig. 5.

It is evident, then, that *wherever there are tensile or compressive stresses there will also be shearing stresses, except on particular planes perpendicular to the principal stresses.* It is evident too that a tensile (or compressive) stress may be the resultant of a shearing stress and a tensile (or compressive) stress. Tensile and compressive stresses may also result from

---

[1] See Merriman's *Mechanics of Materials,* Greene's *Structural Mechanics* Alexander and Thompson's *Applied Mechanics* or Rankine's *Applied Mechanics.*

shearing stresses and pure shearing stress from tensile and compressive stresses of equal intensities acting at right angles to each other[1].

Practically, it is seldom necessary to find the resultant of several stresses, but in addition to the three simple stresses, three others are distinguished, which are due to a non-uniform distribution of tension, compression and shear. The different kinds of stress are,

1. Tensile. Molecules pulling against each other.
2. Compressive. Molecules pushing against each other.
3. Shearing. Molecules sliding past each other.
4. Bending. A combination of tension and compression in different parts.
5. Buckling. A combination of compression and bending.
6. Torsional. Shearing by twisting.

Tensile stresses occur in trusses; shearing and bending stresses in simple beams and girders; buckling stresses in the compression members of all beams and in columns; and torsional stresses are usually avoided.

Combinations of the above *stresses* are of frequent occurrence and are usually treated as being simply superimposed, but this is not always strictly correct.

13. Distribution of Stress. The ordinary cases of the distribution of the intensity of stress are illustrated in Fig. 6. Cases (e), (f), and (g) are combinations of the other cases. *Beyond the elastic limit the distribution of stress is different except for cases (a) and (b).*

Practically, it is difficult to get these ideal distributions of stress. The following are some of the variations from ideal conditions.

(a) The material may not be of homogeneous structure as in wood, for example; indeed any material will vary somewhat from perfect homogeneity.

(b) There may be initial stresses due to unequal heat treatment; this is particularly true of cast iron in which the outer parts are in compression, due to the cooling of the inner parts

---

[1] For investigations of interesting conditions of stress, see works on mechanics.

Art. 13.   DISTRIBUTION OF STRESS.   11

after the outer have solidified; the resistance of the outer parts to the contraction of the inner produces initial tension in the latter.

Initial stresses may be largely eliminated by annealing or by stresses which are large enough to produce considerable permanent set.

(c) There may be undiscoverable defects, such as blowholes

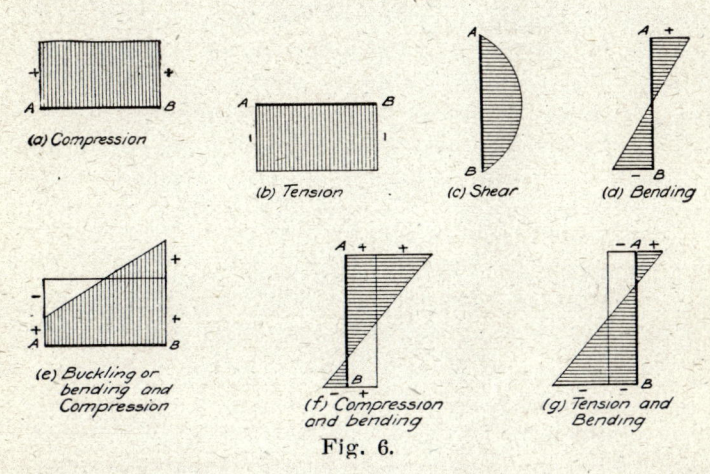

(a) Compression
(b) Tension
(c) Shear
(d) Bending
(e) Buckling or bending and Compression
(f) Compression and bending
(g) Tension and Bending

Fig. 6.

in castings, which might have the same effect as an eccentric application of the load.

(d) It is difficult to apply a force exactly in the axis of a tension or compression piece so as to produce a uniform distribution of stress.

(e) If there is any interference with the transverse deformation of a tension or compression piece, the longitudinal deformations will be changed. If there be a hole or a notch (Fig. 7) in a tension piece, the *unit strength* on a section through the notch or hole will be greater than for a plain piece; the material outside of the notch, near it, acts like a transverse force to prevent contraction of the cross section. This effect disappears when the notch is made long enough, but near the point of transition, from the smaller to the larger sections, there will be a non-uniform distribution of stress; the transition should be a gradual one.

Fig. 7.   In a block under compression, there is always friction on the faces to which the external forces are applied, and this interferes with lateral expansion.

(f) The form of the cross section has some influence upon the distribution of stress and deformation, because the fibers do not act independently as is ordinarily assumed; that is, a bar of circular cross section will not offer exactly the same resistance as one of rectangular cross section having the same area; nor will one bar, whose area is equal to the total area of four bars, offer the same resistance as the four bars.

Since the parts of a solid body can not be deformed independently, there is, even within the elastic limit, a constant tendency to equalize the stress on any section. As soon as one part is deformed more than another it throws more stress upon adjacent parts, but abrupt changes of section should always be avoided in order that the stress may be uniformily distributed.

14. Tensile and Compressive Stresses. Tensile and compressive stresses are alike except that they act in opposite directions; they are *normal stresses*. Forces which elongate a body in the direction of their action, produce tensile stresses in it, while those which compress it, produce compressive stresses. The intensity of stress in either case is determined by equation (1), page 6. It is important to note, however, that when the ratio of the length to the least lateral dimension of a piece in compression, exceeds a not well defined amount—when the piece is a *column* and not a *block*—there will be buckling stress; this is treated under columns in Chapter IX.

15. Shearing Stresses. Forces which deform a body by moving parallel surfaces past each other, produce shearing stresses in it; these are *tangential stresses*. Scissors and shears produce shearing stresses in a single plane as nearly as may be. In Fig. 8, there are shearing stresses in the bolt along the planes AB and CD.

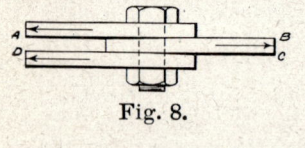

Fig. 8.

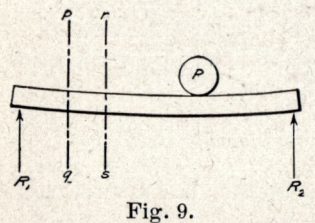

A weight on a beam as in Fig. 9, produces shearing stresses at *every* cross section of the beam because its effect must be transmitted to the supports, producing

Fig. 9.

Art. 16. SHEARS. 13

the reactions R_1 and R_2. This is a case of much practical importance. The shearing stresses may be considered separately from the bending stress which also occurs; if the maximum (principal) stress were wanted at any point, the resultant would have to be found. (76).

16. Shears. *The shear, at any section of a body, is equal to the algebraic sum of all the components of the external forces taken parallel to the section and acting on either side of it,* and is equal to the shearing stress on the section. Thus in Figure 10, the shear (vertical) between R_1 and P_1 equals 4000 lbs. acting up; between P_1 and P_2, 2000 lbs. acting up; between P_2 and A, 1000 lbs. acting down; at the section pq, 1600 lbs. (1000 $+3\times200$) acting down; just to the left of R_2, 2500 lbs. (1600 $+4\frac{1}{2}\times200$) acting down; and just to the right of R_2, there is zero shear (2500−2500), as there should be. In Fig. 9, there is, in like manner an "up" shear on each section between R_1 and P, equal to R_1, and between P and R_2, a down shear equal to R_1-P, (since P is larger than R_1) or to R_2.

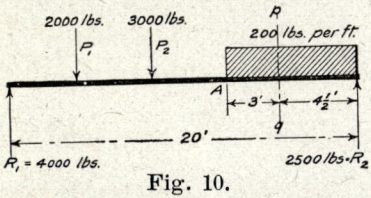

An "up" shear simply denotes that the part to the left of the section tends to move up, past the part to the right, or the part to the right tends to move down, past the part to the left. *Beginning at the right, we get the same results if we apply the terms up and down to the part on the left as before.* Shears are usually spoken of as positive and negative, *an "up" shear, going from left to right, being positive.*

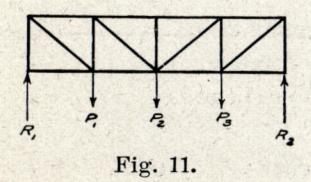

At a load, the shear changes abruptly, sometimes passing through zero, so that *we speak of the shear just to the left or just to the right of the load, never at the load.* Since loads carried by trusses act at the panel points, the shear can change only at the panel points, and is constant in the panels, hence *we speak of the shear in a panel.* In Fig. 11, the shear in the first panel is equal to R_1; in the second panel, to R_1-P_1; in the third, to $R_1-P_1-P_2$; in the fourth, to $R_1-P_1-P_2-P_3$ or to R_2. It is evident, in this case, that the *shears are not resisted by shearing stresses,* but by tension or compression in the diagonal members. The diagonals of the end panels are in tension, because the shear tends to distort the rectangles so as to elongate these diagonals. In this case, as in the cases of Figs. 9 and 10, there is also bending; in fact, shear strictly never occurs except in combination with bending.

17. How Shearing Stresses Occur. In Fig. 5 it was shown how shearing stresses occur in connection with tensile stresses; in like manner, shearing stresses occur with compressive stresses. If, as in Fig. 12, we have a combination of tensile and compressive stresses of equal intensities, acting at right angles to each other, and investigate the stresses on planes making angles of 45 degrees with the directions of these stresses, we shall find simple shearing stresses; on other planes there will be both shearing and normal stresses.

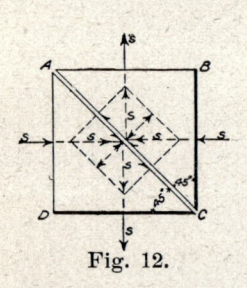

Fig. 12.

Fig. 12 shows how, on both sides of the plane AC, the normal components of the tensile and compressive forces neutralize each other, and how the tangential components are added together: the same result will, of course, obtain for the plane BD. The cube may be conveniently considered as a unit cube so that the stresses on the faces AB, BC, CD, and DA will be unit stresses.

We have, then, under the above conditions, simple shearing stresses, of equal intensity, at right angles to each other. Conversely, if we have shearing stresses of equal intensities acting at right angles to each other, there will be tensile and compressive stresses of equal intensity on planes making angles of 45 degrees with the planes of the shearing stresses. This is shown in Fig. 13, which is the same as Fig. 12, except that the directions of the stresses have been turned through an angle of 45 degrees, and that the diagonal planes are the planes on which simple tensile and compressive stresses act. The figure shows how the compressive stress on plane EG is produced. On FH there will be tensile stresses.

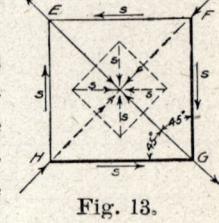

Fig. 13.

The above investigation shows that shearing stresses occur

in pairs at right angles to each other, if there is equilibrium. It would not be possible, in Fig. 13, to have the tangential forces acting on planes EH and FG without those on EF and HG, for the former form a couple which would turn the cube in a clockwise direction. It follows that, *wherever, in an elastic solid, a transverse shearing stress occurs, there is also a longitudinal shearing stress of equal intensity; the resultants of these, upon planes at angles of 45 degrees with the shearing stresses, are equal tensile and compressive stresses.* It may easily be shown (**Fig. 12**) that the intensities of these three kinds of stress are the same (76).

If the cubes of Figs. 12 and 13 be taken indefinitely small, the stresses may, *in any case*, be considered as uniformly distributed over the faces of the cube, and the above principle holds even if there are also tangential forces (Fig. 12) or normal forces (Fig. 13) acting on the faces, or both kinds acting on the front and rear faces.

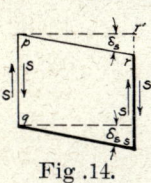

Fig. 14.

In the beam of Fig. 9 we found a vertical shear, which would evidently produce a deformation of the part between any planes as pq and rs, as shown in Fig. 14. But according to the above principle, there must also be horizontal shearing stresses; that the deformation will be as shown in Fig. 14 is evident from Fig. 13, which presents the condition of any small cube in the beam, and shows that the diagonal EG will be lengthened and the diagonal FH shortened. There are also bending stresses in a beam, as shown in Chapter VI, where it is again proven that there are horizontal shearing stresses in beams.

18. Shear Modulus. Since a shearing stress moves the molecules in one section parallel to those in an adjacent section, the resulting deformation, between any two parallel sections, will be as shown in Fig. 14. The angle δ_s is the measure of the deformation which is $r'r$ in the distance pr'; *unit deformation* is, therefore,

$$\frac{rr'}{pr'} = \tan \delta_s = \delta_s \text{ (in circular measure)},$$ since the deformations, within the elastic limit, are very small.

The relation between unit deformation and unit stress is constant, within the elastic limit, and is determined by experiment as in tension.

$$\delta_s = \frac{s_s}{E_s} \text{ or } E_s\, \delta_s = s_s \qquad (3)$$

E_s, the shear modulus, may also be determined theoretically from the cases shown in Figs. 5 or 12, if Poisson's ratio is known. This theoretic relation is,

$$E_s = \frac{1}{2}\frac{m}{(m+1)}E = \frac{2}{5}E, \text{ when } m = 4 \text{ or Poisson's ratio equals } \frac{1}{4}.$$

19. Work Done in Deforming a Body. Resilience. Since work is measured by the product of the force acting and the distance through which it acts, the work done in elongating a steel bar, for example, is equal to the elongating force times the elongation. If the force is gradually applied, it increases from zero to the final value W, and its mean value is $\frac{1}{2} W$. If the accompanying elongation is δL, the total work done is $\frac{1}{2} W \delta L$; if this be divided by the volume AL, we have,

Work done per unit volume $= \frac{1}{2} s\, \delta$

If s does not exceed the elastic limit, this will also represent the potential energy in the bar per unit volume, or the energy restored when the load is taken off or when the bar springs back, and is called the *resilience*.

Resilience per unit volume

$$= \tfrac{1}{2} s\, \delta = \tfrac{1}{2}\frac{s^2}{E}, \text{ from } eq.\ 2, \text{ page } 7. \qquad (4)$$

The term resilience is also applied to designate the work done on a body stressed beyond the elastic limit (21).

The work done by an instantaneously applied force W would be $W \delta L$, and hence it will produce twice the stress, on the same bar, that a gradually applied force produces. If the stress is doubled, the deformation is also momentarily doubled (within the elastic limit). This has been of importance in selecting working stresses.

If the load is applied with impact by a weight W falling through a height h, the work done at the instant of impact, will equal Wh, and it will be spent upon the falling weight, the body struck, and its supports; how much is spent on the body struck would be difficult to determine

The resilience is a good measure of the shock-resisting qualities of a material. To compare various materials in this respect,

Art. 19.   RESILIENCE.   17

substitute the elastic limit for s in equation (4). The elastic resilience of a steel having an elastic limit of 40000 lbs. per square inch equals $\dfrac{40000 \times 40000}{2 \times 29000000} = 27.6$ inch-pounds per cubic inch. The elastic resilience of a cast iron having an elastic limit of 12000 lbs. per square inch equals $\dfrac{12000 \times 12000}{2 \times 12000000} = 6.0$ inch-pounds per cubic inch[1].

---

[1] For the resilience of beams see Art. (88), and for a discussion of the whole subject, see Chapter VI of Johnson's *Materials of Construction*.

QUESTIONS AND PROBLEMS. CHAPTER I.

1. What is statics?
2. May a structure be composed of simple beams, girders, and trusses? What are the constituent parts of a truss called?
3. Which members are the web members of a truss?
4. When is the force of the wind taken as a live load?
5. Give three examples of a concentrated load and three of a distributed load.
6. How may impact stresses be measured?
7. What were the main conclusions at which Prof. Turneaure arrived, in his investigations of the vibrations of railway bridges?
8. What is the total equivalent static stress in a member of a bridge truss, for which the dead-load stress is 70000 lbs., the live-load stress 200000 lbs., and the impact stress is taken as $\frac{300}{300 \times L}$ times the live load stress, L being 150 in this case.

Ans., 403300 lbs.

9. What are the principal uses to which the materials mentioned in Art. 6 are put? Which of these materials is the heaviest? Which are brittle? Which are ductile? Which has the greatest strength?
10. What, according to Johnson's *Materials of Construction*, is the elastic limit of steel? Of long-leaf pine? Of steel piano wire?
11. What is the stress per square inch in a steel tension member which carries a stress of 64000 lbs., and whose area of cross section is 6.4 sq. ins.? What total stress will it carry if the working stress is 12000 lbs. per sq. in.?
12. If the coefficient of expansion of steel is 0.0000065 and of concrete 0.0000055, what kind of stress will be induced, by a fall of temperature, in a bar of steel imbedded in the center of a block of concrete, if the adhesion is perfect? What kind in the concrete?
13. If $E = 29000000$, what will be the total elongation of a steel bar 20 ft. long, having a section 6 in. $\times 1\frac{1}{2}$ in., and carrying a stress of 108000 lbs. in tension?

$$\frac{W}{A} = s = \frac{108000}{6 \times 1\frac{1}{2}} = 12000 \text{ lbs. per sq. in.}$$

$$\delta = \frac{s}{E} = \frac{12000}{29000000} = 0.000413 \text{ in.}$$

$$\delta L = 0.000413 \times 12 \times 20 = 0.099 \text{ in.}$$

QUESTIONS AND PROBLEMS. CHAPTER I.

14. If $E = 30000000$, and the elastic limit of a steel bar 10 ft. long is 36000 lbs. per sq. in., what will be the elongation per inch at the elastic limit? What the total elongation?
Ans., 0.0012″ and 0.144″.

15. An iron bar 30 ft. long stretches 0.18 in. under a stress per square inch of 14000 lbs.; what is the value of E?   28000000.

16. The length of a steel compression member in a truss is 247 in., the area of its cross section is 60 sq. in., and its contraction of length during the passage of the live load is 0.0247 in. What is the live-load stress, E being 29000000?   Ans., 174000 lbs.

17. If a street railway rail be supposed to be rigidly held at its ends, what kind of stress will be induced by a fall of temperature of 60° F.? What will the intensity of stress be if the modulus of elasticity is 30000000 and the coefficient of expansion 0.0000065?   Ans., 11700 lbs. per sq. in.

18. If a plate girder be anchored at each end to rigid walls so that it can not expand or bend, what stress per sq. in. will be induced by a rise of temperature of 100° F.? $E = 29000000$ and the coefficient of expansion $= 0.0000065$.
Ans., 18850 lbs. per sq. in.

19. Is the stretch of a twisted wire hoisting cable elastic or only partly elastic? Why?

20. A steel column for an office building is made 250 ft. long; how much will it be shortened when the average unit compression in it is 10000 lbs. per sq. in., E being 30000000? What will be the contraction if the column is cast iron under an average stress of 8000 lbs. per sq. in., E being 12000000?
Ans. 1 in.   2 in.

21. If a tension member be made of two bars of steel, each $6'' \times 1''$, and two bars of iron, each $6'' \times \frac{3}{4}''$, so that the elongation is the same for all when the total stress is 252000 lbs.; what will be the stress per square inch in each bar if E is the same for all? What if $E = 31000000$ for steel and 27000000 for iron?
Ans., 12000 lbs. per sq. in.   11064 lbs. per sq. in. for iron and 12702 for steel.

22. If E is 12000000 for cast iron, what should be the elongations of a bar one square inch in cross section and 30 inches long, when the loads on it are 3000 lbs., 6000 lbs., and 9000 lbs., if the metal is perfectly elastic under these loads?
Ans., 0.0075″, 0.015″ and 0.0225″.

23. Which is the stiffer, steel with a unit stress of 12000 lbs. per sq. in. and $E = 30000000$, or iron with a unit stress of 10000 lbs. and $E = 27000000$? How do they compare? Ans. As 4 to 3.7.

24. A steel piano wire 4250 ft. long with an 8 lb. plumb-bob was let down a mine shaft; when the 8 lb. bob was exchanged for a 50 lb. bob, the observed elongation was 15 ft. What was the change of stress per square inch, the cross-sectional area of the wire being 0.00038 sq. in.? What was the modulus of elasticity of the steel? Was the elastic limit exceeded?

Ans., 110500 lbs. per sq. in. 31,330,000.

25. If in Fig. 5, Art. 12, the section is 2"x3" and $P = 72000$ lbs., what is the maximum principal stress per sq. in.? What will be the shearing stress per sq. in. on planes making angles of 45° with the axis? On what planes is the unit shearing stress a maximum? How does it compare with the maximum unit tensile stress?

Ans. 12000 lbs. per sq. in. max. tension. 6000 lbs. per sq. in. max. shear.

26. What kinds of stresses are found in simple beams?

27. May a combination of bending and tensile stresses result in tensile stress over the entire section? Illustrate.

28. What is the maximum unit stress in a steel bar 7 ft. long, whose section is 3"x6", when the compressive load on it is 180000 lbs.?

29. What is the difference between shear and shearing stress?

30. Will a notched bar elongate more or less than a plain one?

31. What is the shear in the middle panel of a truss of five equal panels, and carrying equal panel loads at each panel point?

32. What is the shear at the middle of a beam, supported at its ends, and carrying a uniformly distributed load over its entire length?

33. Prove that the intensity of shearing stress on the plane AC, Fig. 12, Art. 17, is equal to s.

34. What is the deflection at the middle of an I beam, supported at its ends, due to shear only, for a load at the middle such that the shearing stress per square inch (which is assumed uniformly distributed over the web) is 4000 lbs.? The span is 20 ft. and $E_s = 12000000$. Ans., 0.04".

35. A steel bar is 8 ft. long and two square inches in cross section; its elastic limit is 30000 lbs. per sq. in. and $E = 29000000$: what must be the cross section of a cast iron bar of the same length so that it will have the same elastic resilience, the elastic limit being 10000 lbs. per sq. in. and $E = 12000000$.

Ans. 7.43 sq. in.

36. In problem 12, what will be the ratio of the unit stress in the steel to that in the concrete, for a unit deformation ∂ if E_c and E_{st} are, respectively, the moduli of elasticity of concrete and steel?

CHAPTER II.

STRESSES AND DEFORMATIONS BEYOND THE ELASTIC LIMIT

20. Non-elastic Stress and Deformation. For stresses above the elastic limit, the deformation is chiefly permanent, and deformations and stresses are not proportional—the deformation increases faster than the stress. Since working stresses are well within the elastic limit, stresses and deformations beyond it are of little importance in designing structures, but are important in interpreting tests of materials. The character of the relation which exists between stresses and deformations, may be seen best if they are plotted on a stress-deformation diagram.

21. Stress-deformation Diagrams. Fig. 15 shows a stress-deformation diagram of a piece of soft steel tested in tension. In accordance with Hooke's Law, OA is a straight line, AA' being equal to the elastic limit, which, in this case, is practically the limit of proportionality between stress and deformation. Above A the deformations increase faster than the stresses, and at B the material may be said to flow, because no increase of stress (or even a less stress) is required to continue the deformation. The point B is called the YIELD POINT because the metal "breaks down" at this point; it is the "elastic limit" in commercial testing and is determined by the drop of the scale beam of the testing machine; it is, therefore, much more conveniently gotten than the point A.

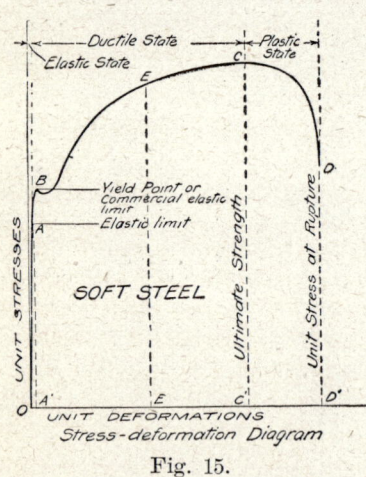

For iron and structural steel, the points A and B are usually close together, but for some ductile materials there is considerable difference between the stress at the elastic limit and at the yield point. Timber and brittle materials like hard steel, cast iron, and stone, do not have a yield point, and for them the limit of proportionality is determined from stress-deformation diagrams.

The vertical ordinates of the stress-deformation diagram measure the *unit* stresses accompanying the deformations measured by the corresponding abscissas. Thus EE' is the unit stress when OE' is the *unit* elongation. AA' is the *unit* stress at the elastic limit, and this is what is usually meant by the elastic limit; OA' is the corresponding elongation. It will be observed that the elastic deformation is very small part of the total OD' CC' is the ULTIMATE STRENGTH or maximum unit stress shown in the test; it is not the unit stress at the point where rupture takes place. DD' is the unit stress just before rupture takes place; this is less than the ultimate strength because the area of the cross section of the test piece decreases. The stresses in the diagram are per unit of original area which is what the engineer wants. The actual intensity of stress *increases* up to the point of rupture[1].

Since $E = \frac{s}{\delta}$, the tangent of the angle which OA makes with OD' represents the modulus of elasticity. Since the elastic resilience per unit volume is equal to $\frac{1}{2} s \delta$ (19), it is represented by the area of the triangle OAA'. The total resilience per cubic inch is represented by the area of $OABECDD'$, and is approximately $AA' \times OD' + \frac{2}{3}(CC' - AA') OD'$.

Testing machines are sometimes fitted with appliances for automatically drawing stress-deformation diagrams[2].

22. Ductility and Plasticity. After the yield point is passed (Fig. 15), the metal seems to harden, and it again requires an increase of stress to increase the deformation, but a given increase of stress will produce a much greater elongation (time being a factor) than when the stress is below the elastic limit. The deformation is now chiefly permanent, and the test piece is more or less uniformly elongated throughout its length, and its cross section is diminished; it is very ductile.

When the ultimate strength is reached, a local contraction

---

[1]Unwin's *The Testing of the Materials of Construction*, or Goodman's *Mechanics Applied to Engineering*.

[2]For complete tensile and compressive stress-deformation diagrams of steel, iron, cast-iron, and timber see Johnson's *Materials of Construction* Chapter II, or Johnson's *Modern Framed Structures*, Chapter VIII.

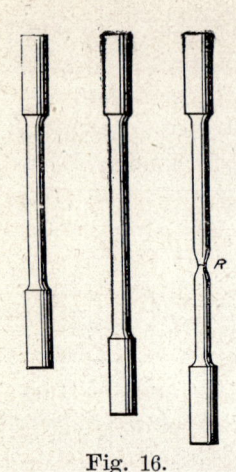

begins—the piece "necks down"—and the elongation also becomes largely local. This is shown in Fig. 16, rupture occuring at R. This is the plastic state; the deformation is all permanent or non-elastic.

Ductility and plasticity are important qualities in structural materials, especially in structures subject to impact stresses. Brittle materials break off short without giving any warning of failure. These qualities are measured in a tensile test by the percentage of elongation and the percentage of reduction of area at the fracture. For structural steel, the percentage of elongation in 8 inches (including fracture) is 20% to 30% and the reduction of area about 40% to 60%; the larger figures apply to the softer steel.

Fig. 16.

23. Ultimate Strength. By ultimate strength is meant the *greatest* unit stress which a test piece will show in a test, and is obtained by dividing the maximum load on the piece by its original area. The ultimate strength in tension, according to this definition, is easily determined as explained in Art. 21, and has been determined by many experiments on many kinds of material; it is one of the results obtained in all commercial testing of iron and steel. The ultimate strengths in pure compression (in short blocks, not in columns), and in shear are of less importance, and have been less definitely determined for various materials. It is difficult to produce shearing stresses without bending stresses. In compression, the character of failure depends very much upon the kind of material; ductile and plastic materials, like soft steel, copper, lead, asphalt, etc., will expand laterally almost without limit, so that the intensity of stress reckoned on the original area is much larger than the real stress; fibrous materials, like wrought iron and wood, will split on account of the lateral expansion, that is, they actually fail in tension; brittle materials, like cast iron, brick, stone, etc., fail with little lateral expansion and usually by shearing on oblique planes, the friction on the plane of failure, and on the faces to which the pressure is applied, having considerable influence. In both compression and tension, any interference with the lateral deformation, in-

Art. 23   ULTIMATE STRENGTH.   25

creases the ultimate strength, and decreases the longitudinal deformation. In compression, the ratio of height to lateral dimension has a marked influence on the ultimate strength.

Ultimate strength in compression has no definite meaning unless the conditions of the test are fully specified[1]. This is true in a lesser degree for tension also; a bar of steel of large cross section, for example, will show a lower ultimate strength than one of small cross section. The usual tensile tests of steel and iron are not exactly comparable because the test pieces vary somewhat in shape and size, for practical reasons.

For the purposes of the engineer, the *limit of strength* is determined by that load which produces the first sign of fracture or lateral flow. This limit, in both tension and compression, is the yield point for such materials as have a yield point, and in steel and iron, is about the same for both kinds of stresses.

Some materials (timber, wrought iron, stratified stone) do not have the same strength in all directions.

ULTIMATE STRENGTHS[2].

	TENSION	COMPRESSION
Rivet Steel	48000 to 58000	....
Soft Steel ....[3]	52000 to 62000	....
Medium Steel	60000 to 70000	....
Cast Iron—extreme values	10000 to 40000	50000 to 150000
Cast Iron—ordinary f'ndry	15000 to 20000	60000 to 90000
Timber—endwise. Dry....	6000 to 12000	4000 to 9000
White Oak and Longleaf Pine	10000 to 12000	5000 to 9000
Wrought Iron	45000 to 55000	....

[1] For a discussion of this point see Kent's *Mechanical Engineer's Pocket-book*, Johnson's *Materials of Construction*, and Burr's *Elasticity and Resistance of the Materials of Engineering*.

[2] For detailed information with regard to ultimate strengths, see Burr's *Elasticity and Resistance of the Materials of Engineering*, Johnson's *Materials of Construction*, Ewing's *Strength of Materials*, Kent's *Mechanical Engineer's Pocket-book*, and the Cambria Steel Co.'s Hand-book.

[3] A single grade of steel, having an average ultimate strength of about 60000 lbs. per sq. in., is now being specified by a number of engineers. Nickel-steel containing 3¼% of nickel, having an ultimate strength of 85000 lbs. to 100000 lbs., and a minimum elastic limit of 50000 lbs., has been specified for the eye-bars of the Blackwell's Island Bridge, now being built over the East River in New York.

The ultimate strength of *structural steel* may be said to be included between the limits of 50000 and 70000 lbs. per sq. in., the allowed variation for any particular grade being from 8000 to 10000 lbs. per sq. in. The ultimate strength of steel may vary from about 48000 lbs. per sq. in. in the softest kind up to nearly 400000 lbs. per sq. in. in hard drawn wire.

24. Factor of Safety. To obtain working unit stresses for use in designing structures, it was and is still, to a large extent, the practice of engineers to divide the ultimate strength by a factor, varying from 3 to 10, called the *factor of safety*. Thus, if the ultimate strength of the steel used be 60000 lbs. per sq. in., and the factor of safety be taken as 5, the working stress will be 12000 lbs. per sq. in.

The *choice of a factor of safety* involves many considerations such as the *impossibility of knowing accurately the amount and effect of all loads and stresses, undiscoverable and unavoidable defects in material and workmanship, and deterioration due to corrosion and wear.*

The distribution of the load and its possible future increase are nearly always more or less uncertain. Then too a structure, or certain parts, may be liable to receive accidental shocks as well as those which are incidental to varying loads; these produce impact stresses which are especially uncertain (5).

Even when the loads are definitely known, theory is frequently not adequate to the determination of the resulting stresses except upon certain assumptions. Unavoidable eccentric stresses are seldom calculated, but they have an influence upon the choice of a factor of safety.

The factor of safety is always taken less for wind load stresses and for combinations of stresses which can only occur at rare intervals, than for other stresses.

The factor of safety is always taken greater for materials which vary greatly in quality than for those which are uniform and may be depended upon to be nearly as determined by tests. The qualities of stone, timber and cast iron are much less uniform than those of steel and wrought iron.

There will be imperfections in workmanship as well as in material which no amount of inspection and testing can eliminate. Working stresses must be based upon available material and workmanship.

Art. 24. FACTOR OF SAFETY. 27

A steel structure over a railway will suffer much more from corrosion than one over a highway or one entirely enclosed. Neglect of repairs may result in injury to parts not subject to wear ordinarily.

A temporary structure is given a smaller factor of safety than a permanent one for numerous reasons.

The damage that would result from the failure of one structure or part might be much greater than from the failure of another.

It is plain that the choice of a factor of safety depends upon the judgment of the engineer, and an inexperienced designer should be guided by precedent, which usually means by some standard specification. Specifications do not give factors of safety at all but working stresses directly, and those may vary so much that it is scarcely proper to speak of a factor of safety. Working stresses may be based upon the elastic limit instead of on the ultimate strength; this is a rational basis if the material has a yield point or definite elastic limit.

Specifications treat stresses in different ways, resulting in widely different working unit stresses, as illustrated below for a tension member of a truss for a railway bridge, designed in accordance with three different specifications. The discrepancy in results is usually much larger.

	STRESS	UNIT	AREA REQUIR'D
Dead load	75300		
Live load	218500		
Total	293800	12000	24.48 sq. ins.
Dead load	75300	20000	3.76
Live load	218500	10000	21.85
			25.61 sq. ins.
Dead load	75300		
Live load	218500		
Impact	142000		
Total	435800	17000	25.63 sq. ins.

In the last case the working unit is applied to an equivalent static stress, while in the other cases an allowance is made for impact in the working stress, the allowance in the second case being equivalent to 100% of the live load stress. In specifications of the last type, there is practically but one working unit stress, while in others there may be many; in one case the impact is allowed for by varying the impact stress, and in the other (to some extent) by using different unit stresses for different parts[1].

The usual factors of safety for iron and steel structures are 4 and 5, being 4 for buildings in general and for ordinary highway bridges. For cast iron the factor of safety is usually taken as 8, in columns. The factor of safety for timber is 4 to 10, depending on the kind of stress[2]

In any case, the factor of safety should be such as to bring the working stress well within the elastic limit. The important point is to have an *equal* margin of strength for all parts of a structure.

25. Peculiar Properties of Iron and Steel in the Non-elastic State.

When stressed beyond the elastic limit, iron and steel show some very interesting qualities. A stress which produces an appreciable permanent set in a body is said to overstrain it. In order to understand the phenomena of overstrain, it should be remembered that with increasing ultimate strength in steel, there goes decreasing ductility, that is, less elongation. Steel of high ultimate strength is called hard steel. The ultimate strength of steel, in manufacture, is chiefly regulated by the pecentage of carbon—the more carbon, the harder the steel. Steel is also made harder by heating and quenching in a cooling bath. It has been found that overstrain also hardens steel in a remarkable way, but impairs elasticity, and if repeated often produces "fatigue." Rest and heat restore elasticity.

26. Shifting of the Elastic Limit.

If a bar of steel or iron be stressed *beyond the yield point,* the stress removed, and then immediately applied again, it will be found that the elastic limit has been very much lowered but that the yield point has been raised, and is now equal to the maximum previous stress. If, however, a period of rest intervenes between the loadings, the elastic limit will also rise (time being an important factor) and may even reach the new yield point; the yield point also rises a

---

[1]For a comparison of the main features of a number of railway bridge specifications see an article by the author in *Engineering News,* Vol. 50, p. 444.

[2]See "Cambria."

little[1]. The period of rest allows the metal to harden, and this hardening will be greater if, in place of relieving the stress, it is held stationary. It is thus possible, by repeated applications of increased loads, to raise the yield point nearly up to the point of rupture, at the same time raising the ultimate strength and decreasing the ductility so that the fracture of a piece of soft steel will resemble that of hard steel.

If the stress exceeds the elastic limit but not the yield point, the elastic limit is immediately *raised*, and by a repetition of such stress, the yield point is also raised.

It has been found that if there has been overstrain in tension, the elastic limit in compression is lowered and vice versa. If this lowered elastic limit is raised again by a stress producing a small permanent set, the elastic limit for the opposite kind of stress falls to zero[2]. Ordinary periods of rest do not seem to have any effect in this case, but gradually increasing stresses, alternating between tension and compression, establish new elastic limits considerably lower than the original elastic limits. These have been called *natural elastic limits*, the original elastic limits being supposed to be artificially raised by the rolling of the metal.

A very interesting method of restoring elasticity and raising the elastic limit is given in Ewing's *Strength of Materials*. "When a piece of iron or steel has had its elasticity broken down by overstraining, it will make a very complete recovery if heated for a few minutes to a temperature such as that of boiling water. When the overstrained piece has been immersed in a bath of boiling water it is found to have practically perfect elasticity up to a new yield point, which is higher than the load used in the process of overstraining."

"A remarkable experiment may be made by taking a bar of mild steel and stretching it in the first instance just up to the primitive yield point, then heating it for a few minutes up to 100°C to produce elastic recovery, then stretching it again just up to its new yield point, then heating again to 100°C and so on. Each step raises the elastic limit, and notwithstanding its natur-

---

[1] See Burr's *Elasticity and Resistance of the Materials of Engineering*, pp. 247-250, for results of experiments made by Professor Bauschinger. For a statement of Bauschinger's conclusions, see Greene's *Structural Mechanics*, p. 166.

[2] For stress-deformation diagrams, showing these remarkable phenomena, see Johnson's *Materials of Construction*, Figs. 436 and 437.

ally plastic quality the bar may in this way finally be caused to break with a fracture resembling that of hard steel, with comparatively little total extension or contraction of section at the fracture, and under a total load much greater than that which could be applied in an ordinary test."

27. Hardening Effects of Non-elastic Deformation. After a piece of iron or steel has undergone a permanent set, it is hardened, that is, it is less ductile and its ultimate strength is increased. This hardening is of great practical importance, and may be considered a benefit as in cold-rolled or cold-drawn shafting and in wire for certain pupuses, or an injury as in wire for other purposes, and in steel hammered or bent cold, or subjected to other severe treatment like punching and shearing. A very narrow strip of metal contigious to a punched hole or a sheared edge is hardened so much as to make it brittle. Under stress, this hardened portion is not capable of deforming as much as the other metal, and therefore causes a non-uniform distribution of stress and a reduction of ultimate strength. The softer and thinner the metal, the less the injury; for the best class of work, it is the practice to remove this hardened part, in medium steel, by reaming out punched holes and planing off sheared edges.

All of the effects of non-elastic stress may be much modified or entirely obliterated by annealing, that is, by heating to redness and cooling slowly. Wire is annealed for certain purposes which require a soft wire and, in this manner, any piece whose uniformity has been disturbed by cold working or partial heating is restored.

28. Fatigue of Iron and Steel. If in place of a few applications of increasing stresses, as explained in Art. 26, many applications of the same stress are made, the elastic limit is raised if the stresses do not approach too closely the original ultimate strength, and will be raised considerably higher than the applied stresses if these are not very much above the original elastic limit[1]. With continuously repeated stresses above the rising *yield point*, rupture will finally occur at a stress much below the original ultimate strength, and with a fracture like that of a brittle material or like that of a piece of steel with an artificially

---

[1] This was investigated by Bauschinger; for the results of his experiment's, see Unwin's *The Testing of the Materials of Construction*, Chapter XII.

raised ultimate strength, as explained in Art. 26. This is the more remarkable because if a piece brought nearly to the point of rupture in this way, is tested in the ordinary way, it will show no loss of strength or ductility. This corresponds with practical experience for it has been noticed that failures occur after many years of service, yet when such metal is tested in the ordinary way, it shows no loss of strength. What the nature of the deterioration is, has not been satisfactorily explained, but it is called fatigue.[1] There seems to be no alteration of structure except just at the surface of fracture.

"Fatigue" experiments have been made by Woehler[2], Spangenberg[3], Bauschinger[4], Baker[5], and others, but further experiments are necessary to satisfactorily settle some disputed points. All these experiments show that the number of repetitions of a variation of stress, which a piece of metal will endure before rupture, depends upon the *range of stress*; the range of stress is the greater the further the maximum is from the ultimate strength. If for bar iron, for example, the range of stress is from 0 to about 32000 lbs per sq. in., it will stand from five to ten million repetitions; in order to stand as many repetitions when the upper limit is 49000 lbs. per sq. in., the range of stress must not exceed about 19000 lbs. per sq. in., that is, it will be from 30000 to 49000 lbs. per sq. in. The range of stress for stresses alternating between tension and compression is the *sum of the two,* and, in this case, for equal resistance, each stress is somewhat more than half of that for stress of one kind with a lower limit of zero.

The experiments also show that for stresses *within the elastic limit* or yield point (natural elastic limits for alternating stresses), *there is no "fatigue."* The yield point should, therefore, be considered the limit of strength as stated in Art. 23. Since it has been the custom to base working stresses on the ultimate strength, it was the practice of some engineers to base

---

[1] Prof. Johnson, in his *Materials of Construction*, Chapter XXVII, explains "fatigue" by saying that some of the millions of incipient defects or "micro-flows" gradually extend their weakening influence.

[2] See Unwin's *The Testing of Materials of Construction* and the *Transactions of the American Society of Civil Engineers*, Vol. 41, p. 222.

[3] See Burr's *Elasticity and Resistance of the Materials of Engineering*, p. 844.

[4] See Unwin's *The Testing of Materials of Construction* and Greene's *Structural Mechanics*, p. 160.

[5] See Unwin's *The Testing of Materials of Construction*

working stresses for bridges upon the range of stress in order to take account of "fatigue," but this has been largely abandoned. According to this practice, working stresses were determined from a formula commonly called the Launhardt Formula, which for stresses of one kind was of the form

$$\text{working stress} = a \left(1 + \frac{\text{minimum stress}}{\text{maximum stress}}\right)$$

which usually also provided for impact and such other things as a factor of safety makes provision for, "a" being a constant depending upon the judgment of the engineer writing the specification. Since working stresses are always taken well within the elastic limit, "fatigue" need not be considered in designing structures; moreover, the influence of periods of rest between loadings must be considerable[1]. Some engineers who used the "Launhardt Formula" neglected "fatigue," but used this formula as an impact formula. There have not been enough experiments like those mentioned in Art. 5 to determine the proper allowance to make for impact stresses in bridges.

It is generally agreed that if sufficient impact stress is included with dead and live load stresses, a working stress equal to about half the elastic limit affords ample security when good steel is used.

---

[1] For an extensive discussion of this whole matter, see the *Transactions of the American Society of Civil Engineers*, Vol. 41, p. 166.

QUESTIONS AND PROBLEMS. CHAPTER II.

1. Which is the more important to the designer, the elastic limit or ultimate strength?

2. If a floor carrying a constant load were supported by steel rods, what objection would there be to having the stress in these rods exceed the elastic limit? What objection would there be to having the stress in a member of a truss exceed the elastic limit?

3. What is the difference between natural elastic limit, true elastic limit, limit of proportionality, yield point, and commercial elastic limit?

4. Name three materials that do not strictly follow Hooke's Law and one that does, but does not have a yield point.

5. Why does a piece of steel pulled in a testing machine break, if the load does not increase up to the time of rupture?

6. What is the total resilience of a piece of steel 8″ long and $\frac{1}{2}$ sq. in. in cross section, if its ultimate strength is 60000 lbs. per sq. in., its elastic limit 30000 lbs. per sq. in., and its elongation 2″? Ans., 50000 in. lbs.

7. Up to what point are deformations practically perfectly elastic? Between what points are they wholly permanent?

8. Name four substances that will show definite failures when tested in compression, and five that will not.

9. What conditions have a marked influence upon the value of the ultimate strength in compression?

10. Why is the yield point the limit of strength for the purposes of the engineer?

11. What experiments upon the strength of American timbers have been the most extensive?

12. What values for the ultimate strength in tension, compression and shear does Rankine give for wrought iron?

13. What material has an ultimate strength in compression greater than that in tension? And in what material is this relation reversed?

14. When may the factor of safety for dead and live load stresses be the same?

15. Why are factors of safety for stone, timber and cast iron taken greater than for steel?

16. Why should not a highway bridge have as large a factor of safety as a railway bridge?

17. Why is the factor of safety for wind stresses taken smaller than for other stresses?

18. Does a "factor of safety of 5" mean that it would require five times the calculated stress to cause failure?

19. What factor of safety would you use in designing the girders for a traveling crane?

20. In what ways may steel be hardened? Is it possible to harden steel without increasing its ultimate strength?

21. How great must be the intensity of stress in a steel bar to impair its elasticity? How great to raise the elastic limit?

22. In what case do ordinary periods of rest not restore impaired elasticity? How may elasticity be quickly restored without lowering the yield point?

23. Is the metal near a punched hole hardened more on one side of the plate than on the other? See Johnson's *Materials of Construction*, Chap. XXVI.

24. What is annealing and what effect does it have?

25. What effect would a very large number of repetitions of stress, above the elastic limit and below the yield point, have upon the ultimate strength? What upon the elastic limit? How does this correspond with the effect of a single stress?

26. What does the "Launhardt Formula" take account of?

27. What would be a good working stress for dead load stress alone? For equal equivalent static alternating stresses?

28. What working stresses would you use in designing a railway bridge?

CHAPTER III.

THE LAWS OF EQUILIBRIUM AND THEIR APPLICATION.

29. The Problem. The problem to be considered is that of keeping structures and their parts at *rest* or in *equilibrium*. In order to hold a structure in equilibrium, it is necessary that the external forces acting on it shall be in equilibrium. In order that *any part* of a structure shall be in equilibrium, it is necessary that the internal forces (stresses), or internal and external forces acting on it shall be in equilibrium. This is a problem in statics (if the structure is *statically determinate*); the unknowns are the reactions and the stresses, and these are determined so as to satisfy the condition of equilibrium by means of the simple laws of equilibrium expressed in the form of equations.

If all the external forces acting on a structure are fully known, the stresses in it can be found, and from these the deformation of any part or the deflection at any point. *The external forces should, therefore, be determined first*; these are the loads and reactions.

Live loads for bridges and buildings are usually taken from standard specifications; dead loads must be estimated when not specified, and are taken uniformly distributed or concentrated, depending upon the construction. Having the loads, the reactions at the supports and the stresses are determined by the application of the laws of equilibrium. Before stating these certain properties and relations of forces will be defined.

30. Properties and Relations of Forces. Three things are necessary to fully determine a force; its magnitude, its point of application, and the direction in which it acts. The point of application is not important, and may be considered to be any point in the line of action of a force. The *line of action* of a force is a line of indefinite length, passing through the point of application in the direction of the force, any part of which laid off to some scale will represent the magnitude of the force; an arrow placed on the line representing the force fully determines the direction in which the force acts. Only *co-planar forces*—forces whose lines of action are in the same plane—will be considered.

Concurrent forces are those whose lines of action intersect in one point.

The *moment of a force* is a measure of its tendency to rotate a body about an axis or a point, and is equal to the magnitude of the force multiplied by the perpendicular distance of its line of action from the axis or point (foot-pounds or inch-pounds).

The *center or origin of moments* is the point about which any force may have a tendency to turn a body.

The *lever arm* of a force is the perpendicular distance from its line of action to the center of moments.

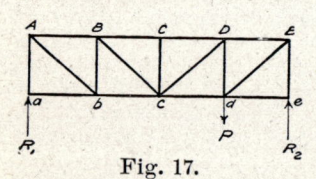

In Fig. 17, the moment of R_1 about e is $R_1 \times ae$; of P about e is $P \times de$; and of R_1 about D is $R_1 \times ad$ or $R_1 \times AD$.

A *couple* consists of two equal and parallel forces acting in opposite directions. The *moment of a couple* is the same about *any* point in its plane, and is equal to *one* of the equal forces multiplied by the perpendicular distance between their lines of action. Fig. 18 shows two parallel forces P acting in opposite directions, forming a couple. Take any point whatever as a and draw a line from it perpendicular to the lines of P. The total moment about a is equal to the algebraic sum of the moments of each force taken separately.

$$P \times ad - P \times ab = P(ad - ab) = P \times bd.$$

Taking any other point as c, the total moment is

$$P \times cd + P \times cb = P(cd + cb) = P \times bd.$$

If either b or d be taken as the center of moments, the moment of one force becomes zero and the total moment is again $P \times bd$. This exhausts all the possible cases, and proves that the moment of the couple is $P \times bd$ for *any* center of moments.

Equivalent systems of forces are such as may be substituted for each other without changing the effect.

The *resultant* of a system of forces is the simplest system that is equivalent to it. *The resultant of any number of co-planar forces is a single force or a couple.* See Art. 34.

The *equilibrant* of a system of forces is the simplest system that will hold the given system (or its resultant) in equilibrium. If the resultant is a single force, the equilibrant is in every re-

Art. 31. TWO FORCES IN EQUILIBRIUM. 37

spect the same except that it acts in the opposite direction. *If the resultant is a couple, it is only necessary that the equilibrant be a couple of equal moment tending to turn in the opposite direction;* the forces of the two couples may make any angle with each other and be of different magnitudes. In Fig. 18, if $P = 1000$ lbs. and $bd = 5$ ft., the moment of the couple is 5000 foot-pounds, and it can be held in equilibrium by another couple acting on the same body in the opposite direction, located anywhere in the same plane, so long as the moment of the latter is 5000 foot-pounds.; for example, by forces of 5 lbs., 1000 ft. apart or 100 lbs., 50 ft. apart.

No single force can hold a couple in equilibrium, and no single force can be an equivalent of a couple. A simple case is that shown in Fig. 19, where the wind load P produces the reactions H whose sum equals P thus forming a couple; another couple must act at the supports, and its moment is $Vb = Pa$. Fig. 20 shows an exactly similar case. If there be more than one parallel load, the resultant of the loads with the direct reaction will form a couple, thus reducing to the same case.

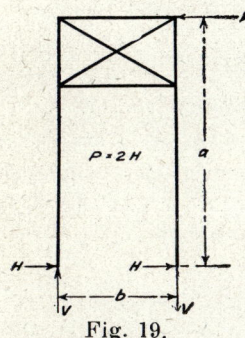

Fig. 19.

In Fig. 20, if the wind force P were just sufficient to overturn the car, the right-hand reaction V' would be zero, and the resisting couple would be the weight of the car acting at its center of gravity, and the upward pressure of the left-hand rail V. In this case V would equal W, the weight of the car, and the arm of the couple would be $\frac{1}{2} b$.

The *components* of a force are any forces of which the given force is the resultant. It is often *convenient* to resolve a force into two components, especially two components at right angles to each other. It is also sometimes convenient to work with the resultant of two or more forces in place of the forces themselves.

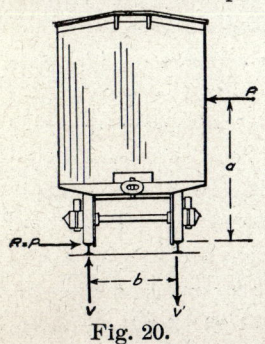

Fig. 20.

31. Two Forces in Equilibrium. In order that two forces may be in equilibrium, it is not only necessary that they be equal and act in opposite directions, but they must have the same line of action; if their lines of action be parallel, they form a couple which will produce rotation.

32. Three Forces in Equilibrium. The resultant of two forces is shown in magnitude and direction by the diagonal of a parallelogram whose adjacent sides represent the given forces in magnitude and direction as shown in Fig. 21. The equilibrant is the same as the resultant except that it has an opposite direction. It is, however, necessary that the line of action of R or E pass through the point F, the common point in the lines of the components P_1 and P_2.

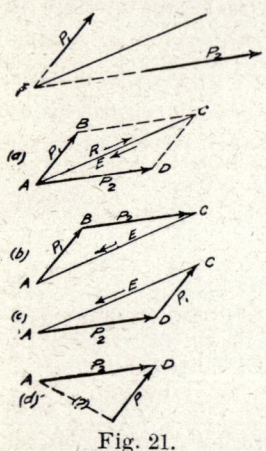

The resultant or equilibrant may also be found by simply constructing one of the triangles ABC or ACD, Fig. 21 (b) and (c). It is necessary that the directions of the given forces follow each other. Fig. 21 (d) shows a wrong construction because the directions of P_1 and P_2 are opposite in going around the triangle.

Fig. 21.

A triangle which represents three forces in magnitude and direction is called a FORCE TRIANGLE. It is evident that the force triangle does not represent the *location* of the forces with respect to each other.

If the forces in a force triangle all have the same direction they represent a concurrent system in equilibrium, and any one force is the equilibrant of the other two. If the direction of any one is opposite to that of the other two, it is their resultant. It follows that a component may be greater than a resultant.

Although *the force triangle* represents concurrent forces, it is, nevertheless, *the foundation of graphic statics,* as will be seen by what follows; by its means the resultant of any number of forces may be found, first finding the resultant of two of them, then the resultant of this resultant and a third force, and so on.

Three non-concurrent forces can not be in equilibrium, because the resultant of two of them would have to be equal to the third and in the same line of action; this makes them concurrent because the resultant passes through the point of intersection of the lines of action of the first two. Fig. 22 shows

Art. 33. FOUR FORCES IN EQUILIBRIUM.

three non-concurrent forces P_1, P_2, and P_3 forming a closed triangle, but these cannot be in equilibrium because even if P_3 should happen to be equal and opposite to R, as shown, they form a couple. If P_3 intersects R, the triangle will not close.

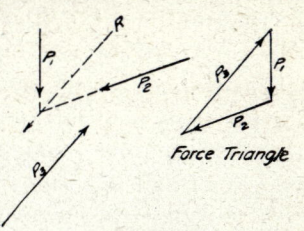

Fig. 22.

Three parallel forces may, however, be in equilibrium, as is clear in the case shown in Fig. 17; they may be considered concurrent, intersecting at infinity.

It is important to note that *when three forces are in equilibrium, their lines of action intersect in a point.* In Fig. 23, P is the resultant of the wind load on one side of a roof; it is desired to determine the reactions R_1 and R_2 applied at A and B so that R_2 will be vertical. R_1 passes through C because the three forces are to be in equilibrium. Now the force triangle may be drawn, because one side P, and the directions of all are known. This determines the magnitudes of R_1 and R_2 as shown.

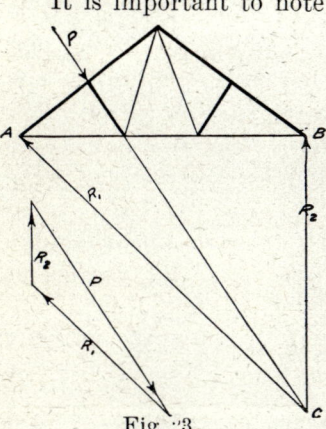

Fig. 23.

33. Four Forces in Equilibrium. If four forces are in equilibrium, the resultant of any two must be the equilibrant of the other two. This is evident for concurrent forces. For non-concurrent forces see Fig. 24. The directions of the four forces

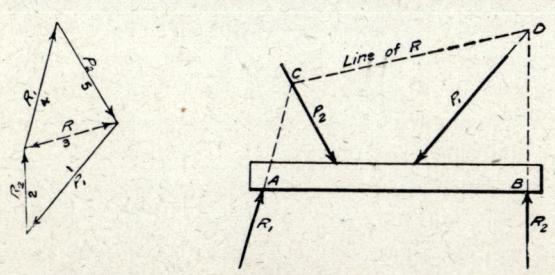

Fig. 24.

P_1, P_2, R_2, and R_1, and the magnitude of one of them, say P_1, are known. The resultant of P_1 and R_2 passes through D and must be the equilibrant of R_1 and P_2; it must, therefore, pass through C also. Draw the two force triangles 123 and 453 (with R as a common side), in the order in which the lines are numbered; the intersections determine the magnitudes of P_2, R_1 and R_2. We thus have a force quadrilateral[1], the diagonal line representing two equal and opposite forces.

This procedure evidently does not apply when the forces are parallel. For a method of solution which will give R_1 and R_2 and the direction of R_1, when P_1 and P_2 are fully known, see Art. 46, Fig. 39.

34. Any Number of Forces in Equilibrium. Fig. 25 shows a body acted upon by the force P at m. If at any point n, two equal and opposite forces parallel to the line of P and each equal to P, be introduced they can not change the effect. P is then equivalent to a force P parallel to it acting at *any* point n and a couple whose moment is Pa.

It follows that *any force may be considered as acting parallel to itself through any point if a couple is introduced whose moment is equal to the product of the force into the distance through which it has been supposed to be moved.* This principle is of much practical importance.

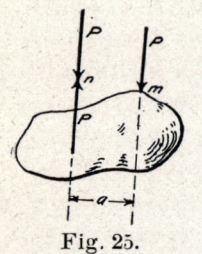

Fig. 25.

Fig. 26 shows a number of non-concurrent forces which have been treated in the above manner; each one has been shifted to a common point O, so that there results a system of concurrent forces and a system of couples. *The system of couples may be reduced to a single couple* (30) *whose moment is*

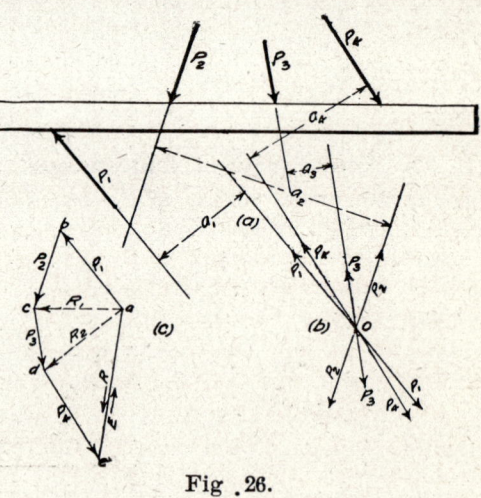

$$M = P_1 a_1 - P_2 a_2 - P_3 a_3 + P_4 a_4, \text{ etc.}$$

Fig. 26.

---

[1]This is the method of Culmann, the founder of graphic statics.

The concurrent forces may be reduced to a single force R. See Fig. 26(c) and Art. 35.

Any number of non-concurrent forces are, in general, equivalent to a single force and a couple. These are again reducible to a single force unless $R = 0$, in which case the resultant is a couple.

In the special case when $R = 0$, the resultant is a couple, and in the special case when $M = 0$, the resultant is a single force (30).

FOR COMPLETE EQUILIBRIUM
$$R = 0 \text{ and } M = 0.$$

These conditions will now be shown graphically, remembering that R refers to the concurrent forces and M to the couples.

35. Force Polygon. The resultant R will now be found, that is, the resultant of half the forces at O in Fig. 26. This may be done by means of the force triangle (32). In Fig. 26(c) the resultant of P_1 and P_2 is R_1; of R_1 and P_3 is R_2; of R_2 and P_4 is R. The given forces are not in equilibrium since their resultant is not zero. The equilibrant is ea. It is important to note that the given forces must be drawn so as to follow each other in direction in each triangle, and this results in having their directions the same around the polygon $abcdea$, when E is one of them. This polygon is the FORCE POLYGON and it follows that,

When a number of forces form a closed polygon, they are in equilibrium if their directions around the polygon are the same (clockwise or anti-clockwise), and any one is the equilibrant of all the others. If any one force has an opposite direction to that of all the others, it is their resultant.

It is evidently not necessary, in drawing a force polygon, to draw the intermediate resultants, R_1, R_2, etc., but only to lay out, in magnitude and direction, one force at the end of the preceding one. If the polygon closes the forces are in equilibrium; if not, the closing line will be the equilibrant or resultant. If the forces had been numbered in a different order, the appearance of the polygon would have been entirely different, but the equilibrant would have been the same (Fig. 26c).

It remains to find the value of M if the forces are non-concurrent. If they are concurrent the point O (Fig. 26) may be taken at their common point of intersection, in which case the arms a of the couples all become zero and $M = 0$. *For concurrent forces, therefore, the number of independent equations of equilibrium is one less than for non-concurrent forces.*

36. Location of Resultant. The resultant of P_1, P_2, P_3, and P_4 is easily located in the space diagram Fig. 27; for the resultant of P_1 and P_2 must pass through m and be parallel to R_1 in Fig. 26(c); the resultant of R_1 and P_3 must pass through n and be parallel to R_2 in Fig. 26(c); and the resultant of R_2 and P_4, which is the resultant of all the given forces in this case, must pass through o parallel to R or ea; $m\,n\,o\,p$ is the resultant polygon. If a force equal to E is applied in the line op, there will be complete equilibrium. *If it is applied parallel to op, as in qr, the resultant is a couple, because E is equal to R.* If it is applied at an angle to op, the force polygon will not close and there will be neither equilibrium of translation nor of rotation.

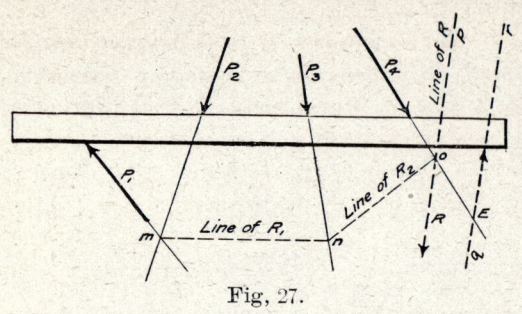

When the forces are parallel, or when the intersections m, n, o fall beyond the drawing, this method of locating the resultant fails. A method which is applicable in *all cases* will now be given.

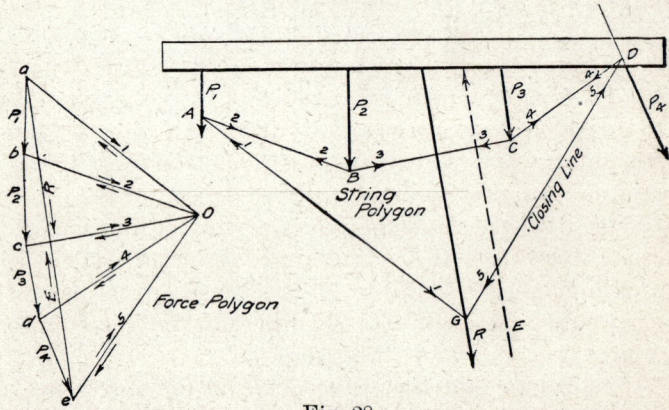

37. The String Polygon. In Fig. 28 there are four nearly parallel forces. The force polygon gives the equilibrant E, or the resultant R, in amount and direction. But to find the location of E or R in the space diagram it is necessary to resort to what is known as the string polygon, because the forces are so nearly parallel that their intersections will not fall within the limits of the drawing. Two forces, 1 and 2, may be introduced at any point A in the line of action of P_1, such that they will equilibrate P_1. This may be done by drawing any convenient force triangle aOb and the lines through A parallel to 1 and 2 (Oa and bO). The arrows within the triangle show the proper direction for equilibrium

Where the line of 2 intersects P_2 (at B), introduce two forces 2 and 3 such that they will equilibrate P_2 and one of them be equal and opposite to the force 2 used at P_1. These will be the forces 2 and 3 from the force triangle bOc. In a like manner P_3 and P_4 are equilibrated by the force 3 and 4 at C, and the forces 4 and 5 at D from triangles cOd and dOe. There remains yet unbalanced only forces 1 and 5 and therefore the equilibrant of these must be the resultant of the whole system. It must be equal to R of the force polygon and must pass through G, the intersection of strings 1 and 5, in the space diagram. Since R passes through G for complete equilibrium, E must pass through G in an opposite direction. If E were parallel to R, as shown in Fig. 28, the resultant would be a couple, because $E = R$ in the force polygon.

The polygon $ABCDGA$ is called a *string polygon*[1]; its sides are the *strings,* and these are drawn parallel to the components 1, 2, 3, etc. of the force polygon, which are called *rays*. The point O is called the *pole*. The last line drawn in the string polygon is called the *closing line,* since it closes the polygon if all the forces are in equilibrium. If the last and first strings do not intersect on the line of one of the forces, there can not be equilibrium, for they represent the lines of action of forces in the force polygon, which form a triangle. Therefore, WHEN THE STRING POLYGON CLOSES, THE RESULTANT IS A SINGLE FORCE; WHEN THE FORCE POLYGON CLOSES, THE RESULTANT IS A COUPLE; AND WHEN BOTH POLYGONS CLOSE, THE RESULTANT IS ZERO—THERE IS COMPLETE EQUILIBRIUM, THAT IS $R = 0$ AND $M = 0$.

The pole O is so chosen as to give good intersections (not acute) in the string polygon for locating the points B, C, etc.

The above demonstration may be carried through by resolving each of the given forces into two components; the arrows on the rays will be reversed.

38. Properties of the String Polygon. The string polygon represents only lines of action of forces whose magnitudes are

---

[1] Also called a funicular polygon and an equilibrium polygon. The force polygon is also an equilibrium polygon.

given in the force polygon. Forces are scaled from the force polygon and distances from the space diagram, or string polygon.

An infinite number of string polygons may be drawn in a given case, because the point A (Fig. 28) may be taken anywhere in the line of action of P_1, and the pole O may also be chosen at any convenient point, but the point G will always fall upon the line of action of E if there is complete equilibrium. The string polygon is simply a device for locating the point G. If the directions of the components are carefully noted, it will be found that they all balance each other; for example, 1 acts toward O as a component of P_1 and away from O as a component of E. This means that if the string polygon were a frame there would be stresses in it equal to the components 1, 2, 3, 4 and 5 (7). (Compression in AG; tension in AB). Such an imaginary frame is useful in finding reactions as will be explained later (47).

If the five forces of Fig. 28 are in equilibrium, any one may be considered the equilibrant of all the others (35), and any string may be considered the closing line of the equilibrium polygon. It is evident that the equilibrant of P_1, P_2 and P_3 would pass through the intersection of the lines of action of 1 and 4, and of P_1 and P_2, through the intersection of the lines of 1 and 3.

Further properties of the string polygon are explained in Chapters IV and V.

Fig. 27 shows a string polygon which results when the pole is chosen at one of the apexes of the force polygon; it is called a *resultant polygon*. The pole is at a Fig. 26 (c).

39. The Laws of Equilibrium. To insure equilibrium among the forces acting upon a structure or upon any part of it, as explained in Art. 29, it is only necessary to write the equations of equilibrium and solve for the unknowns. These equations are the very foundation of the whole subject, and are given in Art. 34; for practical application, however, they are stated as follows:

1. Σ HORIZONTAL COMPONENTS $= 0$. (5)
2. Σ VERTICAL COMPONENTS $= 0$. (6)
3. Σ MOMENTS $= 0$. (7)

or

1. Σ Components acting toward the right $=$
   Σ " " " " " left. (5a)
2. Σ " " " " up $=$
   Σ " " " " down. (6a)
3. Σ Clockwise Moments $= \Sigma$ Anti-clockwise Moments. (7a)

Art. 40   METHODS OF APPLICATION.   45

The terms "horizontal" and "vertical" are used because the loads which act on structures are usually weights which act vertically, and because it is usually convenient to resolve inclined forces into horizontal and vertical components, but it is understood that the terms may be applied to *any forces at right angles to each other*.

That equations 5 and 6 make $R=0$ is shown in the force polygon, Fig. 29.

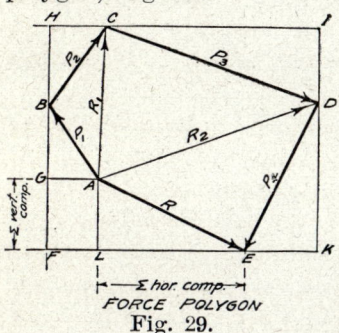

Forces (or components) or moments acting in opposite directions to have opposite signs in any *member* of the above equations. It is burdensome to use an adopted convention with regard to signs, and *it is usually convenient to place the known quantities on one side of the equation and the unknowns, whose directions may not be known,* on the other side. To illustrate the rule, the simple case shown in Fig. 17 gives

$$R_1 + R_2 = P \text{ or } R_1 - P + R_2 = 0 \text{ or } P - R_1 - R_2 = 0.$$

FORCE POLYGON
Fig. 29.

Knowing the line of action of a force but not its direction, it may be entered in the equation of equilibrium with a + sign, upon the assumption that it acts in the corresponding direction; if the solution makes a − quantity of it, it acts in the opposite direction from that assumed.

40. Methods of Application of the Equations of Equilibrium. Having written the equations of equilibrium, it becomes a simple matter to calculate stresses. But the beginner will find his greatest difficulty in writing these equations. To do this successfully requires the strictest adherence to some *method*. The following is an outline of a method which is easily remembered, and it is very essential to remember to apply it:

1. *Make a good sketch* (preferably to scale) giving all the elementary dimensions of the structure, and completely locating all loads by means of proper dimension lines not confused with anything else. A poor sketch is usually misleading, and the time used in making it, worse than wasted.

2. *Take time to consider the problem in all its bearings.* Time spent in deciding upon a method of attack is always well

spent, while a blind attack results in failure and disappointment. The simplest method is also usually the one requiring the least work and is, for that reason, the safest.

3. *Keep all solutions in neat shape, avoiding confusion*; mistakes will be easier found and corrected. For this purpose it is necessary to have always an extra sheet of scratch paper.

4. *Consider the reasonableness of the result.* Even a beginner will have some bounds beyond whch a result will appear unreasonable, and with experience these bounds are very much narrowed. See that results are in proper units. A force times a distance can not equal pounds.

5. *Use no short cuts.* Short cuts come with practice, but with a beginner they lead to mistakes and useless work.

6. *Use some check.* A check may consist of a rough inspection of the numerical operations, the determination of an unknown by two different methods, a solution by another method, a reversed solution, a comparison of various results, a comparison with a solution of a similar problem, or a repetition of the work. It is not a sin to err, but it is a sin to allow the error to remain undiscovered, and sometimes the consequences may be serious.

7. *Avoid useless refinement.* An error of 50 lbs. in a stress, as calculated from the assumed data, (for a bridge or a building) is much to be preferred to having such stress expressed in odd figures or fractions of a pound. Some judgment should be brought to bear in such matters.

8. *For each unknown, decide upon a method of application of the equations of equilibrium and adhere to it.* The unknowns are the magnitudes of reactions and stresses and sometimes also the directions of the reactions. It is not necessary to adhere to one method of application in a particular problem, but it is very essential not to get them confused in getting a particular unknown.

The equations of equilibrium may be applied in six ways, namely, algebraically[1] *or graphically,*

1. TO THE STRUCTURE AS A WHOLE.
2. TO ANY ONE JOINT.
3. TO ANY PART OF THE STRUCTURE CUT OFF FROM THE REST.

The first method considers the whole structure in equilibrium

---

[1] "Analytically" is sometimes used in place of this term, but both methods are analytic.

and is, therefore, applicable for finding *reactions only*. *These are evidently independent of the shape of the structure,* and may often be conveniently gotten by considering one or more resultants of the loads, in place of the loads themselves.

The conditions at the supports must be known. If a beam, supported at its two ends, for example, is not free to move longitudinally at one support, the reactions are *statically indeterminate,* and it is useless to write equations of equilibrium; **but the assumption of such freedom is usually on the safe side.**

The *second method* evidently applies only **to trusses** but both stresses and reactions (in certain cases) may be gotten by its means. The forces dealt with are concurrent, their lines of action meeting at the center of the joint. In this method only two of the equations are independent as explained in Art. 35. For an explanation as to which equations to use, see Art. 41.

The *third method* is called the *method of sections,* and is applicable in finding stresses in all sorts of structures and the only method for finding stresses in simple beams and girders.

If a structure is cut in two by a plane or curved section, either part must be in equilibrium, if the *forces cut off* are considered like external forces. This method, then, reduces to the first method, the only difference being that in one case the whole structure is considered and in the other a part of it. It may also be considered to reduce to the second method when the part cut off includes but a single joint.

It is very important to leave out of consideration altogether any forces acting on that part of the structure which has been discarded, and to include all those acting on the other part—loads, reactions and *stresses.* To avoid confusion the beginner should invariably erase the discarded part, or place a piece of paper over it when writing the equations of equilibrium.

It is evident that, since a section may be taken through any part of the structure, as many sections as are necessary to find all stresses desired may be made successively. *It is useless, however, to consider any section cutting more than three unknowns, because there are but three independent equations.*

41. Which Equations of Equilibrium to Use. A choice may be made of any of the following combinations of the equations of equilibrium in solving for *three* unknowns.

1. Two resolution and one moment equation.
2. One resolution and two moment equations[1].
3. Three moment equations[2].

Since there must be equilibrium for any center of moments, it is plain that an infinite number of moment equations may be written. That any three of them or any two of them are independent is not so apparent from what precedes. If the moment of the resultant is zero for *any* point, it can not be a couple, because the moment of a couple is the same for every point. If the sum of the moments is zero for two different points, therefore, the line of action of the resultant passes through these points; *this fixes its direction*; it remains to impose another condition making it equal to zero. If the moment of the resultant is zero for any point not in its line of action, the resultant must be zero; or if it has no component in any *one* direction it is zero; it has no component in one direction if the forces are in equilibrium and the components are inclined to it or parallel to it.

Graphically combinations 2 and 3 are of no importance, because they involve more labor than the first combination.

It is plain that, with the exceptions noted, any one of the three combinations of the three equations of equilibrium may be used; it is simply a matter of convenience. The applications will be illustrated under the different methods.

When the forces are *concurrent,* there are only two independent equations, as follows:

1. Two resolution equations.
2. One resolution and one moment equation.
3. Two moment equations.

These equations have various advantages and disadvantages in their practical use. The resolution equations involve the determination of sines and cosines, while the moment equations involve the calculation of moment arms. Except in special cases, the unknowns are found by elimination between several resolution equations, while a moment equation may always be written containing but one unknown, if the center of moments is chosen upon the line of action of an unknown force, or at the intersection of two unknown forces. *The moment equations are the simplest for*

---

[1] The centers of moments must not be in a line perpendicular to the components.

[2] The centers of moments must not be in the same straight line.

such unknown stresses whose lever arms are equal to some elementary dimension of the structure. Lever arms may sometimes be taken by scale from a proper drawing—this should be done in any case as a check—when the method becomes partly graphic. A *combination* of resolution and moment equations is usually the most convenient for many structures.

42. Statically Indeterminate Cases. In general, the three equations of equilibrium will suffice to determine three unknowns. These may be the magnitudes or directions of three forces, the magnitudes of two and the direction of one, or the directions of two and the magnitude of one. If there are other unknowns the structure is satically indeterminate unless geometrical conditions yield a further relation between unknowns; for example, it is sometimes evident that two unknowns are equal.

If the conditions of concurrency or parallelism are imposed upon the forces, only two unknowns can be found as explained in Art. 35. It follows that *two stresses may be determined at each joint of a truss.* It does not follow, however, that a structure is statically indeterminate, if by proceeding from joint to joint, a joint is found where there are more than two unknown stresses; it depends upon the total number of unknown stresses and the total number of joints. If j is the number of joints in a truss, $2j$ unknowns may be found; if it is supported at its ends, it will require, in general, three equations to determine the reactions. Therefore, if the number of members is less than or equal to $2j-3$, . (8) the truss is statically determinate. This is illustrated in the truss of Fig. 30. For any system of loads, the reaction R_1 having been calculated, stresses 1 and 13 may be found at joint 1; there remain then two unknowns at joint 2 which may likewise be determined. The same procedure applies at joint 13 after which there remain three unknowns at joints 12, 3 or 4 and four at joints 14 or 5 but the truss is not statically indeterminate because

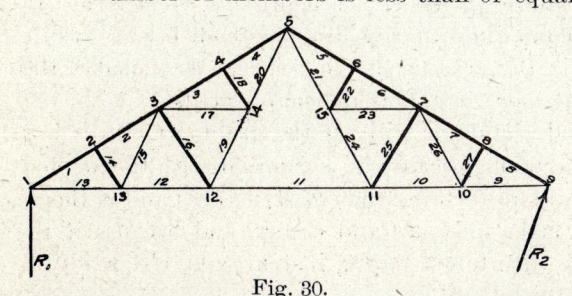

Fig. 30.

$2j - 3 = 30 - 3 = 27 =$ number of members. If another member were added without adding any more joints, it would be indeterminate. The stresses in this case are easily gotten by using a combination of the second method with the method of sections (56).

Statically indeterminate structures are generally avoided. The distribution of stress in them depends upon the relative stiffness of their parts. The stresses are determined by means of the principle of virtual work or least work. See Chapter XVIII.[1]

43. Comparison of Graphic and Algebraic Methods. In comparing graphic and algebraic methods, it should be understood that the slide rule is used in the latter by all experienced calculators, and that the matter of relative accuracy is unimportant, excepting certain graphic solutions. If two lines make an acute intersection with each other, the point of intersection can not be accurately located, and the resulting error may be too great. The same objection holds for intersections found by means of long lines whose directions may be slightly in error. These objections arise particularly in the use of the string polygon, but the force polygon is its own check, for it will not close if the work is not accurate. With careful work, proper instruments, and proper scales, it is seldom necessary to redraw a force polygon.

The greater the number of different inclinations of forces (external and internal) to be dealt with, the more the use of the graphic method is to be commended, and the greater the liability to error in the algebraic method. The more angles there are to deal with, the more laborious the algebraic methods become, while this has no effect in the graphic method, except as it makes the diagrams somewhat more irregular or complicated.

An experienced calculator will use the graphic methods less than an inexperienced one, because he is familiar with the method of calculating stresses in certain kinds of structures and is therefore less liable to make mistakes and errors, and because it requires considerable time to get paper, instruments, etc. ready to use the graphic methods.

Graphically, the method of application of the equations of equilibrium to any one joint is, by far, the most important, because it deals with force polygons, and the method of sections is the least important.

---

[1] Prof. Heller died before the completion of this book.

The advantages and disadvantages of the two methods for finding reactions and the four methods for finding stresses, together with those resulting from the use of the different equations of equilibrium, will be brought out in what follows.

44. Rules to be Observed in the Use of the Graphic Methods. In order to measure forces, it is necessary to use a scale. For this purpose a decimal scale (an engineer's scale) is necessary—one divided into tenths, twentieths, thirtieths, fortieths, fiftieths and sixtieths of an inch. It is not necessary to know how many pounds an inch represents, but the scales for distances and forces should be given on the drawing as a "scale of 10," a "scale of 40," etc. By placing the given scale upon a line representing a known quantity, it is at once apparent how an unknown quantity should be read.

The scaling of stresses should not be complicated by requiring scaled distances to be multiplied or divided by 2, 3 or 4, except that, when convenient, such a scale may be chosen as will require scaled stresses to be multiplied or divided by two. Stresses should be scaled as closely as may be, estimating between divisions. Good instruments should be used. Triangles and straight edges should be tested before using. Soft paper should be avoided.

Truss and stress diagrams should not be drawn on separate sheets, and for all ordinary problems the sheet need not be larger than 8"x10", and the diagrams should not be allowed to run off the sheet. A little preliminary sketching will serve to indicate where a diagram should be started.

Prick points made with a fine needle point should locate *all* intersections.

A well sharpened *hard* pencil should be used for drawing all lines and these should not be "inked in," unless the intersections are protected by small circles made with a bow pen.

Truss diagrams should be laid out accurately to as *large a scale* as the sheet will permit, and great care should be taken in transferring the direction of any member to the stress diagram.

Stress diagrams (force polygons) should be drawn to as *small a scale* as is consistent with the required degree of accuracy in reading stresses. If stress and truss diagrams are both large, it will be found difficult to transfer directions from one to the other.

If inks of different colors are used, say red for the lower chord, black for the upper chord, and blue for the web, the diagrams will be much clearer than when made with a single color.

QUESTIONS AND PROBLEMS. CHAPTER III.

1. How are live loads determined? Dead loads? Wind loads? Reactions? Stresses?

2. In applying the laws of equilibrium, are external and internal forces treated alike?

3. Illustrate the things which fully determine a force. Must it always be assumed that there is a rigid connection between a force and the body upon which it acts?

4. Must concurrent forces have the same point of application?

5. When there is actual rotation produced by a force, where is the center of moments taken?

6. If the resultant of the two forces of a couple be regarded as an infinitely small force, what must be its lever arm to make its moment equal to that of the couple? Why is the moment of a couple the same for any center in its plane?

7. What are the simplest systems of forces that are equivalent to any system of co-planar forces?

8. If in Fig. 20, $P = 10000$ lbs., $a = 8.5$ ft., and $b = 5$ ft., what must be the weight of the car to just balance the wind load? What will the vertical reactions be if the car weighs this amount?
Ans. 34000 lbs.; 0 and 34000 lbs.

9. Into how many sets of two components at right angles to each other may a given force be resolved?

10. If the dead load stress in a certain member of a truss is 15000 lbs. tension, what will be the stress in it if the live load produces 24000 lbs. compression?

11. Give three very fundamental statements in graphic statics which are derived from the parallelogram of forces.

12. If three forces are in equilibrium, prove by means of the force triangle which represents them, that the algebraic sums of the horizontal and of the vertical components are zero. Draw a rectangle which will circumscribe the triangle.

13. Resolve a force into two components by drawing a force triangle, so that both components shall be greater than the given force.

14. Show how to find the magnitude of the equilibrant of any two forces (not parallel) and the location of its line of action.

15. In Fig. 24 mark the order in which the magnitudes of the forces are determined when P_2 is the known force.

16. A force of 8000 lbs. acts 6 inches from the center of a wall; if it be taken as acting at the center of the wall, what will be the moment of the couple which must be introduced?

17. A force of 6000 lbs. acts vertically downward and a force of 10000 lbs. vertically upward; their lines of action are 5 ft. apart; what is their resultant, and how far from the line of action of the greater force is its line of action?   Ans. $7\frac{1}{2}$ ft.

18. What are the conditions for complete equilibrium of a body acted upon by a system of forces—algebraically and graphically?

19. What is the foundation of the force polygon?

20. If the direction of two forces in the force polygon were opposite to that of all the other forces, what would it indicate?

21. What is the fundamental principle used in drawing a resultant polygon? A string polygon?

22. If in Fig. 24 R_1, P_2, and P_1 were known, what would $ACDB$ be?

23. What is the function of the string polygon in Fig. 28? In Fig. 32? In Fig. 43? In Figs. 63 and 64?

24. How are the points A and O chosen in Fig. 28?

25. If the string polygon of Fig. 28 is considered as a framed structure, to what will the stress in BC be equal? In GD?

26. How may the closing line in Fig. 42 be made horizontal? In Fig. 28?

27. Where is the resultant of the loads in Fig. 43 located? In Fig. 61? In Fig. 64?

28. What is the difference between the string polygon and the resultant polygon?

29. If there is complete equilibrium when $R=0$ and $M=0$, why are there three independent equations?

30. Which of the eight directions given in Art. 40 plainly lead to a saving of time? Which to reliable results? Which to accuracy?

31. By which of the six methods of application of the equations of equilibrium are reactions obtained? By which stresses?

32. In Figs. 59 and 60, do the arrows on the members cut by the section represent the forces exerted by the part shown upon the other part, or vice versa?

33. Show how a curved section would be more convenient than a straight one in getting stress PQ in Fig. 53.

34. What combinations of the equations of equilibrium may be used in getting reactions? In getting stresses by the methods of sections and of joints?

35. What is the simplest method of getting the stress D_2 in Fig. 50?

36. What are the disadvantages in the use of the resolution equations of equilibrium? Of the moment equations?

37. Are reactions usually found graphically or algebraically? In what cases should a graphic method of finding stresses be used, and which one?

38. What is meant by a statically indeterminate structure? How may the truss of Fig. 52 be made statically indeterminate as regards stresses? As regards reactions?

39. What tools are necessary for drawing stress diagrams? What are the points upon which particular care should be bestowed?

CHAPTER IV.

APPLICATION OF THE LAWS OF EQUILIBRIUM TO THE STRUCTURE AS A WHOLE.

REACTIONS.

45. Reactions. Reactions will now be determined both algebraically and graphically for a number of different cases.

As stated in Art. 42, three unknown quantities may be determined from the three equations of equilibrium. In general there are two unknowns involved in each reaction, its magnitude and direction; therefore, even in the simplest case of a beam with two supports and vertical loads, some other condition must be introduced which will determine one of the four unknowns. The usual assumption is that there is no friction at one of the supports. This determines the direction of that reaction,—if there is no friction its direction must be perpendicular to the surface of the support. In practice this condition is never fully met.

46. Reactions for a Single Force. Fig. 31 shows a beam carrying a load P and supported at its ends A and B. The reactions, R_1 and R_2, will be vertical if the support at one end is such that the beam is free longitudinally.

Since all the forces are vertical there are no horizontal components. Applying the other two equations of equilibrium, we have Σ vert. comps. $= 0$

$$R_1 - P + R_2 = 0 \text{ or } R_2 = P - R_1$$

For Σ moments $= 0$, the center of moments may be taken at any convenient point; if it is taken at B, the moment of R_2 is zero and we have R_1 directly from

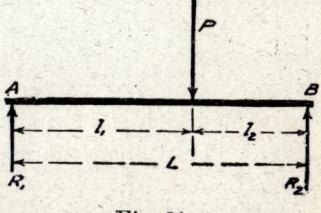

$$R_1 L - P l_2 = 0 \text{ or } R_1 = P \frac{l_2}{L}$$

Fig. 31.

This value of R_1 substituted in the equation above will give the value of $R_2 = P - P\dfrac{l_2}{L} = P\dfrac{l_1}{L}$. As a *check*, with center at A, from Σ moments $= 0$,

$$R_2 L = P l_1 \text{ or } R_2 = P\dfrac{l_1}{L}.$$

This illustrates the law of the lever, to which the student should become accustomed so that it will be unnecessary to think of the moment equations. Thus, if (Fig. 31) $L = 20$ ft., and $l_1 = 12$ ft., and $l_2 = 8$ ft., $R_1 = \tfrac{8}{20}P = \tfrac{2}{5}P$, and $R_2 = \tfrac{12}{20}P = \tfrac{3}{5}P$. As a check, $R_1 + R_2 = (\tfrac{2}{5} + \tfrac{3}{5})P = P$.

Graphically, the problem is to find two vertical forces R_1 and R_2, which will be in equilibrium with P.

It is only necessary to draw a closed string polygon and a corresponding force polygon. The three forces P, R_1, and R_2 must act through the apexes of the string polygon. In Fig. 32, draw the strings 1 and 2 from C parallel to the equilibrants (bO and Oa) of P; where these strings intersect R_1 and R_2 in D and E, there must be apexes of the string polygon; hence $DCED$ is the string polygon. Drawing nO parallel to DE, it is the ray corresponding to the string DE and therefore cuts off the forces R_1 and R_2 in the force polygon which is $abna$, a straight line, since the forces are parallel. The student should prove that there is equilibrium as was done in Art. 37.

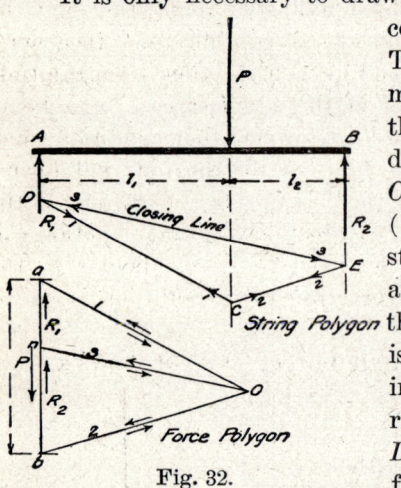

Fig. 32.

It is evident that $P = R_1 + R_2$; the line nO, drawn parallel to the closing line, divides P into two parts equal to R_1 and R_2.

Exactly the same procedures apply to any kind of a truss supported at its ends, because *reactions are independent of the form of the structure.*

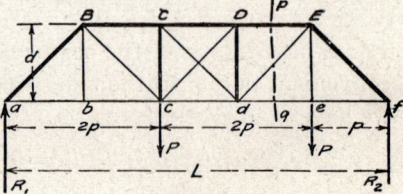

In Fig. 33, the panels

Fig. 33.

Art. 46.   REACTIONS FOR A SINGLE FORCE.   57

being of equal length, the resultant of the two loads evidently acts at d and is $2P$, so that

$$R_1 = \tfrac{2}{5} 2P = \tfrac{4}{5} P \text{ and } R_2 = \tfrac{3}{5} 2P = \tfrac{6}{5} P.$$

$$R_1 + R_2 = (\tfrac{4}{5} + \tfrac{6}{5}) P = 2P \text{ (check)}.$$

Graphically the solution would be exactly like that of Fig. 32, using the resultant $2P$ acting at d.

Let Fig. 34 represent a ladder supported by a wall at B. If the friction between the wall and the ladder be neglected, R_2 will be horizontal and the line of R_1 must pass through C because R_2, P, and R_1 are in equilibrium. The magnitudes of R_1 and R_2 may be found from a force triangle.

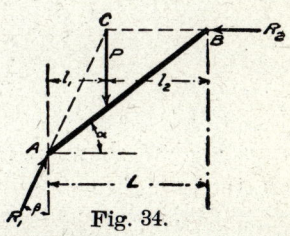

Fig. 34.

This may also be solved by passing a string polygon through the one known point A of R_1 as shown in Fig. 35.

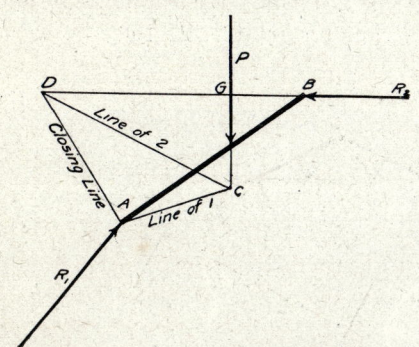

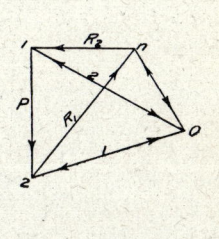

Fig. 35.

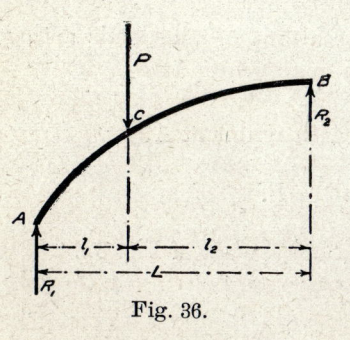

Fig. 36.

The case of Fig. 36 is the same as that of Fig. 31. If R_2 were horizontal, it would be the same as that of Fig. 34 and R_1 would be inclined.

Algebraically, Fig. 34, from Σ vert. comps. $= 0$, $R_1 \cos \beta = P$, and from Σ hor. comps. $= 0$, $R_1 \sin \beta = R_2$, and from Σ moms. $= 0$ with center at A, $R_2 \times L \tan \alpha$

$= Pl_1$. To eliminate between these equations, makes this method somewhat laborious. This case is similar to that of Fig. 23.

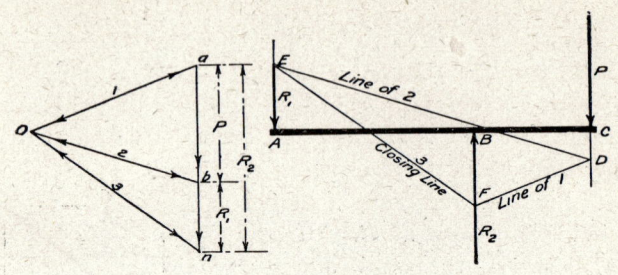

Fig. 37.

Fig. 37 shows a cantilever beam with supports at A and B, the part BC extending beyond the support B.

Taking moment about B, $R_1 \times AB = P \times BC$ and with A as a center, $R_2 \times AB = P \times CA$. As a check, $R_2 = R_1 + P$.

Graphically a string polygon is drawn beginning at D. On parallel to the closing line gives the force polygon, $abna$.

If the truss in Fig. 38 is fixed at both supports A and B, the reactions are statically indeterminate. If they be assumed

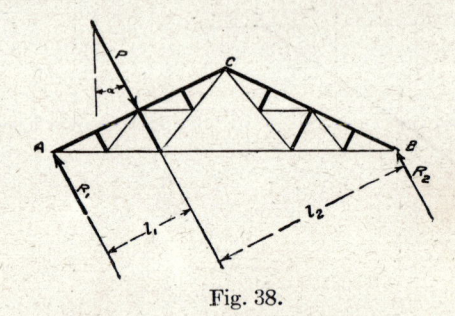

Fig. 38.

parallel to the load, which is the resultant of the loads acting at the joints in the line AC, we have, with center at B,

$$R_1(l_1+l_2) = Pl_2; \quad \text{and with center at } A,$$

$$R_2(l_1+l_2) = Pl_1. \quad R_1 + R_2 = P.$$

Graphically the problem is the same as that of Fig. 32.

Usually when the ends of the truss are both fixed they are

Art. 46.   REACTIONS FOR A SINGLE FORCE.   59

fastened to the tops of columns at A and B, in which case it is customary to assume the horizontal components of the reactions equal. This would *not* give parallel reactions in Fig. 38.

In Fig. 39, P_1 is the resultant of the wind loads at the joints of AC and P_2 of the vertical loads at the joints of AC and

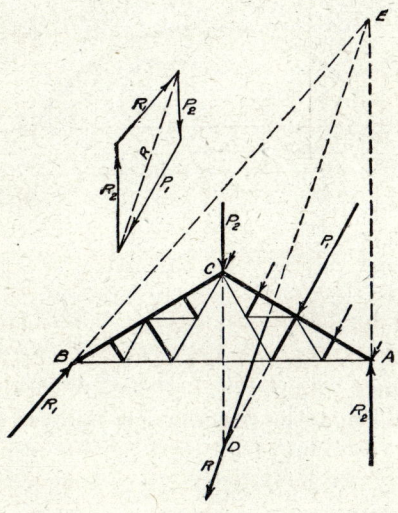

Fig. 39.

CB. This case may be reduced to that of Fig. 23 by finding the resultant R, of P_1 and P_2; it must pass through D. Now R_1, R, and R_2 being in equilibrium, must meet in the point E. This gives the direction of R_1 and the force polygon determines the amounts of R_1 and R_2 (33).

Should any of the intersections be very acute, resort should be had to the string polygon, but the original forces should not be used unless their resultants are not readily located.

A *hinge* is a joint about which the parts of a structure are free to turn; it is assumed to be frictionless and, therefore, the moment at its center is zero for a structure in equilibrium.

Fig. 40 shows a symmetrical three-hinged arch with a single load P on the left half. Considering the right half by itself it is evident that there are but two forces acting upon it, the reaction R_2 and the pressure of the left half through the hinge at C. Since two forces to be in equilibrium must act in the same straight line, the line of R_2 must pass through the center hinge at C. This determines the point D, and since R_1

is in equilibrium with P and R_2 its line of action passes through D. The force polygon gives the magnitudes of R_1 and R_2.

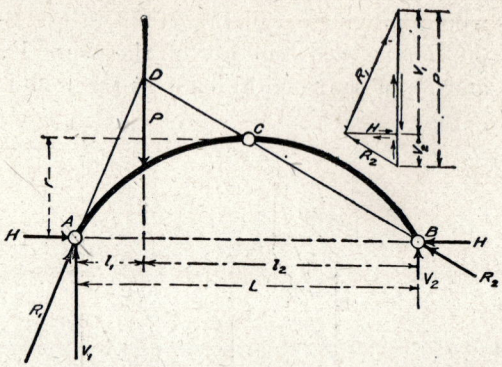

Fig. 40.

In like manner, reactions may be found for a load on the right hand half. By finding the resultant of the two reactions at A (for example) we get the reaction for both loads. If there are a number of loads, the case may be reduced to the above by first finding the resultant of all the loads on each half.

Algebraically, we have from Σ hor. comps. $= 0$

Hor. comp. $R_1 =$ hor. comp. $R_2 = H$

From Σ vert. comps. $= 0$,

$P =$ vert. comp. $R_1 +$ vert. comp. $R_2 = V_1 + V_2$.

From Σ moms. about $C = 0$ (considering only half the arch),

$Hr = V_2 \times \tfrac{1}{2} L$ or $Hr + P(\tfrac{1}{2} L - l_1) = V_1 \times \tfrac{1}{2} L$.

Three of these equations determine the unknowns H, V_1, and V_2. R_1 is the resultant of H and V_1 and R_2 of H and V_2. Equations may, of course, be written with centers at A or B.

In this case, just as in that of Fig. 31,

$$V_1 = P\frac{l_2}{L} \text{ and } V_2 = P\frac{l_1}{L}$$

Substituting V_2 in the equation above,

$$Hr = \tfrac{1}{2} P l_1 \text{ and, } H = \tfrac{1}{2} P \frac{l_1}{r}.$$

47. Reactions for Any Number of Loads. The reaction for a number of loads may be gotten by finding the reaction for each load separately and adding these reactions, or by finding

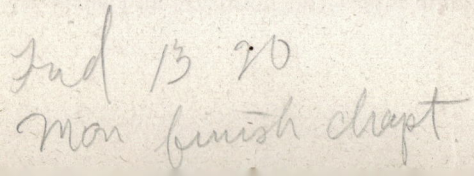

Art. 47. REACTIONS FOR ANY NUMBER OF LOADS. 61

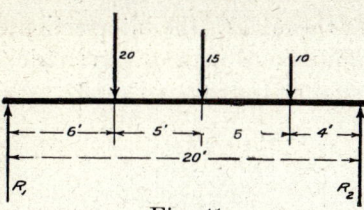

Fig. 41.

the location of the resultant of the loads thus reducing the problem to that of finding reactions for a single load.

In Fig. 41, the location of the resultant of the three loads is not apparent, therefore the first method is the better. By the law of the lever,

$$R_1 = \tfrac{4}{20}10 + \tfrac{9}{20}15 + \tfrac{14}{20}20 = 22\tfrac{3}{4}.$$
$$R_2 = \tfrac{6}{20}20 + \tfrac{11}{20}15 + \tfrac{16}{20}10 = 22\tfrac{1}{4}.$$
$$R_1 + R_2 = 22\tfrac{3}{4} + 22\tfrac{1}{4} = 45 = 20 + 15 + 10;\ check.$$

Applying the equations of equilibrium *directly*,
$$20\ R_1 = 20\times14 + 15\times9 + 10\times4 = 455\ \text{from which}$$
$$R_1 = \tfrac{455}{20} = 22\tfrac{3}{4}$$
$$20\ R_2 = 10\times16 + 15\times11 + 20\times6 = 445\ \text{from which}$$
$$R_2 = \tfrac{445}{20} = 22\tfrac{1}{4}$$

Graphically, the problem is to divide the equilibrant of the three loads into two parts, R_1 and R_2, such that when acting at A and B respectively, they will balance the loads.

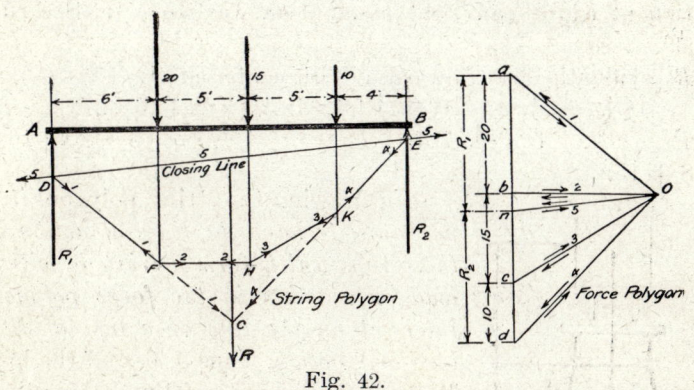

Fig. 42.

The force polygon (Fig. 42) *abcda* gives the equilibrant *da*. To find the point *n*, draw the equilibrium polygon *DFHKED* and *On* parallel to *ED*. The ray 5 corresponds with the string DE —— the closing line. The force polygon *abcdna* closes, and $dn = R_2$, and $na = R_1$. R_1, 1, and 5 are in equilibrium at D, also R_2, 5, and 4 at E.

The student should prove that there is equilibrium as was done in Art. 37.

REACTIONS FOR ANY NUMBER OF LOADS. Art. 47.

The resultant of the loads passes through C, the intersection of 1 and 4, since 1 and 4 are in equilibrium with ad (triangle adO). The string polygon DEC is similar to that of Fig. 32.

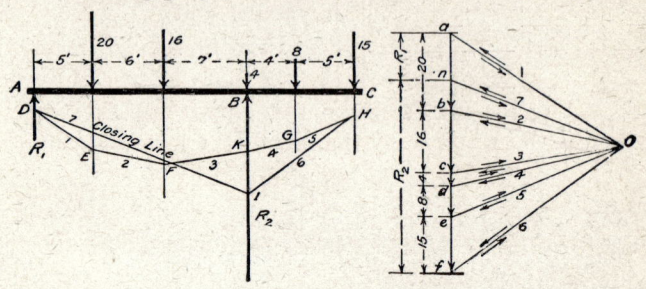

Fig. 43.

Fig. 43 shows a cantilever beam, the part BC extending beyond the support. The loads 20 and 16 will produce an upward reaction at A, while the loads 8 and 15 produce a downward reaction. The direction of the resultant R_1 is in doubt. Assuming R_1 to act upward, and with center at B,

$$18R_1 - 20 \times 13 - 16 \times 7 + 8 \times 4 + 15 \times 9 = 0$$

$R_1 = \tfrac{205}{18}$. Since this is plus as was assumed in writing the equation of equilibrium, the assumption was correct. See rule Art. 39.

R_2 evidently acts upward. With center at A,

$$18 R_2 = 20 \times 5 + 16 \times 11 + 4 \times 18 + 8 \times 22 + 15 \times 27.$$

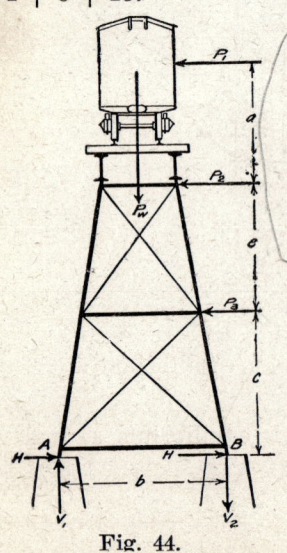

$R_2 = \tfrac{929}{18}$. As a check $R_1 + R_2 = \tfrac{205}{18} + \tfrac{929}{18} = 63 = 20 + 16 + 4 + 8 + 15$.

In drawing the string polygon, *it is necessary to have the lines of action of those rays which form a triangle with a load or reaction in the force polygon, intersect on the line of action of that load or reaction.* Thus 5, 6, and the load 15 form the triangle efO and their lines of action intersect at H.

nO, parallel to the closing line, determines R_1 and R_2.

Fig. 44 shows a trestle bent with foundations at A and B, and wind loads P_1, P_2, and P_3; the resultant of the entire weight is P_w and acts in the axis of symmetry. It is convenient to use only

Fig. 44.

Art. 47. REACTIONS FOR ANY NUMBER OF LOADS. 63

the horizontal and vertical components of the reactions, and it is *assumed* that the horizontal components are equal (46).

The direction in which V_2 will act depends upon the relative magnitudes of the horizontal and vertical loads. If it acts downward as shown, the structure must be anchored.

From Σ hor. comps. $= 0$, we get,
$$P_1 + P_2 + P_3 = 2H; \qquad (a)$$
from Σ vert. comps. $= 0$, we get,
$$P_w = V_1 - V_2; \qquad (b)$$
from Σ moms. $= 0$, with center at A, we get,
$$P_1(a+e+c) + P_2(e+c) + P_3 c - \tfrac{1}{2}b\, P_w - V_2 b = 0. \qquad (c)$$

The moments of the other forces (H and V_1) are zero. Equation (a) gives the value of H; equation (c), that of V_2; and equation (b), that of V_1. As a check a moment equation for B may be written.

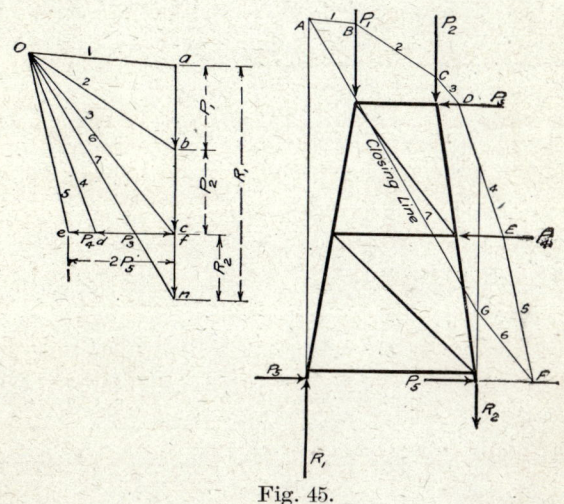

Fig. 45.

A problem quite similar to this is solved graphically in Fig. 45. The force polygon is *abcdefna* and the string polygon is *ABCDEFGA*.

The reactions R_1 and R_2 act in opposite directions.

48. Reactions for Uniform Loads. *A uniformly distributed load may be conceived to be a series of equal infinitely small concentrated loads infinitely small and equal distances apart.* In Fig. 46, the resultant of these loads would equal W and act at the middle of the beam, so that, *by symmetry*, each reaction is $\tfrac{1}{2}W$.

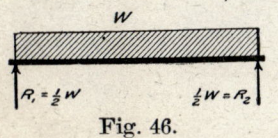

Fig. 46.

In Fig. 47 the resultant of the uniform load acts at its middle or 14 ft. from A and 6 ft. to the left of B.

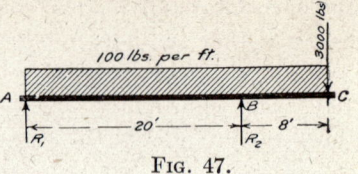

Fig. 47.

$$M_A = 3000 \times 28 + 2800 \times 14 - 20R_2 = 0$$
$$R_2 = \tfrac{123200}{20} = 6160 \text{ lbs.}$$

Assuming R_1 to act upward,
$$M_B = 20R_1 - 2800 \times 6 + 3000 \times 8 = 0.$$
$$R_1 = -\tfrac{7200}{20} = -360; \; R_1 \text{ acts } downward.$$

Graphically, the solution of this problem is like that of Fig. 43, the resultant of the uniform load being used as one load, and the 3000 lbs. as another.

QUESTIONS AND PROBLEMS CHAPTER IV.

1. Upon what equation of equilibrium is the law of the lever based?

2. If a beam is supported at its quarter point what must be the ratio of the load at the end of the short arm to that at the end of the long arm when the beam is balanced, neglecting the beam's own weight? If the beam is 20 ft. long and weighs 50 lbs. per ft., what load, at its end, will be required to balance it.

3. What are the reactions for a beam 20 ft. long, supported at its ends, weighing 100 lbs. per ft., and having a load of 15000 lbs. at 5 ft. from one end?

4. Find R_1 and R_2, Fig. 33, for $P = 20000$ lbs. Also for the same panel load at each of the joints b, c, d, and e.

5. Draw a truss of eight equal panels similar to that of Fig. 33 and number the intermediate joints, from right to left. Find the values of R_1, for a load P at 1, at 1 and 2, at 1, 2, and 3, etc.

6. If the truss of Fig. 33 consists of 5 panels at 20 ft. each, what will be the panel loads at c and d produced by a load 44 ft. from R_1, so placed upon the floor of the bridge that 6000 lbs. will be carried to one truss? What will be the reactions produced at the ends of the truss? What will be the reactions produced at the ends of a girder having a span of 100 ft., by a load of 6000 lbs. located 44 ft. from one support?

7. Show how the construction of Fig. 39 will be modified for the wind load on the other side of the roof.

8. What will be the horizontal and vertical components of the reactions for a symmetrical three-hinged arch having a span of 160 ft., and a rise of 40 ft., for a load of 80000 lbs. at 40 ft. from one support. (Apply the equations of equilibrium and do not use formulas).

9. Take the figures representing the loads in Fig. 43 as thousands of pounds, and find the reactions when these loads are combined with a uniform load of 400 lbs. per foot.

10. In the above case, what will be the shear at 15 ft. from A? At 7 ft. from C?

11. Find all the reactions for Fig. 49 when $P = 30000$ lbs., $h = 20$ ft., and $b = 16$ ft.

12. How would you find the reactions in Figs. 51 and 53 when the panel loads and panel lengths are unequal?

13. Is there any distinction between loads and reactions so far as the string polygon is concerned?

14. How would you find the location of the resultant of the loads in Fig. 61?

15. Calculate H, V_1, and V_2, Fig. 44, for $P_1 = 13500$ lbs., $P_2 = 6000$ lbs., $P_3 = 4000$ lbs., $a = 13.5$ ft., $e = 20$ ft., $c = 18$ ft., $b = 20$ ft., and $P_w = 24000$ lbs.

CHAPTER V.

APPLICATION OF THE LAWS OF EQUILIBRIUM TO A PART OF A STRUCTURE.

STRESSES.

49. Stresses. The stresses in the members of a truss are found by applying the laws of equilibrium to parts of the truss. These parts may be single joints or larger portions of the structure.

As explained in Art. 40, the application of the equations of equilibrium to one joint of a truss at a time, involves only concurrent forces. Graphically, we deal with force polygons only. Any joint may be treated graphically or algebraically, but there is usually nothing to be gained by using both methods for one truss.

When larger portions of the structure are considered in calculating stresses, it is called the method of sections. The stresses in the members cut by the section dividing the truss into two parts are obtained. This method is of considerable importance, especially the algebraic application, on account of its ready application to the forms of trusses usually used. This is the only method applicable for finding stresses in solid beams and girders.

When a single joint of a truss is considered, there are but two independent equations of equilibrium, the forces being concurrent. The solution must therefore begin at a joint where there are but two unknown quantities.

The reactions are first determined by the methods of Chapter IV.

50. Stresses in the Simplest Form of Truss. Stress Diagrams. Fig. 48 shows a triangular truss carrying a single load at its apex. To find the stresses (the reactions being known) it is only necessary to draw a force polygon for each joint. In this case, there are three forces at each joint, two being unknown. Laying out P to some suitable scale and drawing a force triangle for joint 2, stresses D_1 and D_2 are determined. Since these three forces are in equilibrium the direction of the arrows is clockwise as determined by the known direction of P. Transferring the directions of D_1 and D_2 to the truss diagram, we find they act *toward the joint*.

Laying out R_1 and drawing L and D_1 parallel to their directions in the truss diagram, the force triangle for joint 1, determines the stresses L and D_1. The directions are counter-clockwise as determined by R_1; transferring these to the truss, D_1 acts *toward the joint* and L *away from the joint*.

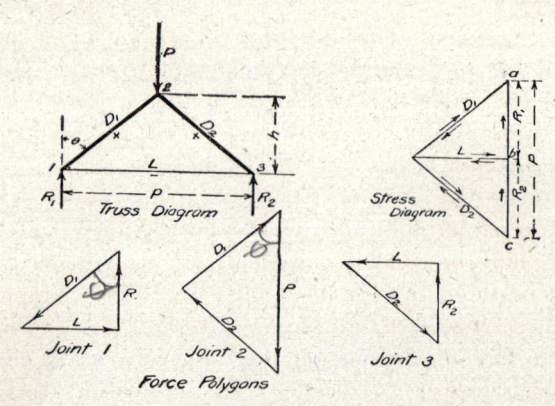

Fig. 48.

Treating joint 3 in like manner, it is found that each one of the stresses has been determined twice. To avoid this unnecessary labor, the force polygons (triangles in this case) may be drawn in one diagram, called a *stress diagram*,[1] as shown.

Starting with any known force, in the stress diagram, the direction in which any stress acts at a certain joint, can be determined by going around the force polygon for that joint. Since the lines are common to two joints, the directions which they show will be opposite to each other; *if these directions are toward the two joints in the truss diagram, the stress is evidently compressive, and if they are away from them, the stress is tensile* (7). Thus are the stresses fully determined.

Tensile and compressive stresses may be distinguished from each other by means of arrows in the truss diagram, or by lines of different colors, or by any other convenient sign. The usual signs used are $+$ and $-$ (as shown in Fig. 48), which have noth-

---

[1] Stress diagrams are also called Cremona diagrams, Maxwell diagrams, and reciprocal figures.

Art. 50.   STRESSES IN THE SIMPLEST TRUSS.   69

ing whatever to do with the signs in the equations of equilibrium. In this book *the $+$ sign is used to denote compression,* and *the $-$ sign to denote tension.* This convention is often reversed; practice is not uniform on this point. In mechanics, the $+$ sign is nearly always used to denote tension.

In drawing a stress diagram, it is not necessary to draw it joint by joint. The method of procedure is as follows:

1. Lay out the force polygon for the external forces. This will be a straight line for parallel forces but, since the polygon must close, the line will be traversed twice in going over all loads and reactions.

2. Draw lines parallel to the outer members (upper and lower chords); these will go through the points in the force polygon in which the adjacent outer forces in the truss diagram meet. If a number of members lie between two adjacent forces, the lines parallel to them in the stress diagram will all go through the same point. See Figs. 48 to 53.

3. Complete the stress diagram by drawing a *succession* of lines parallel to the inner members.

4. Determine the character of each stress by going around the force polygon for each joint, starting with a konwn force or stress. The character of each stress, together with its scaled amount *should be put on the truss diagram.*

It will be found that, if the external forces have been laid out in a clockwise direction, the order of the forces at any joint will be in a clockwise direction, as determined by the force polygon, and vice versa.

Algebraically, we have

At joint 1, $D_1 \cos \theta = R_1$ $\qquad\qquad D_1 = R_1 \sec \theta$
$\qquad D_1 \sin \theta = L = R_1 \tan \theta$

Or considering joint 1, with a center of moments at joint 2,

$$M_2 = \tfrac{1}{2} p R_1 - L h = 0 \qquad L = R_1 \frac{\tfrac{1}{2} p}{h} = R_1 \tan \theta$$

and with a center of moments at joint 3,

$$M_3 = R_1 p - D_1 p \cos \theta = 0 \qquad D_1 = R_1 \sec \theta$$

The stresses D_1 and L were first determined by two resolution equations and then by two moment equations. They may also be gotten by means of one resolution and one moment equation. It is to be noted that the equation in M_2 determines an unknown without finding a function of an angle, it being assumed that h is a known dimension of the truss.

The angle θ should always be measured from the direction of the loads, and its functions should always be expressed as ratios of lengths and thus used on the slide rule[1]. This necessitates the calculation of the lengths of the diagonal members which may easily be done by means of a table of squares.

The stress D_2 is equal to D_1 because the truss is symmetrical. They may also be gotten at joint 2 from $D_1 \sin\theta = D_2 \sin\theta$; hence $D_1 = D_2$ and $2D_1 \cos\theta = P$; $D_1 = \frac{1}{2} P \sec\theta$ which is the same as was gotten above since $R_1 = \frac{1}{2}P$. Using a moment equation we have,

$$M_3 = \frac{1}{2}pP - D_1 p\cos\theta = 0; \quad D_1 = \frac{1}{2} P \sec\theta$$

All stress diagrams are simply extensions of the above simple case excepting a few apparently statically indeterminate cases (42).

51. Stresses in a Crane. Fig. 49 shows a crane with supports at A and B and carrying a single load P.

The reaction at A is shown divided into its vertical and horizontal components R and H. The reaction at B is assumed to be horizontal.

The vertical reaction at A must be equal to P from Σ Vert. Comp. $=0$, and H at A equals H at B from Σ Horiz. Comp. $=0$.

By moments about A,

$$Hh = Pb \quad \text{and} \quad H = \frac{b}{h} P.$$

The stresses in the members may be obtained by resolutions at the joints.

Joint 2. $\quad U \sin\alpha = H \qquad U = H \dfrac{l_v}{b} \text{(tension)}$

$\qquad\qquad U \cos\alpha = V = H \dfrac{l_v a}{b\, l_v} = H \dfrac{a}{b} \text{(tension)}$

Joint 3. $\quad D \sin\beta = H \qquad D = H \dfrac{l_D}{b} \text{(compression)}$

It is to be noted that those equations have been chosen which involve but two forces, and it thus becomes a very simple matter to determine the character of the stress. Thus the horizontal

---

[1] An exception to this rule is the case of $\theta = 45°$. $\sin 45° = \cos 45° = 0.707$; $\tan 45° = 1.000$; $\sec 45° = 1.414$.

Art. 52. STRESSES IN AN UNSYMMETRICAL TRUSS. 71

component of U at joint 2 must act *away from the joint* to balance H.

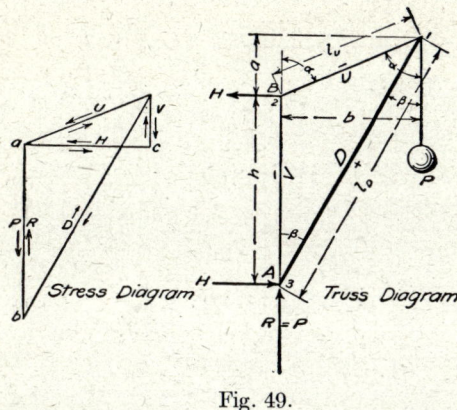

Fig. 49.

The stresses may be checked by writing other equations of equilibrium, as follows:

Joint 1. $U \sin \alpha = D \sin \beta$.
            $U \cos \alpha + P = D \cos \beta$.
Joint 3. $D \cos \beta = P + V$.
            $M_1 = Pb - H(a+h) + Vb = 0$.

The above equations are but solutions of the triangles in the stress diagram. The force polygon of external forces is *abaca*. The force polygon for joint 1 is PDU; for joint 2, HUV; and for joint 3, $RHVD$.

52. Stresses in an Unsymmetrical Truss Unsymmetrically Loaded. Fig. 50 shows a truss of three equal panels with parallel chords, and supports at joints 1 and 7. The reactions are readily found as explained in Chapter IV.

Graphically the force polygon for external forces is *abcda*. The force polygon for each joint is easily followed and the signs of the stresses determined. These are also readily found by inspection because the truss is a beam supported at its ends; it bends so that the upper chord is shortened and the lower chord lengthened; hence the upper chord members are in compression and the lower chord members in tension. The diagonals are determined by the shears in the panels; thus, the shear in panel 1–3 shortens D_1, the shear in panel 3–5 (2000 lbs. up) lengthens D_2, and the shear in panel 5–7 lengthens D_3. V_1 is in tension because it must be directly opposite to P_1.

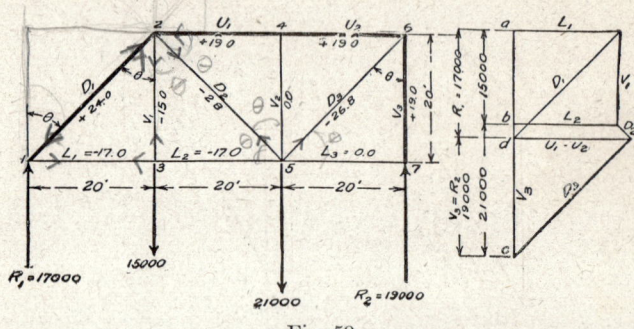

Fig. 50.

The algebraic solution is as follows:

$\theta = 45°$. $\operatorname{Sin}\theta = \cos\theta = 0.707$. $\operatorname{Sec}\theta = 1.414$. $\operatorname{Tan}\theta = \mathbf{1.000}$.

At joint 4, from Σ vert. comps. $= 0$, we have $V_2 = \mathbf{0}$, and at joint 7, from Σ hor. comps. $= 0$, we have $L_3 = 0$. These two stresses will, therefore, not appear in the stress diagram.

Joint 1. $D_1 = R_1 \sec\theta = 17000 \times 1.414 = 24000$ lbs. $(+)$.
  $D_1 \sin\theta = L_1 = 24000 \times 0.707 = 17000$ lbs. $(-)$.
Joint 3. $V_1 = P_1 = 15000$ lbs. $(-)$.
  $L_1 = L_2 = 17000$ lbs. $(-)$.
Joint 2. $D_1 \cos\theta - V_1 = D_2 \cos\theta$. $D_2 = D_1 - V_1 \sec\theta$.
  $D_2 = 24000 - 15000 \times 1.414 = 2800$ lbs. $(-)$.
  $U_1 = D_1 \sin\theta + D_2 \sin\theta = 26800 \times 0.707 = 19000$ lbs. $(+)$
Joint 4. $U_1 = U_2 = 19000$ lbs. $(+)$.
Joint 7. $V_3 = R_2 = 19000$ lbs. $(+)$.
Joint 6. $D_3 \cos\theta = V_3 = 19000$.
  $D_3 = 19000 \times 1.414 = 26800$. $(-)$.
Joint 5. $D_2 \cos\theta + D_3 \cos\theta = P_2 = 21000$ lbs.
  $(2800 + 26800)0.707 = 21000$ lbs. Check.

Only resolution equations have been used above, but in some cases the moment equations are even simpler. Thus, for joint 1, $M_2 = 20R_1 - 20L_1 = 0$; hence $L_1 = R_1$.

53. Bow's Notation. The method of lettering most frequently used for graphic solutions is one devised by Bow. By

Art. 54.   STRESSES IN A ROOF TRUSS FOR WIND LOAD.   73

this method, in the truss diagram the spaces between the forces (both external and internal) are lettered and a force or stress is designated by the two letters adjacent to it. This causes the letters in the force or stress diagram to come at the intersections, so that a stress is represented by a line with letters at its ends. This method is used only for graphic stress determinations. Bow's notation will be used for the graphic solution in the following article.

54. Stresses in a Roof Truss for Wind Load. Fig. 51 shows a roof truss with a normal wind load on one side of the roof. It is assumed that the support at E is on rollers or is free

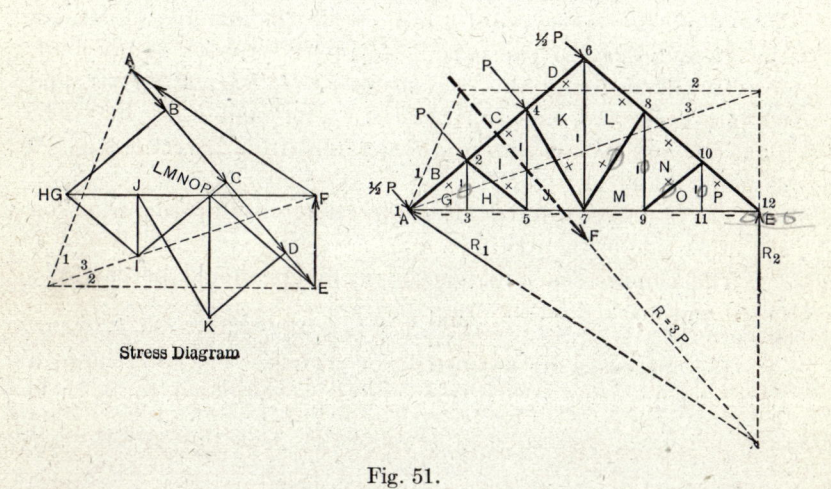

Fig. 51.

to slide without friction. Therefore, the reaction R_2 will be vertical.

When there are so many different inclinations of members and external forces, the reactions as well as the stresses are best obtained graphically.

When the loads are symmetrical as in this case, their resultant may be located immediately, and if the intersection of this resultant and R_2 comes within the limits of the drawing and is not too acute, the reactions may be determined, by the force triangle $AEFA$ as in Figs. 23 and 39. If the intersection of the resultant and R_2 cannot be used, the reactions may be determined by passing a string polygon through the *only known point* in R_1 as shown by the dotted lines. The closing line 3 cuts off the value of EF or R_2 on the vertical from E in the force polygon.

Using the external force diagram thus constructed and beginning at joint 1 or 12 the stress diagram may be constructed. The external forces in the force diagram must be laid off in order proceeding around the truss diagram either clockwise or counter-clockwise. Whichever direction is used in the beginning must be adhered to throughout the solution. With this system of notation it is not necessary to put arrows on the stress diagram, as the order of the letters, beginning with the direction of any known force, indicates the direction of the other forces, thus $ABCDEFA$ proceeds around the truss clockwise and gives the correct directions of all the external forces in the stress diagram. The same is true of the stresses at any joint.

It will be found that the stresses GH, LM, MN, NO, and OP are each zero, and that $EL=EN=EP$ and $FM=FO=FP$. That GH and OP are zero is also apparent from Σ vert. comp.$=0$ at joints 3 and 11.

The stresses will be altogether different for the wind on the other side of the roof.

The compression and tension members should be carefully noted and marked on the truss diagram.

55. Stresses in a Cantilever Truss. Fig. 52 shows a bracket supporting two loads, and it is supposed to be held

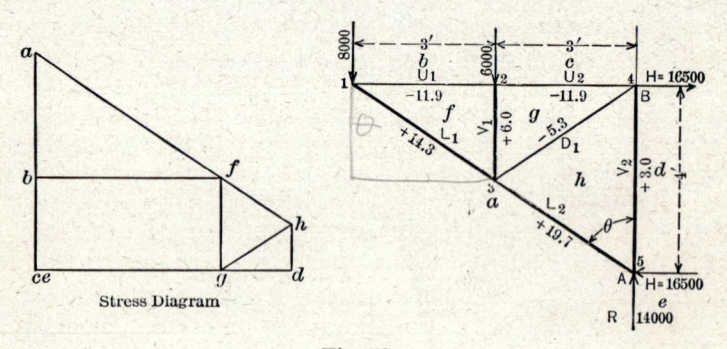

Fig. 52.

in such a way at B that there can be only a horizontal reaction at that point.

From Σ vert. comp.$=0$, the vertical component of the reaction at A must be equal to the sum of the two loads. By taking moments about A, $4H = 8000 \times 6 + 6000 \times 3 = 66000$ ft. lbs., from which $H = 16500$ lbs. The H at A must equal the H at B, as they are the only horizontal forces.

For the algebraic solution the functions of the angles should be expressed in terms of the lengths of the members of the truss (50). The diagonal length here $= \sqrt{3^2 + 2^2} = \sqrt{13} = 3.6$ ft.

$$\sin \theta = \frac{3}{3.6} \quad \cos \theta = \frac{2}{3.6}$$

By resolutions at the joints the following stresses are found:

Joint 1. $L_1 \cos \theta = 8000 \quad L_1 = 8000 \frac{3.6}{2} = 14400$ lbs. $(+)$

$L_1 \sin \theta = U_1 = 8000 \frac{3.6}{2} \times \frac{3}{3.6} = 12000$ lbs. $(-)$

Joint 2. $V_1 = 6000$ lbs. $(+)$

$U_2 = U_1 = 12000$ lbs. $(-)$

Joint 5. $L_2 \sin \theta = H = 16500$ lbs. $L_2 = 16500 \frac{3.6}{3} = 19800$ lbs. $(+)$

$L_2 \cos \theta - 14000 = V_2 = 19800 \frac{2}{3.6} - 14000 = -3000$ lbs. $(+)$

Joint 4. $D_1 \cos \theta = V_2 = 3000 \quad D_1 = 3000 \frac{3.6}{2} = 5400$ lbs. $(-)$

$D_1 \sin \theta + U_2 = H = 16500$ lbs.

$D_1 = (16500 - 12000) \frac{3.6}{3} = 5400$ lbs. $(-)$. *Check.*

Graphically, using Bow's notation, the force polygon of external forces is *abcdea*. The stress diagram may be constructed, beginning either at joint 1, 4, or 5. The scaled stresses are given on the truss diagram in 1000-lb. units.

56. Stresses in a Compound Fink Roof Truss for Vertical Loads. Fig. 53 shows the case mentioned in Art. 42 as being apparently statically indeterminate. The external force diagram is laid out and the stress diagram started, beginning at joint 1. There is no difficulty until joint 4 is reached, when it is found that there are more than two unknowns at each of the remaining joints. If joints 6 and 7 be next used, the *tentative* stress diagrams $DEQ'P'D$ and $P'Q'R'O'P'$ may be drawn, using any value for EQ'. This will give the true value of PQ, as it lies between the parallel lines DP' and EQ'. Now if joint 5 be considered, it is seen that O must lie on a line parallel to ON of the truss, from N of the stress diagram, and that also it must lie at the apex of the triangle $O'P'Q'$, which has its base $P'Q'$ in the lines DP' and EQ'. From this the true locations of the other parts of the stress diagram are evident.

The stresses will be the same in symmetrical members of the truss, as the loads are symmetrical, but both halves of the

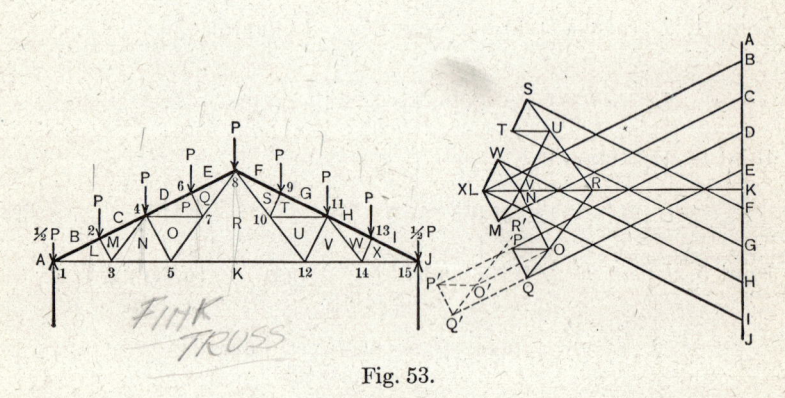

Fig. 53.

stress diagram should be drawn, in order to check the work. The completed diagram should close.

57. Stresses in Solid Beams. The method of sections must be used for finding the stresses in solid beams and girders (49). Fig. 54 shows a solid beam (stick of timber or girder) cut by a section pq. *Either the part to the left or to the right of pq may be considered, but not both.* Considering the part to the left of pq, and writing equations of equilibrium between the *forces acting on this part, we have*

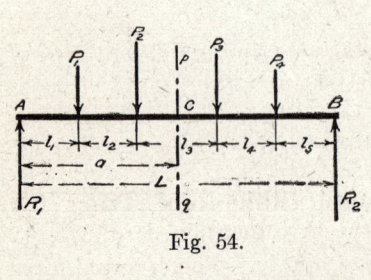

Fig. 54.

Σ vert. comps. $= 0 = R_1 - P_1 - P_2 -$ shearing stress at section: or *the shear at the section = the shearing stress at the section.*

Σ moments about $C = 0 = R_1 a - P_1(a - l_1) - P_2(a - l_1 - l_2) -$

moment of the stresses at the section; or *the bending moment at the section = the moment of resistance at the section.*

The distribution of the shearing and bending stresses over the cross section is discussed under the theory of flexure, Chapter VI.

Fig. 55 shows a similar case with a uniform load.

Σ vert. comps. $= 0 = R_1 - wa$ — shearing stress at the section pq; or the shear at the section = the shearing stress at the section $= R_1 - wa$.

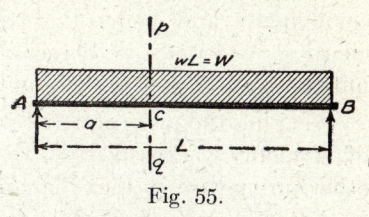

Σ moments about $C = 0 = R_1 a - wa \times \tfrac{1}{2}a$ — moment of the stresses at the section; or the *bending moment at the section = the moment of resistance at the section.* $M = M_R = R_1 a - \tfrac{1}{2}wa^2$.

The uniform load to the left of the section is wa; it is treated as a concentrated load at its center of gravity; hence its lever arm is $\tfrac{1}{2}a$ and in the bending moment for uniform load there will always be a term of the form $\tfrac{1}{2}wa^2$.

58. Stresses in Trusses. Algebraic Solution. In a truss it is also often convenient to speak of the shear at a section (in a panel since this is constant) and the bending moment at a section (at a joint since this is the most convenient point in finding the resisting stresses), but these are resisted by *members* in direct tension and compression.

In Fig. 56, for example, the part to the left of the section which cuts the stresses U, D, and L is considered. The shear in the panel is resisted by the vertical components of U and D (Σ vert. comps. $= 0$). The bending moment at any point is resisted by the sum of the moments of U, D, and L about the same point.

In Fig. 33, the chords being parallel they take no shear, so that, taking successive sections, the vertical component of $aB =$

R_1, the vertical component of $Bc = R_1$, the vertical component of $dE = R_1 - P$, the vertical component of $Ef = R_2$. These equations determine the diagonal stresses. Getting their horizontal components and using the horizontal resolution equation, the chord stresses may be determined by taking successive sections, but these are more easily found from the moment equation.

Taking the more general case of Fig. 56, to find L, the center of moments is chosen at C, the point of intersection of the two other unknowns, so that their moments are zero. There being no loads to the left of the section, in this case, the only forces left are L and R_1.

For $M_c = 0$, $R_1 \times 2p = L \times d$ or $L = R_1 \dfrac{2p}{d}$.

For finding U, the center of moments is taken at E.
$$M_E = 0 \text{ or } R_1 \times 3p = U \times c \qquad U = R_1 \frac{3p}{c}.$$

For D, the center of moments is taken at the intersection A, of U and L.
$$M_A = 0 \text{ or } R_1 a = Db \text{ or } D = R_1 \frac{a}{b}.$$

The *directions* of U. L, and D are obtained by a consideration of the direction which the resisting moment must have. *A stress acting toward the part under consideration is compressive and one acting away from it is tensile.*

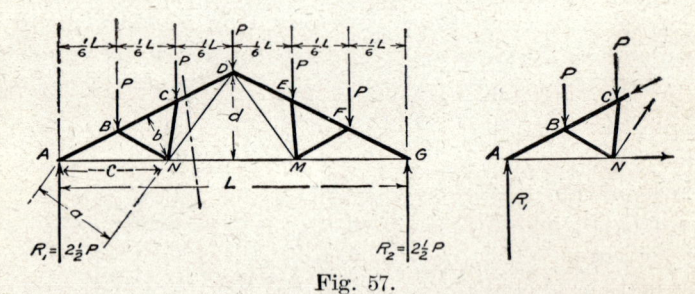

Fig. 57.

In Fig. 57, if a section is taken through three members only, and the left hand portion considered, as shown, there are six forces in equilibrium, namely, R_1, P at B, P at C, CD, ND, and NM.

$$M_D = 0 \text{ or } NM \times d = R_1 \times \tfrac{1}{2}L - P(\tfrac{1}{6}L + \tfrac{2}{6}L)$$
$$M_A = 0 \text{ or } ND \times a = P(\tfrac{1}{6}L + \tfrac{2}{6}L)$$
$$M_N = 0 \text{ or } CD \times b = R_1 \times c - P(c - \tfrac{1}{6}L) + P(\tfrac{1}{3}L - c)$$

Art. 59. STRESSES IN A TRUSS WITH PARALLEL CHORDS. 79

In a truss of this kind, the calculation of the lever arms is tedious; they may be taken by scale if a proper scale drawing of the truss is made, but the stresses are usually gotten graphically from a stress diagram (56). The above method is quite convenient for some members—NM, for example.

This method of finding the stress in the lower chord member 5–12 of Fig. 53 is sometimes used in connection with the graphic solution, the computed value being scaled off on the stress diagram, thus locating the point R directly without the auxiliary diagram (42).

59. Stresses in a Truss With Parallel Chords. Fig. 58 shows a truss of five equal panels carrying a load at each upper joint. The diagonal length is $\sqrt{18^2 + 20^2} = 26.9$ ft. Sec $\theta = \frac{26.9}{18}$. Tan $\theta = \frac{20}{18}$.

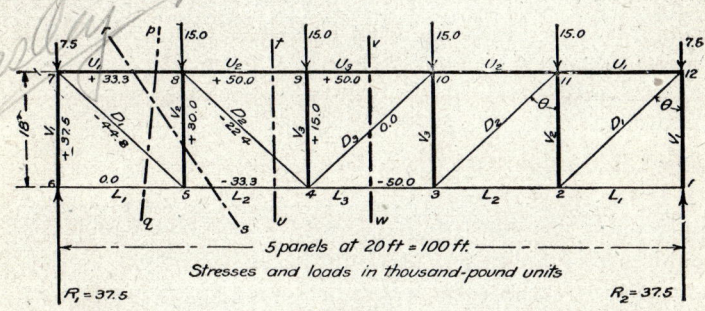

Fig. 58.

Section pq. Σ vert. comps. $= 0$ or shear in panel 7–8 $=$ vert. comp. $D_1 = R_1 - \frac{1}{2}P = 2P = 30000$ lbs.

$D_1 = 30000 \sec \theta = 30000 \frac{26.9}{18} = 44800$ lbs. $(-)$

$M_5 = 0$ or $(R_1 - \frac{1}{2}P) 20 = 18 U_1 = 30000 \times 20$

$U_1 = \frac{30000 \times 20}{18} = 33300$ lbs. $(+)$

$M_7 = 0$ or $18 L_1 = 0$. That L_1 is zero is also apparent at joint 6 from Σ horiz. comp. $= 0$.

Section rs. Σ vert. comps. $= 0$ or $R_1 - \frac{1}{2}P = V_2 = 30000$ lbs.

Section tu. Shear in panel 8–9 $=$ vert. comp. $D_2 = R_1 - 1\frac{1}{2} P$.

$D_2 = 15000 \sec \theta = 15000 \frac{26.9}{18} = 22400$ lbs. $(-)$

$M_4 = 0$ or $(R_1 - \frac{1}{2}P) 40 - P \times 20 = 18 U_2$.

$$U_2 = \frac{30000 \times 40 - 15000 \times 20}{18} = 50000 \text{ lbs. } (+)$$

$M_8 = 0$ or $(R_1 - \tfrac{1}{2}P)\, 20 = 18L_2 = 30000 \times 20.$

$$L_2 = \frac{30000 \times 20}{18} = 33300 \text{ lbs. } (-)$$

Section vw. Σ vert. comps. $= 0$ or shear in panel 9-10 $=$ vert. comp. $D_3 = 0$. Hence $D_3 = 0$.

$M_4 = 0$, or $30000 \times 40 - 15000 \times 20 = 18U_3.$

$$U_3 = \frac{30000 \times 40 - 30000 \times 10}{18} = 50000 \text{ lbs. } (+)$$

$M_{10} = 0$ or $30000 \times 60 - 15000(40+20) = 18 L_3.$

$$L_3 = \frac{30000 \times 60 - 30000 \times 30}{18} = 50000 \text{ lbs. } (-)$$

Since the loads are symmetrical about the center line, and $D_3 = 0$, the stresses will be symmetrical. It will be noted that the stresses U_1 and L_2 are equal and opposite as they should be in order that the sum of the horizontal components, for section rs, shall be zero. Likewise must $U_2 = L_3$ and $U_3 = L_3$. It is also apparet at joint 9 that $U_2 = U_3$ and $V_3 = 15000$ lbs.

The *signs of the stresses are apparent* upon inspection. The top chord is in compression, the bottom chord in tension, the diagonals in tension, and the verticals in compression.

If the loads were applied at the lower joints in place of the upper ones, the signs of the stresses would be the same, but V_3 would be zero (joint 9), V_2 would be decreased by P, and V_1 by $\tfrac{1}{2}P$. *The stress in each post is decreased by the amount of load transferred from its upper to its lower end.*

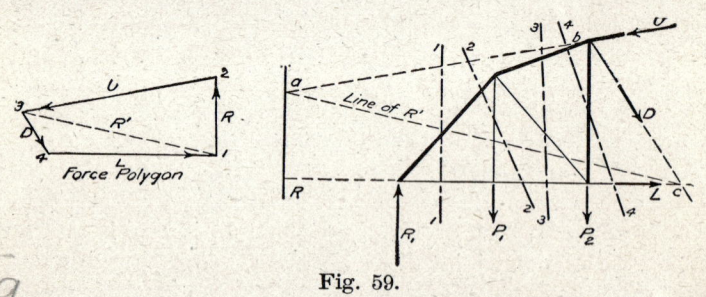

Fig. 59.

60. Graphical Solution by Sections. Culmann's Method. Fig. 59 shows a part of a truss cut off by a section for the purpose of finding the stresses U, D, and L. R is the resultant of the external forces R_1, P_1, and P_2; thus the system is reduced to four forces in equilibrium—R, U, D,

Art. 60.   GRAPHICAL SOLUTION BY SECTIONS.   81

and L. R may be found by drawing force and string polygons (see Fig. 37), and U, D, and L may be found by the method of Art. 33 as shown in the force polygon of Fig. 59. The resultant of U and R is R' and must pass through a; the resultant of L and D must also equal R', but be opposite in direction; and must pass through c. Then ac determines the direction of R'. In the force polygon R is laid out to scale and through its extremities lines are drawn parallel to the directions of U and R', thus determining their amounts from the force triangle 1-2-3; in like manner, from R' and lines parallel to the directions of D and L, the force triangle 1-3-4 is formed.

Three independent solutions are possible by means of the following combinations:

R with U and D with L (as shown).
R with L and D with U.
R with D and U with L.

Combinations giving acute intersections, either in the force or space diagrams should be avoided. When this is not possible, it is possible to find the three stresses by using two convenient components in place of R.

By taking successive sections all the stresses may be found, or any three stresses gotten by some other method may be readily checked. In the former case, by combining the various force polygons, a stress diagram is formed, but the construction is not so simple as that of Art. 54. If, however, the sections are taken in the order indicated in Fig. 59, there will be but two unknowns in each case, and the construction reduces to that of Art. 54.

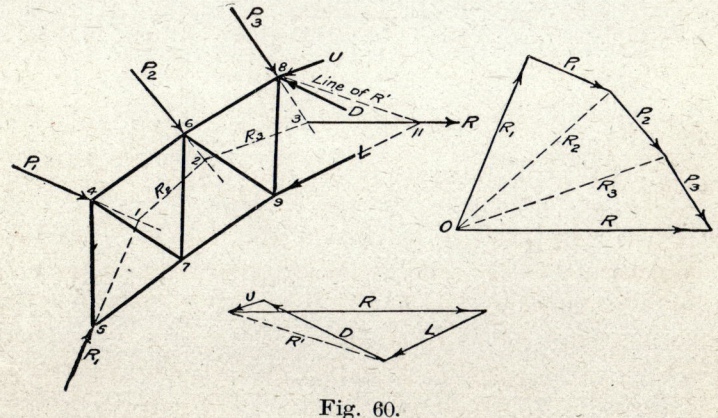

Fig. 60.

82 THE GRAPHIC METHOD OF SECTIONS. Art. 61.

Fig. 60 shows a case in which R is determined by means of a resultant polygon and Fig. 61, a case in which R is determined by a string polygon, 1-2-6.

61. Graphical Solution. The Method of Sections by Moments. In Culmann's method, stresses are determined by means of force polygons, that is, the resolution equations of equilibrium are used. In order to use the moment equation, we resort to the string polygon.

Fig. 61 shows a simple truss with vertical loads and reactions. The force polygon of external forces is $abcdena$. The shear diagram is drawn opposite it and shows how the shear changes at the panel points and passes through zero at joint 7 or at load P_3. From any pole O draw the rays 1 to 5, and in the

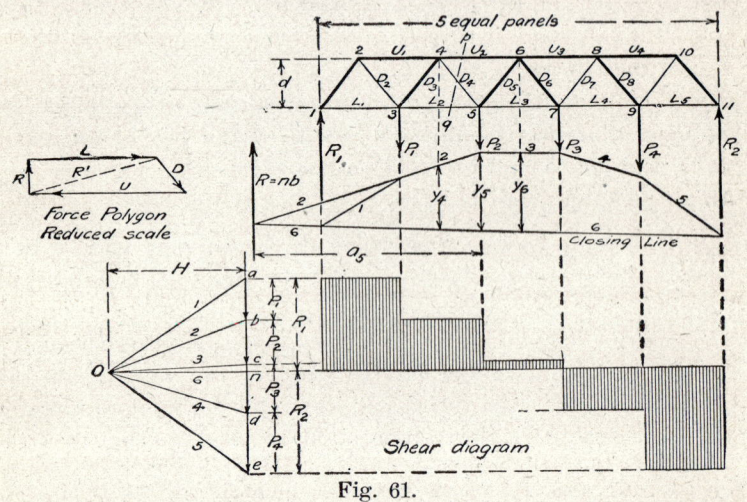

Fig. 61.

space diagram, the corresponding strings; string 6 determines ray 6 and point n.

To find stress U_2, for example, take section pq and center of moments at joint 5, then

$$M_5 = 0 \text{ or } U_2 \times d = R_1 \times 2p - P_1 \times p.$$

The moment of the external forces (R_1 and P_1) is equal to the moment of their resultant R, which from the force polygon ($nabn$) is equal to nb. R acts at the intersection of strings 2 and 6—triangle $nbOn$—and its lever arm is a_5. The above equation becomes

$$U_2 d = R a_5$$

Art. 61.   THE GRAPHIC METHOD OF SECTIONS.   83

From the similar triangles formed by *rays* 2 and 6 and strings 2 and 6 with R and y_5, we have

$$\frac{R}{y_5} = \frac{H}{a_5} \text{ or } Ra_5 = Hy_5$$

Hence $U_2 d = Hy_5$.

Thus we get a value for the sum of the moments of the external forces to the left of any section by scaling an ordinate between two strings, for O may be so chosen that H is some convenient quantity like 100 or 1000 lbs.

This is not true for non-parallel forces unless a string polygon is drawn for each section, which would be very laborious. For parallel forces H is the same for any resultant.

H, the perpendicular distance from the pole to any force, is called the *pole distance* of the force, although it is really a force; the product Hy_5 will be the same, no matter which is called the force or the distance, so long as the scale of forces is used in the force polygon and the scale of distances in the string polygon or space diagram.

To find U_2 then, it is simply a matter of scaling y_5, locating the decimal point, and dividing by d (the lever arm of U_2). U_2 may also be found by constructing any two similar triangles, for $U_2 : H :: y_5 : d$.

For L_2, the section is the same as for U_2 and, therefore, R will be the same; the center of moments is joint 4 and $L_2 d = Hy_4$.

For L_3, the external forces are R_1, P_1, and P_2, whose resultant is nc; since 3 and 6 are components of nc, the ordinate y_6 will be measured between strings 3 and 6 on a line through the center of moments which is at joint 6.

Since R_1 is always one of the external forces, *the ordinate y will always be measured from the closing line to that string which is parallel to the other component of the resultant of the forces.* Thus if the moment of R_1 about joint 6 were wanted, the ordinate would extend from the closing line to string 1 produced.

For the truss of Fig. 61, the diagonal stresses can not be found (the center of moments being at infinity) unless the chord stresses are found first and then used in the equation of equilibrium for the diagonal stress. If the centers of moments for the diagonals are taken at the middle of the top or bottom panels, their lever arms will be $d' = d \sin\theta$. For D_4, $D_4 \times d' + L_2 \times d = Hy_5$,

the center of moments being in U_2 directly above joint 5. Now L_2d being equal to Hy_4, we have
$$D_4d' = H(y_5 - y_4)$$

Drawing a line through the upper extremity of y_4 parallel to string 6, it cuts off, on y_5, the distance $y_5 - y_4$; constructing two similar triangles upon this distance, D_4 is determined.

62. Stresses in a Derrick. The crane or derrick shown in Fig. 49 is usually supported by several wire rope guys

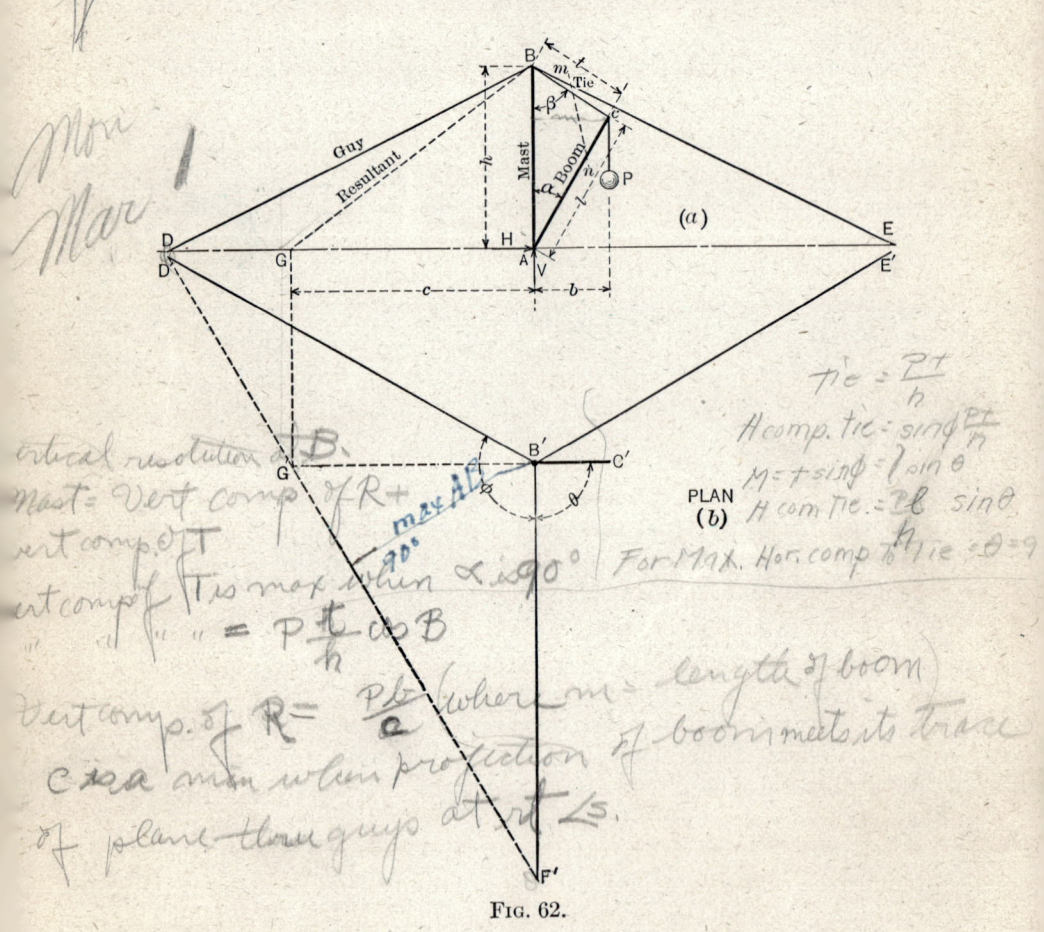

Fig. 62.

attached at B and running down to anchorages at some distant points, or by two *stiff legs* attached at the same point. Thus in the common derrick the reaction at B is not horizontal.

Fig. 62 shows a horizontal and vertical projection of a derrick with three guys. This is the fewest number that the derrick could have and be stable in all positions of the boom unless some of the guys were stiff, or capable of taking compression as well as tension. Also the maximum angle between any two adjacent guys must not equal 180° or the derrick will not be stable for certain position of the boom.

The stresses in the members of the derrick will vary for different positions of the boom, both horizontally and vertically, and the problem is to find the position of the boom which will give maximum stresses in each member.

Maximum stress in the boom. The boom may be raised and lowered by means of the tie BC. Taking a section mn through the tie and the boom, and a center of moments at B,

$$AC \times h \sin \alpha = P \times l . \sin \alpha,$$

$$AC = \text{Stress in boom} = P \frac{l}{h} \quad \ldots \ldots \ldots \ldots \ldots (a)$$

This is independent of the angle α, therefore the stress in the boom is constant for any given load.

Maximum stress in the tie. With the same section as before, and a center of moments at A,

$$BC \times h \sin \beta = P \times t \sin \beta,$$

$$BC = \text{Stress in tie} = P \frac{t}{h} \ldots \ldots \ldots \ldots \ldots \ldots (b)$$

From this it is seen that the stress in the tie is a maximum when the length t of the tie is a maximum. This would occur when the boom is hanging vertically downward, if such a position were possible. Usually the boom cannot drop below a horizontal position.

Maximum stress in the mast. By considering the joint B' in the horizontal projection, Fig. 62 (b), it is evident that the guy $B'E'$ is not in service as long as the angle $D'B'C'$ or $F'B'C'$ does not exceed 180°, also the resultant of the stresses in the guys $B'D'$ and $B'F'$ must lie in the plane of the two guys and directly opposite to the tie $B'C'$. Again considering joint A of the elevation, by vertical resolutions,

$$BA = \text{Stress in mast} = V - AC \cos \alpha.$$

$$V = P + P\frac{b}{c} \qquad\qquad b = l\sin\alpha$$

$$BA = P + P\frac{l\sin\alpha}{c} - P\frac{l\cos\alpha}{h}\dots\dots\dots(c)$$

From this equation it is evident that for a maximum stress in the mast, c should be a minimum. This occurs when the boom is swung so that the angle $B'G'F'$ is 90°.

Also if the boom cannot drop below a horizontal position it is evident that the maximum stress in the mast occurs when $\alpha = 90°$, or the boom is horizontal. ($Sin\,\alpha$ is maximum.)

If it is possible to drop the boom below a horizontal position the position for a maximum stress in the mast may be found by differentiating equation (c) and setting the first differential equal to zero.

$$\frac{d(BA)}{d\alpha} = \frac{Pl}{c}\cos\alpha + \frac{Pl}{h}\sin\alpha = 0.$$

$$\frac{\cos\alpha}{c} = -\frac{\sin\alpha}{h} \quad\text{or}\quad \frac{\sin\alpha}{\cos\alpha} = \tan\alpha = -\frac{h}{c}.$$

This gives the value for α for a maximum stress in the mast.

Maximum stress in a guy. The position of the boom in elevation should be such as to produce a maximum vertical component to the resultant of the stresses in the two guys in action.

$$\text{Vert. comp. of restulant} = P\frac{b}{c}.$$

From this it is seen that the boom should be horizontal.

The position of the boom in plan may be obtained from resolutions at B' normal to one of the guys, using horizontal components. To obtain the stress in $B'D'$ we will take resolutions normal to $B'F'$.

$$D'B'\cos(\phi - 90°) = B'C'\sin\theta,$$

$$D'B' = B'C'\frac{\sin\theta}{\cos(\phi - 90)}.$$

This is evidently a maximum when $\sin\theta$ is a maximum, or when $\theta = 90°$. In words the stress in one guy is maximum when the boom is rotated so that it stands perpendicular to the horizontal projection of one of the other guys.

Art. 63.   THE STRING POLYGON AS A MOMENT DIAGRAM.   87

63. The String Polygon as a Moment Diagram. When the forces acting on a structure are all parallel, as in Fig. 61, H is constant and the moment at any section is proportional to the ordinate of the string polygon. The string polygon is, therefore, quite similar to the moment diagram, especially if the pole O is chosen on a horizontal line through n, so that the closing line will be horizontal. For example, if $H = 10000$ lbs. and y scales 34.5 ft., the moment is 345000 ft. lbs., while in the moment diagram the moment would be scaled directly and this scaled distance would have exactly the same length as y if the scales were properly chosen.

The string polygon is of greater importance in theory than in practice; it furnishes a graphic representation of the variation of the moment.

64. The Graphic Method of Sections for Uniform Loads. According to Art. 57 (Fig. 55) the bending moment at any section of a beam distant x from the left support is, for uniform load, $M_x = R_1 x - \frac{1}{2} w x^2$. This shows that M_x may be represented

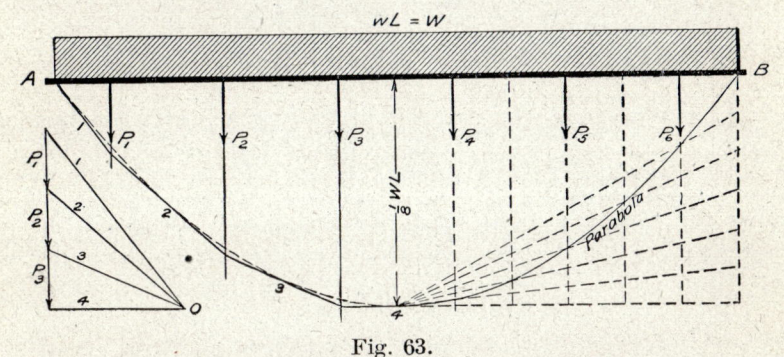

Fig. 63.

by ordinates to a parabola whose maximum ordinate is at the middle of the beam and is equal to

$$M_{\frac{1}{2}L} = \frac{1}{2}wL \times \frac{1}{2}L - \frac{1}{2}wL \times \frac{1}{4}L = \frac{1}{8}wL^2 = \frac{1}{8}WL.$$

The parabola may be constructed by the method shown for the right half of the beam, Fig. 63, or by constructing a string polygon as shown. The load is divided into a number of equal parts, and each part is considered as a concentrated load acting at its center of gravity. This is equivalent to the procedure for finding the moment at any of the sections of division and, therefore, the string polygon will give the correct moments at these sections. An inscribed curve, tangent to the string polygon (Fig. 63) is the string polygon for uniform load.

In truss bridges the uniform load is transformed into concentrated loads (panel loads) at the panel points, and the *apexes* of the string polygon will lie on a parabola.

65. Moment Areas. In Fig. 64 the moment at any section as tt or ss is Hy, y being the ordinate made by the string polygon in the section. The area enclosed by the string polygon is called the *moment area*. The moments represented by the ordinates

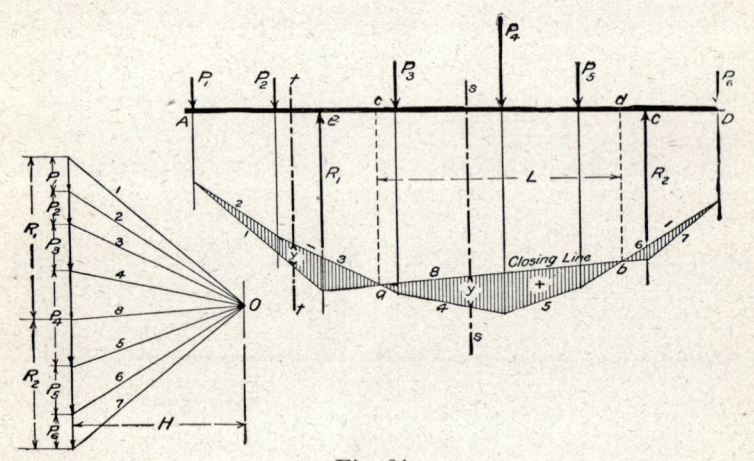

Fig. 64.

above the closing line are of opposite sign to those below the closing line. Moments which make a beam concave on the upper side (produce compression in the upper fibers) are usually called plus moments.

A moment area gives a graphic representation of the bending moment at every section of a beam and is, of course, applicable to trusses as well as solid beams. Thus at sections through points a and b, the moment is zero and at load P_4, it is a maximum. Between the points c and d, the moment is positive, and beyond them it is negative; these points of zero moment are dividing points of contrary flexure. The part cd of length L is exactly like an ordinary beam of the same length supported at its ends, because the moments at the supports are zero. The end reaction of such a beam, at c, can be gotten from the location of P_3, P_4, and P_5, but it is also equal to the shear at c which is $R_1 - P_1 - P_2$.

QUESTIONS AND PROBLEMS. CHAPTER V.

1. What is the difference between a stress diagram and a force polygon?

2. Explain fully how the signs of stresses are determined when algebraic methods are used and when graphic methods are used.

3. What should be the uniform practice with regard to the angles giving the inclinations of the members of a truss and their functions?

4. Find, graphically, the stresses in a truss like that of Fig. 61, with panel loads, at joints 3, 5, 7, and 9, of 15000 lbs. each, the panels being 15 ft. and the depth d, $7\frac{1}{2}$ ft. Also for a single load at joint 9 such that $R_1 = 1000$ lbs.

5. Find the stresses in problem 4 algebraically and compare the results.

6. Take a truss similar to that of Fig. 51 with a span of 60 ft. (six panels of 10 ft. each), a height at the center of 15 ft., and vertical panel loads at joints 2, 4, 6, 8, and 10 of 6400 lbs. each. Find the stresses algebraically and graphically and compare them.

NOTE.—This style of truss is called a Howe truss. When the diagonal web members are inclined in the opposite direction, it is a Pratt truss. The instructor may assign individual problems by varying the span, the pitch, and the panel load. The above truss is one-fourth pitch because the ratio of height to span is $\frac{1}{4}$.

7. Find the stresses in the truss of problem 6 when the support is at joint 9 in place of joint 12 and a half panel load is added at joint 12.

8. If the reaction R_1 were known, would it be possible to draw a stress diagram for a full arch like that shown in part in Fig. 60?

9. What is the bending moment at the middle of a beam of 24 ft. span for a load of 8000 lbs. at its middle?

10. What is the maximum bending moment in the above beam for a load of 9000 lbs. 8 ft. from one support? What the maximum shear?

11. At which load, in the beam of Fig. 41, is the bending moment a maximum?

12. At which joint of the truss, Fig. 50, is the bending moment a maximum? Where does the shear pass through zero?

13. What is the bending moment at the middle of a beam of span L, carrying a uniform load W? What the shear?

14. What is the bending moment in a beam of 20 ft. span at 4 ft. from one support for a uniform load of 400 lbs. per ft.? What the shear?

15. In the method of sections, the sections are taken so as to cut how many members? Where are the centers of moments taken?

16. In Fig. 57, take a section and write a moment equation for the stress in BC.

17. Find the stresses in the truss of Fig. 50 by the algebraic method of sections.

18. Find the stresses in the truss of Fig. 61 by the algebraic method of sections for the data given in Problem 4.

19. Calculate U_2 and V_2, Fig. 52, by the method of sections.

20. Find U_2, D_4, and L_2, Fig. 61, for the data given in problem 4, by Culmann's method.

21. For the same data as above, find the chord stresses by the method of Art. 61.

22. Find, graphically, the maximum moment in the beam of Fig. 42, for loads of 18, 40, and 24 in place of 20, 15, and 10, respectively.

23. Find the stresses in the truss of problem 6, by the algebraic method of sections.

CHAPTER VI.

STRESSES IN BEAMS AND GIRDERS.

66. Classification of Beams. According to Art. 2, beams are of three kinds, simple beams, girders, and trusses. Simple beams and girders may be called *solid beams* to distinguish them from trusses, which are trussed beams.

Simple beams usually have a uniform cross section from end to end. Timber beams usually have a rectangular cross section and steel beams an I-shaped one.

Girders may have a uniform or variable cross section; the variation may be due to a variable depth or to a difference in length of flange plates.

I beams, channels, Z bars, and girders have webs and flanges. See Fig. 1, Art. 2.

Beams may be classified in accordance with the manner in which they are supported.

1. Supported at both ends (commonest case)—simply resting on the supports so as not to interfere with elastic bending.
2. Fixed at both ends so that the *axis at these points* does not change direction when the beam bends.
3. Fixed at one end and free at the other (cantilever). Case 2 becomes case 3 when one support is removed.
4. Fixed at one end and supported at the other. This case is intermediate between cases 1 and 2, or 1 and 3.
5. Continuous over three or more supports.

In practice the condition of fixity at the supports is not met with except when the beam is continuous over the supports and loaded beyond them; in other cases the fixity is only partial and the beam is often considered as simply supported. "Fixed ends" implies freedom to change length due to elastic deflection and changes of temperature, which is the usual condition in the other cases.

Beams may have straight axes or curved axes as in arches.

67. General Consideration of Stresses in Solid Beams.

In the most general case of forces acting in any direction and in any position on a bar, there will be produced, on any section, tensile or compressive stresses (normal), shearing stresses (tangential, bending stresses (normal), and torsional stresses (tangential). In special cases, any one of these stresses, or any combination of two or three of them may occur. According to the usual assumption, these stresses may be investigated independently and the results of like kind, for any point, may be added. In Chapter IX combinations of bending and tensile or compressive stresses are treated. In this chapter only the usual cases of simple bending and shearing stresses are treated. When these two are combined, it is seldom necessary to find the resultant principal stress (12); a method of doing this is, however, given in Art. 76 and the lines of principal stress, for a certain case, are shown in Art. 77.

Ordinarily, beams have loads acting perpendicular to their axes; they may be spoken of as vertical loads and horizontal beams. When the loads are inclined to the axis of a beam, there will be a combination of bending, shearing, and tensile or compressive stresses—the horizontal components producing the latter. Stresses are investigated upon sections perpendicular to the axis of a beam. In arches the shearing stress acts in a radial direction, and, in general, there will be shearing, bending, and compressive stresses upon the radial sections. In beams with straight axes, provision must ordinarily be made to resist *the shear and the bending moment* (57), and these are treated independently although, in general, both shearing and bending stresses act upon each particle. Like provision must be made in trusses, but in this case the shear is not resisted by shearing stresses, but by tensile or compressive stresses in the web members and inclined chord members (58).

68. Bending Stress in Solid Beams. Theory of Flexure.

In the special case shown in Fig. 65, the shear between the loads is zero, and in this part of the beam there is only bending stress. Stresses in solid beams are investigated

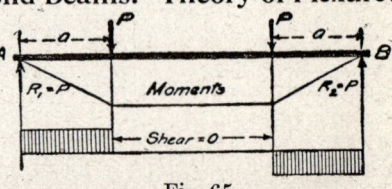

Fig. 65.

on planes perpendicular to the axis of the beam by the method of sections, as explained in Art. 57. It was there shown that the

Art. 68.   BENDING STRESS IN SOLID BEAMS.

bending moment at a section (the sum of the moments of the external forces to the left of the section) is equal to the moment of resistance at the section (the sum of the moments of the stresses at the section). That the bending moment is equivalent to the moment of a couple is shown in Fig. 66, where R at c is the resultant of all the external forces to the left of section mn; this is *equivalent to a force R at the section and a couple whose moment is Ra* (34). To resist the single force, the shearing stress, $S = R$ (Σ vert comps. $= 0$); to resist the couple, it is only necessary that there be stresses at the section forming an opposite couple of equal moment (30). Since there may be many couples fulfilling this condition, the distribution of the bending stresses is statically indeterminate. The distribution of the bending stresses over the cross section of a beam is assumed to be in accordance with the *theory of flexure*.

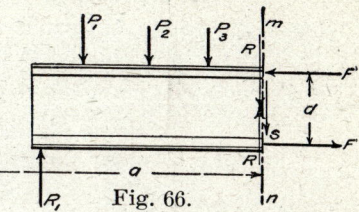

It is a matter of common experience that a load placed on a beam will bend it. In some cases the bending may not be apparent, but it nevertheless takes place on account of the elasticity of the material. Fig. 67 shows, to an exaggerated degree, the bending in the simple case of Fig. 65. If before the beam is loaded, two vertical lines were marked on each face, BB and $B'B'$, Fig. 67, it would be found that when the beam is bent, these lines are no longer parallel to each other, but that the distance between them (in this case) is diminished in the upper part of the beam and increased in the lower part. If the upper part of the beam is compressed and the lower part elongated, there must be an intermediate surface in which the length of the fibers is unchanged; this is called the *neutral surface* and is indicated by the line N_1N_1. The line in which the neutral surface intersects any cross section as NN (Fig. 67) is called the *neutral axis*.

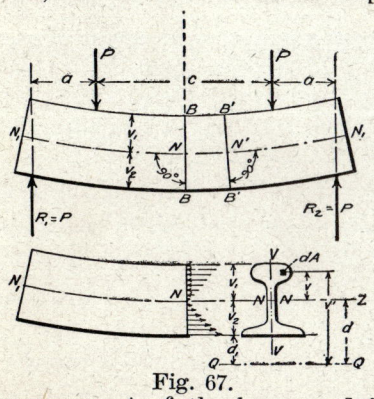

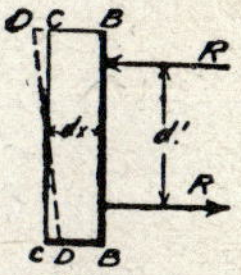

The *assumptions in the theory of flexure* are:

1. Originally plane cross sections will be planes after bending takes place.

2. The modulus of elasticity is constant throughout the beam. It follows that it is the same for tension and compression (for there will evidently be both kinds of stresses), and the stress must nowhere exceed the elastic limit (11).

3. The fibers do not act upon each other but independently.

When bending takes place, the fibers between any two cross sections are compressed above the neutral surface (Fig. 67) and elongated below it. According to the first assumption the change of length of the fibers is directly proportional to their distances from the neutral axis, as shown in Fig. 68, *DD* being originally parallel to *BB*.

Under the second assumption, Hooke's law (8) must hold for all parts; it therefore follows that the unit stresses vary directly as the deformations, that is, *the intensity of the bending stress increases directly as the distance from the neutral axis as shown in Fig. 67*. This simply means that if the stress *per square inch* is 150 lbs. at a distance of one inch from the neutral axis, at a distance of two inches it will be 300 lbs., at a distance of 10 inches, 1500 lbs., etc. The *total* stress at a certain distance from the neutral axis will, of course, depend upon the *width* of the cross section.

Since the moment of resistance must be equivalent to the moment of a couple, the resultant of the tensile stresses must equal the resultant of the compressive stresses, which makes "the sum of the horizontal components" zero because all other forces are vertical.

It is evident that the *maximum intensity of stress* will occur in the fiber which is most remote from the neutral axis. The stress per square inch upon this fiber must not exceed the working stress, and if the cross section is made of such dimensions and such shape that the unit stress in the extreme fiber is equal to the working stress, the moment of resistance will equal the bending moment, and the problem is solved.

The first assumption upon which the theory of flexure is based has the merit of being the simplest which can be made under the given circumstances. The second assumption limits its application to certain materials, and to stresses within the elastic limits. It has been found, by careful experiments, that originally plane cross sections remain plane and perpendicular to the neutral surface, and that the length of the neutral surface does not change; and this is practically true for stone, which does not follow Hooke's law, even when it is, at the same time, also subject to shearing stresses. Stone, concrete, and cast iron do not meet the requirements of the theory of flexure because they do not follow Hooke's law; the discrepancy is particularly large for cast iron, but the error is on the side of safety.

The influence of shearing stresses which are usually combined with bending stresses is discussed in Art. 87.

The third assumption can, of course, not be in accord with the facts. Since there is tension on one side of the neutral axis and compression on the other, there will be transverse contraction and expansion (9), and the interaction of the fibers will be different from that in pure tension and compression, because the the stress on the inner fibers is less than on the outer ones. Since the contraction and expansion decrease to zero at the neutral axis, the inner fibers interfere with both the transverse and longitudinal deformations of the outer fibers (13).

The effect of the interactions of the fibers depends upon the form of the cross section, but the assumption is on the side of safety; the interference with the deformations of the outer fibers makes the maximum stress less than the theory of flexure indicates. The more the area of the cross section is concentrated into two narrow strips parallel to the neutral axis, the less the discrepancy. The error is greater with a rectangular than with an I-shaped cross section. With a cross section, unsymmetrical about the neutral axis, this axis would have a sligthly different location from that indicated by the theory of flexure; if this were not so, the "sum of the horizontal components" would not be zero, because there would be a greater resistance on that side of the neutral axis where there is a greater proportion of fibers vertically over each other (Above NN, Fig. 67).

Under the usual working stresses, the assumptions in the theory of flexure are practically correct for all materials of construction and their adoption has been all but universal. It should be remembered, however, that long compression flanges of beams should be stayed against transverse buckling, and that when bending and shearing stresses are combined, the limitations pointed out in Arts. 87 and 67 must also be observed.

69. Bending Stresses and Moments of Resistance for a Beam of Rectangular Cross Section. The moment is the same at any section *between* the loads, of the beam in Fig. 65, because the forces on either side of such section form a couple (30). The bending moment is, therefore Pa, and M_R must equal Pa, that is, $M = Pa = M_R$.

M_R is easily found for a *rectangular* cross section as shown in Fig. 69. If the maximum allowed stress in the extreme fibers be 1000 lbs. per sq. in., the width of the section 10″, and its depth 18″, then the average unit stress *in tension and compression* is 500 lbs. per sq. in.; these stresses act over an area of $10 \times 9 = 90$ sq. ins.; hence the total tension below and the total compression above the neutral axis equals $R = 90 \times 500 = 45000$ lbs. It is evident that the neutral axis must be in the middle of the section in order that this condition of equilibrium may hold.

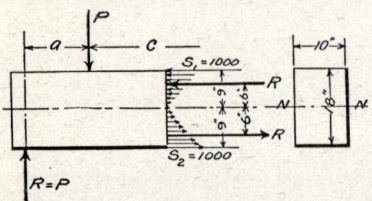

Fig. 69.

These resultants of 45000 lbs. each act at the centers of gravity of the stress diagrams; and since these are triangles (for constant width), they act at two thirds of the altitudes from the vertexes, or at 6″ from the neutral axis. The lever arm of the couple is then 12″ and its moment is $45000 \times 12 = 540000$ in. lbs. $= M_R$.

If $a = 4.5$ ft., P should not be greater than $\frac{45000}{4.5} = 10000$ lbs.

In the same manner a general formula may be deduced. The average unit stress is $\tfrac{1}{2} s_1$; it acts over an area $\tfrac{1}{2} bh$; $\tfrac{1}{4} s_1 bh$ is one force of the couple, and its lever arm is $\tfrac{2}{3} h$; its moment is $\tfrac{1}{6} s_1 bh^2 = M_R$.

This value of M_R will be again gotten from the general formula for M, applicable to any cross section, which will now be deduced.

70. Moment of Resistance for a Beam of Any Cross Section. Referring to Fig. 67, v denotes the vertical distance, from the neutral axis, of any element of area, and s the corresponding unit stress. Having decided upon the maximum unit stress (working stress) to be allowed in the extreme fibers—s_1 or s_2—

Art. 70.   MOMENT OF RESISTANCE OF A BEAM.

the unit stress at unit distance from the neutral axis is $\frac{s_1}{v_1}$ or $\frac{s_2}{v_2}$ and at a distance v,
$$s = s_1 \frac{v}{v_1} \text{ or } s_2 \frac{v}{v_2} \tag{9}$$

If an infinitesimal area dA be considered, the stress over it will be constant and equal to sdA, and its moment about the neutral axis will be $vsdA$. (The center of moments may be taken at any point since the moment of resistance is equivalent to the moment of a couple). Summing up the moments of all the elementary stresses, $M_R = \int_{-v_2}^{+v_1} vsdA$.

Opposite signs for the parts above and below the neutral axis simply denote that the stresses are of opposite sign, as they should be, to make the moments of the *same* sign[1] (Fig. 68).

Substituting the value of s from equation (9),
$$M_R = \frac{s_1}{v_1} \int_{-v_2}^{+v_1} v^2 dA = \frac{s_2}{v_2} \int_{-v_2}^{+v_1} v^2 dA$$
$$= s_1 \frac{I}{v_1} = s_2 \frac{I}{v_2} \tag{10}$$

in which $I = \int_{-v_2}^{+v_1} v^2 dA$ (11)

I is called the *moment of inertia* of the cross section; it is a "second moment," while $\int vdA$ is the first or *statical moment*. The moment of inertia accounts for the fact that the stress varies as the distance from the neutral axis, and that the moment of this stress about the neutral axis varies in the same way.

Since v appears as a square, the moment of inertia of the lower as well as the upper part of the cross section is positive, and they are *added* together.

It is evident that the more the area is disposed *away from* the neutral axis, the greater will be the moment of inertia, and the greater the moment of resistance. For this reason steel beams and girders have I-shaped cross sections; the average unit stress is much greater than in rectangular cross sections of the same height and area. Fig. 70 shows four different ways in which four angles and a plate may be riveted together to from a

---

[1] It does not follow that the moment of the resultant of the tensile stresses equals that of the compressive stresses, about the neutral axis; this is true for sections symmetrical about the neutral axis, but it is not necessary in order to satisfy the conditions of equilibrium; it is only necessary that the total tension shall equal the total compression, and that the moment of resistance shall equal the bending moment.

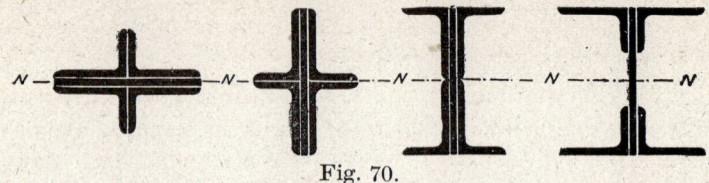

Fig. 70.

beam, and the manner in which the strength is increased by moving the area away from the neutral axis, NN.

Equation (10) is perhaps the most valuable in the entire subject of stresses, and the student should be as familiar with its use as with the use of the ordinary multiplication table.

If v_1 is greater than v_2, s_1 will be the maximum unit fiber stress (working stress) and vice versa. *The extreme fiber governs the section.*

Perhaps the most convenient form in which to remember equation (10) is, since $M_R = M$,

$$\frac{M}{s_1} = \frac{I}{v_1} \text{ or } \frac{M}{s_2} = \frac{I}{v_2} = \text{section modulus.} \qquad (12)$$

This is most frequently written in the form (dropping the subscripts), $s = \frac{Mv}{I}$.

In any case this equation must be solved by trial, because both I and v depend upon the section, unless a table of section moduli is available. $\frac{I}{v}$ is called the section modulus because it is a measure of the sections value in resisting bending. The tables for rolled shapes given in the rolling-mill handbooks give the section moduli and for these, equation (12) furnishes a direct solution as the following example shows.

A beam of 20 ft. span carries a total uniform load of 9000 lbs. The maximum moment will evidently be at mid-span and is equal to $\frac{9000 \times 20}{8} = 22500$ ft. lbs. (64). If the maximum allowed fiber stress is 16000 lbs. per sq. in., the required section modulus $= \frac{22500 \times 12}{16000} = 16.9$ in.^{3} (The moment must be in in. lbs. in order to divide it by lbs. per sq. in.). According to column 8, Cambria p. 158, this requires a $9'' \times 21.0$ lb. I beam.[1] An $8'' \times 25.25$ lb. beam has nearly the required section modulus but it weighs more; while it meets the requirements, the $9''$ I is not only more economical but stronger and stiffer. Stiffness is

---
[1] The beam must be properly stayed against transverse buckling (68).

sometimes an important consideration as in the case of floor beams carrying plaster.

A similar calculation usually *fully determines* the size of a beam to carry a given load, except in certain cases, of long or very short beams (76).

If v_1 and v_2 are not equal, the section moduli for tension and compression are not equal. If the working stresses in tension and compression are the same, that one governs whose extreme fiber is the farther from the neutral axis, and this is the one given in the handbooks for unsymmetrical sections. The other one may be easily calculated from the moment of inertia which is also given for various axes. How to calculate the moment of inertia for any section about any axis is explained in Art. 72.

71. Location of the Neutral Axis. The neutral axis is located by the requirement that the total tension on a cross section must equal the total compression, or that the algebraic sum of the normal stresses must be zero, that is,

$$\int_{-v_2}^{+v_1} s\, dA = 0,$$ which from equation (9) becomes $\dfrac{s_1}{v_1} \int_{-v_2}^{+v_1} v\, dA = 0.$

This can be true only when

$$\int_{-v_2}^{+v_1} v\, dA = 0 \tag{13}$$

This is the algebraic sum of the *moments of the areas* about the neutral axis, and requires that the moment of the area above the neutral axis shall balance the moment of the area below it; in other words, *the neutral axis must pass through the center of gravity of the cross section.*

Unless otherwise particularly specified, the moment of inertia of a cross section is referred to an axis through its center of gravity.

The location of the center of gravity of the sections of rolled shapes is given in the handbooks. For other areas the engineering pocket-books, or any book on theoretical mechanics may be consulted.[1] The location of the neutral axis, or center of gravity, is determined below for a few cases.

The *center of gravity* of an area is simply the point about which it would balance if it had weight which was uniformly

---

[1] See Goodman's *Mechanics Applied to Engineering*, chapter III, and "Cambria".

distributed over the area; it is the *point of application of the resultant* of all the elements of an area treated like forces and may, therefore, be found algebraically or graphically.

It follows that the center of gravity is always on an axis of symmetry. Thus in Fig. 67, the center of gravity is on VV; it is only necessary to find v_1 or v_2.

In equation (13) v is the distance of any element of area from an axis through the center of gravity. But since it is the location of this axis that is to be found, moments can not be taken about it. Moments may be taken about any parallel axis as QQ, Fig. 67. Now $\int_{d_1}^{d_1+v_1+v_2} v' dA = A(v_2+d_1)$, in which v' is measured from QQ. Since d_1 may be any assumed distance, it may be zero, whence

$$v_2 = \frac{1}{A} \int_0^{v_1+v_2} v' dA \qquad (14)$$

The center of gravity of a rectangular cross section lies, of course, at the middle of its height, but applying equation (14)

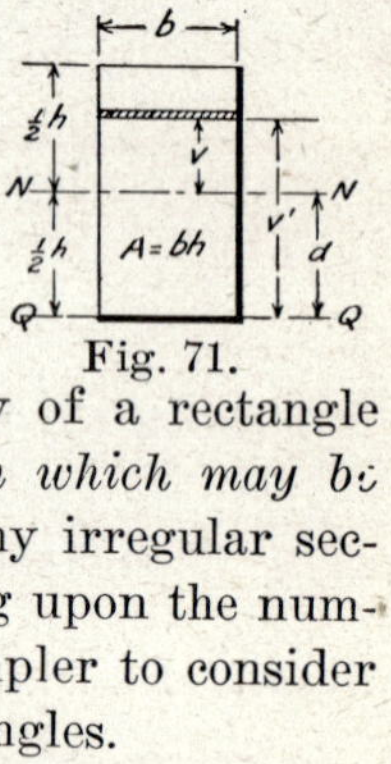

$$d = \frac{\int_0^h v' dA}{bh} = \frac{\int_0^h v' b dv'}{bh} = \frac{\tfrac{1}{2}bh^2}{bh} = \tfrac{1}{2}h.$$

Fig. 71.

Since the location of the center of gravity of a rectangle is known, *the center of gravity of any section which may be divided into rectangles, is easily calculated.* Any irregular section may be thus treated, the accuracy depending upon the number of divisions made. It will sometimes be simpler to consider a section as a combination of rectangles and triangles.

Fig. 72 shows an area which may be divided into two rectangles whose areas are

$$6 \times \tfrac{1}{2} = 3.00 \text{ sq. in.}$$
$$8 \times 1 = 8.00 \text{ sq. in.}$$
$$A = 11.00 \text{ sq. in.}$$

Taking moments about QQ
$$Ad = 11.00 d = 3 \times 8.25 + 8 \times 4.0 = 56.75$$
From which $d = 5.16$ inches.

Fig. 72.

The center of gravity may be found with fewer figures if we take moments about an axis through the center of gravity of one of the parts, when the moment of this part becomes zero. In the above case, with axis $Q'Q'$

$$11\,d' = 8 \times 4.25 = 34.00 \text{ and } d' = 3.09 \text{ in.}$$

This is the same location as found above for,

$$d = 8.25 - d' = 8.25 - 3.09 = 5.16 \text{ in.}$$

A steel shape, whose properties are given in the handbooks, should not be divided in the above manner. Referring to Fig. 73 and "Cambria" p. 174, the center of gravity of the angles is 0.75 in. from the back of the longer leg. Taking moments about axis QQ,

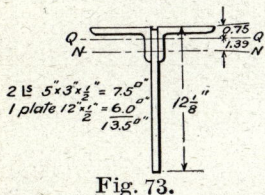

Fig. 73.

$$13.5\,d = 6(6.125 - 0.75) = 6 \times 5.375 = 32.25 \text{ and } d = 2.39 \text{ in.}$$

For a triangle, Fig. 74, the application of equation (14) is as follows.

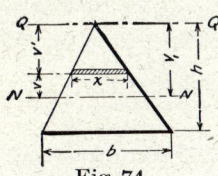

Fig. 74. 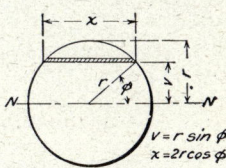   Fig. 75.

$$v_1 = \frac{1}{\frac{1}{2}bh} \int_0^h v'x\,dv'$$

This becomes, since $x : b :: v' : h$ and $x = \frac{b}{h}v'$,

$$v_1 = \frac{2}{h^2} \int_0^h v'^2\,dv' = \frac{2}{h^2} \times \tfrac{1}{3}h^3 = \tfrac{2}{3}h.$$

72. Moments of Inertia. Having located the center of gravity of an area, the moment of inertia about an axis through it (the neutral axis) is found by means of equation (11). I is a quantity of the fourth order—the square of a distance times an area.

For a *rectangle*, Fig. 70,

$$I = \int_{-\frac{1}{2}h}^{+\frac{1}{2}h} v^2 b\,dv = \tfrac{1}{3}b(\tfrac{1}{8}h^3 + \tfrac{1}{8}h^3) = \tfrac{1}{12}bh^3 \qquad (15)$$

This value should be remembered as it is frequently used.

For a *triangle*, Fig. 74,

$$I = \int_{-\frac{1}{3}h}^{+\frac{2}{3}h} v^2 x \, dv \qquad x = \frac{b}{h}\left(\tfrac{2}{3}h - v\right)$$

$$I = \frac{b}{h}\int_{-\frac{1}{3}h}^{+\frac{2}{3}h} (\tfrac{2}{3}hv^2 - v^3)\,dv = \frac{b}{h}\left(\tfrac{2}{9}h \times \tfrac{8}{27}h^3 - \tfrac{1}{4}\times \tfrac{16}{81}h^4 + \tfrac{2}{9}h \times \tfrac{1}{27}h^3 \right.$$
$$\left. + \tfrac{1}{4}\times \tfrac{1}{81}h^4\right) = \tfrac{1}{36}bh^3$$

or one-third as much as for a rectangle of the same base and height.

For a *circle*, Fig. 75,

$$I = \int_{-r}^{+r} v^2 x\,dv = 4\int_0^{\frac{1}{2}\pi} r^2 \sin^2\phi \; r\cos\phi \; r\cos\phi\, d\phi$$

$$I = 4r^4 \int_0^{\frac{1}{2}\pi} \sin^2\phi \cos^2\phi\,d\phi = \tfrac{1}{4}\pi r^4$$

The moment of inertia is four times that of one quadrant. In like manner I for a rectangle is twice that for half of it, and it follows that I for a rectangle about one edge is $\tfrac{1}{24}bh^3$ in which h is twice the height, that is

$$h = 2h_1 \text{ and } I = \tfrac{1}{24}b(2h_1)^3 = \tfrac{1}{3}bh_1^3$$

It is often necessary to find moments of inertia for axes parallel to the neutral axes. In Figs. 72 and 73, for example, the neutral axis NN of the combination is the one about which the moments of inertia of the elements of area (rectangles and angles) is desired. Equation (11) is applicable; thus in Fig. 67,

$$I_a = \int_{-v_2}^{+v_1}(v+d)^2\,dA = \int_{-v_2}^{+v_1} v^2 dA + 2d\int_{-v_2}^{+v_1} v\,dA + d^2\int_{-v_2}^{+v_1} dA$$

Since $\int_{-v_2}^{+v_1} v^2 dA = I$, $\int_{-v_2}^{+v_1} v\,dA = 0$ and $\int_{-v_2}^{+v_1} dA = A$

[See equations (11) and (13)].

$$I_a = I + Ad^2 \qquad (16)$$

This equation is of much practical importance and the student should be familiar with its meaning. Equation (16) means that the moment of inertia of any area, about an axis parallel to the neutral axis, is equal to the moment of inertia of the area about its neutral axis, plus its area times the square of the distance between the axes.

The same result may be gotten as above by integrating $I_Q = \int_{d_1}^{d+v_1} v'^2 dA$, and these operations are applicable to any kind of area, Figs. 71 to 74, for example.

Moments of inertia of irregular areas may be gotten approximately by dividing them into a number of rectangles, or mechanically by means of a moment planimeter. The moments of inertia of angles, channels, Z bars, etc. should be taken from the handbooks.

To find the moment of inertia of the cross section shown in Fig. 72, about its neutral axis NN, equations (15) and (16) are used, the area being treated as two rectangles as was done in finding d.

$$I = \tfrac{1}{12} bh^3 = \frac{6}{12 \times 8} + \frac{8^3}{12} = 42.73$$
$$Ad^2 = 3 \times 3.09^2 + 8 \times 1.16^2 = \underline{39.41}$$
$$I \text{ for axis } NN = 82.14 \text{ in.}^4$$

For the section of Fig. 73 refer to Cambria.

$$I = \tfrac{1}{12} \times \tfrac{1}{2} + 12^3 \text{(for plate)} + 2 \times 2.58 \text{ (for angles)}$$
$$= 72.0 + 5.16 \qquad\qquad\qquad\qquad = 77.16$$
$$Ad^2 = 6 \times (6\tfrac{1}{8} - 0.75 - 2.39)^2 + 7.5 \times 2.39^2 \qquad = \underline{96.30}$$
$$I \text{ for axis } NN \qquad\qquad\qquad\qquad\qquad = 173.46 \text{ in.}^4$$

It is often more convenient to find I by subtraction than by addition; thus for a ring whose external radius is r_1 and internal radius r_2, $I = \tfrac{1}{4} \pi (r_1^4 - r_2^4)$.

73. Oblique Loading. In what precedes it was assumed that the neutral axis is perpendicular to the plane of the bending moment. In Fig. 67 the plane of the bending moment cuts the cross section in VV, an axis of symmetry. On account of this symmetry, the plane of the resisting moment is evidently coincident with that of the bending moment, and it follows that the neutral axis is perpendicular to this plane, since the moment of resistance is a moment about it. This may also be true if the section has no axis of symmetry as is shown by the following consideration. In Fig. 67, the origin of a rectangular sytem of coördinates is at the center of gravity of the section and the axis of Z is coincident with the neutral axis. Since the external forces lie in the plane whose trace is the axis of V, the sum of their moments about this axis is zero; the sum of the moments of the stresses about this axis must also be zero, that is,

$$\int s dA z = 0$$

Substituting the value of s from equation (9), $\frac{s_1}{v_1}\int vz dA = 0$ or

$$\int vz dA = 0 \qquad (17)$$

When equation (17) holds, the plane of the bending moment and that of a moment equivalent to the sum of the moments of the bending stresses are coincident. In Fig. 67, there is, in the second quadrant, an element of area for every one, similarly located, in the first quadrant. The product vz is plus in the first quadrant and minus in the second, hence $\int vz dA$, for these quadrants is zero. Similar reasoning applies for the third and fourth quadrants; therefore, *when the plane of the bending moment cuts the cross section of a beam in an axis of symmetry, the* $\int vz dA = 0$; *this is also true when there are similar areas similarly situated in the first and fourth quadrants, and in the third and second quadrants,* as shown in Fig. 76, because $\int vz dA$ for these quadrants cancel each other, and therefore $\int vz dA = 0$. If the plane of the bending moment corresponds with ZZ, we have the case of symmetry. For these two cases the neutral axes are at right angles to each other. The similar axes for a single angle of equal legs are shown in Fig. 77.

Fig. 76.

A Z-bar cross section does not have an axis of symmetry, but there are also two axes, at right angles to each other, each of which will be the neutral axis when the other is the trace of the plane of the bending moment. For these axes $\int vz dA = 0$ as will be seen by reference to Fig. 78. For the axes $V_1 V_1$ and $Z_1 Z_1$, $\int v_1 z_1 dA = 0$ for the web, since they are axes of symmetry; for the flanges this is not true because $v_1 z_1$ is minus for both of them. Now if the axes be turned so as to take some position

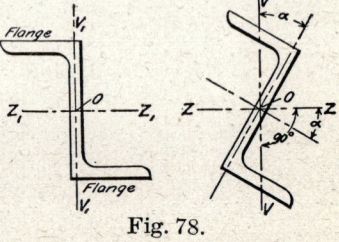

Fig. 77.

Fig. 78.

VV and ZZ, some of the area passes into the first and third quadrants (plus) and some passes out of the second and fourth (minus); there must be some position of the axes for which the plus value of $\int vzdA$ is equal to the minus value and therefore $\int vzdA = 0$, and the neutral axis is perpendicular to the plane of the bending moment.

If the following values are calculated for any two rectangular axes as V_1V_1 and Z_1Z_1, for example, viz. $\int v_1^2 dA = I_{z1}$, $\int z_1^2 dA = I_{v1}$, and $\int v_1 z_1 dA = I_{v1z1}$, the $\int v^2 dA = I_z$ may be found in terms of these quantities and the angle a. Differentiating with respect to a and putting the first differential coefficient equal to zero, it will be found that I_z is a maximum or a minimum, when a is determined by this equation:

$$tan\, 2a = \frac{2I_{v1z1}}{I - I_{z1}} \qquad (18)$$

Equation (18) will give two values of $2a$ differing from each other by 180°, or two values of a differing by 90°. These two values locate two axes, *at right angles to each other,* about which the moment of inertia is a maximum or a minimum. These may be distinguished from each other by inspection; thus in Fig. 76, I_z is a maximum and I_v is a minimum; the corresponding axes are called *principal axes. Every cross section, no matter what its shape may be, has two principal axes.*

Equation (18) shows that when $I_{vz} = 0$, $a = 0$ and 90°, that is the principal axes coincide with the axes of V_1 and Z_1. Since it has been shown that $I_{vz} = 0$ when one axis is an axis of symmetry, it follows that *an axis of symmetry is a principal axis.* See Figs. 67, 76 and 77. An axis at right angles to an axis of symmetry is a principal axis, since it has been shown that principal axes make an angle of 90° with each other and that, in this case, $I_{vz} = 0$.

For angles of unequal legs, and for Z-bars, the principal axes are located in the Cambria handbook.

In practice, sections having at least one axis of symmetry are usually used for beams, and they are so placed that a principal axis lies in the plane of the outer forces. A common exception to this is the case of a roof purlin, which has an axis of symmetry

106   OBLIQUE LOADING.   Art. 73.

parallel to the roof while the load, which it carries to the roof trusses, acts vertically. This is illustrated for a timber purlin in Fig. 79.

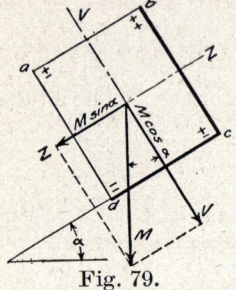

In order to find the maximum fiber stress, it is not necessary to find the position of the neutral axis. The bending moment is M and its plane is vertical. If it is resolved into two components whose planes contains the principal axes (as shown), the extreme fiber stresses for each component may be calculated, according to equation (10), and the results added algebraically.

Fig. 79.

$$s = \frac{M\cos\alpha}{I_z}v + \frac{M\sin\alpha}{I_y}z \qquad (19)$$

$M\cos\alpha$ produces compression at a and b, and tension at d and c. $M\sin\alpha$ produces compression at b and c, and tension at a and d. The maximum resultant compression will evidently be at b and the maximum tension at d.

A single channel is frequently used as a roof purlin, as shown in Fig. 80. For a quarter-pitch roof (rise equals one-fourth of the span), $\alpha = 26°\ 34'$. Knowing the span and the load, M is easily calculated. Assuming $M = 68000$ in. lbs., in this case, $M\sin\alpha = 68000 \times 0.447 = 30400$ in. lbs., and $M\cos\alpha = 68000 \times 0.894 = 60900$ in. lbs. The other quantities of equation (19) are given in the Cambria handbook.

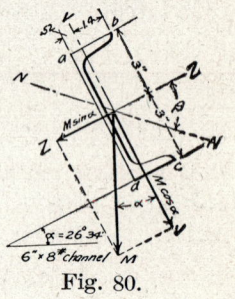

Fig. 80.

s at $b = \dfrac{60900}{13.0} 3 + \dfrac{30400}{0.70} 1.4 = 74800$ lbs. per sq. in.

s at $d = \dfrac{60900}{13.0} 3 + \dfrac{30400}{0.7} 0.52 = 36600$ lbs. per sq. in.

At c and a, the stresses will be less, because the two terms will have opposite signs.

Since these stresses exceed 16000 lbs. per square inch, the usual working stress, the channel is too small, although as commonly designed, the maximum stress is found to be less than 16000 lbs. per sq. in. This stress is calculated as if the plane of M coincided with that of the principal axis, in which case

$$s = \frac{M}{I}v = \frac{68000}{13} 3 = 15700 \text{ lbs. per sq. in.}$$

The above discrepancy may be much reduced, as it often is.

Art. 74. RELATION BETWEEN MOMENT AND SHEAR.

by preventing deflection in the direction of the axis of Z; this cancels $M\sin\alpha$ and then equation (10) is applicable.

It is evident that the position of the neutral axis is not needed in getting the maximum fiber stress, but it may easily be found from equation (19), if the moments of inertia about the principal axes are known (I_v and I_z). If the coördinates, v' and z', of a fiber on the neutral axis are substituted in (19), s must be zero and $\sin\alpha \dfrac{z'}{I_v} = -\cos\alpha \dfrac{v'}{I_z}$ or

$$\frac{v'}{z'} = -\tan\alpha \; \frac{I_z}{I_v} = \tan\beta \tag{20}$$

in which β is the angle between the neutral axis and the axis of Z.

In the above case, Fig. 80, $\tan\beta = -0.5\dfrac{13.0}{0.7} = 9.28$ and $\beta = 83°\;51'$. β determines the direction of the neutral axis and the *deflection* must be in a direction perpendicular to it.

When the direction of the neutral axis is not known, it may, in certain cases, be doubtful which are the extreme points; this is easily determined by calculating the stresses from equation (19)[1].

74. Relation Between the Bending Moment and the Shear at Any Cross Section of a Beam.

A very important and very simple relation exists between the bending moment and the shear. Fig. 81 shows a beam supported at its ends and carrying concentrated loads, but *the same relation holds in beams loaded and supported in any manner*. R is the resultant of the forces to the left of the section pq.

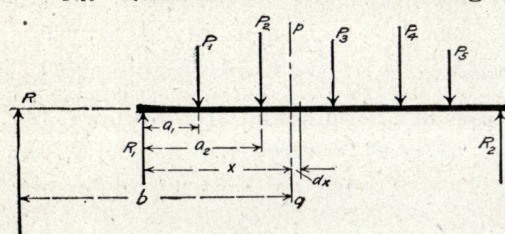

Fig. 81.

$$R = S_x = R_1 - \Sigma^x P \quad \text{and} \quad M_x = Rb = R_1 x - \Sigma_0^x P\,(x-a)$$

For the section at a distance dx from pq,

$$M_x + dM_x = R\,(b+dx) = S_x(b+dx)$$

and the increase of the moment is $dM_x = S_x dx$. The rate of increase of the moment along the beam is therefore,

$$\frac{dM_x}{dx} = S_x \tag{21}$$

---

[1] For a more general discussion of this general case of bending, with examples, see *Johnson's Modern Framed Structures* p. 154, or German works on technical mechanics or the statics of construction.

The same result is obtained by differentiating the value of M_x above and substituting S_x for its value.

$$\frac{dM_x}{dx} = R_1 - \Sigma_0^x P = S_x.$$

The importance of this simple relation is apparent when it is remembered that the moment is constant, is a maximum, or is a minimum when $\frac{dM_x}{dx} = 0$. It follows that,

1. Where the shear is zero or passes through zero, the moment is constant or is a maximum or a minimum.

2. Where the shear is uniform, the *increase* of the moment is uniform.

3. That the area of the shear diagram to the left of any section is equal to the moment at the section since

$$\int dM = \int S dx = M.$$

The shear and moment diagrams of Figs. 94 to 112 should be carefully compared to understand these relations. It should be remembered that the moment is not a maximum where it passes from a positive to a negative value, and that the shear becomes zero or passes through zero at a support.

That the moment is dependent upon the shear (a resultant) and the distance through which it acts is shown in Fig. 81, where $M_x = Rb$.

75. Shearing Stresses in a Solid Beam. In addition to the bending stresses (normal) at a section, there are, in general, also shearing stresses (tangential) in order that "the sum of the vertical components" shall be zero as was shown in Art. 57. The shear (the sum of the vertical components of the external forces) is equal to the shearing stress (the sum of the vertical components of the internal forces).

It is usually assumed that shearing stresses are uniformly distributed over the cross section of a beam. This is a reasonable assumption for an I-shaped section and perhaps also in certain other cases as will be pointed out below.

As was shown in Art. 74, the shear and the bending moment are dependent upon each other: it follows that the shearing stresses and bending stresses are interdependent and that the distribution of the shearing stress depends upon the distribution of the bending stress, that is, upon the theory of flexure.

In order to fully investigate the stresses at any point of a

Art. 75. SHEARING STRESSES IN A SOLID BEAM.   109

beam, three planes should be passed through it. In the usual case, which is the only one here considered, the cross section is symmetrical about the plane of the bending moment, and there is no variation of stress parallel to the neutral axis, or perpendicular to the plane of the bending moment. It remains to find how the stress varies vertically, and horizontally lengthwise of beam. That there are horizontal shearing stresses will now be shown. If we find how the horizontal shearing stresses are distributed, the distribution of the vertical shearing stresses will be known because, according to Art. 17, their intensities at any point must be equal.

A numerical case will be first worked out and a general formula derived afterward.

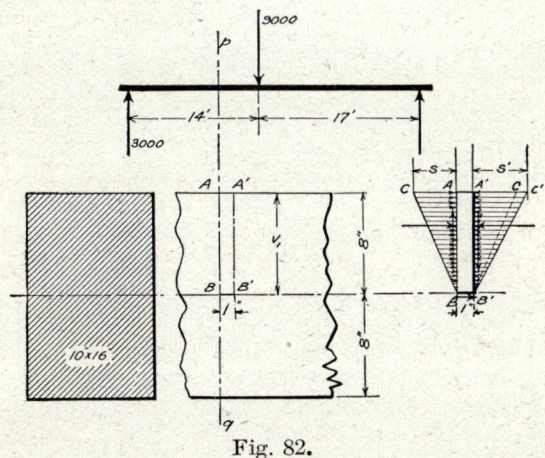

Fig. 82.

Considering the simple case of a rectangular beam, $10'' \times 16''$, carrying a single load as shown in Fig. 82, the shearing stresses at all sections between the left reaction and the load will be alike, because the shear at each section is 3000 lbs. It follows that the horizontal shear does not vary lengthwise of the beam, in this part of it.

Considering two cross sections AB and $A'B'$, one inch apart the difference in the bending moments is 3000 in. lbs. If the equilibrium of a block cut out by these two sections and the neutral plane be considered, the forces acting upon it come from the stresses cut in these three planes as illustrated in Fig. 82.

The *difference* in the extreme fiber unit stresses is $A'C' - AC$

and this is, according to equation (12), $s_1 = \dfrac{Mv_1}{I} = \dfrac{3000 \times 8}{\frac{1}{12} \times 10 \times 16 \times 16 \times 16}$ $= \dfrac{900}{128} = 7.03$ lbs. per sq. in. The mean difference in unit stress upon the planes $A'B'$ and AB is one half of this or 3.515 lbs. per sq. in., and the total difference of stress is $3.515 \times 8 \times 10 = 281.2$ lbs. acting towards the left. This can be balanced by a shearing stress on the plane BB' only. The area of this plane is 10 sq. ins., hence the intensity of the horizontal shear at the neutral axis is $281.2 \div 10 = 28.12$ lbs. per sq. in. This is just 50% greater than the mean unit shear on the cross section, because that is $\dfrac{3000}{10 \times 16} = 18.75$ lbs. per sq. in.

The horizontal shear evidently decreases from the neutral axis outward, because the difference in the normal stresses on AB and $A'B'$ decreases. At the upper and lower edges of the cross section, it becomes zero, hence the vertical shear is also zero at these edges. This is evident also, if the action of shear at a section is considered. Fig. 83 shows the movement which tends to take place at a section AB. It is seen that there is no resistance to the downward movement of an extreme particle at F; likewise there would be none to C moving up, if there were no external forces applied at D. Such forces are applied at certain sections of pins and rivets used in connecting parts of trusses and girders, and modify the distribution of the shearing stress in an unknown manner. The usual assumption of uniform distribution seems to be justified by experiment.

Fig. 83.

When a cross section is curved at any point of its perimeter the *shearing stress must act tangentially,* because the normal component must be zero, since the condition in its direction is the same as at the upper and lower edges of a rectangular section.

Fig. 84 shows a cross section symmetrical about the plane of the shear S. At the points P', the shearing stress must act tangentially and it is usually *assumed* that the resultant of all the shearing stresses, acting at the points of a horizontal line, goes

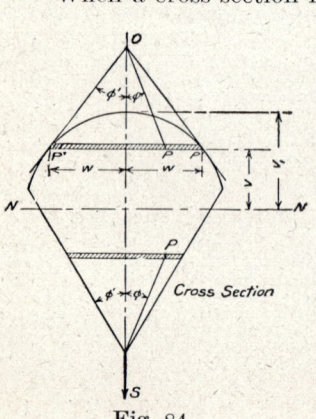

Fig. 84.

Art. 75.   SHEARING STRESSES IN A SOLID BEAM.   111

through the point O and is opposite to S. This makes the vertical components of the unit stresses along $P'P'$ equal, and since the horizontal components increase toward the points P', the intensity is greatest at these points.

To derive a general formula for s_s at *any point* of a cross section, the procedure is similar to that for the numerical case above. In place of taking the two sections one inch apart, as in Fig. 82, they will be taken a distance dx apart, so that the stress in this distance may be considered of constant intensity, and the horizontal section will be taken a distance v above the neutral axis. The longitudinal stress on an element of area $2w$ wide and dv deep is $2wdvs$ and the total stress, above the horizontal section is $\int_v^{v_1} 2wsdv$. Substituting for s its value from equation (12), the total stress on one end of the block is $\frac{M}{I} \int_v^{v_1} 2wvdv$; the total stress on the other end of the block is $\frac{M'}{I} \int_v^{v_1} 2wvdv$. The difference between these stresses is equal to the horizontal shear on the area $2wdx$. $M' - M = dM = Sdx$ according to equation (21); therefore, $\frac{M'-M}{I} \int_v^{v_1} 2wvdv = \frac{Sdx}{I} \int_v^{v_1} 2wvdv =$ total horizontal shear. $s_s' = \frac{S}{2wI} \int_v^{v_1} 2wvdv =$ unit shear in a **strip** whose sides are vertical $= s_s \cos\phi$ in a strip whose sides are not vertical (Fig. 84). Therefore,

$$s_s = \frac{S}{2w\cos\phi\, I} \int_v^{v_1} 2wvdv = \frac{SM_s}{2w\cos\phi\, I} \qquad (22)$$

in which M_s is the statical moment of that part of the section lying above a horizontal line through the point where s_s is to be calculated.

For a *rectangular cross section* ϕ becomes zero and $\cos\phi = 1$. Equation (22) reduces to $s = \frac{S}{b \times \frac{1}{12}bh^3} \int_v^{v_1} bvdv$ When $v = 0$, that is, for stress at the neutral axis,

$$s_s = \frac{12L}{bh^3} \int_0^{\frac{1}{2}h} vdv = \frac{12S}{bh^3} \times \frac{h^2}{8} = \frac{3}{2}\frac{S}{A} \qquad (23)$$

This shows that *the unit shearing stress at the neutral axis of a rectangular cross section is 50% greater than the mean value.* This corresponds with what was found in the numerical example above.

When $v = \frac{1}{2}h$, $s_s = 0$ as was found above from general considerations.

For a *circular cross section* equation (22) becomes, *for points on the circumference,*

$$s_s = \frac{S}{2r\cos^2\phi' I} \int_{r\sin\phi'}^{r} 2r\cos\phi' \, r\sin\phi' \, r\cos\phi' \, d\phi' =$$

$$\frac{Sr^2}{\cos^2\phi' I} \int_{\phi'}^{\frac{\pi}{2}} \sin\phi' \cos^2\phi' \, d\phi'$$

$I = \frac{1}{4}\pi r^4$ (68) and for stress at the neutral axis, $\phi = 0$, and s_s is constant over the full width, so that

$$s_s = \frac{4S}{\pi r^2} \int_0^{90°} \sin\phi' \cos^2\phi' \, d\phi' = \frac{4}{3}\frac{S}{\pi r^2} = \frac{4}{3}\frac{S}{A} \tag{24}$$

This shows that *the unit shearing stress at the neutral axis of a circular cross section is 33 1-3% greater than the mean value.*

Equation (22) is not applicable to an I section on account of the sudden change in width at the junction of the flange and web. For such a section the usual assumption of *uniform distribution of the shearing stresses, over the section of the web only,* is on the side of safety. These stresses must be zero at the upper and lower edges of each flange, but since the flanges take some stress, the effect is to approximate to a uniform distribution of stress vertically. Thus the actual maximum unit stress will be about the same as the unit stress on the assumption.

According to the above investigation, the shearing stress is the greatest at the neutral axis and becomes zero at the upper and lower edges. The law of variation between these extremes depends upon the cross section. For a rectangular cross section, the stresses vary as the ordinates to a parabola whose middle ordinate is $\frac{3}{2}\frac{S}{A}$. This is is illustrated in Fig. 85.

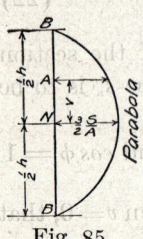

Fig. 85.

76. Resultant of Bending and Shearing Stresses. Principal Stresses in Beams. The bending and shearing stresses in beams and girders have so far been considered separately, and it has

Art. 76.   PRINCIPAL STRESSES IN BEAMS.   113

been shown that, in general, both occur at any point in a beam. The question arises, why is the resultant stress—the principal stress (12) —not calculated?

According to Art. 75, the shearing stresses increase from the neutral axis outward, and according to Art. 68, the bending stresses increase in an opposite direction. In the outer fibers, the bending stresses are a maximum and the shearing stresses zero; at the neutral axis the reverse is the case. The maximum resultant stress occurs somewhere between the neutral axis and outer fiber, and its intensity might be greater than the maximum intensity of the bending stress, depending upon the form of cross section. The common I section is an unfavorable one in this respect. Since it is unknown how shearing stresses are distributed over an I section, calculations must always be made upon certain assumptions; such calculations indicate that, within certain limitations, the bending and shearing stresses may be considered separately, and, in simple beams, the shearing stresses need not be considered at all (See example Art. 70).

The resultant stress is evidently less in a beam uniformly loaded (supported both ends) than in one carrying a concentrated load, because in the one-case the maximum shear comes at the supports, and the maximum moment at the center section, while in the other these sections coincide. (See Figs. 101 and 96. Also compare shear and moment diagrams for other cases.) Suppose a beam to be designed to resist the maximum moment caused by a *single load*; if now the span be decreased, the moment becomes smaller, and the shear remains the same. It is evident that in *very short* beams, the bending stresses are negligible as compared with the shearing stresses, and the usual procedure is not applicable. This is especially true for timber beams. The resistance to shear in sections parallel to the fibers being the least, short timber beams sometimes fail (at the neutral axis) in horizontal shear. A similar failure might occur in very short I beams heavily loaded, because the web is thin.

For example, if a timber beam $12'' \times 12''$ has a span of 4 ft. and carries a load of 24000 lbs. at its middle, its extreme fiber stress is $s = \dfrac{Mv}{I} = \dfrac{12000 \times 24 \times 6}{\frac{1}{12} \times 12 \times 12^3} = 1000$ lbs. per sq. in. (Eq. 10). The maximum unit shearing stress is $\dfrac{3}{2} \times \dfrac{12000}{12 \times 12} = 125$ lbs. per sq. in. (Eq. 23). Now if the working stresses are 1000 lbs. in the extreme fiber and 100 lbs. in shearing with the grain, the beam is overstrained in shear. (See Cambria p. 361). The shear is the same near the load as at the end and therefore the maximum resultant unit stress may be greater than either of the above. How to calculate this principal stress will now be shown. This is of importance only in exceptional cases and for theoretical considerations.

It has been shown that on a vertical section of a beam there are normal and tangential stresses, and on a horizontal section there are tangential stresses. If equations are written giving the stresses on a plane making an angle ϕ with the vertical section, in terms of these stresses on vertical and horizontal planes, the value of ϕ which will make the normal stress on the inclined plane a maximum can be easily found.

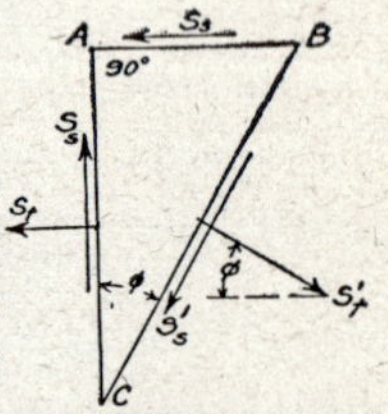

Fig. 86 shows the face of a triangular block, taken indefinitely small, so that the unit stresses on the three surfaces whose traces are AB, AC, and BC may be taken constant. The plane whose trace is AC is taken in a vertical section on the tension side of a beam. The *unit stresses* and not the total stresses are shown in the figure. It should be remembered that there is no variation in stress perpendicular to the plane of the paper, that there are no stresses on the front and rear faces of the block, and that the unit shearing stresses on AB and AC are equal (17). Fig. 86 is a representation of the various stresses in a beam.[1] The problem is to find that value of ϕ which will make s_t' a maximum (Also s_s').

Fig. 86.

Taking dA as the area of the plane whose trace is BC, the equilibrium of the block requires the sum of the horizontal and vertical components of the forces to be separately equal to zero. The area of the plane $AB = dA \sin \phi$ and of AC, $dA \cos \phi$.

From the sum of the horizontal components
$s_t' dA \cos \phi - s_s' dA \sin \phi - s_s dA \sin \phi - s_t dA \cos \phi = 0.$
Canceling the factor dA, this equation becomes,

$$s_t' \cos \phi - s_s' \sin \phi - s_s \sin \phi - s \cos \phi = 0. \qquad (a)$$

In like manner from the vertical components,

$$s_t' \sin \phi + s_s' \cos \phi - s_s \cos \phi = 0. \qquad (b)$$

---
[1] This is a special case of the general problem in which there is also a normal stress on AB.

Art. 76.   PRINCIPAL STRESSES IN BEAMS.   115

Multiplying the first equation by $cos\,\phi$ and the second by $sin\,\phi$, and adding, s_s' is eliminated.

$s_t'\,cos^2\phi - s_s'\,sin\,\phi\,cos\,\phi - s_s\,sin\,\phi\,cos\,\phi - s_t\,cos^2\phi = 0.$
$s_t'\,sin^2\phi + s_s'\,sin\,\phi\,cos\,\phi - s\,sin\,\phi\,cos\,\phi = 0$
$s_t' = s_t\,cos^2\phi + 2\,s_s\,sin\,\phi\,cos\,\phi$ which reduces to
$s_t' = \tfrac{1}{2}s_t\,(1+cos\,2\,\phi) + s_s\,sin\,2\,\phi$ (25)
$s_s' = \tfrac{1}{2}s_t\,sin\,2\,\phi + s_s\,cos\,2\,\phi$ (26)

Equation (26) is gotten by multiplying (*a*) by $sin\,\phi$, (*b*) by $cos\,\phi$, subtracting, and introducing the angle $2\,\phi$.

From (25), *for a maximum or a minimum s_t'*

$$\frac{ds_t'}{d\phi} = -s_t\,sin\,2\,\phi + 2\,s_s\,cos\,2\,\phi = 0 \qquad (c)$$

$$tan\,2\,\phi = 2\,\frac{s_s}{s_t} \qquad (27)$$

Tan $2\,\phi$ has the same value for two angles differing from each other by 180°; therefore ϕ has two values differing by 90°, one of which locates the plane upon which s_t' is a maximum, and the other the plane upon which s_t' is a minimum. By substituting the value of $2\,\phi$ from (27) in (25) these values are determined. From (*c*) or (27),

$$sin\,2\phi = \pm\frac{2s_s}{\sqrt{s_t^2+4s_s^2}}\,;\ cos\,2\phi = \pm\frac{s_t}{\sqrt{s_t^2+4s_s^2}}.$$

These values in equation (25) give

$$s_t'\begin{pmatrix}max\\min\end{pmatrix} = \tfrac{1}{2}s_t \pm \frac{\tfrac{1}{2}s_t^2+2s_s^2}{\sqrt{s_t^2+4s_s^2}} = \tfrac{1}{2}s_t \pm \tfrac{1}{2}\sqrt{s_t^2+4s_s^2} \qquad (28)$$

The larger value is the maximum principal stress and the smaller value the minimum principal stress (12). *These will be of opposite sign,* because the negative term is greater than the positive term; this means that one is tension and the other compression. On the compression side of a beam s_t is replaced by s_c and s_t' by s_c'.

If equation (28) gives the values of the *principal* stresses, the value of ϕ from equation (27) should make $s_s' = 0$ in equation (26); that this is true is apparent by comparing equations (*c*) and (26).

When s_s is zero as it is in the extreme upper and lower fibres, equation (28) becomes $s_t' = s_t$ or 0; the resultant stress is equal to the bending stress—tension in this case—and the compressive stress is zero. Now the principal stresses lie in the horizontal and vertical planes, as is also shown by equation (27).

When $s_t = 0$, as it does at the neutral axis, equation (28) becomes $s' = \pm s_s$ and equation (27) gives $\phi = 45°$ and $135°$, which agrees with the conclusions in Art. 17. At the neutral axis the principal stresses are equal, of equal intensity with the shearing stresses, and act on planes making angles of 45° with the neutral plane.

From equation (26), for maximum or minimum s'_s

$$\frac{ds_s'}{d\phi} = -s_t \cos 2\phi - 2s_s \sin 2\phi = 0 \qquad (d)$$

$$\tan 2\phi = -\frac{s_t}{2s_s} \qquad (29)$$

This value is the negative cotangent of the angle determined by equation (27), therefore the value of 2ϕ for maximum or minimum s_s' differs from that for maximum or minimum s_t' by 90°, and the values of ϕ differ by 45°. This fact has already been brought out for points on the neutral axis.

By comparing equations (d) and (25), it is apparent *that s_t' does not become zero when s_s' is a maximum or minimum;* its value is $s_t' = \frac{1}{2}s_t$; this is true in the case of Fig. 5, Art. 12, when the inclination of AB is 45°, as may readily be proven.

By substitution in equation (26) from equation (29),

$$s_s'\binom{max}{min} = \pm \tfrac{1}{2}\sqrt{s_t^2 + 4s_s^2} \qquad (30)$$

Equation (30) shows that the maximum and minimum values of the shearing stresses are numerically equal, which agrees with the conclusions of Art. 17.

77. Lines of Principal Stress. Knowing the intensity of the shearing stress (s_s) and the bending stress (s_t or s_c) at any point in a vertical section of a beam, the inclinations of the planes on which the principal stresses act may be gotten from equation (27); these will also be the inclinations of the lines of principal stress, because they are at right angles to each other. Curves having these inclinations for every point through which they pass are lines of principal maximum and principal minimum stress. Fig. 87 shows approximately the location of such lines in a beam, supported at its ends and carrying a load at the center.

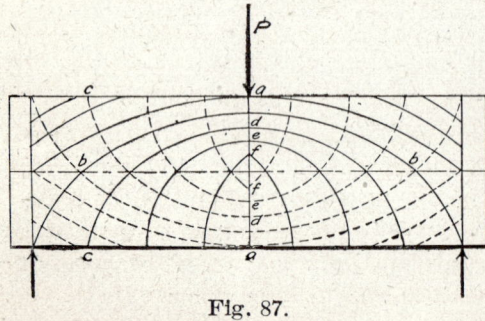

Fig. 87.

Art. 78. WORKING STRESS FOR COMPOUND STRESS.

The dotted lines are lines of tension, and the full lines, lines of compression. The former are evidently lines of maximum principal stress below the neutral plane, and of minimum principal stress above it. The reverse is the case for the compression lines.

In accordance with the previous article, these lines cross each other at angles of 90° and the neutral plane at angles of 45°. The stresses along them gradually decrease from the central plane to their ends, at the upper and lower edges. At a the shearing stress is zero, the bending stress alone acts, and the line is horizontal; toward the neutral axis, the influence of the shearing stresses increases, and that of the bending stress decreases, bringing the line to an inclination of 45° at b, where the shearing stresses alone act; above the neutral plane the compressive stresses gradually reduce the tension to zero at c, and the line becomes vertical. At d, e, and f, the lines are inclined, owing to the influence of the shearing stress.

In a beam carrying uniform load the lines would all be horizontal at the middle section, because the shear is zero, and the curves would be flatter, because the shear *increases toward the supports.*

If the lines of maximum and minimum shear were drawn they would cross the lines of principal stress at angles of 45°

78. Working Stress for Cases of Compound Stress. It was pointed out in Art. 13 that transverse forces, acting upon the sides of a bar in tension or compression, interfere with the longitudinal deformation so that it is no longer proportional to the longitudinal stress. There is a similar state of things in a beam, the shearing and bending stresses resulting in tensile and compressive stresses acting at right angles to each other.

Working stresses are based upon experiments in simple tension, compression, and shear, for which cases equation (2), $E\delta = s$, holds. When stress and deformation are not directly proportional to each other, the question arises, Shall the working stress be based upon the intensity of the maximum stress or upon the maximum deformation? Experiments alone can determine this, and these are beset with such difficulties that authorities do not agree, as yet, upon this matter. The weight of authority seems to be in favor of considering the maximum *deformation.* in the line of principal stress, as the best basis for a working stress. Having calculated this, as explained below, an *equivalent direct stress* is used as a working stress.

Knowing δ_{max}, $s_w = E\, \delta_{max}$.

For the case of Art. 76,

$$\delta'_t (\max) = \frac{1}{E}\left[s' (\max) - \frac{1}{m} s'_t (\min) \right]$$

$$\delta'_c (\max) = \frac{1}{E}\left[s'_c (\max) - \frac{1}{m} s'_c (\min) \right].$$

Substituting $\frac{s_w}{E}$ for δ_{max}

$$s_w = s'_t (\max) - \frac{1}{m} s'_t (\min) \text{ or } s_w = s'_c (\max) - \frac{1}{m} s'_c (\min) \quad (31)$$

At the neutral axis of a beam, the shearing stresses are principal stresses, and their values are $+s_s$ and $-s_s$ from equation (30), s_t being 0.

These values in equation (31) give

$$s_w = s_s + \frac{1}{m} s_s \text{ or } s_s = \frac{m}{m+1} s_w \quad (32)$$

that is, theoretically, the working stress in shear should be $\frac{4}{5}$ of that in tension, when $m = 4$ or Poisson's ratio is $\frac{1}{4}$; it is, however, always taken less than this, and usually low enough so that the shearing stress may be taken as uniformly distributed over a cross section (75).

79. Stresses in Girders. All of the preceding general discussion of solid beams applies, of course, to girders. In Fig. 66 are shown the forces acting upon a part of a girder to the left of the section mn. The *shearing stress* $S = R$; this is assumed to be uniformly distributed over the area of the cross section of the web only (75). Therefore,

$$A_w = \frac{S_{max}}{s_s} = ht \quad (33)$$

This equation determines the area of the web; its depth, h, is determined by considerations of economy; its thickness, t, is never made less than $\frac{1}{4}''$, and for railway bridges seldom less than $\frac{3}{8}''$.

Since there are compressive stresses in the web (77), it is usually stiffened, because its ratio of depth to thickness is much greater than for I beams. The unknown influence of the tensile stresses acting at right angles to the compressive stresses, makes a calculation of the buckling stresses impossible.

The bending stress in a girder may be calculated by means

of equation (12), which must be solved by trial, as there are no tables of section moduli as there are for I beams. In order to avoid the labor of calculating the moment of inertia of each section which may be tried, the calculation is much simplified by making *two assumptions*.

1. The stresses in the flanges (tension and compression) are uniformly distributed over their areas and their resultants, therefore, act at the centers of gravity of the flanges.

2. That the depth of the web, h, may be set equal to d, the distance between centers of gravity of the flanges.

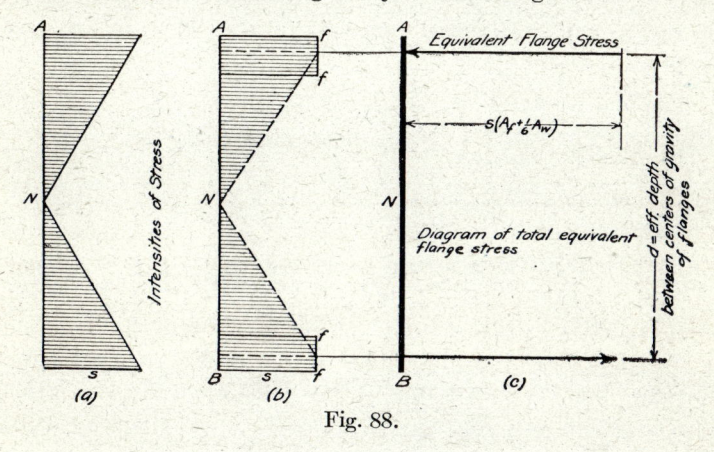

Fig. 88.

Fig. 88 (a) shows the actual distribution of the *intensity* of bending stress over the cross section, while Fig. 88 (b) shows the effect of the assumptions, with the diagrams for the intensities of stress in flanges and web superimposed. Fig. 88 (a) corresponds with the formula $M = s\dfrac{I}{v}$; so does Fig. 88 (b) so far as the web is concerned, except that the second assumption changes its depth a little. The depth of the web is sometimes equal to that of the cross section; it is sometimes less and sometimes greater than d. The diagram for each flange is a rectangle, which results from the first assumption, and which is the same thing as neglecting the moment of inertia of the flange about its own axis, in comparison with that about the neutral axis of the whole cross section; equation (16) becomes $I_N = Ad^2 = 2A_f(\tfrac{1}{2}d)^2$, and from equation (10), $M_R = s\dfrac{2A_f(\tfrac{1}{2}d)^2}{\tfrac{1}{2}d} = sA_fd$.

That this is true may be easily seen by reference to Fig. 88 (b);

sA_f is the stress in each flange, and d is the lever arm of a *couple*, whose moment is the moment of resistance of the flanges.

The moment of resistance of the web $= s\dfrac{I}{v} = s\dfrac{\frac{1}{12}th^3}{\frac{1}{2}h} = \frac{1}{6}sth^2 = \frac{1}{6}sA_w h = \frac{1}{6}sA_w d$ by the second assumption.

The total moment of resistance is
$$M_R = s(A_f + \tfrac{1}{6}A_w)d = M \tag{34}$$
which shows that one-sixth of the area of the web may be treated *like* flange area, that is, the couple formed by the stresses in the web may be replaced by an *equivalent couple* ($\tfrac{1}{6}sA_w d$) whose forces ($\tfrac{1}{6}sA_w$) act in the centers of gravity of the flanges, so that there results a stress diagram as shown in Fig. 88 (*c*). Now it is plain that the

Equivalent flange stress $= \dfrac{M}{d}$ (35)

Equivalent flange area $= \dfrac{equiv.\ flange\ stress}{s_t}$ (36)

Flange area proper (net one flange) $=$
equiv. flange area $- \tfrac{1}{6} A_w$ (37)

Flange area proper (net one flange) $=$
equiv. flange area $- \tfrac{1}{8} A_w$ (38)

Equation (37) is used when there is no allowance to be made for rivet holes in the web; equation (38) makes an approximate allowance for a vertical line of rivet holes in the web; (these occur at stiffeners); an exact allowance can be made by deducting the moment of inertia of the areas cut out of the web by the rivet holes on the tension side from the total moment of inertia of the web.

The moment of resistance of the web is sometimes neglected, in which case the equivalent flange stresses and areas become the actual ones, and the term in A_w drops out of equations (37) and (38).

Since d, the *effective depth*, can not be calculated until the flanges are known, an approximate value, or the depth of the web, may be used for the first trial. Two or three trials will usually give a flange that is exact.

Equation (36) determines the *net* area of the tension flange, that is, the gross area less that cut out by the rivet holes.

The *top flange* is usually made the same as the bottom flange (gross areas alike), but it must be held against sidewise buckling, if it is long. There are many points in the design of girders whose discussion would be foreign to the purpose of this article.

80. Beams Stressed Beyond the Elastic Limit. When the extreme fiber stress in a beam is greater than the elastic limit of the material, the theory of flexure is no longer applicable, and the equations based upon it are not applicable. The discrepancies between the theory of flexure and the facts in the case are negligible within the elastic limit, but not beyond it. *The stresses do not increase uniformly from the neutral axis outward,* even though the deformations may sensibly do so; Hooke's law does not hold. Hence experiments on the ultimate strength of beams can not confirm or disprove the theory of flexure.

If the extreme fiber unit stress at rupture is calculated by equation (10), it will be found to be much greater than the ultimate strength in tension or compression, unless there is considerable difference in these, in which case it will lie *between* them; its value will depend upon the form of the cross section to a large extent. Timber being stronger in tension than in compression, fails on the compression side of a beam; the reverse is true with cast iron. For a rectangular cross section s_u in a cast iron beam will be nearly twice the ultimate strength in tension.

The discrepancy between the ultimate strength in bending as determined by equation (10), and the ultimate strength in tension or compression, is explained as follows:

1. The stresses do not increase outward from the neutral axis as rapidly as for stresses within the elastic limit.

2. The neutral axis moves toward the stronger side as the stresses increase, since equilibrium requires the total tension to be equal to the total compression.

3. The interaction of the fibers, preventing transverse deformation as explained in the third assumption under the theory of flexure (68), has a much greater influence for stresses beyond the elastic limit than for stresses within it; in both cases this influence is such as to increase the strength of the beam in bending.

4. The influence of the shearing stresses is greater beyond the elastic limit than within it.

5. The usual ultimate strength in tension is not the real

strength, on account of the contraction of area. In a beam there is very little contraction on the tension side, or expansion on the compression side.

The adequacy of this explanation is disputed by some authorities, because certain experiments have shown that the neutral axis moves very little in a cast iron beam, and that the ultimate strength in bending does not differ greatly from that in tension, for stone and concrete, provided the latter is determined accurately, which is a difficult matter to do.[1]

Equations applicable beyond the elastic limit have been developed, but for the sake of simplicity, the form of equation (10) is used to compare the ultimate strengths of beams. Thus, if a beam having a certain length and cross section is loaded until rupture occurs in the extreme fiber, the moment may be calculated from the breaking load and length, and v and I are known; from these may be calculated $s_u = \frac{Mv}{I}$. s_u is an experimental constant, for a certain kind of material, and may be used to calculate the breaking load for other beams of the same material, having different lengths and cross sections. If the forms of the cross sections are different, the results may be largely in error, particularly for cast iron. s_u is called the *modulus of rupture in cross-breaking*.

Steel and iron really have no modulus of rupture in cross-breaking, because they do not rupture like stone, wood, and cast iron, but bend indefinitely; for them the elastic limit is the proper limit of strength.

---

[1] See Föppl's *Technische Mechanik*, Vol. III § 22a.

QUESTIONS AND PROBLEMS. CHAPTER VI. 123

1. What constitutes the web and what the flanges of a plate girder? Are there corresponding parts in a truss?

2. Illustrate five cases of beams supported in different ways. May one span of a continuous beam be considered as fixed at its ends?

3. Why are stresses in beams investigated on sections perpendicular to their axis? What kinds of stresses are found on these sections, in general?

4. Are the three equations of equilibrium applicable in beams having only vertical loads?

5. What, according to the theory of flexure, is the relation between the unit elongations of fibers in a beam at distances of 2 inches and 12 inches from the neutral axis? What is the relation between the unit stresses in these fibers? What law is involved?

6. Upon what does the variation of the total stress on a cross section of a beam depend?

7. State the facts contrary to the first assumption in the theory of flexure. To the second. To the third.

8. To what is the moment of resistance of a rectangular cross section equal? Derive this from the general formula.

9. What is the difference between the moment of inertia and the statical moment of the area of a cross section? How should a given area be disposed with respect to the neutral axis in order that either may be as large as possible?

10. What is the greatest stress in a timber floor joist, 3"x12", if the maximum moment is 12000 ft. lbs.?

11. What are the unit stresses in the extreme upper and lower fibers of a beam composed of two angles 6"x4"x$\frac{1}{2}$", the longer legs being vertical, and the maximum moment being 138800 in. lbs.?   Ans. 7930 and 16000 lbs. per sq. in.

12. Upon what does the section modulus depend?

13. What are the section moduli in problem 11?

14. Do the section moduli given in the Cambria handbook equal $\frac{I}{v}$ for I beams and channels?

15. What is the section modulus of a 10"x30.0 lb. I beam for an axis through its center of gravity parallel to the sides of the web?

16. If 16000 lbs. per sq. in. is the working stress, what

size of I beam should be used as a floor joist, in which the maximum moment is 93300 ft. lbs. Ans. 18″x55.0 lbs.

17. Where is the neutral axis located in the sections of Fig. 70.

18. Prove that the neutral axis in the beam of problem 11 is located as given in "Cambria."

19. Find the location of the neutral axis of a section composed of an 18″x60.0 lb. I beam, having a 12″x20.5 lb. channel riveted to its upper flange, through the web of the channel (flanges down). Make a complete sketch.
Ans. 11.19 in. from lower edge.

20. What is the moment of inertia of the section given in problem 19? Ans. 1221.5 in.^{4}

21. What is the extreme fiber stress in the beam whose section is given in problem 19 if the maximum is moment 105000 ft. lbs.? Ans. 11460 lbs. per sq. in.

22. What is the moment of inertia of a triangular area of height h and base b about its base?

23. In the fourth section of Fig. 70, what is the moment of inertia of one of the angles about the axis NN, through the center of gravity of the section? Of the four angles? Of the plate? Of the entire section?

24. What is the moment of resistance of the web of a plate girder which is 48″ deep and $\frac{3}{8}$″ thick, when the extreme fiber stress is 10000 lbs. per sq. in.?

25. What will be the maximum moment allowed in the beam of problem 23 if the working stress is 12000 lbs. per sq. in.? What in a beam whose cross section is shown in Fig. 73?

26. In what cases is the neutral axis perpendicular to the plane of the bending moment?

27. What is the axis of a beam? The neutral axis? The neutral plane?

28. What is the location of the principal axes of a 6″x4″x $\frac{3}{8}$″ angle?

29. If in the problem illustrated in Fig. 80, a timber purlin 4″ wide by 10″ deep is substituted, what will be the extreme fiber stresses?

30. What is the location of the neutral axis in problem 29?

31. Find where the shear passes through zero in Fig. 81

when the span is 36 ft., $P_1=80$, $P_2=120$, $P_3=60$, $P_4=40$, $P_5=112$, $a_1=5$ ft., $a_2=11$ ft., $a_3=20$ ft., $a_4=24$ ft., and $a_5=32$ ft. Find the maximum moment. Where is the moment a minimum?

32. Illustrate a case in which the shear is uniform over a part of a beam, along which the increase of the moment is uniform.

33. Construct a shear diagram for problem 31, and find the area of that part to the left of the section of maximum moment.

34. What is the unit shearing stress at the neutral axis, in a vertical section of a timber beam 12"x12", if the total shear at the section is 43200 lbs.? What is the unit horizontal shearing stress at the same point?

35. At what points in a circular cross section is the shearing stress zero? At what points is it a maximum? In what direction does the shearing stress at the circumference act?

36. At what points in a beam is the bending stress a principal stress? Can a shearing stress be a principal stress in a beam? At what points are the resultants of shearing stresses principal stresses?

37. When does the shearing stress in a beam become more important than the bending stress?

38. What is the direction of lines of maximum and minimum shear at the neutral plane?

39. What are the principal stresses in the web of an I beam at a point where the bending stress is 11000 lbs. per sq. in., and the shearing stress 2800 lbs. per sq. in.?

40. In the above problem, what is the equivalent simple stress according to equation (31)?

41. What is the function of the web in a plate girder? Of the flanges?

42. Do the assumptions made in calculating stresses in plate girders give results too large or too small? What is the value of these assumptions?

43. How is the effective depth of a girder determined?

44. What is the effective depth of a girder having a 56"x 5-16" web and 2 angles 6"x6"x$\frac{3}{8}$" in each flange, the extreme depth outside of flanges being 56$\frac{1}{4}$"? What is the equivalent flange stress if the moment is 480000 ft. lbs.? What is the

required net area of the flange proper, if the working stress in tension is 10000 lbs. per sq. in.?

Ans. 52.97 in. effective depth. 108800 lbs. equiv. flange stress. 7.96 or 8.69 sq. ins. flange area (net).

45. If in the above problem, the maximum shear is 48000 lbs., what is the maximum shearing stress per square inch?

46. If the modulus of rupture in cross-breaking of Georgia pine is 7000 lbs. per sq. in., what will be the bending moment in a beam at rupture, its cross section being 10″ wide and 12″ deep?

CHAPTER VII.

DEFLECTION OF BEAMS AND GIRDERS.

81. Equation of the Elastic Line. The bending stresses in a beam shorten the fibers on one side, and lengthen them on the other side, of the neutral plane; the result is, the beam is bent, that is, it is deflected from its unstrained position; its axis forms a curve, called the *elastic line*.

Only elastic deflections are of importance, because working stresses are taken well within the elastic limits. It is sometimes important to know the elastic deflection of a beam or girder, although this is quite small in properly designed work.

Since the bending stresses are determined according to the theory of flexure, the equation of the elastic line must be based on this theory. The origin of coördinates is usually taken at a support, y being the deflection at a distance x from it. The amount of the deflection evidently depends upon the length of the beam, the manner in which it is supported, and the load which it carries; these are taken account of by M. It also depends upon the elastic property of the material, and the amount and distribution of material in the beam; these are taken account of by E and I respectively. The *equation of the elastic line* must therefore be a relation between y, x, M, E, and I. It is evident too that y, the deflection, increases when M increases, and decreases when E and I increase.

A general equation of the elastic line is easily derived. Fig. 89 represents a piece of a beam in which the bending caused the sections AB and CD, a distance dx apart, to make an angle $d\phi$ with each other. A fiber at a distance v from the neutral plane NN, originally dx long, is increased in length an amount $v\,d\phi$, and the *unit*

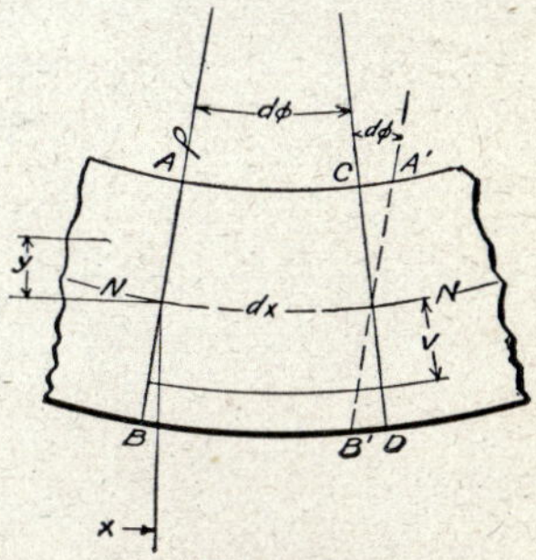

Fig. 89.

deformation is $\frac{vd\phi}{dx}$, which according to equations **(2)** and **(12)** gives

$$\frac{vd\phi}{dx} = \frac{s}{E} = \frac{Mv}{EI} \qquad (a)$$

This reduces to

$$d\phi = dx \frac{M}{EI} \qquad (b)$$

In order to get ϕ in terms of x and y, the radius of curvature ρ, of the elastic line is introduced; this is the distance from the neutral plane to the intersection of AB and CD produced. Since $\rho d\phi = dx$, $d\phi = \frac{dx}{\rho}$ and equation (b) becomes

$$\frac{1}{\rho} = \frac{M}{EI} \text{ or } M = \frac{EI}{\rho} \qquad (c)$$

From the calculus [1]

$$\rho = \frac{\left[1 + \left(\frac{dy}{dx}\right)^2\right]^{\frac{3}{2}}}{\frac{d^2y}{dx^2}} = \frac{1}{\frac{d^2y}{dx^2}}$$

Since the deflections are very small, $\frac{dy}{dx}$, the tangent of the angle which the elastic line makes with the axis of x, is a very small quantity, and its square is negligible.

Equation (c) becomes

$$EI \frac{d^2y}{dx^2} = -M \qquad (39)$$

The minus sign is gotten by adopting the following conventions with regard to the moment and the deflection. It is usual to call a *moment positive when it bends the beam so that it will be concave on its upper side,* as is the case in a beam supported at its ends. The deflection is always downward and is usually called positive, that is, *y is positive downward.* Now, in a beam supported at its ends, $\frac{dy}{dx}$ will be plus at the origin (the left support), will decrease to zero and then become minus, that is, it decreases over the whole length of the beam, and $\frac{d^2y}{dx^2}$ must therefore be negative. M is positive over the whole length of the beam; *therefore the two sides of equation* (39) *have opposite signs.* This will be found to be true in any case, including beams in which the moment changes from positive to negative, or vice versa.

Equation (39) is called the *differential equation of the elastic*

---
[1] See Edwards' Differential Calculus, page 137.

Art. 81. EQUATION OF THE ELASTIC LINE. 129

line. Expressing M in terms of x and integrating twice, an equation giving y in terms of x—the *equation of the elastic line*—is gotten. The first integration gives $\frac{dy}{dx}$, the *slope of the elastic line.*

A differential equation must be written for each segment of a beam into which the loads divide it, because the expression for M is different in each segment. Thus in a beam supported at its ends and carrying a single load, the terms in x, of the values of M, for the two segments are different; the curve of the elastic line is continuous past the load, but two equations are required to express it. When there are a number of loads on a beam, the evaluation of the constants of integration becomes burdensome.

The constants of integration are evaluated by means of the limiting conditions. At the supports $y = 0$; at fixed ends $\frac{dy}{dx} = 0$; at the juncture of two segments, y and $\frac{dy}{dx}$ from one equation are equal to y and $\frac{dy}{dx}$ from the other equation.

The deflection at any point due to several loads is the resultant of those due to the loads considered separately. The equations of the elastic line for all the usual cases of simple loading accompany Figs. 94 to 105. The manner of their derivation is given below, for several cases.

82. Deflection of a Cantilever Beam for a Load at its End. Fig. 94 shows a beam fixed at the left end and carrying a load P at the free end. The maximum moment is evidently at the support, and is equal to $-PL$ (concave on lower side). From "the sum of the vertical components equals zero," $R_1 = P$. Taking a section at a distance x from the support, the bending moment is $-P(L-x)$, considering the part to the right of the section. The same result is, of course, obtained by considering the left-hand part; in this case $M_x = -PL + Px = -P(L-x)$.

From equation (39)

$$EI \frac{d^2y}{dx^2} = P(L-x)$$

$$EI \frac{dy}{dx} = P(Lx - \tfrac{1}{2}x^2) + (C = 0)$$

Since $\frac{dy}{dx} = 0$ when $x = 0$, C must also be zero. If the load were not at the end of the beam, the part to the right of the load would not be bent. The above equation would give the slope of this part when the value of x at the load is substituted. When the deflection at the load is known, the deflection at the end can be readily determined. Integrating again

$$EIy = P(\tfrac{1}{2}Lx^2 - \tfrac{1}{6}x^3) + (C_1 = 0)$$

When $x = 0$, $y = 0$ and therefore $C_1 = 0$.

The maximum deflection evidently occurs at the end when $x = L$.

$$y_{max.} = \frac{P}{EI}(\tfrac{1}{2}L^3 - \tfrac{1}{6}L^3) = \frac{PL^3}{3EI} \text{ at } B.$$

The slope at $B = \dfrac{dy}{dx} = \dfrac{P}{EI}(L^2 - \tfrac{1}{2}L^2) = \dfrac{PL^2}{2EI}$

83. Deflection of a Beam Supported at its Ends and Uniformly Loaded. Fig. 101 shows a beam with a uniform load W. The bending moment at a distance x form the left support is $M_x = \tfrac{1}{2}Wx - \tfrac{1}{2}wx^2$.

Since $w = \dfrac{W}{L}$ this becomes $M_x = \tfrac{1}{2}W\left(x - \dfrac{x^2}{L}\right)$

From equation (39)

$$EI\frac{d^2y}{dx^2} = \tfrac{1}{2}W\left(\frac{x^2}{L} - x\right)$$

$$2EI\frac{dy}{dx} = W\left(\frac{x^3}{3L} - \tfrac{1}{2}x^2\right) + C$$

Since $\dfrac{dy}{dx} = 0$ evidently, when $x = \tfrac{1}{2}L$,

$$0 = W\left(\frac{\tfrac{1}{8}L^3}{3L} - \tfrac{1}{2} \times \tfrac{1}{4}L^2\right) + C \text{ and } C = \tfrac{1}{12}WL^2$$

$$2EIy = W\left(\frac{x^4}{12L} - \tfrac{1}{6}x^3 + \tfrac{1}{12}L^2x\right) + (C_1 = 0)$$

$$y = \frac{W}{24EI}\left(\frac{x^4}{L} - 2x^3 + L^2x\right)$$

The deflection is evidently a maximum when $x = \tfrac{1}{2}L$.

$$y_{max} = \frac{W}{24EI}(\tfrac{1}{16}L^3 - \tfrac{1}{4}L^3 + \tfrac{1}{2}L^3) = \frac{5WL^3}{384EI}$$

If the load on a 10″x25.0 lb. I beam having a span of 20 ft. is 13000 lbs., uniformly distributed, the deflection at the middle will be

$$y_{max} = \frac{5 \times 13000 \times 240 \times 240 \times 240}{384 \times 29000000 \times 122.1} = 0.66 \text{ in.}$$

With the *same total load* on a span of 10 ft., the deflection of this beam would be only one-eighth as much, since the deflection varies as the cube of the length.

84. Deflection of a Beam Supported at Its Ends and Carrying a Single Load at Any Point.

Fig. 96 shows a beam carrying a load P at distances l_1 and l_2 from the supports.

For the segment AC

$$M_x = R_1 x = P \frac{l_2}{L} x$$

Equation (39) becomes

$$EI \frac{d^2 y}{dx^2} = - P \frac{l_2}{L} x$$

$$EI \frac{dy}{dx} = - \tfrac{1}{2} P \frac{l_2}{L} x^2 + C \tag{a}$$

$$EI y = - \tfrac{1}{6} \frac{l_2}{L} x^3 + Cx + (C_1 = 0) \tag{b}$$

When $x = 0$, $y = 0$, and therefore $C_1 = 0$. In order to evaluate C, it is necessary to find y and $\frac{dy}{dx}$ for the segment CB; this may be done by taking A as the origin, but if B is taken as the origin, the equations will be exactly similar to those above. Imagining the beam turned end for end,

$$EI \frac{d^2 y_1}{dx_1^2} = - P \frac{l_1}{L} x_1$$

$$EI \frac{dy_1}{dx_1} = - \tfrac{1}{2} P \frac{l_1}{L} x_1^2 + C' \tag{c}$$

$$EI y_1 = - \tfrac{1}{6} P \frac{l_1}{L} x_1^3 + C' x_1 + (C_1' = 0) \tag{d}$$

C and C' may be evaluated by means of the conditions at the load where, when $x = l_1$ and $x_1 = l_2$, $y = y_1$ and $\frac{dy}{dx} = - \frac{dy_1}{dx_1}$. The deflection is positive in both cases, but since x and x_1 have been taken positive in opposite directions, the slopes from equations (a) and (c) will be the same if they are given opposite signs. From (a) and (c)

$$\tfrac{1}{2} P \frac{l_2}{L} l_1^2 - C = - \tfrac{1}{2} P \frac{l_1}{L} l_2^2 + C' \tag{e}$$

From (b) and (d)

$$- \tfrac{1}{6} P \frac{l_2}{L} l_1^3 + C l_1 = - \tfrac{1}{6} P \frac{l_1}{L} l_2^3 + C' l_2 \tag{f}$$

Multiplying (e) by l_2 and subtracting (f) from it

$$P \frac{l_1 l_2}{6 L} (3 l_1 l_2 + 2 l_2^2 + l_1^2) = C (l_1 + l_2)$$

$$C = P \frac{l_1 l_2}{6 L} (l_1 + 2 l_2).$$

This value of C in equation (b) gives

$$y = \frac{P l_1 l_2}{6 EIL} \left(l_1 x + 2 l_2 x - \frac{x^3}{l_1} \right) \tag{g}$$

132   DEFLECTION OF A BEAM.   Art. 85.

y at $C = \dfrac{Pl_1^2 l_2^2}{3EIL}$ but y_{max} occurs in the longer segment where $\dfrac{dy}{dx} = 0$. From equation (a) $\tfrac{1}{2} P \dfrac{l_2}{L} x^2 = P \dfrac{l_1 l_2}{6L}(l_1 + 2l_2)$, and

$$x = \sqrt{\tfrac{1}{3}(l_1^2 + 2l_1 l_2)} \text{ where } y \text{ is a maximum.}$$

Fig. 95 shows a special case of the above $(l_1 = l_2)$, but the equation of the elastic line may easily be deduced independently. The elastic line is evidently horizontal at the middle of the beam.

85. Deflection of a Beam Carrying a Number of Loads[1]. It is evident from the preceding case that the evaluation of the constants of integration in the equation of the elastic line would become increasingly burdensome as the number of loads increased. Equation (39) must be written for each segment. Finding the location of the section at which the maximum deflection occurs might be practically impossible by this method, but the deflection at a *particular* section may be obtained by taking the sum of those calculated for each load separately.

The deduction of the equation of the elastic line for simple cases of combined loading does not become very involved, particularly if the loading is symmetrical about the middle of a beam, whose end conditions are alike. Thus the cases of Arts. 83 and 84 might be combined, or a uniform load might be combined with that given in Art. 81.

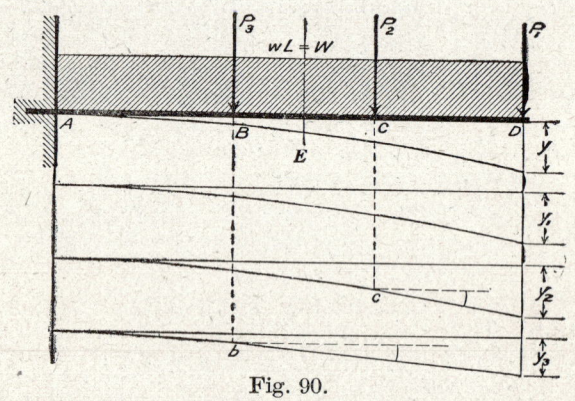

Fig. 90.

Fig. 90 shows a cantilever beam carrying four loads. The deflection at the end consists of four parts; y is due to the uni-

---
[1] For a complete general discussion of this subject, with numerical examples, see Mueller-Breslau's *Graphische Statik*, Vol. II, Part 2.

Art. 85.   DEFLECTION OF A BEAM.   133

form load (Fig. 100), y_1 to P_1 (Fig. 94), y_2 to P_2, and y_3 to P_3. The *deflection at C* due to P_2 is a case similar to that of P_1 at the end; the effect of P_2 at the *end* is found from the slope of the elastic line at C (82). In a similar way, the effect of P_3 is found. The total deflection at the end is $y+y_1+y_2+y_3$. By adding the ordinates of the four curves, at any section, the ordinate of the elastic line is obtained.

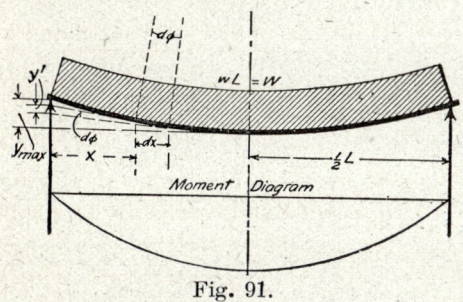

The deflection at a particular section may be gotten by a single integration. If in Fig. 89 tangents be drawn to the elastic line, NN, at the two sections, the angle between them will be $d\phi$, because they are perpendicular to AB and CD. This is illustrated in Fig. 91 for a particular case. $xd\phi = y'$ and $y = \int_0^{\frac{1}{2}L} xd\phi$ Substituting the value of $d\phi$ from equation (*b*), Art. 81

$$y = \int \frac{Mxdx}{EI} \tag{40}$$

When E and I are constant, they may be placed outside of the integral sign. $\int Mdx$ is evidently the area of the moment diagram, and $\int Mdx\, x$ is the *statical moment of this area* about an axis passing vertically through the *origin*.

The advantage of equation (40) lies in its applicability to beams carrying more than one load, for the statical moment of the area of any part of the moment diagram is easily gotten. It should be noted that equation (40), in the case of Fig. 91, really gives the deflection of the support from the tangent.

The application of equation (40) to the case shown in Fig. 91 is as follows: From Art. 83 $M = \frac{1}{2}W\left(x - \frac{x^2}{L}\right)$; E and I are constant.

$$y_{\max} = \frac{1}{EI}\int_0^L Mxdx = \frac{W}{2EI}\int_0^{\frac{1}{2}L}\left(x^2 - \frac{x^3}{L}\right)dx$$

$$= \frac{W}{2EI}\left(\tfrac{1}{3}\times\tfrac{1}{8}L^3 - \tfrac{1}{4}\times\tfrac{1}{16}L^3\right) = \frac{5\,WL^3}{384\,EI}$$

which is the same as was deduced from the elastic line equation, Art. 83.

86. Deflection of a Beam or Girder Having a Variable Cross Section.[1] When the cross section of a beam varies continuously, I may be expressed in terms of x in equation (39). The equation of the elastic line may then be deduced as in the cases above, if the integrations are possible.

In a *girder with flange plates*, the cross section changes abruptly at the ends of these plates. The sections of abrupt change are similar to sections at which concentrated loads are applied. Dealing with the case shown in Fig. 90 in a somewhat different way from that used in Art. 85, the elastic line for the part AB is gotten at once by treating this part as a beam carrying a uniform load of length AB, and a concentrated load at its end B, equal to the sum of all the other loads. The slope at B being calculated, the deflection at D, due to the bending of AB, may be obtained. The parts BC and CD would be treated in a similar manner. If there were an abrupt change of section at E, the segment BC would be divided into two parts, because I changes at E and is a factor in the deflection formula. The slope and deflection at E would be found from the general formulas for $\frac{dy}{dx}$ and y, for a beam of length BC, carrying a uniform load and a load at its end C. See Figs. 94 and 100.

A similar procedure applies to a beam supported at its ends, if the direction of the tangent to the elastic line at some point is known; any part of the beam may be considered like a cantilever beam, the reaction and loads acting in opposite directions.

To find the *maximum deflection* of a beam supported at its ends, the *graphic method* is the simplest and safest except in special cases. In this method the moment diagram is divided into a number of strips, at whose centers of gravity imaginary forces, proportional to the areas of the strips, are supposed to act on the beam. Drawing a string polygon (37) for these loads, the ordinates will represent deflections if the pole distance is taken equal to EI, as is shown by the following comparison between the elastic line and the moment (M').

$$\frac{dy}{dx} = \text{slope.} \qquad \frac{dM'}{dx} = S.$$

$$\frac{d^2y}{dx^2} = \frac{M}{EI}. \qquad \frac{d^2M'}{dx^2} = w.$$

---

[1] See Trans. Am. Soc. C. E., Vol. 51, page 1.

Art. 86.   DEFLECTION OF A BEAM OR GIRDER.   135

If $\frac{M}{EI}$ is taken as the unit load (w) at any point of a beam, then y will be the moment (M') at that point. Graphically, y will be the ordinate in the string polygon, for this imaginary load, if the pole distance is unity; if the pole distance is made equal to EI, then the ordinate of the string polygon will correspond to a unit load equal to M. It follows that *if a string polygon be drawn for a distributed load represented by the moment diagram, this polygon will represent the elastic line, if the pole distance is equal to EI.*

In a girder with flange plates there will be several values of EI, and hence the string polygon must be constructed with different pole distances[1].

87. Deflection of a Beam Due to Shear. In the preceding discussion of the deflection of beams, only the bending stresses were taken into account; it will now be shown that the influence of the shear is negligible except in very short beams, and in plate girders, in certain cases.

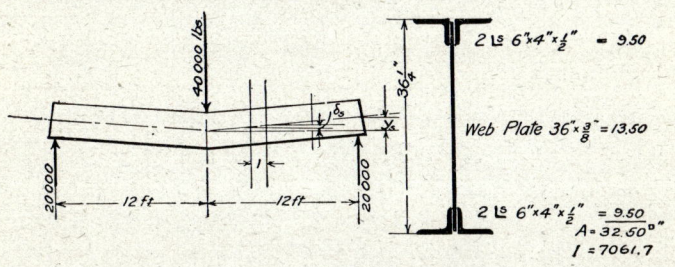

Fig. 92.

Fig. 92 shows the cross section of a girder of 24 ft. span, carrying a load of 40000 lbs. at its middle. Each reaction is 20000 lbs. The shear in the girder, between the support and the load, is constant, and is equal to 20000 lbs. Upon the usual assumption, this shear is resisted by a shearing stress in the web only, which is uniformly distributed over its cross section. The unit stress is therefore $s_s = \frac{20000}{13.5} = 1480$ lbs. per sq. in. By equation (3), the deflection per inch of length of girder is $\delta_s = \frac{1480}{E_s} = \frac{1480}{12000000}$ inches; the deflection in 12 ft. (144 in.) is $y_s = \frac{1480}{12000000} \cdot 144 = 0.0178$ inches.

---

[1] See Mueller-Breslau's *Graphische Statik* Vol. II, Part 2.

136   DEFLECTION OF A BEAM DUE TO SHEAR.   Art. 87.

The deflection due to bending may be calculated from the value of y_{max} in Art. 82, when $L = 12$ ft. $y_b = \dfrac{PL^3}{3EI} = \dfrac{20000 \times 144^3}{3 \times 30000000 \times 7061.7} = 0.094$ inches.

In calculating I, no allowance is made for rivet holes; this will give a result nearer the truth than for a section through rivet holes.

The deflection due to shear is about 19% of that due to bending; this is, however, in the nature of an estimate, on account of the assumption upon which it is based.

In beams having rectangular and circular cross sections, the deflection due to shear is less than in beams having I-shaped cross sections. This deflection is calculated in a different manner, because the shearing stresses are not uniformly distributed over the cross section (75). In the above case of uniform distribution of the shearing stresses vertically, the deflection in a length dx is $dy = \dfrac{s_s}{E_s} dx$, but in general it is $dy = k \dfrac{s_s}{E_s} dx$, in which k is a factor depending upon the form of cross section, and is greater than unity, that is, the deflection is greater than upon the assumption of uniform distribution of stress over the entire area of the cross section. For rectangular cross sections $k = 1.2$, and for circular cross sections $k = 1.185$[1]; for I beams—assuming the stress distributed over the *entire* cross section in accordance with equation (22)—$k =$ about 2.4 for a 3 inch I beam and about 2.0 for a 20 inch I beam.

For a timber beam of width b and depth h, having a span of L ft. and a load P at the middle,

$$y_b = \dfrac{\tfrac{1}{2} P (\tfrac{1}{2} L)^3}{3 EI} = \dfrac{PL^3}{48 E \times \tfrac{1}{12} b h^3} = \dfrac{PL^3}{4 E b h^3}$$

$$y_s = 1.2 \dfrac{\tfrac{1}{2} P}{b h E_s} \tfrac{1}{2} L = 0.3 \dfrac{PL}{E_s b h} = \tfrac{3}{4} \dfrac{PL}{E b h}$$

$$y_b + y_s = \dfrac{PL}{4 E b h} \left(\dfrac{L^2}{h^2} + 3 \right)$$

In the above E_s has been put equal to $\tfrac{2}{5} E$ (78). The last equation shows the following relations:

$\dfrac{L}{h} = 10; \quad 5; \quad 2; \quad 8; \quad 16$

$\dfrac{y_s}{y_b} = \dfrac{3}{100}; \quad \dfrac{12}{100}; \quad \dfrac{75}{100}; \quad \dfrac{4.7}{100}; \quad \dfrac{1.17}{100}.$

---
[1] See Bach's *Elasticitaet und Festigkeit* Chap. IX, § 52.

For a ratio of span to depth of 10, the deflection due to shear is but 3% of that due to bending; when this ratio is 5 the percentage is 12, and as the ratio decreases, the deflection due to shear becomes more important than that due to bending. In *very short beams* it is more rational, therefore, to neglect the bending stress than the shearing stress; this is also indicated by the fact that the assumption, that plane cross sections remain plane after bending, can not be true. The shearing stresses at the upper and lower edges of the cross section are zero and therefore δ_s is zero—the cross section remains perpendicular to the axis of the beam; toward the neutral axis the deformation increases so that the cross section becomes curved.

In beams with circular cross sections—pins of pin-connected trusses, for example—the influence of the shear is somewhat greater than in those with rectangular cross sections.

The above considerations show the limits within which the formulas of Arts. 81 to 86 and Art. 90 are applicable.

88. Resilience of Beams. As explained in Art. 19, resilience is equal to the work of deformation, and elastic resilience is equal to the potential energy stored in a beam.

If the deformation due to shear is neglected, only the bending stress, that is, tension and compression, need be considered Equation (4) is applied to an element of volume, and the total work of deforming the beam is then obtained by integration over the cross section and length of the beam.

Work per unit of volume $= \tfrac{1}{2} \dfrac{s^2}{E} = \tfrac{1}{2} \dfrac{M^2 v^2}{E I^2}$ by substitution from equation (12).

Work per element of volume $= \tfrac{1}{2} \dfrac{M^2 v^2}{E I^2} dx dA$.

Total work of deformation $= \dfrac{1}{2E} \displaystyle\int_0^L \dfrac{M^2}{I^2} dx \int_{-v_2}^{+v_1} v^2 dA$

Since $\displaystyle\int_{-v_2}^{+v_1} v^2 dA = I$ this becomes

Elastic resilience of a beam $= \dfrac{1}{2E} \displaystyle\int_0^L \dfrac{M^2}{I} dx$ \hfill (41)

In deducing the above equation it should be remembered

that M and I may vary along the length of the beam, that is, with x, and v varies in the cross section.

The same result may be gotten by considering the stress sdA on an elementary fiber and the distance $vd\phi$ through which it acts (Fig. 89). The force increases from zero directly as the deformation increases (within the elastic limit), so that the mean force is $\frac{1}{2}sdA$. Substituting the values s and $d\phi$ from equations (12) and (b) Art. 81, and integrating as before, equation (41) results.

An expression for the work done by the shear will be quite similar to equation (4).

Equation (41) is an expression representing the potential energy stored in a beam, and this must be equal to the external work done by the load deforming the beam, if the elastic limit is not exceeded. Thus, in a cantilever beam with a load P at the end,

$$\text{Work} = \tfrac{1}{2} P y_{\max} = \frac{1}{2E} \int_0^L M^2 \, dx = \frac{P^2}{2EI} \int_0^L (L-x)^2 dx$$

I being constant. (See Fig. 94).

Upon integration there results

$$\tfrac{1}{2} P y_{\max} = \frac{P^2 L^3}{2 \times 3 EI} \text{ and } y_{\max} = \frac{PL^3}{3EI}$$

which is the same as was found in Art. 82. The *deflection at a single load* may be thus conveniently gotten. In the case of Art. 84, the integration would have to be between the limits $x = 0$ and l_1, and $x_1 = 0$ and l_2, the total work being the sum of that performed upon the two parts of the beam.

If the deflection at each load is known, the resilience may, of course, be calculated from the external work performed. Thus, in a beam supported at its ends and carrying a load at its middle, the elastic resilience will be equal to $\tfrac{1}{2} P \dfrac{PL^3}{48EI}$ (See Fig. 95 for the deflection). This may be put in terms of the maximum moment or the maximum fiber stress. $M_{\max} = \tfrac{1}{4} PL = \dfrac{s_1 I}{v_1}$;

therefore $P = \dfrac{4 s_1 I}{v_1 L}$ and $P^2 = \dfrac{16 s_1^2 I^2}{v_1^2 L^2}$

$$\text{Resilience} = \frac{8 s_1^2 I^2 L^3}{48 v_1^2 L^2 EI} = \frac{s_1^2 IL}{6 E v_1^2}$$

For a particular form of cross section, a rectangular one for example, this will become

Art. 88. RESILIENCE OF A BEAM. 139

Resilience $= \dfrac{s_1^2 \tfrac{1}{12} bh^3}{6E\tfrac{1}{4}h^2} L = \tfrac{1}{18} \dfrac{s_1^2}{E} bhL = \tfrac{1}{18} \dfrac{s_1^2}{E} V.$

It is to be noted that this equation shows, that for the same form of cross section, the resilience of a beam does not depend upon the size or dimensions of the cross section, or the length of the beam, but only upon its volume.

Since the resilience is a measure of the shock-resisting qualities of a beam, the question arises, What is the resilience of a beam for a load not gradually applied? This case is similar, of course, to that explained in Art. 19. If it were possible to apply a load instantaneously, its velocity being zero when it begins to act on the beam, the total work done would be $P_i y$. If a gradually applied load produces the same deflection, the total work done must be the same, so that

$$\tfrac{1}{2} Py = P_i y \text{ and } P = 2P_i.$$

An instantaneously applied load will, therefore, produce twice the deflection, and consequently twice the stress, that the *same* load gradually applied produces.

When a load is gradually applied, no sensible part of the work done is spent in giving a velocity to the beam, but all the energy becomes potential—the beam is capable of doing work when it springs back. When the same load is applied instantaneously, only half of the energy will have been converted into potential energy, when the deflection is equal to the static deflection; the other half will have given an increasing velocity to the beam and the load, and is converted into potential energy during the last half of the deflection, when the velocity decreases. The beam cannot remain in this extreme position because the deflection is twice that for the load at rest; the potential energy is converted into kinetic energy again, the velocity increasing to the point of the static deflection, and then decreasing to zero deflection, after which, it deflects again, that is, it vibrates past the point of static deflection.

Experience teaches that these vibrations diminish in amplitude and finally cease. This is due to various frictional resistances.

As explained in Art. 5, twice the static deflection never results from suddenly applied loads, but it may be much larger even, if the load falls from a height h. In this case the application of the load is not only instantaneous, but an initial energy equal to Ph must be accounted for. The work done is equal to $P(h+y_1)$ but it is not all spent in deforming the beam; a large percentage of the energy may be spent in deforming the falling body and the beam's supports, and if the elastic limit is exceeded some of the energy is transformed into heat. To determine the effect upon the beam from the load, and height of fall, is a problem of great difficulty, but if the maximum deflection is measured, the stress may be calculated from the static load, which will produce the same deflection.

It is apparent now that the proper way to determine the resilience of a beam is by means of a static load. The usual impact tests which are made upon railway rails serve, at best, only as a comparison of the shock-resisting qualities of the rails tested under the same conditions[1].

It is of practical importance to note that while a defect (a flaw, a crack, or a hole) reduces the static strength of a beam, it reduces its resilience in a much greater degree, so that the factor of safety is much less for moving load than for static load. An abrupt change of section has the effect of concentrating the work done upon the beam, at the weak section.

89. Points of Contrary Flexure. A beam simply supported at the ends, and carrying loads, will be concave on its upper side. If by some means opposite moments are applied at the ends, the slope of the beam, near the supports, will be decreased, and the curvature reversed; near the supports, the beam will be convex on its upper side. The points in the axis of the beam where the curvature reverses (where the curvature is zero, and the radius of curvature infinite) are points of inflection, and are called *points of contrary flexure* or *points of contra-flexure*.

Points of contra-flexure occur in beams with fixed ends, and in beams continuous over supports as shown in Figs. 98, 99, 102, 103, 107, 108, 109, 111, and 112.

The curvature at these points being zero, it follows that the moment is zero, and their location is found by finding the value of x, for which the moment is zero.

---

[1] See Johnson's *Materials of Construction* for a full explanation of resilience.

Art. 89.   POINTS OF CONTRARY FLEXURES.   141

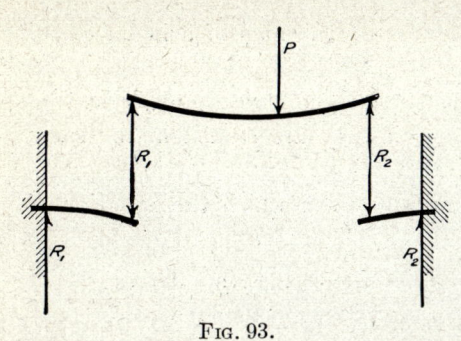

FIG. 93.

It is sometimes convenient to imagine a beam having points of contra-flexure, to be made up of beams simply supported at their ends and cantilever beams. There being no moment at the points of contra-flexure, the cutting of the beam at these points does not affect the stresses, provided the loads or reactions at these points are taken equal to the shear at these points. This is illustrated in Fig. 93 for the case of a beam fixed at both ends. This resolves the case of Fig. 99 into those of Figs. 96 and 94.

142 QUESTIONS AND PROBLEMS. CHAPTER VII.

1. Why is the curve formed by the axis of a beam called the elastic line?

2. Will a steel beam deflect more or less than a cast iron beam of exactly the same size, if they are loaded in the same way?

3. Name the five assumptions upon which the equation of the elastic line is based.

4. What are the difficulties attending the derivation of the equation of the elastic line in certain particular cases?

5. Derive the equation of the elastic line of a cantilever beam carrying a uniformly distributed load. What is the end deflection in this case? What is the end deflection if there is also a load at the end?

6. What is the end deflection of a cantilever beam for a load P_1 at its end and a load P_2 at its middle?

7. How do the deflections of ordinary beams and cantilever beams vary with respect to their lengths?

8. Show how to get y_{max} for the case of Art. 83 from the formula derived in problem 5.

9. If a beam supported at its ends is uniformly loaded, how much must it be raised at the middle in order that each half shall be in the condition of a beam fixed at one end and supported at the other? How many points of contra-flexure will there be in it?

10. How is the location of the point of maximum deflection of a beam found? Why may this be a difficult problem? What is the best method of solving it in complicated cases?

11. What deflection does equation (40) give? How would this equation be used in finding the maximum deflection when the point at which it occurs is not known?

12. Find the maximum deflection for the case of Art. 82, by means of equation (40).

13. What is the maximum deflection of a girder supported at its ends and uniformly loaded, if the cross section varies in such a manner that $\dfrac{M}{EI}$ is constant? Ans. $y_{max} = \tfrac{1}{8} c\, L^2 = \dfrac{ML^2}{8EI}$.

14. Why is the representation of the elastic line analogous

to a moment diagram? What corresponds to the load in the former case?

15. In what case is the deflection due to shear not negligible?

16. What percentage of the *total* deflection is due to shear in a timber beam 12″x12″, having a span of 16 ft. and carrying a load P at the middle? $E_s = \frac{2}{5}E$. Ans. 1.16%.

17. What is the total elastic resilience of the girder shown in Fig. 91 if $E = 29000000$, and the elastic limit of the material is 32000 lbs.? Are there any factors affecting the result prejudicially? Ans. 36400 in. lbs.

18. What is the most economical way of increasing the moment of resistance of a beam? The resilience?

19. For the same live load, which has the greater resilience, a short beam or a long beam, if **the** maximum stress is the same in both?

20. Why does a bridge vibrate?

21. Analyze the beam shown in Fig. 103 in the manner shown in Fig. 93, and compare the maximum moments in the two cases.

CHAPTER VIII.

SPECIAL CASES OF BEAMS AND GIRDERS LOADED AND SUPPORTED IN DIFFERENT WAYS.

90. Explanation of Table. Figs. 94 to 113 illustrate all of the cases of simple loading that an engineer will encounter in ordinary practice. Accompanying these are equations giving general and maximum values of the shears, the moments, and the deflections, and diagrams showing how these vary.

The beam is shown as a single heavy line in its bent condition, thus forming a diagram of deflections. The deflections are determined from the equation of the elastic line, the effect of the shear being neglected (87). The origin of coördinates is usually taken at a support, and in such a manner as to make the equation of the elastic line as simple as possible.

The moments and shears are determined by the application of the equations of equilibrium by the method of sections, the section being taken where the stresses are wanted. The loads all being vertical, there are no horizontal components except for stresses (70). From "the sum of the vertical components equals zero,"

Shear at a section = shearing stress at the section.

Shear = Σ external forces on one side of section.

From "the sum of the moments equals zero,"

Bending moment at a section = moment of resistance.

Bending moment = Σ moments of the external forces, on one side of the section, about a point in the section.

These formulas apply, of course, to any kind of a simple beam or girder in which *E and I are constant,* and when these quantities are not involved, to other beams, some applying to trusses at certain sections.

It is well in applying the formulas to use inches and pounds in calculating deflections, because these correspond with the values of E usually given.

Art. 90.   EQUATIONS FOR VARIOUS BEAMS.   145

$R_1 = P$ $S_{max} = P$
$M = -P(L-x)$
$M_{max} = -PL$ at A
$y = \frac{P}{2EI}(Lx^2 - \frac{1}{3}x^3)$
$y_{max} = \frac{PL^3}{3EI}$ at B

Fig. 94.

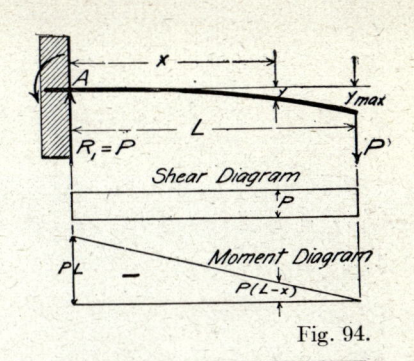

$R_1 = \frac{1}{2}P$ $S_{max} = \frac{1}{2}P$
$M = R_1 x = \frac{1}{2}Px$
$M_{max} = \frac{1}{4}PL$ at C
$y = \frac{P}{16EI}(L^2 x - \frac{4}{3}x^3)$
$y_{max} = \frac{PL^3}{48EI}$ at C

Fig. 95.

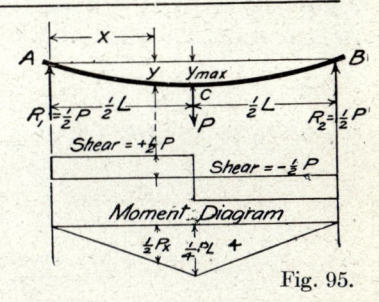

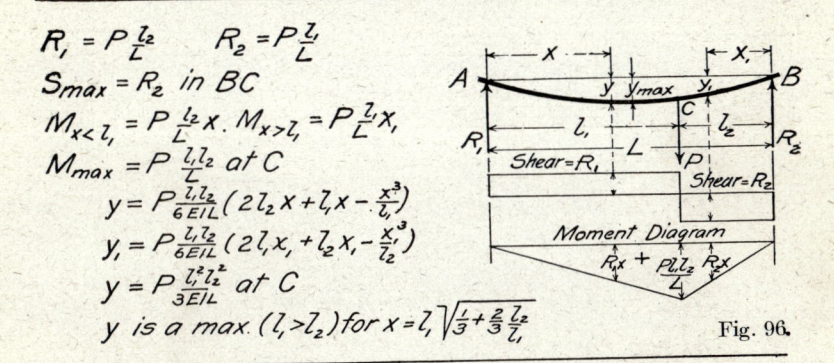

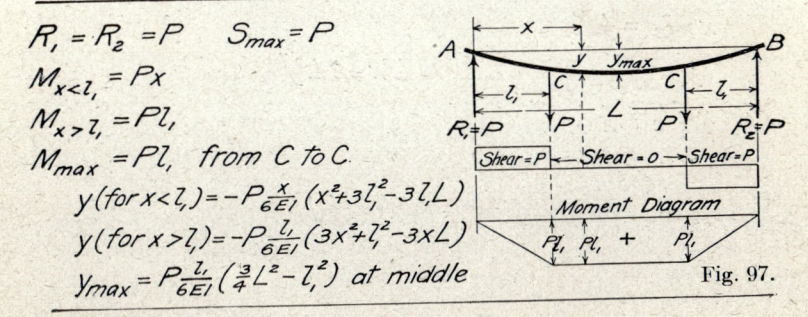

$R_1 = P\frac{l_2}{L}$ $R_2 = P\frac{l_1}{L}$
$S_{max} = R_2$ in BC
$M_{x<l_1} = P\frac{l_2}{L}x$, $M_{x>l_1} = P\frac{l_1}{L}x_1$
$M_{max} = P\frac{l_1 l_2}{L}$ at C
$y = P\frac{l_1 l_2}{6EIL}(2l_2 x + l_1 x - \frac{x^3}{l_1})$
$y_1 = P\frac{l_1 l_2}{6EIL}(2l_1 x_1 + l_2 x_1 - \frac{x_1^3}{l_2})$
$y = P\frac{l_1^2 l_2^2}{3EIL}$ at C
y is a max. $(l_1 > l_2)$ for $x = l_1\sqrt{\frac{1}{3} + \frac{2}{3}\frac{l_2}{l_1}}$

Fig. 96.

$R_1 = R_2 = P$ $S_{max} = P$
$M_{x<l_1} = Px$
$M_{x>l_1} = Pl_1$
$M_{max} = Pl_1$ from C to C
y (for $x<l_1$) $= -P\frac{x}{6EI}(x^2 + 3l_1^2 - 3l_1 L)$
y (for $x>l_1$) $= -P\frac{l_1}{6EI}(3x^2 + l_1^2 - 3xL)$
$y_{max} = P\frac{l_1}{6EI}(\frac{3}{4}L^2 - l_1^2)$ at middle

Fig. 97.

$R_1 = \frac{P}{2L^3}(3L - l_2) l_2^2$

$S_{max} = R_1 \text{ or } R_1 - P$

$M_{x < l_2} = R_1(L - x) - P(l_2 - x)$

$M_{x > l_2} = R_1(L - x)$

$M_{max} = R_1 l$, at C

$M_{max} = R_1 L - P l_2$ at B

$M = 0$ for $x = \frac{P l_2 - R_1 L}{P - R_1}$

For $x > l_2$

$y = \frac{1}{6EI}(R_1 x^3 - 3R_1 L x^2 + 3 P l_2^2 x - P l_2^3)$

For $x < l_2$

$y = \frac{1}{6EI}(R_1 x^3 - 3R_1 L x^2 + 3 P l_2 x^2 - P x^3)$

y is a max. for $x = L\left(1 - \sqrt{\frac{L - l_2}{3L - l_2}}\right)$

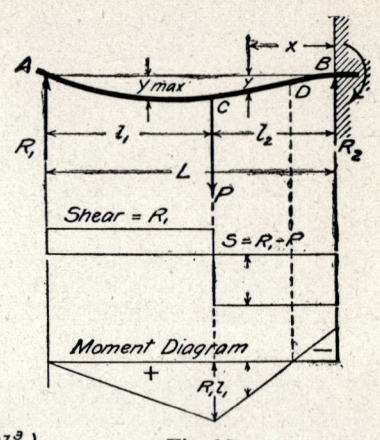

Fig. 98.

When $l_1 = l_2 = \frac{1}{2} L$

$\quad R_1 = \frac{5}{16} P \quad R_2 = \frac{11}{16} P = S_{max}$

$\quad M_{x < l_2} = \frac{1}{16} P(11x - 3L)$

$\quad M_{x > l_2} = \frac{5}{16} P(L - x)$

$\quad M_{max} = +\frac{5}{32} PL$ at C and $-\frac{3}{16} PL$ at B

$\quad M = 0$ for $x = \frac{3}{11} L$

For $x > l_2 = \frac{1}{2} L$

$\quad y = \frac{P}{96 EI}[5x^3 - 15 L x^2 + 12 L^2 x - 2L^3]$

For $x < l_2 = \frac{1}{2} L$

$\quad y = \frac{P x^2}{96 EI}(9L - 11x)$

$\quad y_{max} = \sqrt{\frac{1}{5}}\left(\frac{PL^3}{48 EI}\right)$ for $x = L\left(1 - \frac{1}{\sqrt{5}}\right)$

Art. 90.   EQUATIONS FOR VARIOUS BEAMS.   147

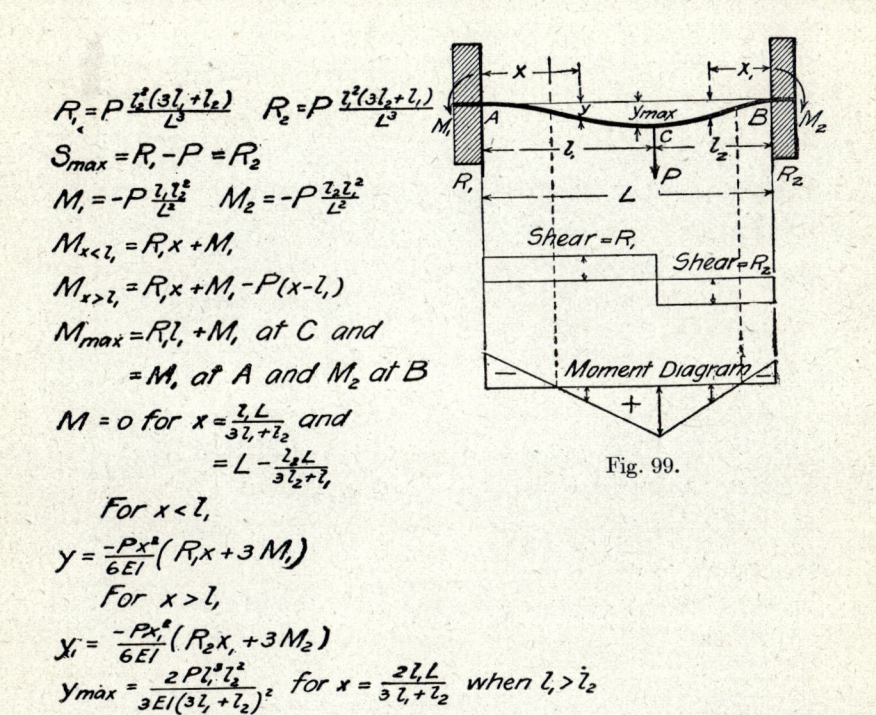

$R_1 = P \dfrac{l_2^2(3l_1 + l_2)}{L^3}$ $R_2 = P \dfrac{l_1^2(3l_2 + l_1)}{L^3}$

$S_{max} = R_1 - P = R_2$

$M_1 = -P \dfrac{l_1 l_2^2}{L^2}$ $M_2 = -P \dfrac{l_2 l_1^2}{L^2}$

$M_{x<l_1} = R_1 x + M_1$

$M_{x>l_1} = R_1 x + M_1 - P(x - l_1)$

$M_{max} = R_1 l_1 + M_1$ at C and

$\qquad = M_1$ at A and M_2 at B

$M = 0$ for $x = \dfrac{l_1 L}{3 l_1 + l_2}$ and

$\qquad = L - \dfrac{l_2 L}{3 l_2 + l_1}$

Fig. 99.

For $x < l_1$

$y = \dfrac{-Px^2}{6EI}(R_1 x + 3 M_1)$

For $x > l_1$

$y_1 = \dfrac{-Px_1^2}{6EI}(R_2 x_1 + 3 M_2)$

$y_{max} = \dfrac{2 P l_1^3 l_2^2}{3 E I (3 l_1 + l_2)^2}$ for $x = \dfrac{2 l_1 L}{3 l_1 + l_2}$ when $l_1 > l_2$

When $l_1 = l_2 = \tfrac{1}{2} L$

$\qquad R_1 = \tfrac{1}{2} P = R_2 = S_{max}$

$\qquad M_1 = -\tfrac{1}{8} PL = M_2$

$\qquad M_{x<l_1} = \tfrac{1}{2} P(x - \tfrac{1}{4} L)$

$\qquad M_{x>l_1} = \tfrac{1}{2} P(x_1 - \tfrac{1}{4} L)$

$\qquad M_{max} = \pm \tfrac{1}{8} PL$ at $C, A,$ and B

$\qquad M = 0$ for $x = \tfrac{1}{4} L$ and $\tfrac{3}{4} L$

$\qquad y = \dfrac{-Px^2}{6EI}(\tfrac{1}{2} x - \tfrac{3}{8} L)$ for $x < \tfrac{1}{2} L$

$\qquad y_{max} = \dfrac{PL^3}{192 EI}$ at $x = \tfrac{1}{2} L = l_1$

$R_1 = W = wl = S_{max}$
$S = R_1 - wx = W - wx$
$M = -\tfrac{1}{2}w(L-x)^2$
$M_{max} = -\tfrac{1}{2}wL^2 = -\tfrac{1}{2}WL$ at A
$y = \dfrac{W}{24EIL}(x^4 - 4Lx^3 + 6L^2x^2)$
$y_{max} = \dfrac{WL^3}{8EI}$ at B

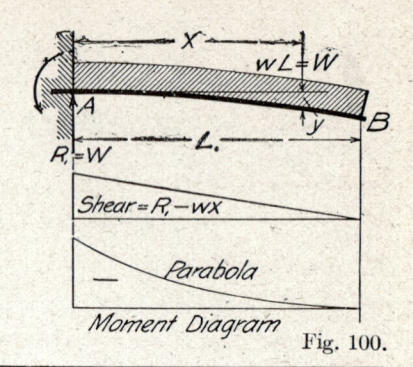

Fig. 100.

$R_1 = \tfrac{1}{2}W = S_{max}$
$S = \tfrac{1}{2}W - wx = w(\tfrac{1}{2}L - x)$
$S = 0$ at center for $x = \tfrac{1}{2}L$
$M = \tfrac{1}{2}Wx - \tfrac{1}{2}wx^2 = \tfrac{1}{2}wLx - \tfrac{1}{2}wx^2$
$M_{max} = \tfrac{1}{8}WL = \tfrac{1}{8}wL^2$ at center
$y = \dfrac{W}{24EIL}(x^4 + L^3x - 2Lx^3)$
$y_{max} = \dfrac{5WL^3}{384EI}$ at center

Fig. 101.

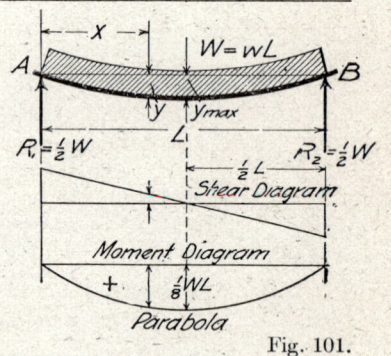

$R_1 = \tfrac{3}{8}W \quad R_2 = \tfrac{5}{8}W$
$S = R_1 - w(L-x) = \tfrac{3}{8}W - w(L-x)$
$S_{max} = \tfrac{3}{8}W - W = -\tfrac{5}{8}W$ at B
$S = 0$ at $x = \tfrac{5}{8}L$
$M = \dfrac{W}{8}(4\tfrac{x}{L} - 1)(L-x)$
$M_{max} = -\tfrac{1}{8}wL^2 = -\tfrac{1}{8}WL$ at B
$\quad = \tfrac{9}{128}wL^2 = \tfrac{9}{128}WL$ for $x = \tfrac{5}{8}L$
$M = 0$ for $x = \tfrac{1}{4}L$
$y = \dfrac{Wx^2}{48EI}(1 - \tfrac{x}{L})(3L - 2x)$
$y_{max} = \dfrac{WL^3}{185EI}$ for $x = 0.5785L$
$y = \dfrac{WL^3}{187EI}$ for $x = \tfrac{5}{8}L$
Point of contra-flexure at D

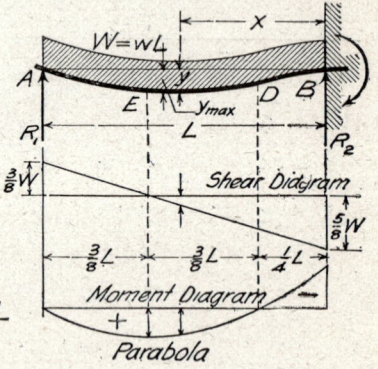

Fig. 102.

Art. 90.   EQUATIONS FOR VARIOUS BEAMS.   149

$R_1 = \frac{1}{2}W = S_{max}$
$S = \frac{1}{2}W - wx = w(\frac{1}{2}L - x)$
$S = 0$ at center for $x = \frac{1}{2}L$
$M = \frac{1}{2}W(x - \frac{x^2}{L} - \frac{1}{6}L)$
$M_{max} = -\frac{1}{12}WL$ at A and B
$\quad = \frac{1}{24}WL$ at C for $x = \frac{1}{2}L$
$M = 0$ for $x = 0.2113L$ and $0.7887L$
$y = \frac{Wx^2}{24EI}(L - 2x + \frac{x^2}{L})$
$y_{max} = \frac{WL^3}{384EI}$ at C
Points of contra-flexure at D

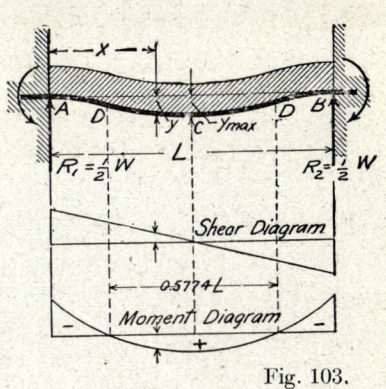

Fig. 103.

$R = W = S_{max}$
$S = \frac{W}{L^2}x^2$
$M = -\frac{1}{3}\frac{W}{L^2}x^3$
$M_{max} = -\frac{1}{3}WL$ at B
$y = \frac{W}{12EI}(L^2x - \frac{x^5}{5L^2})$
$y_{max} = \frac{WL^3}{15EI}$ at B
Deflection $= y_{max} - y$

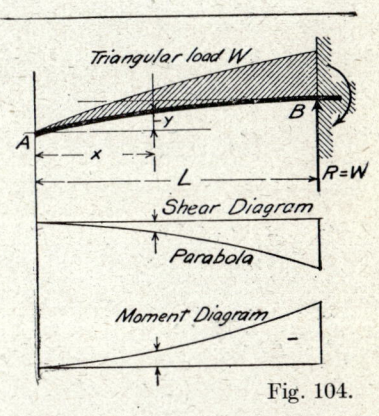

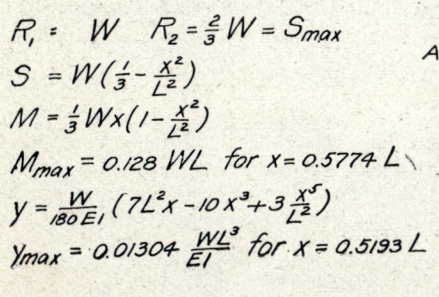

Fig. 104.

$R_1 = W \quad R_2 = \frac{2}{3}W = S_{max}$
$S = W(\frac{1}{3} - \frac{x^2}{L^2})$
$M = \frac{1}{3}Wx(1 - \frac{x^2}{L^2})$
$M_{max} = 0.128\,WL$ for $x = 0.5774L$
$y = \frac{W}{180EI}(7L^2x - 10x^3 + 3\frac{x^5}{L^2})$
$y_{max} = 0.01304\frac{WL^3}{EI}$ for $x = 0.5193L$

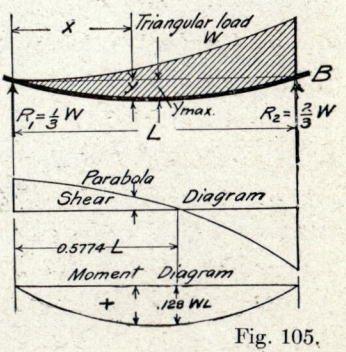

Fig. 105.

EQUATIONS FOR VARIOUS BEAMS.

$R_1 = \frac{l_3 + \frac{1}{2} l_2}{L} W \qquad R_2 = \frac{l_1 + \frac{1}{2} l_2}{L} W$

$S_{AC} = R_1 \qquad S_{CD} = R_1 - w(x - l_1)$

$S_{max} = R_1$ (for $l_1 < l_3$)

$S = 0$ for $x = l_1 + \frac{R_1}{w}$

$M = R_1 x$ for AC

$\quad = R_2(L - x)$ for DB

$\quad = R_1 x - \frac{1}{2} w(x - l_1)^2$ for CD

$M_{max} = R_1 (l_1 + \frac{1}{2} \frac{R_1}{w})$ for $x = l_1 + \frac{R_1}{w}$

Fig. 106.

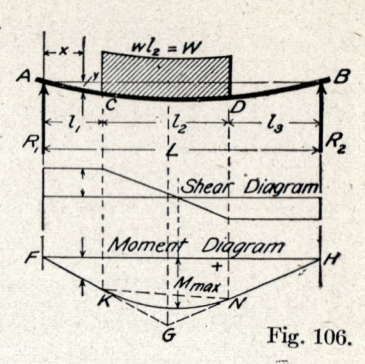

When $l_3 = l_1$

$R_1 = \frac{1}{2} W = R_2 = S_{max}$

$S_{AC} = \frac{1}{2} W \qquad S_{CD} = \frac{1}{2} W - w(x - l_1)$

$S = 0$ for $x = l_1 + \frac{1}{2} l_2 = \frac{1}{2} L$

$M = R_1 x$ for AC and $R_1 x - \frac{1}{2} w(x - l_1)^2$ for CD

$M_{max} = \frac{1}{2} W(l_1 + \frac{1}{4} l_2)$ for $x = l_1 + \frac{1}{2} l_2 = \frac{1}{2} L$

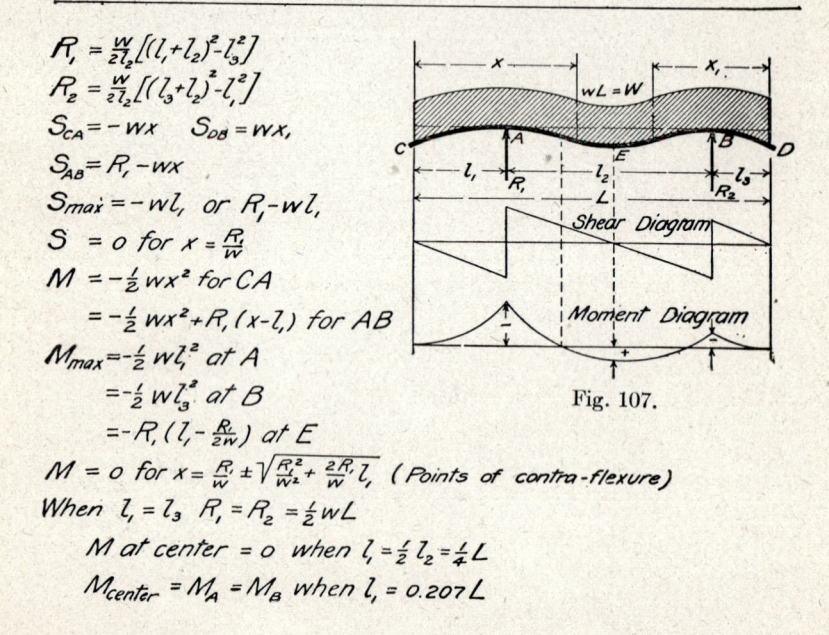

$R_1 = \frac{w}{2 l_2}[(l_1 + l_2)^2 - l_3^2]$

$R_2 = \frac{w}{2 l_2}[(l_3 + l_2)^2 - l_1^2]$

$S_{CA} = -wx \qquad S_{DB} = wx_1$

$S_{AB} = R_1 - wx$

$S_{max} = -wl_1$ or $R_1 - wl_1$

$S = 0$ for $x = \frac{R_1}{w}$

$M = -\frac{1}{2} wx^2$ for CA

$\quad = -\frac{1}{2} wx^2 + R_1(x - l_1)$ for AB

$M_{max} = -\frac{1}{2} wl_1^2$ at A

$\quad = -\frac{1}{2} wl_3^2$ at B

$\quad = -R_1(l_1 - \frac{R_1}{2w})$ at E

$M = 0$ for $x = \frac{R_1}{w} \pm \sqrt{\frac{R_1^2}{w^2} + \frac{2 R_1}{w} l_1}$ (Points of contra-flexure)

When $l_1 = l_3 \quad R_1 = R_2 = \frac{1}{2} wL$

$\quad M$ at center $= 0$ when $l_1 = \frac{1}{2} l_2 = \frac{1}{4} L$

$\quad M_{center} = M_A = M_B$ when $l_1 = 0.207 L$

Fig. 107.

Art. 90.   EQUATIONS FOR VARIOUS BEAMS.   151

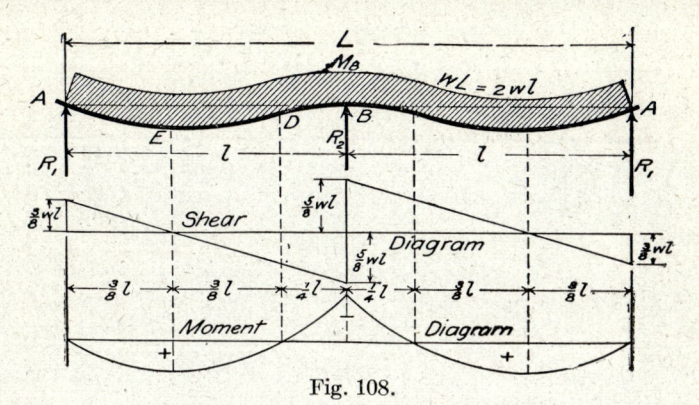

Fig. 108.

$R_1 = \frac{3}{8} wl \qquad R_2 = \frac{5}{4} wl$
Each half is the case shown in Fig. 101.

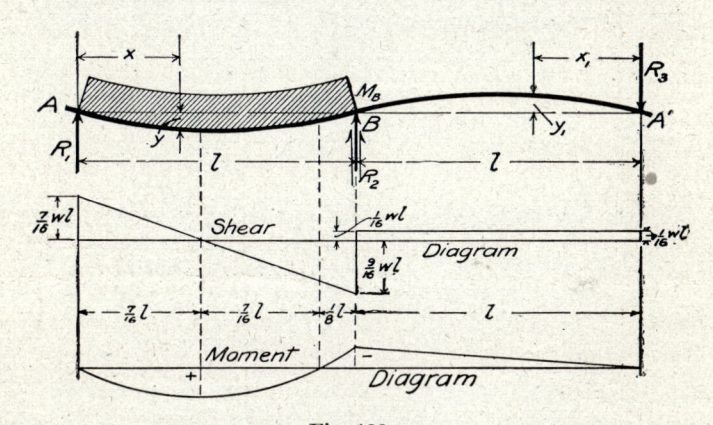

Fig. 109.

$R_1 = \frac{7}{16} wl \qquad R_2 = \frac{5}{8} wl \qquad R_3 = \frac{1}{16} wl$

$S = R_1 - wx = \frac{7}{16} wl - wx \quad \text{or} \quad S = \frac{1}{16} wl$

$S_{max} = \frac{9}{16} wl \qquad S = 0 \text{ at } x = \frac{7}{16} l \text{ and } x = l$

$M = R_1 x - \frac{1}{2} wx^2 = wx(\frac{7}{16} l - \frac{1}{2} x) \quad \text{or} \quad M = -R_3 x_1$

$M_{max} = \frac{49}{512} wl^2 \text{ for } x = \frac{7}{16} l \text{ or } -\frac{1}{16} wl^2 \text{ for } x = l$

$M = 0 \text{ for } x = \frac{7}{8} l.$ Point of contra-flexure

Any number of spans

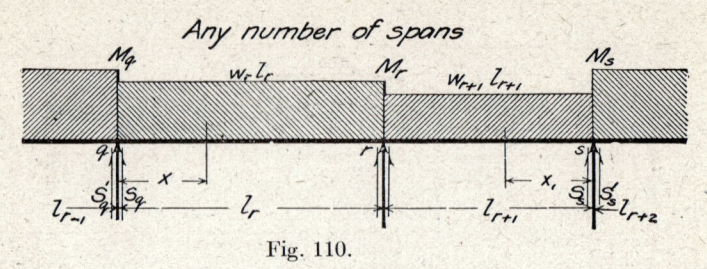

Fig. 110.

$$M_q l_r + 2M_r(l_r + l_{r+1}) + M_s l_{r+1} = -\tfrac{1}{4}(w_r l_r^3 + w_{r+1} l_{r+1}^3)$$
$$M = M_q + S_q x - \tfrac{1}{2} w_r x^2 = M_r \text{ when } x = l_r$$
$$S = S_q - wx \qquad S_q l_r = M_r - M_q + \tfrac{1}{2} w_r l_r^2 \qquad R_q = S_q + S_q'$$

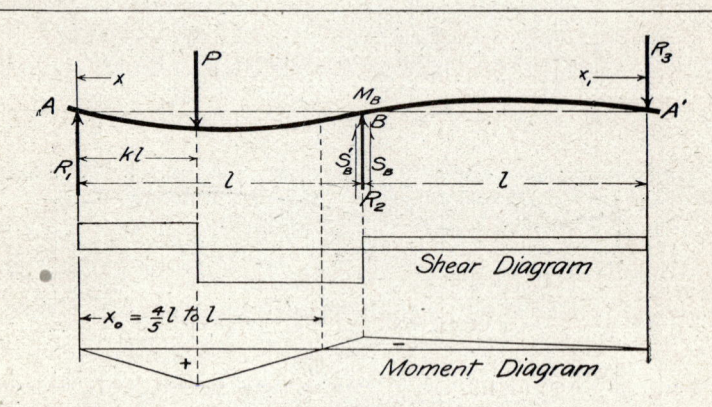

Fig. 111.

$$R_1 = \tfrac{1}{4} P(4 + k^3 - 5k) \qquad R_3 = \tfrac{1}{4} P(k^3 - k)$$
$$R_2 = \tfrac{1}{2} P(3k - k^3) = S_B + S_B'$$
$$S = R_1 \text{ or } R_1 - P = S_B' \text{ or } R_3$$
$$S_{max} = R_1 \text{ or } R_1 - P \qquad S = 0 \text{ at the load}$$
$$M = R_1 x \text{ or } R_1 x - P(x - kl) \text{ or } R_3 x_1$$
$$M_{max} = R_1 kl \text{ at the load or } -R_3 l \text{ at } B$$
$$M = 0 \text{ for } x = x_0 = \tfrac{4}{5 - k^2} l = \tfrac{4}{5} l \text{ to } l \quad \text{Point of contra-flexure}$$
$$x = x_0 \text{ when } k = \sqrt{5 - 4\tfrac{l}{x}} = k_0$$

Art. 90.   EQUATIONS FOR VARIOUS BEAMS.   153

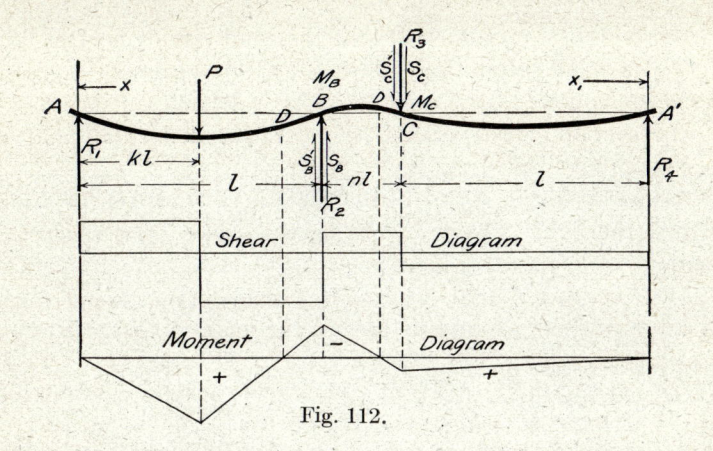

Fig. 112.

$H = 4 + 8n + 3n^2$

$R_1 = P[1 - k - (k - k^3)\frac{2+2n}{H}]$

$R_2 = \frac{P}{H}[Hk + (k-k^3)(5 + 2n + \frac{2}{n})] = S'_B + S_B$

$R_3 = \frac{P}{H}[(k-k^3)(3 + n + \frac{2}{n})] = S'_C + S_C$

$R_4 = \frac{P}{H}(k-k^3)n = S_C \quad S'_B = P - R_1$

$S = R_1 \text{ or } R_1 - P \text{ or } S_B = S'_C \text{ or } R_4 = S_C$

$M = R_1 x \text{ or } R_1 x - P(x - kl) \text{ or } R_4 x, \text{ or } R_4 x_1 - R_3(x_1 - l)$

$M_{max} = R_1 kl \text{ at load, or } -[R_1 l - Pl(1-k)] \text{ at } B \text{ or } R_4 l \text{ at } C$

$M = 0 \text{ for } x = x_0 = \frac{P}{P - R_1} kl \text{ in span } AB$

$x = x_0 \text{ when } k = \sqrt{1 + \frac{H}{2 + 2n}(1 - \frac{l}{x})} = k_0 \text{ Span } AB$

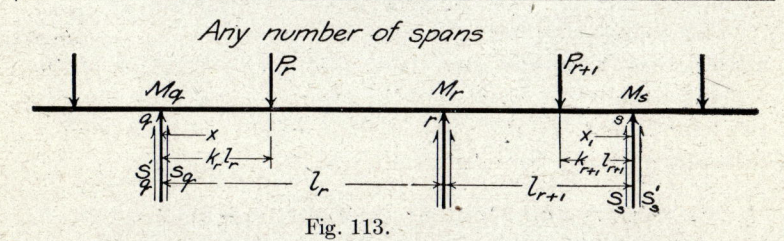

Any number of spans

Fig. 113.

$M_q l_r + 2 M_r (l_r + l_{r+1}) + M_s l_{r+1} = -\sum P_r (k_r - k_r^3) l_r^2 - \sum P_{r+1}(k_{r+1} - k_{r+1}^3) l_{r+1}^2$

$M = M_q + S_q x \text{ or } M_q + S_q x - P_r(x - k_r l_r) = M_r \text{ when } x = l_r$

$S = S_q \text{ or } S_q - P_r. \quad S_q l_r = M_r - M_q + P_r l_r (1 - k_r) \quad R_q = S_q + S'_q$

It should be remembered that the condition of perfect fixity at the ends of beams is seldom found in practice, except in beams continuous over a support as in a double cantilever.

In certain constructions, the greatest deflection, and not the maximum fiber stress will govern.

Some cases not shown in the table may be gotten by simply turning the figure upside down, making loads of reactions and reactions of loads.

The student should, whenever possible, avoid using formulas in numerical problems; the fundamental principles should be applied.

91. Shear and Moment Diagrams. The shear and moment diagrams, Figs. 94 to 112, are laid out from horizontal lines, the ordinates on opposite sides of these lines having opposite signs. *It is usual to consider a shear acting upward on the part to the left of a section as positive,* and such shears are laid out *above* the base line. For the same reason, *bending moments which make a beam concave on its upper surface (as in an ordinary beam) are positive,* but are laid out *below* the base line.

These diagrams are convenient in showing how the shear and moment vary along a beam, and may be constructed by laying out ordinates calculated from the general equations given, or by the graphic methods of chapter V. They are particularly instructive in showing that where the shear passes through zero, the moment is a maximum (or minimum), and that the points of zero moment are points of contra-flexure (89). The area of the shear diagram to the left (or right) of a section, is equal to the ordinate of the moment diagram at the section (74).

The shear and moment diagrams may usually be drawn after several ordinates have been laid out, because their character is usually apparent upon inspection of the general equations for S and M; the moment diagram for uniform load, for example, is always bounded by a parabola.

92. Shears and Moments in Cantilever Beams. Fig. 94. If the origin is taken at the free end, $Px = M_x$ and $M_{max} = PL$ evidently. If the origin is taken at the fixed end $M_x = P(L-x)$ or $M_x = M_A - R_1 x = PL - Px = P(L-x)$, the sign of M_A being evident. This shows that if there is a moment at a support, it must not be neglected, if that point is in that part of the structure which is under consideration. The same principle holds at any section of a beam (74), so that if the shear and moment at any section are known, the shear and moment at any other section may be found. See Figs. 110 and 113.

If a timber beam acts as a cantilever 20 ft. long with a load of 3000 lbs. at its end,

$M_{max} = 3000 \times 20 = 60000$ ft. lbs. $= 720000$ in. lbs., neglecting the beam's own weight for the sake of simplicity.

From equation (12), if the working stress is 1500 lbs. per sq. in.,

$$\frac{720000}{1500} = 480 = \frac{I}{v} = \frac{\frac{1}{12}bh^3}{\frac{1}{2}h} = \frac{1}{6}bh^2$$

If h is assumed as 16 in., $b = \frac{6 \times 480}{16 \times 16} = 11.25$ in.

A commercial size would be 12"x16", making the extreme fiber stress

$$s = \frac{Mv_1}{I} = \frac{720000 \times 8}{\frac{1}{12} \times 12 \times 16 \times 16 \times 16} = 1405 \text{ lbs. per sq. in.}$$

The shear is 3000 lbs. at each section. The mean unit shear is $\frac{3000}{12 \times 16} = 15.6$ lbs. per sq. in. The maximum shearing stress (at the neutral axis) is $15.6 \times 1\frac{1}{2} = 23.4$ lbs. per sq. in. (75), which is much smaller than what is usually allowed. (Cambria p. 361).

Fig. 100. The origin is taken at A; the same results can, of course, be gotten if it is taken at B.

In this case the shear diagram is a straight line since $S = R_1 - wx$ is the equation of a right line. The equation for M is that of a parabola.

$$M = w(L-x) \times \tfrac{1}{2}(L-x) = \tfrac{1}{2}w(L-x)^2.$$

It will be noted that the maximum deflection is much less than in the above case, for the same total load.

Fig. 104. The equations for a triangular load are easily derived, if it is remembered that its center of gravity is at $\tfrac{1}{3}L$ from B.

93. Shears and Moments for a Beam Supported at Both Ends. Fig. 96. The reactions are gotten by the law of the lever, and the shears are equal to them. $M_{max} = R_1 l_1 = R_2 l_2$ at the load, where $S = 0$. y_{max} does not occur at the load but where $\frac{dy}{dx} = 0$, which is evidently in the longer segment.

Fig. 97. The reactions are apparent. The moment between the loads must be constant, because the shear is zero (74), or because the external forces form a couple whose moment is Pl, for *any* section between the loads (30).

Fig. 101. This is perhaps the commonest case. The reactions are apparent. The shear at the middle $= R_1 - \frac{1}{2}wL = \frac{1}{2}wL - \frac{1}{2}wL = 0$, and must vary uniformly between the ends and this point. The moment is, of course, a maximum at the middle and is

$$R_1 \times \tfrac{1}{2}L - \tfrac{1}{2}wL \times \tfrac{1}{4}L = M_{max} = \tfrac{1}{8}wL^2 = \tfrac{1}{8}WL \qquad (42)$$

This value is the same as the general equation will give when $x = \frac{1}{2}L$.

Equation (42) is important because it is used very frequently. $\frac{1}{8}WL$ is the middle ordinate of the parabola.

If a girder 25 ft. long carries a total uniform load of 4000 lbs. per lineal foot,

$w = 4000$ lbs. $W = 4000 \times 25 = 100000$ lbs. $L = 25$ ft.

$R_1 = R_2 = S_{max} = 50000$ lbs.

Shear at middle $= 50000 - 4000 \times 12\frac{1}{2} = 0$.

$M_{max} = \frac{1}{8}WL = \frac{1}{8} \times 100000 \times 25 = 312500$ ft. lbs.

Moment at 5 ft. from one end $= 50000 \times 5 - 5 \times 4000 \times 2\frac{1}{2} = 200000$ ft. lbs.

Comparing the moment produced by a uniform load with that produced by a concentrated load at the middle, it is found that a beam will carry twice as much load when it is uniformly distributed as when it is concentrated half way between the supports.

Fig. 106. Under the uniform load, the moment diagram is parabolic. If the load were concentrated at the middle of CD, the diagram would be FGH; if at C and D, it would be $FKNH$.

94. Combinations of Concentrated and Uniform Loads on Cantilever Beams and Beams Supported at the Ends.

Since the weight of the beam itself is usually taken as a uniform load, the case of a beam carrying concentrated loads only does not occur.

Finding the shears and moments in a cantilever beam for any combination of uniform and concentrated loads, applied on any part of the beam, is simply a matter of adding together the results gotten for each load considered separately, or applying the equations of equilibrium. This is also the case for combinations of loads on beams supported at both ends, but, in general,

Art. 94.   CONCENTRATED AND UNIFORM LOADS.   157

the section at which the maximum moment occurs is not apparent from a consideration of the loads separately. The maximum shear is equal to the greater reaction, and after this has been determined, the *section of maximum moment* is easily gotten, because it is *located where the shear passes through zero.* If, for example, the cases of Figs. 101 and 96 are combined as shown in Fig. 114, the shear passes through zero at 14 ft. from A, and $M_{max} = 14000 \times 14 - 1000 \times 14 \times 7 = 98000$ ft. lbs.

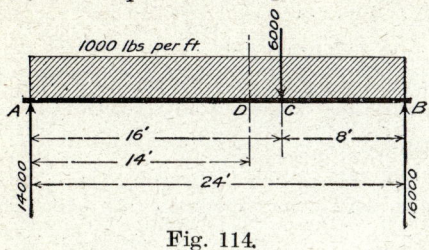

Fig. 114.

In Fig. 115 the shear passes through zero at the load and $M_{max} = 9000 \times 16 - 500 \times 16 \times 8 = 80000$ ft. lbs.

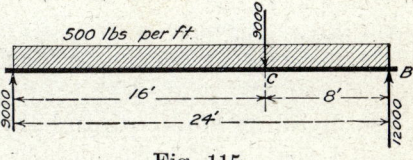

Fig. 115.

The same rule applies when there are any number of loads on the beam. *With nothing but concentrated loads, the shear must evidently pass through zero at a load, and therefore the moment is a maximum under some load.* This is also evident if a moment diagram is drawn.

95. Bending Moments and Shears for Beams Having Fixed Ends. In order that the end of a beam may be fixed, there must be a moment at the support of such magnitude as to keep the elastic line horizontal at the support, as was explained in Art. 89, and acting as shown in Figs. 94, 98, 99, 100, 102, 103, and 104. This condition is imposed by making $\frac{dy}{dx} = 0$ at the fixed end. In Fig. 99, for example,

$M_{x<l_1} = R_1 x - M_1$ $\qquad$ $M_{x>l_1} = R_1 x - M_1 - P(x - l_1)$

Putting these values into the differential equation of the elastic line, two values of $\frac{dy}{dx}$ and two values of y will be gotten. The conditions to be fulfilled are, $y = 0$ when $x = 0$; $y = 0$ when $x = l_1 + l_2$; $\frac{dy}{dx} = 0$ when $x = 0$; $\frac{dy}{dx} = 0$ when $x = l_1 + l_2$; at C, y for one segment is equal to y for the other segment; and at C, $\frac{dy}{dx}$ for one segment is equal to $\frac{dy}{dx}$ for the other. These six conditions determine the four constants of integration, R_1, and M_1.

Since it is necessary to use the equation of the elastic line to determine the reactions and end moments, they are statically indeterminate, that is, they depend upon the deformation of the beam. In the above case, knowing any *two* of the quantities R_1, R_2, M_1, and M_2, the moment and shear at any section are statically determinate, that is, they are gotten by means of the equations of equilibrium. When $l_1 = l_2$, $R_1 = R_2$ and $M_1 = M_2$ by symmetry, that is, the equations for the two segments become identical.

Knowing M_1 and R_1, the points of contra-flexure are located by putting the above values for the moments equal to zero and solving for x. Knowing the location of the points of contra-flexure, it may be convenient to treat the beam as made up of two cantilevers supporting a beam similar to that shown in Fig. 96 (89).

96. Bending Moments and Shears for Continuous Beams. Fig. 108 shows a two-span continuous beam. If the middle support be lowered, the beam will deflect and the load on the middle support will decrease, finally becoming zero when the deflection is equal to $\frac{5WL^3}{384EI}$; the beam becomes discontinuous and now has a single span $L = 2l$ (Fig. 101).

If the middle support be raised, the load on the end supports will decrease, finally becoming zero when the end deflections are $\frac{wl^4}{8EI}$, and the beam becomes a double cantilever (Fig. 100).

These considerations show that the reactions, and therefore the shears and moments depend upon the deformation of the beam, that is, upon the elastic line, just as for beams having fixed ends, and are therefore statically indeterminate; beams with fixed ends may, in fact, be considered as special cases of continuous beams, as will now be shown from the simple case of Fig. 108.

In this case, the elastic line must be horizontal at the middle support on account of symmetry. Imposing this condition by means of the equation of the elastic line, together with the condition of zero deflection at the supports, the reactions are determined and the moments may be gotten as in ordinary beams.

Art. 96. CONTINUOUS BEAMS. 159

In place of using this method, which is quite similar to that outlined in the previous article, the equation of the elastic line will be used *indirectly* as suggested above.

Since the beam is horizontal at the middle, each arm may be considered like a cantilever carrying a uniform load acting downward, and a load at the end acting upward, such that the end deflection will be zero. (Or the beam may be considered as one simply supported at the ends, with a uniform load and a concentrated load (R_2) acting in opposite directions).

The deflection at the end is

$\frac{wl^4}{8EI}$ for the uniform load (Fig. 100).

$\frac{R_1 l^3}{3EI}$ for the reaction (Fig. 94).

and these must be equal.

$$\frac{R_1 l^3}{3EI} = \frac{wl^4}{8EI} \text{ whence } R_1 = \tfrac{3}{8} wl.$$

Since, by symmetry, the end reactions are the same, the middle reaction $R_2 = 2wl - \tfrac{3}{4} wl = \tfrac{5}{4} wl$. These results are the same as those given with Fig. 102, and the deduction of the other equations will be exactly the same in both cases. The deduction of some of the equations may be simpler if the origin is taken at A. Each arm is resolvable into a beam supported at its ends of $\tfrac{3}{4} l$ span, and a cantilever of length $\tfrac{1}{4} l$. The maximum moment in the former is $\tfrac{1}{8} \times \tfrac{3}{4} wl \times \tfrac{3}{4} l = \tfrac{9}{128} wl^2$, which is the same as that obtained from the general equation when $x = \tfrac{5}{8} l$. In like manner, from the cantilever, the moment at the center support is $-\tfrac{1}{4} wl \times \tfrac{1}{8} l - \tfrac{3}{8} wl \times \tfrac{1}{4} l = -\tfrac{1}{8} wl^2$.

Fig. 98 shows a case similar to a continuous beam of two equal spans *symmetrically* loaded, and the equations are deducible in a manner similar to the above. The cases of Figs. 99 and 103 are the same as one span of a continuous beam of an indefinitely large number of equal spans, similarly loaded, and the equations may be checked by applying the general equation for continuous beams which will now be deduced (97).

It should be noted in Fig. 108 that the shear on either side of R_2 is not equal to the reaction, but the reaction is equal to the numerical sum of the shears. The moment is a maximum at three of the points where the shear passes through zero, one of these moments being negative and the other two positive.

If the middle support were raised, the end reactions would

decrease uniformly, so that if it were raised half as much as necessary to make the reactions zero, that is, if it were raised a distance $\frac{wl^4}{16EI}$ the end reactions would be $\frac{3}{16}wl$; if it were lowered a distance $\frac{2.5wl^4}{384EI}$ the center reaction would be $\frac{5}{8}wl$.

97. General Equations for Continuous Beams.[1] It was shown in Art. 95 that the stresses in a span of a continuous beam become statically determinate when the *moments* at the supports are known; if, therefore, an equation can be deduced involving the moments at *three successive supports,* a continuous beam of n spans having $n+1$ supports and $n-1$ unknown moments at supports (the moments at the end supports being zero), will furnish $n-1$ equations from which to determine the $n-1$ unknowns.

Such an equation (for uniform loads) was published by *Clapeyron* in 1857 and, as in the special cases above, is based on the equation of the elastic line. The deduction of this equation for *uniform load* follows.

Fig. 110 shows two successive spans of a continuous beam of an indefinite number of spans; M_q, M_r, and M_s are the moments at the supports; S_q is the shear just to the right of q and S_s is the shear just to the left of s. The moments at the supports may be assumed positive.

For span qr

$$M_x = M_q + S_q x - \tfrac{1}{2} w_r x^2 \tag{a}$$

$$M_r = M_q + S_q l_r - \tfrac{1}{2} w_r l^2 \tag{b}$$

$$S_q l_r = M_r - M_q + \tfrac{1}{2} w_r l^2 \tag{c}$$

$$-EI\frac{d^2y}{dx^2} = M_q + S_q x - \tfrac{1}{2} w_r x^2 \text{ from } (a) \text{ and } (39) \tag{d}$$

$$-EI\frac{dy}{dx} = M_q x + \tfrac{1}{2} S_q x^2 - \tfrac{1}{6} w_r x^3 + C_1 \tag{e}$$

$$-EIy = \tfrac{1}{2} M_q x^2 + \tfrac{1}{6} S_q x^3 - \tfrac{1}{24} w_r x^4 + C_1 x + (C_2 = 0) \tag{f}$$

When $x = l_r$, $y = 0$ and (f) becomes

$$0 = \tfrac{1}{2} M_q l_r^2 + \tfrac{1}{6} S_q l_r^3 - \tfrac{1}{24} w_r l_r^4 + C_1 l_r \text{ and}$$

$$C_1 = -\tfrac{1}{2} M_q l_r - \tfrac{1}{6} S_q l_r^2 + \tfrac{1}{24} w_r l_r^3 \tag{g}$$

At r, from (g) and (e), when $x = l_r$

$$-EI\frac{dy}{dx} = M_q l_r + \tfrac{1}{2} S_q l_r^2 - \tfrac{1}{6} w_r l_r^3 - \tfrac{1}{2} M_q l_r - \tfrac{1}{6} S_q l_r^2 + \tfrac{1}{24} w_r l_r^3$$

---

[1] For a complete treatment of the continuous beam with variable moment of inertia, see Howe's *The Theory of the Continuous Girder.* For a graphical treatment of the continuous beam see Eddy's *Researches in Graphical Statics.*

Art. 97. EQUATIONS FOR CONTINUOUS BEAMS.

$$-EI\frac{dy}{dx} = \tfrac{1}{2}M_q l_r + \tfrac{1}{3}S_q l^2 - \tfrac{1}{8}w_r l^3 \qquad (h)$$

Multiplying (c) by $\tfrac{1}{3} l_r$ and substituting in (h)

$$-EI\frac{dy}{dx} = \tfrac{1}{2}M_q l_r + \tfrac{1}{3}M_r l_r - \tfrac{1}{3}M_q l_r + \tfrac{1}{6}w_r l^3 - \tfrac{1}{8}w_r l_r^3$$

$$= \tfrac{1}{6}M_q l_r + \tfrac{1}{3}M_r l_r + \tfrac{1}{24}w_r l_r^3 \qquad (i)$$

For the span rs, by analogy,

$$-EI\frac{dy}{dx_1} = -\tfrac{1}{6}M_s l_{r+1} - \tfrac{1}{3}M_r l_{r+1} - \tfrac{1}{24}w_{r+1} l_{r+1}^3 \qquad (k)$$

At the middle support (i) and (k) must be equal.

$$M_q l_r + 2M_r(l_r + l_{r+1}) + M_s l_{r+1} = -\tfrac{1}{4}(w_r l_r^3 + w_{r+1} l_{r+1}^3) \qquad (43)$$

This equation expresses what is called the *theorem of three moments for uniform load*. In a similar manner, the theorem of three moments for concentrated loads is derived. Its derivation is simplest when the locations of the loads are given as shown in Fig. 113, in which k_r and k_{r+1} are fractions whose values may vary from 0 to 1. The distances kl are sometimes measured toward the right in both spans, in which case, the form of the equation of three moments is different in one term. The equation is (Fig. 113).

$$M_q l_r + 2M_r(l_r + l_{r+1}) + M_s l_{r+1} =$$
$$-\Sigma P_r(k_r - k_r^3)l_r^2 - \Sigma P_{r+1}(k_{r+1} - k_{r+1}^3)l_{r+1}^2 \qquad (44)$$

Applying equation (43) to the case explained in Art. 96,

$$M_q = M_s = 0; \ l_r = l_{r+1} = l; \ w_r = w_{r+1} = w;$$
$$4M_B l = -\tfrac{1}{2}wl^3 \text{ and } M_B = -\tfrac{1}{8}wl^2$$

Taking moments about B,

$$R_1 l - \tfrac{1}{2}wl^2 = M_B = -\tfrac{1}{8}wl^2$$
$$R_1 = \tfrac{1}{2}wl - \tfrac{1}{8}wl = \tfrac{3}{8}wl \text{ as before.}$$

Applying equation (43) to the case of Fig. 109,

$$4M_B l = -\tfrac{1}{4}wl^3 \text{ and } M_B = -\tfrac{1}{16}wl^2.$$
$$R_3 l = M_B = -\tfrac{1}{16}wl^2 \text{ and } R_3 = -\tfrac{1}{16}wl.$$
$$R_1 l - \tfrac{1}{2}wl^2 = M_B = -\tfrac{1}{16}wl^2 \text{ and } R_1 = +\tfrac{7}{16}wl.$$
$$R_2 = wl - R_1 - R_3 = wl - \tfrac{7}{16}wl + \tfrac{1}{16}wl = \tfrac{5}{8}wl.$$
$$S_2 = -R_3 = +\tfrac{1}{16}wl.$$
$$S'_2 = R_2 - S_2 = \tfrac{5}{8}wl - \tfrac{1}{16}wl = \tfrac{9}{16}wl$$
or $S'_2 = R_1 - wl = \tfrac{7}{16}wl - wl = -\tfrac{9}{16}wl.$

These shears act in the same direction, of course; the opposite signs are gotten from opposite ends of the beam.

$$S = R_1 - wx = \tfrac{7}{16}wl - wx$$
$$= 0 \text{ when } x = \tfrac{7}{16}l \text{ or } x = l$$
$$M = R_1 x - \tfrac{1}{2}wx^2 = \tfrac{7}{16}wlx - \tfrac{1}{2}wx^2$$

$= 0$ when $x = \tfrac{7}{8}l$
$M_{max} = \tfrac{49}{256}wl^2 - \tfrac{1}{2} \times \tfrac{49}{256}wl^2 = \tfrac{49}{512}wl^2$ for $x = \tfrac{7}{16}l$
$= -\tfrac{1}{16}wl^2$ when $x = l$

Applying equation (44) twice to the case explained in Art. 95, the same results are gotten. It is necessary to consider the beam as one span of a continuous beam of many equal spans, similarly loaded, as shown in Fig. 116, in order that the elastic line may be horizontal at the supports. There will evidently be but two different moments at supports.

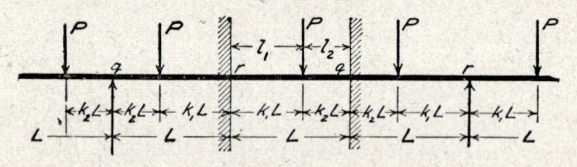

Fig. 116.

$M_s = M_q;\ l_r = l_{r+1} = L;$
$M_q L + 2 M_r \times 2L + M_q L = - Pk_2(1 - k_2^2)L^2 - Pk_2(1 - k_2^2)L^2$
$M_q + 2M_r = - PLk_2(1 - k_2^2) \qquad (a)$

This is for the left-hand and central spans Fig. 116. In like manner, for the right-hand and central spans

$2M_r + 4M_q = - 2PLk_1(1 - k_1^2) \qquad (b)$

Subtracting (a) from (b)
$3M_q = PLk_2(1 - k_2^2) - 2PLk_1(1 - k_1^2)$

Since $k_1 L = l_1 \quad k_1 = \dfrac{l_1}{L}$. Also $k_2 L = l_2 \quad k_2 = \dfrac{l_2}{L}$

$3M_q = Pl_2\left(1 - \dfrac{l_2^2}{L^2}\right) - 2Pl_1\left(1 - \dfrac{l_1^2}{L^2}\right)$
$= Pl_2\left(\dfrac{L^2 - l_2^2}{L^2}\right) - 2Pl_1\left(\dfrac{L^2 - l_1^2}{L^2}\right)$
$= P\dfrac{l_2}{L^2}(l_1^2 + 2l_1 l_2 + l_2^2 - l_2^2) - 2P\dfrac{l_1}{L^2}(l_1^2 + 2 l_1 l_2 + l_2^2 - l_1^2)$
$= P\dfrac{l_1 l_2}{L^2}(l_1 + 2l_2 - 4l_1 - 2l_2) = - 3P\dfrac{l_1^2 l_2}{L^2}$

$M_q = - P\dfrac{l_1^2 l_2}{L^2}$ as given under Fig. 99.

Substituting this value in equation (a) or (b)

$M_r = - P\dfrac{l_1 l_2^2}{L^2}$ as by the method of Art. 95.

Applying equation (44) to the case of Fig. 112,
$2M_B(ni + l) + M_C nl = - P(k - k^3)l^2$ and
$M_B nl + 2M_C(nl + l) = 0$

$M = \dfrac{-n}{2n+2} M_B$ which in the first equation gives

Art. 98. PRACTICAL USES OF CONTINUOUS BEAMS. 163

$$2M_B l(1+n) - \frac{n^2 l}{2n+2} M_B = -P(k-k^3)(n+1)l$$

$$M_B = -2 \frac{Pl}{H}(k-k^3)(1+n) \text{ when } H = 4 + 8n + 3n^2.$$

Multiplying this value by $\frac{-n}{2(1+n)}$

$$M_C = \frac{Pl}{H}(k-k^3)n.$$

The reactions may now be determined from the following equations.

$R_1 l - P(l - kl) = M_B \qquad R_1 l(+nl) - P(l - kl + nl) + R_2 nl = M_C$
$R_4 l = M_C \qquad\qquad R_4(l + nl) - R_3 nl = M_B$

In this case, as in the case of Fig. 111, there must be one negative reaction if the beam is to be continuous.

When there is a *partial uniform load* on any span, it may be divided into a number of equal parts and each part treated as a concentrated load.

98. Practical Uses of Continuous Beams. Continuous beams are avoided, when practical, on account of the uncertainty of the stresses. This uncertainty is due to the difficulty of making the supports fit the unstrained outline of the beam, to the elasticity of the supports, and to the possible settlement of supports. When the supports do not fit the unstrained outline of the beam, they are said to be "out of level." A slight change in the "level" of the supports, may cause marked changes in the stresses (96). If the exact level of the supports were fixed, the stresses could be calculated by means of modifications of equations (43) and (44). These modified equations are obtained by taking the axis of x so that the elevations of the supports will be y_q, y_r, and y_s; then there will appear in the second members of equations (43) and (44), the term $+6EI \left(\frac{y_r - y_q}{l_r} + \frac{y_r - y_s}{l_{r+1}} \right)$

Swing bridges rest upon three or four supports when in the "closed" position, and *one* of the *limiting* conditions for which stresses are calculated is that of a continuous beam. This is the most important application of the above formulas[1]. Sometimes the track of a railway bridge is supported directly by the top chord of a deck-truss bridge, in which case the top chord is a continuous beam with elastic supports; the bending stresses are,

---

[1] See Merriman and Jacoby's *Roofs and Bridges, Part IV,* Wright's *The Designing of Draw-Spans,* and Johnson's *Modern Framed Structures.*

164 LIVE LOADS ON BEAMS. Art. 99.

however, usually calculated upon a simple assumption.[1] Railway rails and long lines of shafting are continuous beams.

When a continuous beam is arranged at certain points (points of contra-flexure, for example) so that it can not take any moment at these points (hinges), it becomes a *cantilever structure*, and the stresses are statically determinate and not affected by small changes in the "level" of the supports.

99. Live Loads on Beams. Since live loads are moving loads, it becomes a question of finding the *position* of the load which will produce the maximum moment or maximum shear at a section of a beam. Having determined the position of the load, the procedure is the same as for stationary or dead load.

It is evident that a single concentrated load moving over a cantilever beam will produce the greatest moment when it is at the free end; moving over a beam supported at both ends, it will produce the greatest moment when it is at the middle of the span, and the greatest shear (at the end) when it is at the support or just to the right of the left support. See the general equations accompanying Figs. 94 and 96.

To determine the proper position of a moving load on a cantilever beam for any maximum stress is usually a very simple matter, and will not be discussed further. The common cases, including both concentrated and uniform loads, will now be considered.

100. Two Concentrated Moving Loads a Fixed Distance Apart. In Fig. 117, P_1 is greater than P_2 and they are a given fixed distance a apart. The resultant R, of P_1 and P_2, should be at the center of the beam for a maximum moment in the beam if it were not for the fact that it always comes under a load as shown by the moment diagram (94), and by the fact that the shear passes through zero at a load. Evidently the maximum moment occurs under the greater load, but this load cannot be at the middle of the span with-

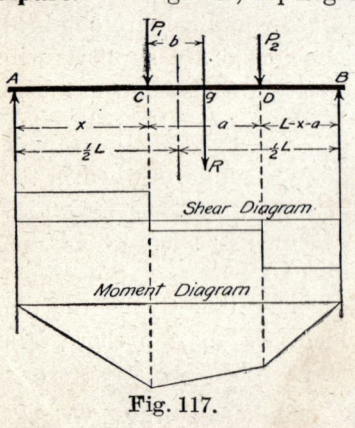

Fig. 117.

---
[1] See the General Specifications of the Am. Ry. Eng. Assoc.

Art. 100. TWO CONCENTRATED MOVING LOADS.

out disregarding the fact that R should be as near the middle as possible. These two factors make it impossible to have the maximum moment at the middle; the center line of the beam must be half way between P_1 and R, as will now be proven.

$$M_c = R_1 x = R \frac{L-(x+b)}{L} x = \frac{R}{L}(Lx - x^2 - bx)$$

$$\frac{dM_c}{dx} = \frac{R}{L}(L - 2x - b) = 0 \text{ when } M_c = M_{max}$$

$x = \tfrac{1}{2}L - \tfrac{1}{2}b$, that is, P_1 is $\tfrac{1}{2}b$ to the left of the center and therefore R must be $\tfrac{1}{2}b$ to right of it. *The load under which the maximum moment occurs must be as far on one side of the center of the beam as the resultant of the loads in on the other side of the center.*

If $P_1 = 36000$ lbs., $P_2 = 28000$ lbs., $L = 40$ ft. and $a = 8$ ft., $36000\ b = 28000\ (a-b) = 28000 \times 8 - 28000b$ and $b = 3\tfrac{1}{2}$ ft., P_1 must be placed $1\tfrac{3}{4}$ ft. to the left of the center line so that R will be $1\tfrac{3}{4}$ ft. to the right of it or $18\tfrac{1}{4}$ ft. from B. Now

$$R_1 = \frac{18\tfrac{1}{4}}{40}(36000 + 28000) = 29200 \text{ lbs. and}$$

$$M_{max} = R_1 x = 29200 \times 18\tfrac{1}{4} = 533000 \text{ ft. lbs.}$$

In a similar manner that value of x may be found which will give a maximum shear, but it is evident that *the maximum shear occurs at the end when the heavier load is there and the other load is on the beam.* In the above example, when P_1 is at A,

$$S_{max} = 36000 + \tfrac{32}{40}\ 28000 = 36000 + 22400 = 58400 \text{ lbs.}$$

101. Any Number of Concentrated Moving Loads Fixed Distances Apart. Fig. 118 shows six loads which move together. The distances between the loads being known, the location of the resultant is found at a distance b from P_4. Exactly the same reasoning will apply as for the case of two loads, and the same rule for the position giving maximum moment will apply; the load must be so placed that the center line of the beam will bisect b, when the maximum

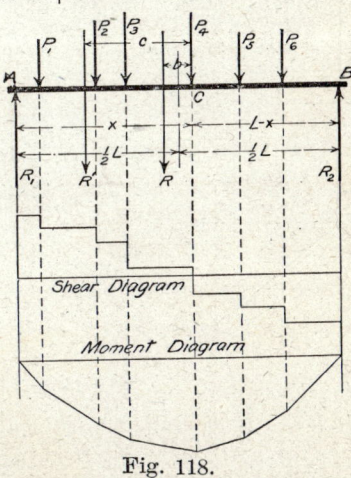

Fig. 118.

moment occurs under P_4. The proof is as follows, R' being the resultant of the loads to the left of C.

$$M_C = R_1 x - R'c = \frac{R}{L}(L - x + b)x - R'c$$

$$\frac{dM_C}{dx} = \frac{R}{L}(L - 2x + b) = 0 \text{ when } M_C = M_{max}$$

$x = \tfrac{1}{2}L + \tfrac{1}{2}b$, that is, P_4 is $\tfrac{1}{2}b$ to the right and R is $\tfrac{1}{2}b$ to the left of the center line.

The maximum moment does not necessarily occur under the load which is nearest the resultant, but might occur under P_3, for example, in which case R would have to be placed on the right of the center line. The moments for both cases should be calculated, and compared.

As the load is not usually turned end for end, the maximum shear may occur at either A or B; there must evidently be a load at A or B, and it is uncertain which load at either end will give the maximum shear. P_2 at A, for example, might produce the maximum shear, in which case P_1 would not be on the beam at all. The shear for each case should be calculated, and the results compared. The maximum shear will be equal to R_1 or R_2, of course.

For a complete discussion of this problem as applied to train wheel loads, see Chapter XIII.

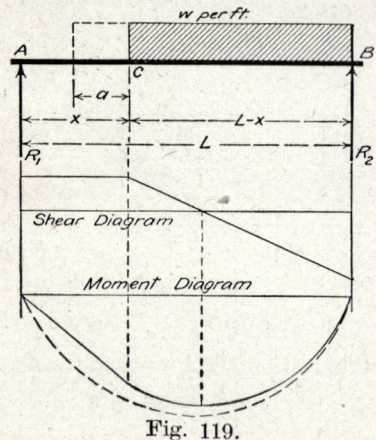

102. A Continuous Uniform Moving Load. A uniform live load is usually assumed to be of indefinite length so that it may come onto a beam from either end and cover the whole beam.

Fig. 119 shows a beam of span L which is to carry a live load of w lbs. per ft. What is the value of a for a maximum moment at C? A load anywhere on the beam will produce a positive moment at C, (Fig. 96), therefore there should be as much load as possible on the beam, that is, the beam should be fully loaded. For maximum moment at any point of a beam supported at its ends, it should have a full load. The maximum moment in the beam occurs, of course, at its middle. See Fig. 101. It may, of course, be proven analytically, that for maximum moment at C, a should equal x.

Fig. 119.

Art. 103.   UNIFORM LIVE AND DEAD LOAD.   167

The dotted moment diagram is for full load; *all* ordinates are longer than for partial load.

The maximum shear in the beam occurs at the end, and is equal to the reaction; it occurs under full load because a load anywhere on the beam will increase R_1 or R_2.

The maximum shear at C occurs when the load extends from C to the farther support, for if there were any load to the left of C, *part* of it would go to R_1 to increase it to R_1', while *all* of it would be subtracted from R_1' to give the shear at C; in other words, it decreases the shear more than it increases it——$S_c = R_1' - wa$. It may easily be proven analytically that a should be zero.

It is often necessary to find the shear at an intermediate section of a girder.

103. Combination of Uniform Live and Uniform Dead Load.

Fig. 120 shows a girder of 50 ft. span; the dead load is 600 lbs. per foot and must, of course, always be a full load; the live load is 2300 lbs. per foot, and is taken as a full load for all moments and for maximum end shear; it is taken as a partial load only for maximum shear at an intermediate section (102).

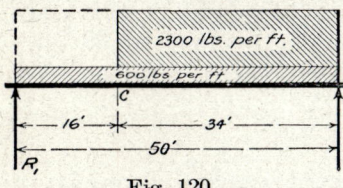

Fig. 120.

The reactions for full load are $(2300+600)25 = 72500$ lbs., and this is the maximum or end shear. The maximum moment is, according to equation (42),

$$\tfrac{1}{8}WL = \tfrac{1}{8} 2900 \times 50 \times 50 = 906250 \text{ ft. lbs.}$$

The maximum moment at 16 ft. from one end is

$$72500 \times 16 - 2900 \times 16 \times 8 = 788800 \text{ ft. lbs.}$$

The maximum shear at 16 ft. from the end is (partial load)
$R_1 - 600 \times 16 = 600 \times 25 + \tfrac{17}{50} 2300 \times 34 - 600 \times 16 = 41600$ lbs.

At the middle of the span, the dead load shear is zero, and the maximum live load shear is (for the load covering half the span)

$$\tfrac{12.5}{50} 2300 \times 25 = 14375 \text{ lbs.}$$

104. Maximum Live Load Shears in a Continuous Beam of Two Spans.

In a two span continuous beam (spans equal or unequal), it is only necessary to consider one section (**in the** left-hand span, for instance) at a distance x from the support, to find the loading which will give the maximum shear at the section. For any section in the other span the reasoning will be the same, or the beam may be considered turned end for end.

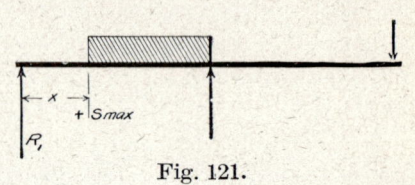

In Fig. 121, the shear at any section in the first span is evidently $S_x = +R_1$ (91). If there were any load to the left of the section, it would increase R_1 (and therefore the shear) but it would decrease the shear more, because **only** part of it goes to the left support (102). Any load to the right of the section would increase R_1 and the shear the same amount. The loading then, for maximum live load shear, so far as the first span is concerned, is the same as for a single span. It remains to consider the effect of loads in the second span. Any load in the second span causes a negative reaction at the left end— Figs. 109 and 111 reversed. This would decrease R_1 and therefore the positive shear at the section; the second span should be free from live load.

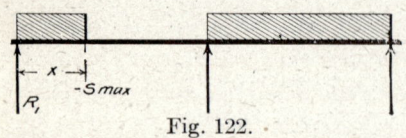

It follows that the second span should be fully loaded for maximum negative shear at the section as shown in Fig. 122. In this case, the first span should be loaded to the left of the section, for while any load in this part will increase the positive reaction (R_1), it will increase the negative shear more. The load in the first span produces a $+R_1$, and that in the second span a $-R_1$, but whichever is the greater, the loading shown in Fig. 122 will give the maximum negative shear.

If the live loads are concentrated loads, they should be confined, as far as possible, within the spaces indicated by the above uniform loads, at the same time bringing as much load as possible near the section. See Chapter XIII.

It may be possible for the live load to advance from both ends, but it may not be possible for it to cover an intermediate space as in Fig. 121; this must be determined in every particular case from the character of the live load.

Art. 105.   MAXIMUM LIVE LOAD SHEARS.   169

105. Maximum Live Load Shears in a Continuous Beam of Three Spans. For a maximum positive shear in one of the outer spans of Fig. 123, the loading should be as shown, because Fig. 112 shows that a load in either end span will pro-

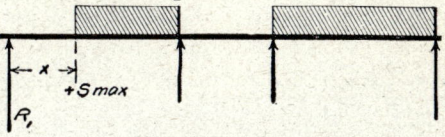

Fig. 123.

duce a positive reaction at *both* ends. The first span is not *fully* loaded, because a load to the left of the section will increase R_1 less than it will decrease the shear. A load in the middle span will evidently produce negative reactions at both ends.

The loading for maximum negative shear at any section in an outer span, must be the complement of that for maximum positive shear or as shown in Fig. 124.

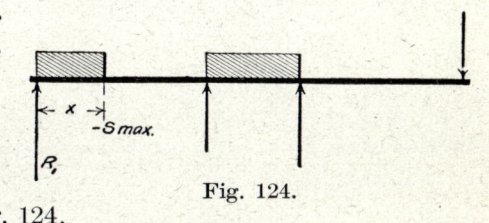

Fig. 124.

The loading for maximum shear in the middle span is easily determined but is seldom needed.

106. Maximum Live Load Moment in a Continuous Beam of Two Spans. In a two span continuous beam, any load in the second span will produce a negative moment in the first span, at any section (Fig. 111 reversed). A load in the first span may produce either a positive or a negative moment, depending upon the location of the load and the section; but since the point of contra-flexure lies between $x = \frac{4}{5}l$ and $x = l$, the moment is always positive for a load anywhere in the first

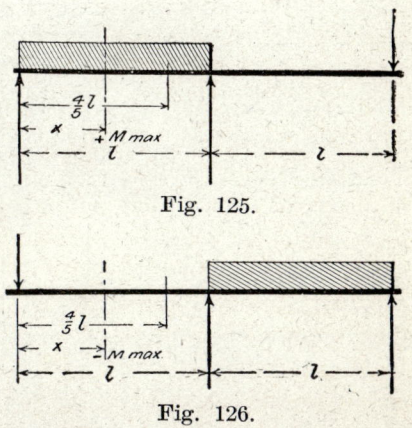

Fig. 125.

Fig. 126.

span, if $x < \frac{4}{5}l$; therefore, for $x < \frac{4}{5}l$, the loadings should be as shown in Figs. 125 and 126.

170 MAXIMUM LIVE LOAD MOMENT. Art. 106.

For $x > \frac{4}{5}l$, a load in the second span will, as before, produce a minus moment; *a load in the first span may produce either a plus or minus moment, depending upon its location.* If the location of P, Fig. 111, is found which will produce zero moment at the section under consideration, all loads to the left of this load will evidently produce a minus moment at the section, and all loads to the right, a plus moment; the loadings, therefore, for the two maximum moments will be as shown in Figs. 127 and 128. A single load at D, a distance k_0l from the left support will give zero moment at a distance x from this support. The value of k_o is given with Fig. 111, for equal spans.

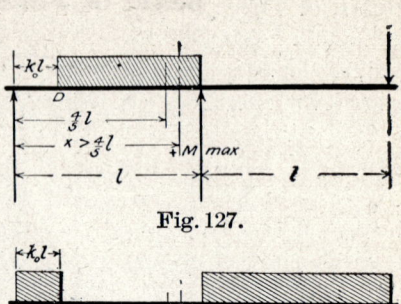

Fig. 127.

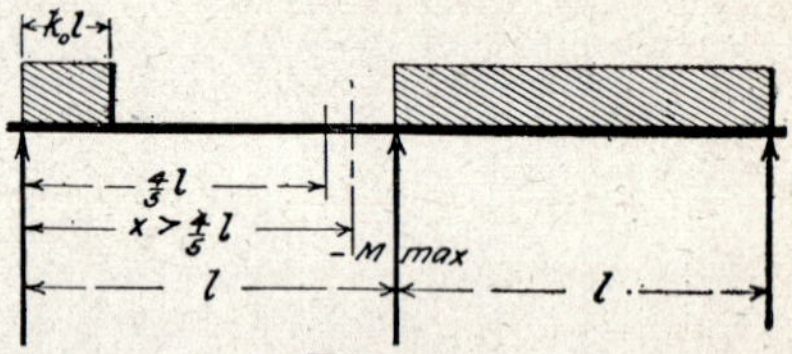

Fig. 128.

107. Maximum Live Load Moment in a Continuous Beam of Three Spans. Only points in the end spans, which are of equal length, will be considered. As shown by Fig. 112, any load in the third span will produce a positive moment at any section of the first span, and any load in the first span will produce a positive moment in the first span at any section to the left of the point of contra-flexure.

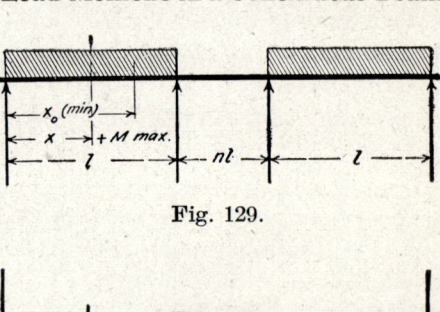

Fig. 129.

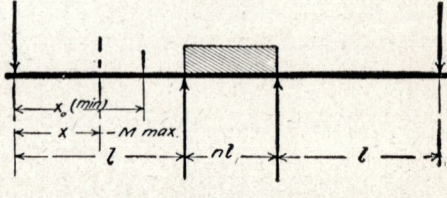

Fig. 130.

Art. 107.   MAXIMUM LIVE LOAD MOMENT.   171

For the end spans there are, therefore, two cases as in a two span bridge. A load in the middle span will evidently produce a negative moment in both end spans. Figs. 129 to 132 show the four cases for any section in the first span. The minimum value of x_0 is gotten by substituting the value of R_1, as given with Fig. 112 in the equation for the general value of x_0 and making $k=0$. $x_0 \text{ (min.)} = \dfrac{H}{H+2+2n} l.$

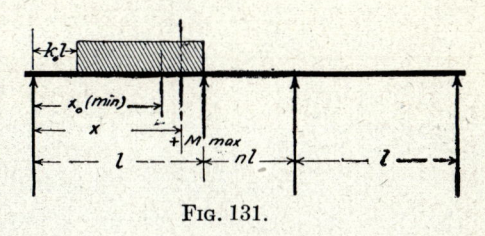

Fig. 131.

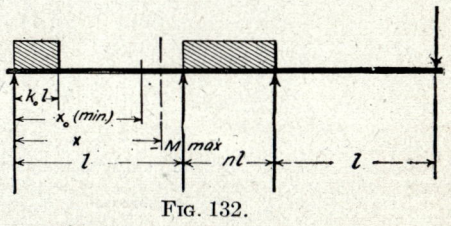

Fig. 132.

The value of k_0 is given with Fig. 112.

QUESTIONS AND PROBLEMS. CHAPTER VIII.

1. Are both the maximum shear and maximum moment required in designing a simple beam? What is required for a girder?

2. Upon what assumptions are the formulas for deflection accompanying Figs. 94 to 113 based?

3. In Fig. 96, find the value of y at C from the equation of the elastic line, for the segment CB, with origin at A.

4. In Fig. 98, what must be the value of l_1 in order that the maximum negative moment shall be equal to the maximum positive moment?

5. In the beams of Figs. 94 to 105, how do the maximum moments vary with the total load? With the length? How do the maximum deflections vary?

6. In Fig. 107, how many points of contra-flexure are there? How many maximum moments?

7. What is the usual convention with regard to signs for shears and moments?

8. Construct a shear and a moment diagram for the case of Fig. 114.

9. A cantilever beam 9 ft. long carries a uniform load of 100 lbs. per ft., and a concentrated load of 6000 lbs. at 3 ft. from the free end, what is the maximum shear? The maximum moment?

10. What size of I beam would you use for a floor joist carrying a total uniform load of 12000 lbs., the span being 20 ft. and the greatest fiber stress allowed 16000 lbs. per sq. in.? What is the greatest load this beam will carry if it is concentrated at mid-span?

11. In problem 10, the deflection is what proportion of the span length?

12. What is the maximum moment in the ties on a railway bridge if the supports are 7 ft. center to center and the rails are taken 5 ft. center to center, the total load on the tie being 18000 lbs.?

13. What is the maximum moment in a vertical beam carrying a water pressure of 15 ft. depth if the beam is supported at its ends, the distance between supports being equal to the depth of water? What if the beam is fixed at the lower end?

14. If in Fig. 114, there is also a load of 12000 lbs. at the middle, what is the maximum moment? The maximum shear?

15. What is meant by a "fixed end"? In which beams, Figs. 94 to 113, are the shears and moments statically indeterminate?

16. What is the maximum moment in a beam supported at its ends for a load P at mid-span? What is the maximum moment if the ends of the beam are fixed, and where does it occur?

17. Where does the maximum moment occur in a beam having fixed ends and carrying a uniform load?

18. What is the maximum moment for live load in the floor beam of a highway bridge, the total uniform load being 40000 lbs. and covering a length of 20 ft., the span length being $21\frac{1}{2}$ ft.? (Fig. 106, $l_1 = l_3 = 9$ in.).

19. If in Fig. 107, $l_1 = l_3 = 8$ ft. and $l_2 = 18$ ft., what will be the moment at the middle of the beam if the load between supports is 2000 lbs. per ft., and the load on the cantilevers is 1500 lbs. per ft.?

20. Does the case shown in Fig. 108 become a statically determinate one when the points of contra-flexure are known?

21. How does the maximum moment in Fig. 108 compare with that in each span when the beam is discontinuous?

22. Deduce the equation of three moments for a uniform load of w per foot on a continuous beam of three spans, l_1, l_2, and l_3.

23. In Fig. 112, what is the value of R_1 when there are two loads, each equal to P, symmetrically situated in the outer spans?

24. Deduce the equations accompanying Fig. 98 from equation (44).

25. A traveling crane has four wheels which run on two crane girders; these in turn are supported on four wheels which run on crane-runway girders. If the load on each crane wheel is 40000 lbs., and the wheel base is 10 ft., what will be the maximum moment from the wheel loads, in a crane girder having a span of 48 ft.? What the maximum shear?

Ans. 770000 ft. lbs. and 71670 lbs.

26. Find, in the above example, the maximum moment

and maximum shear in the crane-runway girder of 20 ft. span. The wheel base is 9 ft. and the load on each wheel is 90000 lbs.

Ans. 540000 ft. lbs. and 139500 lbs.

27. Find the maximum moment and maximum shear in a beam of 19 ft. span for a live load of four equal wheel loads o 40000 lbs. each, the distances center to center of wheels being 5 ft.

Ans. 373200 ft. lbs. and 96800 lbs.

28. What is the maximum live load moment in a girder of 100 ft. span for a uniform live load of 2575 lbs. per ft.? What is the maximum live load moment at 25 ft. from a support?

29. In the preceding problem, what is the shear at 25 ft. from the support for the same loading which gave the maximum moment at this point? What is the *maximum* live load shear at this point?

30. In the preceding problem, find the maximum shear and maximum moment at 25 ft. from the support when the live load is combined with a uniform dead load of 760 lbs. per ft.? What is the maximum shear in the girder in this case?

31. A continuous girder has two spans of 40 ft. each; the dead load is 600 lbs. per ft. and the live load 3000 lbs. per ft. Will it be a continuous beam when the live load covers one arm, if it is impossible to have a negative reaction at the ends? See Figs. 108 and 109.

32. In the preceding example, what will be the dead-load shear at 20 ft. from the end? What the maximum positive and negative live-load shears at the ends?

Ans. −3000 lbs. +52500 lbs. −7500 lbs.

33. In the above example, what will be the maximum positive and negative moments at 20 ft. from the end?

Ans. +540000 ft. lbs. −180000 ft. lbs.

34. At what point on the girder of problem 31 must a concentrated load stand to produce zero moment at 36 ft. from the left support?   Ans. 2.98 ft. from left support.

35. In Fig. 111, what must be the value of k for a maximum moment at the middle support?

Ans. $k = \sqrt{\tfrac{1}{3}}$.

36. If in Fig. 112 there is also a load P at a distance kl from A', will all the reactions be positive?

CHAPTER IX.

STRESSES IN BLOCKS AND COLUMNS.

A piece of material in compression is a *block* when its ratio of length to least width is small. When this ratio is large it is called a *column*, a *pillar*, a *post* or a *strut*. The boundary between these two classes is not a definite one, as will appear from the following discussion.

Arch stones of stone bridges and ordinary masonry pillars are examples of blocks. Compression members of trusses, and posts in buildings are examples of columns. A vertical column is usually called a *post*, and secondary compression members, such as those belonging to the wind bracing, are called *struts*.

108. Concentrated Loads on Blocks. When the load and reaction are uniformly distributed as in Fig. 133 (*a*), the unit stress on any square cross section is $s_c = \dfrac{W}{A}$. When the load is not uniformly distributed, or is concentrated, the stress on any cross section *near the ends*, can evidently not be uniformly distributed, but it may be at some intermediate cross section, provided the line of action of the resultants of the external forces is coincident with the axis of the block.

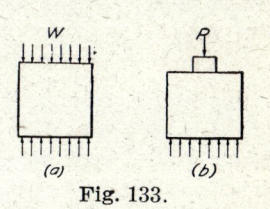

Fig. 133.

Bauschinger's experiments on sandstone blocks show that the smaller the surface of application of the load, that is, the nearer the load approaches a concentrated one, the less the ultimate strength will be.[1] Thus a block of stone will carry more load when loaded as in Fig. 133 (*a*) than when loaded as in Fig. 133 (*b*), as would be expected by analogy with uniformly distributed and concentrated loads on beams.

109. Eccentric Loads on Blocks. Fig. 134 shows a block *CDEF* which is supposed to be loaded with a concentrated load

---

[1] See Johnson's *Materials of Construction*, Chapter III.

P, or such a non-uniform load that its resultant P will be at a distance e from the axis of the block. If two forces, each equal to P and acting parallel with its line of action, be assumed to act in opposite directions at a (in the axis of the block), the effect will not be changed. The load P is therefore equivalent to a concentric load P and a couple whose moment is Pe. (34). The concentric load produces, on an intermediate section AB, a uniform unit stress as shown by the diagram $ABcd$; the couple produces a uniformly varying unit stress (diagram $ABfg$) precisely like that produced upon the section of a beam. (68) (13). The moment of the couple being anti-clockwise the bending stress will be compressive at A and tensile at B; it is zero at the center of gravity of the cross section.

Combining the diagrams for the two kinds of stress there results:

1. Diagram ABh in which the maximum unit tensile stress due to bending is just *equal* to the unit stress due to the direct compression.

2. Diagram $ABno$ in which the maximum unit tensile stress due to bending is *greater* than the unit stress due to direct compression.

Fig. 134.

3. Diagram $ABkm$, in which the maximum unit tensile stress due to bending is *less* than the unit stress due to direct compression.

These values of the maximum unit stress are expressed by the equation
$$s_{\max} = \frac{P}{A} \pm \frac{Mv_1}{I} = \frac{P}{A} \pm \frac{Pev_1}{I} \tag{45}$$

For example, if a load on a stone wall 24 inches thick has an eccentricity of $3\frac{1}{2}$ inches and amounts to 8000 lbs. per lineal foot,
$$s_{\max} = \frac{8000}{12 \times 24} \pm \frac{8000 \times 3\frac{1}{2} \times 12}{\frac{1}{12} \times 12 \times 24 \times 24 \times 24} = 27.8 \pm 24.3$$
$$= + 52.1 \text{ and } + 3.5 \text{ lbs. per sq. inch.}$$

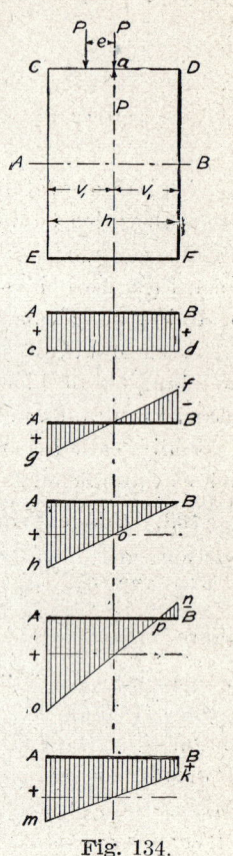

Art. 109.   CONCENTRATED LOADS ON BLOCKS.   177

Both extreme fiber stresses are compressive in this case. The average unit stress is the mean of these two and is 27.8 lbs. per sq. inch, or the same as the uniform unit stress, which is also apparent from an inspection of the diagrams Fig. 134.

The extreme fiber stress at B is zero when

$$\frac{P}{A} = \frac{Pev_1}{I} \text{ or when } e = \frac{I}{Av_1}$$

For a *rectangular cross section* this becomes

$$e = \frac{\frac{1}{12} b h^3}{b h \times \frac{1}{2} h} = \frac{1}{6} h$$

as is evident from the stress diagram ABh whose center of gravity is $\frac{1}{6} AB$ from o or $\frac{1}{3} AB$ from A. (In this case the diagram for the total stress on a cross section is similar to that for unit stress). If the eccentricity of the load is greater than one-sixth of the total width of the section either way from the center, the stress at the further edge becomes tensile. Then to avoid the tensile stresses in masonry, as is usually required, the resultant of the loads must not fall outside of the *middle third* of the width, or more definitely, it must not fall outside of the shaded zone in Fig. 135 (a).

For a circular cross section the above equation will give $\frac{1}{8} d$ as the limit for e, that is the result-

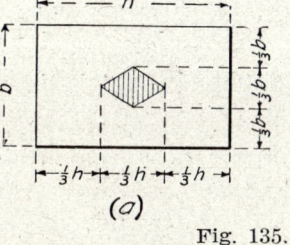

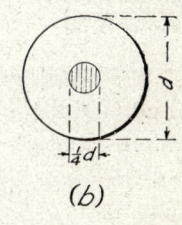

Fig. 135.

ant must not fall outside a central zone whose diameter is equal to $\frac{1}{4}$ the diameter of the cross section. Fig. 135 (b).

When in a rectangular cross section, *no tension is possible*, the stress diagram is still a triangle in the second case, as Apo for example, Fig. 134. The distance of the resultant from A is $\frac{1}{3} Ap = \frac{1}{2}h - e$.

Total stress $= Ap \times b \times \frac{1}{2} s_{max} = 3(\frac{1}{2}h - e) b \times \frac{1}{2} s_{max} = P$.

$$s_{max} = \frac{\frac{2}{3} P}{(\frac{1}{2}h - e) b}$$

As the eccentricity e, increases, the denominator diminishes

178　　CONCENTRATED LOADS ON BLOCKS.　　Art. 109.

and s_{max} increases. When *tension is possible*, e may of course exceed $\frac{1}{2} h$, but when it is not, the maximum eccentricity is limited by the strength of the material. If no tension were possible and e could be made equal to $\frac{1}{2} h$, s_{max} would be infinite.

A case quite similar to the above may be illustrated by means of a bridge pier (Fig. 136) having a horizontal force acting near its top. The horizontal load of 70,000 lbs. is equivalent to a force of 70,000 lbs. acting at g and a couple whose moment is $70,000 \times 26 = 1,820,000$ ft. lbs. The couple produces a uniformly varying pressure upon the foundation and the vertical loads a uniform pressure, so that equation (45) is applicable.

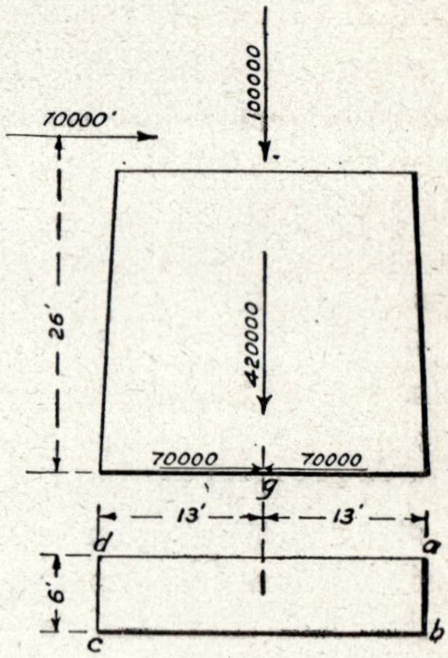

$$\frac{P}{A} = \frac{100,000 + 420,000}{6 \times 26} = 3330$$

$$\frac{Mv_1}{I} = \frac{1,820,000 \times 13}{\frac{1}{12} \times 6 \times 26 \times 26 \times 26} = 2690$$

Pressure along $ab = 2690 + 3330 = 6020$ lbs. per sq. ft. Pressure along $cd = 3330 - 2690 = 640$ lbs. per sq. ft.

Fig. 136.

In equation (45) $I = \int v^2 dA$ is the measure of the cross section's resistance to turning about the neutral axis. If it is assumed that the entire area is concentrated in a single point, then

$$I = Ar^2 \tag{46}$$

in which r is the distance from the axis to the point at which the area would have to be concentrated in order to have the same moment of inertia as the actual moment of inertia; r is called the *radius of gyration*.

Substituting this value of I in equation (45)

$$s_{max} = \frac{P}{A} + \frac{Pev_1}{Ar^2} = \frac{P}{A}\left(1 + \frac{ev_1}{r^2}\right) = s_c\left(1 + \frac{ev_1}{r^2}\right) \tag{45a}$$

$$s_c = \frac{P}{A} = \frac{s_{max}}{1 + \frac{ev_1}{r^2}} \tag{47}$$

s_c is a reduced working unit stress in compression depending upon the maximum allowed unit stress, the eccentricity, and the form and size of the cross section. s_c may be applied to the total stress to find the required area just as s_w is applied in tension or in blocks in compression when the load is concentric.

Equation (47) can best be solved by trial because r depends upon the section which is to be found. Both A and r are unknown.

In Fig. 134 it is evident that one side of the block will be compressed more than the other, and if there is any tension, one side may even be extended. This is similar to the deformation of a beam (68) and the axis must bend. The point a moves toward the left so that the moment is really greater than Pe since the final lever arm is greater than e by the amount of the deflection of the axis between a and the section under consideration. In a block, however, this deflection is so small compared with e that it is negligible.

110. Columns Eccentrically Loaded. If a *column* is eccentrically loaded, the deflection is not negligible as it is in a *block*. As in Fig. 134, the stress at any section is composed of two parts, direct compression and bending. The lever arm of the couple is, however, not e, but $e + y_{max} - y$. Fig. 137. The moment of the couple is $M = -P(e + y_{max} - y)$. y may be found from the differential equation of the elastic line just as for a beam, (81), but in this case the moment is in terms of y and not of x.

Putting $e + y_{max} = e_1$ for convenience,

$$EI\frac{d^2y}{dx^2} = -M = P(e_1 - y)$$

$$2\frac{d^2y}{dx^2}dy = \frac{2P}{EI}(e_1 - y)\,dy$$

Fig. 137.

Integrating:

$$\left(\frac{dy}{dx}\right)^2 = \frac{P}{EI}(2e_1 - y)y + C$$

$\frac{dy}{dx} = 0$ when $y = 0$ hence $C = 0$

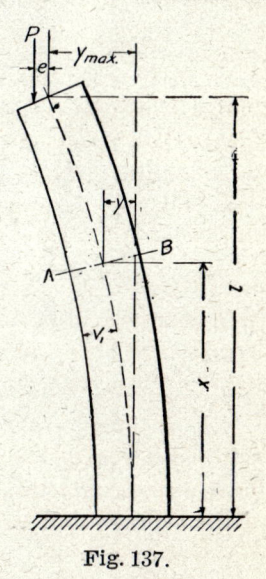

Extracting the square root and transforming

$$\sqrt{\frac{P}{EI}}dx = \frac{dy}{\sqrt{2e_1 y - y^2}} \qquad (a)$$

Integrating again, the equation of the elastic line is:

$$\sqrt{\frac{P}{EI}}x = vers^{-1}\frac{y}{e_1} + C' = vers^{-1}\frac{y}{e+y_{max}} + C'$$

when $x=0$, $y=0$ hence $C'=0$

$$\sqrt{\frac{P}{EI}}x = vers^{-1}\frac{y}{e+y_{max}} \qquad (48)$$

when $x=l$, $y=y_{max}$ and (48) becomes

$$vers\sqrt{\frac{Pl^2}{EI}} = \frac{y_{max}}{e+y_{max}} = vers(\theta\, l) \qquad (b)$$

where $\theta = \sqrt{\dfrac{P}{EI}} = \dfrac{1}{r}\sqrt{\dfrac{P}{AE}} \qquad (49)$

From (b)

$$y_{max} = e\frac{vers\,\theta\, l}{1 - vers\,\theta\, l} = e\frac{1-\cos\theta\, l}{\cos\theta\, l} = e(\sec\theta\, l - 1) \qquad (50)$$

Equation (50) determines the maximum eccentricity which is $e + y_{max}$; having this the eccentricity at any section may be found, it being $e + y_{max} - y$, y being obtained from equation (48). Stresses are found as in a block. The maximum stress will occur in the extreme fibre at the base on the compression or concave side.

$$s_{max} = \frac{P}{A} + \frac{P(e+y_{max})v_1}{I} = \frac{P}{A}\left(1 + \frac{e_1 v_1}{r^2}\right) \qquad (51)$$

$$s_c = \frac{P}{A} = \frac{s_{max}}{1 + \dfrac{e_1 v_1}{r^2}} = \frac{s_{max}}{1 + \dfrac{e\, v_1}{r^2}\sec\theta\, l} \qquad (52)$$

Equations (48), (49), (50), (51), and (52) give complete information with regard to stresses in and deflections of originally straight and homogeneous columns *within the elastic limit.* If the average unit stress allowable is found from equation (52) the area of a column's cross section is determined as simply as that of a tension member. This equation is, however, so difficult of application that *it is not used in practice;* it may be used as an occasional check upon results obtained by the usual methods. $\dfrac{P}{A}$ appears on both sides of the equation (see equation (49)) while v_1 and r also depend upon the section which is to be found.

Art. 110.   COLUMNS ECCENTRICALLY LOADED.   181

If in equation (51) e_1 is put equal to e, that is if the bending is neglected, s_{max} will be the same as for a block (Eq. 45a) and s_c the same as given by equation (47); but according to equation (52) this is true only when $\sec \theta l = 1$ or $\theta l = 0$, and according to equation (49), θl has this value only when $l=0$. It follows that a column may be treated as a block when it is short, the boundary line between the two depending upon l and e (equations (50) and (49)). When y_{max} is small compared with e, y_{max} is negligible.

To show the influence of the bending, y_{max} is given below in terms of e for a column composed of two steel channels 10 in.$\times$20 lbs.$\times$200 inches long. Applying equation (50) for a column fixed at one end;

for $P = 50,000$ lbs. $y_{max} = \left[\sec \left(200 \sqrt{\dfrac{50000}{29000000 \times 157.4}} \right) - 1 \right] e$

$y_{max} = (\sec. 0.662 - 1) e = 0.269 e$

for $P = 100,000$ lbs. $y_{max} = (\sec. 0.936 - 1) e = 0.688 e$
for $P = 150,000$ lbs. $y_{max} = (\sec. 1.146 - 1) e = 1.430 e$
for $P = 200,000$ lbs. $y_{max} = (\sec. 1.324 - 1) e = 3.105 e$
for $P = 250,000$ lbs. $y_{max} = (\sec. 1.478 - 1) e = 9.628 e$
for $P = 270,000$ lbs. $y_{max} = (\sec. 1.540 - 1) e = 30.882 e$
for $P = 281,000$ lbs. $y_{max} = (\sec. 1.570 - 1) e = \infty$

It is to be noted that the influence of the bending increases at first slowly and then very rapidly, so that for the greater loads e is negligible compared with y_{max}. In fact, $y_{max} = \infty$ for a load of only 281,000 lbs., or an average stress of 23,900 lbs. per sq. in., no matter how small the eccentricity may be, so long as it is not zero. This must be interpreted to mean that the equilibrium between the load and the induced stresses is not possible except for loads less than this; under greater loads the column fails. Of course if e is large, the elastic limit may be exceeded for a less load than 281,000 lbs., and it should be remembered that the equations are not applicable beyond the elastic limit. Thus if $e = \frac{1}{2}$ in. and $P = 250,000$ lbs., $y_{max} = 9.628 \times \frac{1}{2} = 4.814$ in. $s_{max} = \dfrac{250000}{11.76} \left(1 + \dfrac{4.814 + 0.5}{13.4} 5 \right) = 63,500$ lbs. per sq. in. Since this exceeds the elastic limit, the deflection would be much greater than that given by the formula and the column would fail.

The important case in which the eccentricity is very small, —for practically concentric loads—will be considered in the next article.

111. Columns Concentrically Loaded. It is practically impossible to apply loads to either tensile or compressive members without a slight eccentricity; this causes the member to bend. In a tensile member the load has a tendency to reduce this bending, but in a compressive member the tendency is just the opposite, and this is of great importance as is shown by experiments, and as will also appear from a discussion of the equations in the preceding article.

An *ideal column* is one having a perfectly straight axis, and the material of which is homogenious and in the same condition throughout. If such a column be loaded concentrically it will not bend. The *practical column* will bend under any load until the load and the stresses are in equilibrium or until the column fails.

If the load is not great enough to cause failure, the column is in stable equilibrium, for if its deflection be changed by applying a small transverse force, and this force is then removed, it will return to its original deflected position. If the load be applied gradually, a point will be reached at which failure takes place suddenly. The load under which stable equilibrium just ceases must, therefore, be the ultimate load which the column will carry. This critical load is easily found from equations (49) and (50), for it is the load which will make $y_{max} = \infty$, which is true when $\theta l = \frac{1}{2}\pi$. As shown by the example in Art. 110, this is quite possible in an ordinary column. From equation (49), which applies to a column fixed at one end and free at the other,

$$\theta l = \tfrac{1}{2}\pi = \frac{l}{r}\sqrt{\frac{P_{max}}{AE}}$$

from which

$$P_{max} = \tfrac{1}{4}\pi^2 A E \frac{r^2}{l^2} \qquad (53)$$

This then is the load that will produce failure when the eccentricity is so small that there is no danger that the elastic limit will be exceeded for a less load, as was illustrated by the example in Art. 110. It should be remembered that initial stresses and bends, and non-homogenity of the material in a column, have an influence quite similar to eccentric loading; when these all happen to have a tendency to produce bending in one direction, they form the most unfavorable case, which must always be assumed. It is assumed, therefore, that care has been taken to have the column straight and the eccentricity very small. Equa-

Art. 111. COLUMNS CONCENTRICALLY LOADED. 183

tion (53) is, therefore, applicable under conditions approaching very closely to the ideal, as it is independent of the eccentricity.[1]

Equation (53) is based upon the maximum deflection and not upon the maximum unit stress. It is much simpler than equation (52) in which it would be impossible to assign a satisfactory value of e for concentric loads. No doubt, when the column fails, the stress has reached the ultimate strength of the material. It has been shown by many experiments on steel,[2] that the yield point is the ultimate strength in *columns,* that is, the stress-deformation diagram does not rise above the yield point in steel.[3] Since the equations do not apply beyond the elastic limit, or limit of proportionality, it will be on the side of safety to call the elastic limit the ultimate strength. When equation (53) gives values of $\dfrac{P_{max}}{A}$ greater than the elastic limit, (as it will for small values of $\dfrac{l}{r}$) it is no longer applicable. Under this formula the column is treated as a block. Equation (53) may be written in the form of equation (54) and must be used in connection with equation (55).

$$s_c = \frac{P_{max}}{A} = \tfrac{1}{4}\pi^2 E \frac{r^2}{l^2} \tag{54}$$

$$s_c = \frac{P_{max}}{A} = s_e \tag{55}$$

s_e is the unit stress at the elastic limit. Applying a factor

---

[1] Prof. Wm. Cain has shown by a rigorous analysis that equation (53) gives the load *on the ideal column* that is just sufficient to keep the column deflected after it has been slightly bent by a transverse force, and he deduces a formula for the amount of the maximum deflection for loads greater than this critical load. This formula shows that a load only a few pounds greater than the critical load will cause a deflection so large that, practically the critical load is the ultimate load. Slight variations from the ideal condition would produce the same result. See Trans. Am. Soc. C. E., Vol. XXXIX, page 96.

[2] See a paper by Chas. Marshall, Trans. Am. Soc. C. E., Vol. XVII, page 53.

[3] See also Johnson's *Materials of Construction*, page 363, for an account of experiments by M. Considère showing that the strength of a column is a function of the elastic limit of the material and is independent of the ultimate strength in either tension or compression.

of safety to s_c, the working unit stress is gotten. The same factor of safety is usually used for all values of $\dfrac{l}{r}$. It is difficult to assign a rational value.

Equations (54) and (55) give the same value of s_c when
$$s_e = \tfrac{1}{4}\pi^2 E \dfrac{r^2}{l^2}, \text{ or when}$$
$$\dfrac{l}{r} = \tfrac{1}{2}\pi\sqrt{\dfrac{E}{s_e}} \qquad (56)$$

That is, equation (56) gives the value of $\dfrac{l}{r}$ at which equation (54) begins to be applicable and equation (55) ceases to be applicable.

It may be noted that the stress due to direct compression is negligible when $\dfrac{e_1 r_1}{r^2}$ in equation (51) is very much greater than unity; this is the case when e_1 is large, that is, when y_{max} is large; but y_{max} is infinite when $\sec\theta l = \infty$ or when equation (54) holds. Long columns, therefore, fail by bending, and short columns by direct compression. In ordinary cases, however, both kinds of stress are combined, and buckling may take place for a load less than P_{max} as given by equation (53); that is, the elastic limit is passed. The difference in these loads depends upon the eccentricity and the initial curvature of the column.

If the effect of the initial curvature be investigated, it will be found to vary in a manner quite like the effect of eccentricity as shown by the application of equation (50). This difference, then, increases as the eccentricity and initial curvature increase.

The effect of the usual variations from theoretical conditions can only be found by experiments. This is discussed in Art. 113.

112. End Conditions. The column shown in Fig. 137 has a fixed end and a free end. At a *fixed end* the direction of the tangent to the elastic curve corresponds with that of the axis of the column before it is bent, that is $\dfrac{dy}{dx} = 0$. When the end of a column is perfectly free to turn so that its end condition has no influence whatever on its bending, the end is said to be *pivoted*. A *round end* would be formed by a hemispherical end on a flat surface; the deflection of the column shifts the point of application of the load slightly. When there is a rocker bearing in place

Art. 112.   END CONDITIONS.   185

of the flat bearing, a round end becomes a *hinged end*. A *hinged end* is also formed by a pin connection in which the clearance between the pin and the pin hole is small. A ball and socket joint is hinged in all directions, while a pin joint is hinged in but one direction. When the end of a column is a plane normal to its axis, and it rests squarely on a plane surface, it is *flat ended*. Under certain conditions a flat end might be a fixed end, but this cannot be accomplished perfectly by fastening the column to its bearing on account of the elasticity of the fastenings.

In structural work, columns have *pin or hinged ends, flat ends, riveted ends* and *fixed ends*. Pivoted ends do not occur. On account of frictional resistance, a pin-ended column occupies an intermediate place between pivoted and flat-ended columns. This frictional resistance depends upon the size of the pin, being largest for large pins. Compression members in riveted trusses are columns with riveted ends. Such columns are usually assumed to be flat-ended. The ends are not fixed on account of the elasticity of the connections and the deflection of the truss. When a truss deflects, the angles between the members change and some bending is induced in them because their ends are not pivoted.

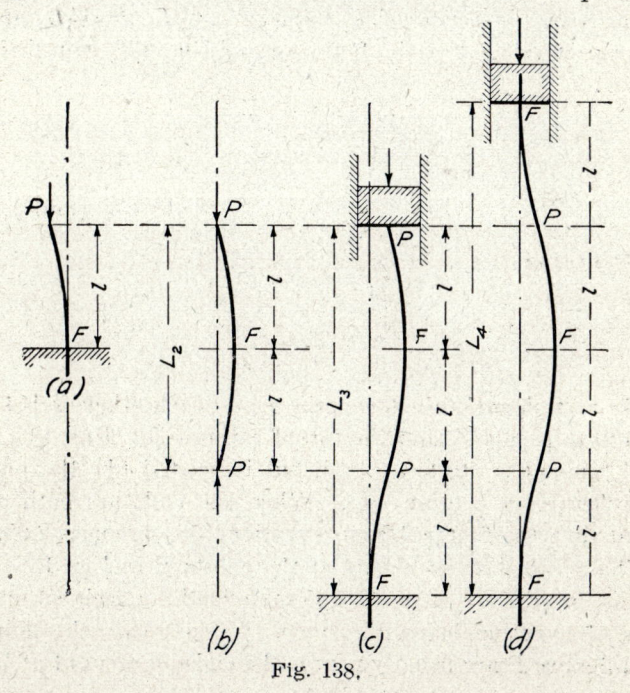

Fig. 138.

In practical column formulas, such assumptions of end conditions are usually made as will be on the side of safety. In theoretical analyses, only the pivoted and fixed end conditions are investigated. Fig. 138 shows that the fundamental cases are really combinations of the simple case of a column fixed at one end and free at the other, provided the ends are not allowed to move sidewise, so as to change their relative lateral positions, for this would, of course, change the curvature.

Figures 138 (*a*), (*b*), (*c*), and (*d*) show, respectively, columns with one fixed end and one free end, with two pivoted ends, with one pivoted and one fixed end and with two fixed ends. The points F are all fixed points because at these the tangent to the elastic curve is vertical; the points P are all pivoted because at these the bending moment is zero. It is evident that the points F and P divide the column (*d*) into four equal parts and it follows, that for the same strength, and for the different end conditions shown in Fig. 138, a column's length should vary as 1:2:3:4.

If it is desired to have the preceding equations apply to columns of cases (*b*), (*c*) and (*d*), and to have them in terms of the total length of the column, it is only necessary to substitute for l its value in terms of L, namely $l=\frac{1}{2}L_2$, $l=\frac{1}{3}L_3$ and $l=\frac{1}{4}L_4$ respectively. For the four cases of Fig. 138, equation (54) becomes:

$$s_c = \frac{P_{max}}{A} = \frac{1}{4}\pi^2 E \frac{r^2}{l^2} \tag{54}$$

$$s_c = \frac{P_{max}}{A} = \pi^2 E \frac{r^2}{L_2^2} \quad \text{(Euler's Formula)}. \tag{57}$$

$$s_c = \frac{P_{max}}{A} = 2.25 \pi^2 E \frac{r^2}{L_3^2} \tag{58}$$

$$s_c = \frac{P_{max}}{A} = 4\pi^2 E \frac{r^2}{L_4^2} \tag{59}$$

For the same lengths the strengths are to each other as 1:4:9:16.

It is to be noted that the top of column (*c*), Fig. 138, is not on the tangent at its lower end, but is located like the point of contra-flexure in column (*d*). When the ends are both on the tangent line, the factor 2.25 in equation (58) becomes 2.05.

The greatest stress occurs at the points F in Fig. 138, and is the same in all four cases, for the same load, on each column, the radius of gyration being the same. In case (*d*), the points of contra-flexure P are usually nearer the ends on account of lack of perfect fixity, and the maximum stress is at the middle of the column. If then the location of the points of contra-flexure are known, the part of the column between them may be treated as a column with true pivoted ends.

Columns do not necessarily bend into the simple curves shown in Fig. 138. In case (b), for example, double and triple flexure occasionally occur, and the column carries a much greater load. Experiments show that these conditions are unstable. With an increase of load the column goes over into the weaker condition of single flexure.[1] Multiple flexure is due to variations from the ideal conditions tending to produce bending in opposite directions in different parts of the column. Its possibility follows from equation (49) because, $\sec \theta l = \infty$ when $\theta l = \frac{1}{2}\pi$, $\theta l = \frac{3}{2}\pi$, $\theta l = \frac{5}{2}\pi$, etc.

In Fig. 138 (b), on account of the symmetry, the tangent to the elastic line is vertical at the middle, and each half of the column is in the condition of a column fixed at one end and free at the other—case (a). This condition will not be changed if the column be cut in two, *provided there is no tension on the convex side*. It follows that *a column may have a fixed end without being fastened*, or that a flat end may be a fixed end. An elastic base, however, will deform until the stresses developed are equal to the pressure from the column. Since this pressure is greater on one side than the other, the column, if free at one end, will lean; the elastic curve will be tangent to the inclined position, and the stresses will be but slightly different from those in the case of a true fixed end. In a column with two fixed ends, for example, any turning of the ends will move the points of contra-flexure toward the ends—the column will approach the condition of a column with pivoted end. If the ends abutted against perfectly *inelastic surfaces*, they would be in the condition of perfect fixity so long as there was no tension on the convex side, near the ends; the intensity of the direct compression would have to be greater than the intensity of the tension due to bending.

$$\frac{P}{A} > \frac{M_r v_1}{I}$$

---

[1] See a report on *Experiments on the Strength of Wrought Iron struts*, by James Christie, Mem. Am. Soc. C. E., Trans. Am. Soc. C. E., Vol. XIII, page 88.

188 END CONDITIONS. Art. 112.

From equation (50)
$$M_v = P(e + y_{max}) = Pe \sec \theta l$$
$$\frac{P}{A} > \frac{Pe \sec \theta l \, v_1}{Ar^2} \text{ or } \frac{e \sec \theta l \, v_1}{r^2} < 1 \qquad (60)$$

If the ends are not fastened but simply press against flat rigid surfaces, there will be the less liability of separation on the convex side, the broader the ends are, for v_1 and r refer to the end surfaces here

A column's support approaches rigidity when it is a large mass like a bridge pier, and when the end of a column is so large that the intensity of pressure on the support is comparatively small. A further difficulty in the practical application of equation (60) lies in the fact that no satisfactory value of e can be assigned to take account of all the variations from ideal conditions.

If the end of the column is forked, as shown in Fig. 139, it will be fixed when

$$\tfrac{1}{2} Pk \gtreqless M$$

M being the bending moment at the end due to the column bending, or this combined with the moment due to transverse loads on the column, the support being assumed *inelastic*.

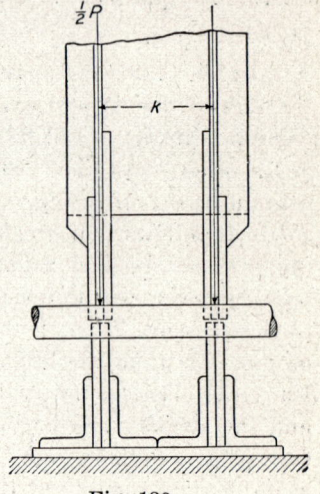

Fig. 139.

When the ends of a column fixed at both ends are not fastened, they will turn as soon as the pressure on the convex side passes zero; the curvature between the points of contra-flexure increases and beyond them it decreases—the points of contra-flexure move toward the ends, and when they arrive at the ends, we have the case of pivoted ends so far as the form of the elastic line is concerned, but on account of the flat ends, the end pressures will be eccentric, as shown in Fig. 140.

It follows that the stress in a flat ended column will be less than in a column with pivoted ends, because the turning of the ends produces an eccentricity tending to reverse the curvature. Equa-

Fig. 140.

tion (51) will give some idea concerning this contingency, but with elastic supports, the column's end will turn under a much less load than when the supports are rigid.

113. Column Formulas. By a column formula is usually meant an equation which gives the average working stress by which the total stress in a column, concentrically loaded, must be divided in order to obtain its area. Finding the required area of a column's cross section is, therefore, a very simple matter, since all specifications give one or more column formulas. It is not as simple, however, as finding the required area of a tension member, because the shortest method of solving the formula, is by trial.

It is assumed that care has been taken to have the column straight and the load concentric, but practically it is impossible to know, in any particular case, how great the variations from ideal conditions are.

If the condition of the column approaches very closely to the ideal, as explained in Article 111, then equations (54), (57), (58), (59) and (55) are applicable, and are used for the practical column by many engineers, particularly in continental Europe. Equation (57), which applies to a column with pivoted ends, was published by Euler in 1759, and is called *Euler's Formula*. The question arises, does the practical column approach the ideal closely enough so that its strength will be but slightly below that given by Euler's Formula? It is only by experiments that the effect of variations from the ideal column can be determined. With experiments on practical columns, a good test of Euler's Formula cannot be made because the end conditions are uncertain, as is apparent from a careful reading of Article 112. Then, too, Euler's Formula is not applicable beyond the elastic limit, but in a steel column the stress at failure does not exceed this limit much.

Most engineers in this country base their column formulas upon experiments, and put them in terms of the maximum allowed unit stress. These experiments eliminate, to a certain extent, the uncertainties as to end conditions, and show rather wide variations from the mean, as would be expected, particularly when multiple flexure occurs. It is highly desirable to have more experiments in order to reduce the discrepancies between various column formulas now in use.

Equation (52) might be used as a column formula if a satisfactory value can be assigned to the eccentricity. If $sec.\ \theta l$ is developed into a series, and the higher powers omitted, equation (52) becomes:

$$s_c = \frac{P}{A} = \frac{s_{max}}{1 + \frac{ev_1}{r^2} + \frac{ev_1}{2r^2}\frac{l^2}{r^2}\frac{P}{AE}}$$

When e is very small—when care has been taken to have the load concentric and the column straight—, $\frac{ev_1}{r^2}$ will be less than e and may be neglected. Since e is unknown, $\frac{ev_1}{2r^2}\frac{P}{AE}$ may be set equal to $\frac{1}{a}$ (since it will be a small fraction) which is to be determined by experiment. We have then the following formula which, in this country is called *Rankine's Formula*.

$$s_c = \frac{P}{A} = \frac{s_{max}}{1 + \frac{1}{a}\frac{l^2}{r^2}} \tag{61}$$

This equation is best solved by trial, since r depends upon the section sought, but the solution is very simple compared with that of equation (52).

Equation (61) represents a curve which is laid in the middle of a field of results, plotted from experiments made upon columns having various ratios of $\frac{l}{r}$. The value of a so determined would not, of course, apply beyond the limits of $\frac{l}{r}$ used in the experiments, or to any other end conditions or kind of material; but it is assumed to apply to any form of cross section. Even within these limitations, a is evidently not a constant, but the formula can be made to represent the experiments very closely between certain limits of $\frac{l}{r}$; this is sometimes better accomplished by putting for s_{max}, a value different from its value in tension. It is not permissible in all cases to omit the higher powers in the development of the series for $sec.\ \theta l$. Rankine's Formula, therefore, is purely empirical. It was originally deduced by *Navier* from equation (51) in a manner which gave a much simpler value of a than that given above, and which shows more clearly that a cannot be a constant, but it is none the less indeterminate theoretically.

Art. 113.   COLUMNS FORMULAS.   191

Many different column formulas have been proposed, but in recent years the *Straight Line Formula* has come into favor with the engineers in this country, because a straight line can be made to represent the experiments as well as any curve, for the usual values of $\frac{l}{r}$ which occur in practice. The *Straight Line Formula* is of the form

$$s_c = \frac{P}{A} = s_{max} - c\frac{l}{r} \qquad (62)$$

In this formula c is the experimental constant and, as in Rankine's Formula, s_{max} is also sometimes chosen to fit the experiments.

Fig. 141 shows in a general way, the relations between the commonest column formulas for steel columns having an elastic limit of 40,000 lbs. per sq. in. A portion of Euler's curve is of no value because it lies above the elastic limit. The ultimate

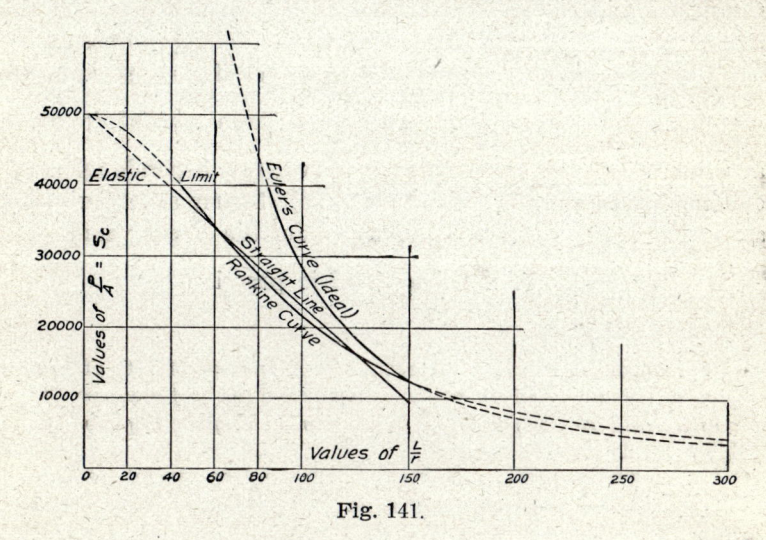

Fig. 141.

strength of a column cannot exceed the elastic limit if its ratio $\frac{l}{r}$ is greater than perhaps 40. If this ratio is less than this limit, it is difficult to determine the point of failure. A block will deform indefinitely, but a column will bend suddenly when the yield point is passed. While the elastic limit is a proper limit of strength, it would evidently not be rational to apply the same factor of safety to it for the shortest columns as for the longer columns. This difficulty is, however, of little importance, as very few practical columns have ratios of $\dfrac{l}{r}$ less than 40 or greater than 150. The portions of the curves shown dotted are of little importance.

Rankine's and the Straight Line formulas are experimental, and Fig. 141 shows that the strength of the practical column is considerably below that of the ideal for the usual values of $\dfrac{l}{r}$, and particularly for those occurring oftenest in practice. No numerical values for the empirical constants are given in these equations, because they vary widely in the formulas as applied to the different sets of experiments that have so far been made.[1] For definite values the student should refer to the various standard specifications.

There is no reason why the Straight Line and Rankine's Curve should cut the vertical axis in the same point or at the particular value of s_c shown in Fig. 141; it is only a question of having these lines represent the average of the experiments within the usual values of $\dfrac{l}{r}$. Neither is there any definite value at which these lines meet Euler's Curve; this depends upon the end conditions and the kind of material. Nearly all experiments show that Euler's Curve is applicable for the larger values of $\dfrac{l}{r}$—values usually above those used in practice.

---

[1] For diagrams showing the results of a number of sets of experiments on columns, and for column formulas fitted to them, see Burr's *Elasticity and Resistance of the Materials of Engineering*, pp. 479 to 506, 6th Edition.

For diagrams showing the results of some very careful tests made by Tetmajer, see Johnson's *Materials of Construction*. Figs. 297 and 298, or Trans. Am. Soc. C. E., Vol. XXXIX, pp. 109 and 111.

For diagrams showing the results of experiments made in this country before 1885, see a paper by Thos. H. Johnson, M. Am. Soc. C. E. in the Trans. Am. Soc. C. E., Vol. XV, page 517. This paper gives the Straight Line formulas which Mr. Johnson proposed.

For the results of some very careful experiments upon columns of single angles, beams, channels, tees, and tubes, see papers by Mr. James Christie, Trans. Am. Soc. C. E., Vol. XIII, pp. 86 and 254.

Art. 114.   COLUMNS IN TOWERS.   193

114. Columns in Towers. Fig. 142 shows a two-story tower, composed of four columns fastened together with bracing. The column being held at the middle, may take on the reverse curvature shown by the dotted line. The point A being a point of contraflexure, will be in the condition of a pivoted end; but if the connection of the strut AB is large and rigid, and if the strut itself has considerable stiffness, there will be a tendency to hold the column in a vertical line at A. The two segments of the column are treated as separate columns with indeterminate end conditions; a safe assumption is that of pivoted ends. The bracing in the vertical planes holds the columns against buckling in two directions *only*. To prevent buckling in a diagonal direction the horizontal braces AC and BD may be used.

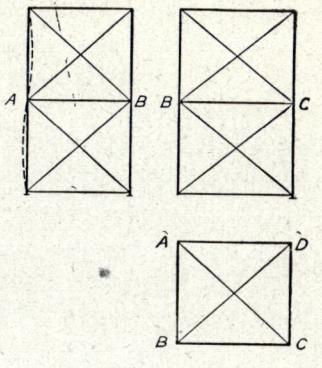

Fig. 142.

If the column AE, Fig. 143, be held against sidewise movement (in all directions) at points A, B, C, D and E, by means of pivoted connections, then *each segment is in the condition of a column with pivoted ends*. Of course initial bends may interfere considerably with the uniform bending indicated by the dotted line, but under the most favorable conditions, the segments are in the same condition if the column is of uniform section and divided into equal lengths.

If the strut connections are not pivoted, the bending will not be so great.

If the load on the column is *eccentric* the effect will be quite different. In this case the small accidental eccentricities are neglected. It is not possible to make an exact solution in a practical case because of the indefinite end conditions, but the cases shown in Fig. 144 will furnish a guide for the judgement. The column is assumed to be continuous, and except in case (*b*), to have pivoted ends. Under the assumption of pivoted ends, the lines of the reaction fall in

Fig. 143.

the axes of the columns. With square ends, they would move toward the load when the lower story of the column is bent so as to be convex toward the loaded side, decreasing the eccentricity; in the opposite case the eccentricity would be increased as the column bends. The effect of y on the moment is neglected.

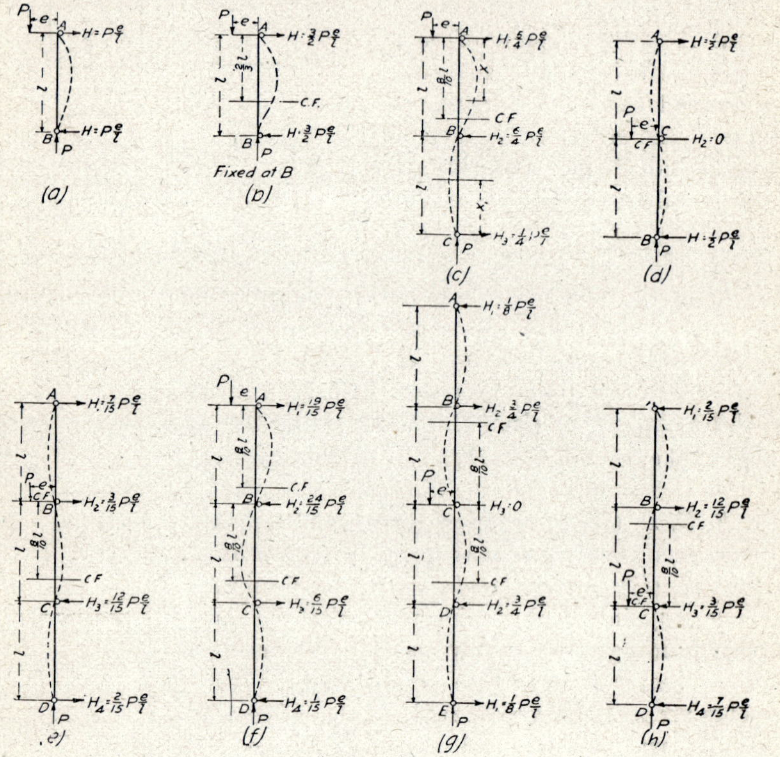

Fig. 144.

The cases of the one story column, (a) and (b), Fig. 144, are given for the sake of completeness. The other cases show that the influence of the eccentric load decreases very rapidly in the stories above or below it, and may be neglected in the third or fourth story from the load. In case (f), for example, the maximum moment in the lower story is $\frac{1}{15}Pe$ at C. The maximum moment in any case occurs at the top of the column when the load is at the top, and is Pe.

The horizontal reactions are gotten by applying the differential equation of the elastic line to each segment. In case (c), for example, there are seven quantities to determine—three reactions

Art. 114. COLUMNS IN TOWERS. 195

and four constants of integration. The conditions for determining these are, the sum of the horizontal components equals zero, the sum of the moments about B equals zero, $y=0$ when $x=0$, $y=0$ when $x=l$, $y_1=0$ when $x_1=0$, $y_1=0$ when $x_1=l$ and $\frac{dy}{dx}$ is the same for $x=l$ and $x_1=l$ excepting signs.

AB $\begin{cases} EI\dfrac{d^2y}{dx^2} = -Pe + H_1 x \\ EI\dfrac{dy}{dx} = -Pex + \frac{1}{2}H_1 x^2 + C \quad \dotfill (a) \\ EIy = -\frac{1}{2}Pex^2 + \frac{1}{6}H_1 x^3 + Cx + (C'=0) \\ C'=0 \text{ since when } x=0 \ y=0 \\ \text{since } y=0 \text{ when } x=l \\ C = \frac{1}{2}Pel - \frac{1}{6}H_1 l^2 \end{cases}$

BC $\begin{cases} EI\dfrac{d^2y_1}{dx_1^2} = H_3 x_1 \\ EI\dfrac{dy_1}{dx_1} = \frac{1}{2}H_3 x_1^2 + C_1 \quad \dotfill (a_1) \\ EIy_1 = \frac{1}{6}H_3 x_1^3 + C_1 x_1 + (C'_1=0) \\ C'_1=0 \text{ since } y_1=0 \text{ when } x_1=0 \\ \text{since } y_1=0 \text{ when } x_1=l \\ C_1 = -\frac{1}{6}H_3 l^2 \end{cases}$

Making $x=l$ in (a) and $x_1=l$ in (a_1)
$-Pel + \frac{1}{2}H_1 l^2 + \frac{1}{2}Pel - \frac{1}{6}H_1 l^2 = -\frac{1}{2}H_3 l^2 + \frac{1}{6}H_3 l^2$
$\frac{1}{3}H_1 l^2 - \frac{1}{2}Pel = -\frac{1}{3}H_3 l^2$
$M_B = 0 = Pe - H_1 l + H_3 l$ or $H_3 l = H_1 l - Pe$

Substituting this value of $H_3 l$ in the preceding equation

$$H_1 = \tfrac{5}{4} P \frac{e}{l}$$

This value in the above equation gives

$$H_3 = \tfrac{1}{4} P \frac{e}{l}$$

$$H_2 = H_1 + H_3 = \tfrac{6}{4} P \frac{e}{l}$$

For the point of contra-flexure

$$Pe - H_1 x = 0 = Pe - \tfrac{5}{4} P \frac{e}{l} x \text{ and } x = \tfrac{4}{5} l$$

Having all the external forces, the moment at any section of the column is easily gotten. When a column has several eccentric loads, the corresponding cases in Fig. 144 may be combined and the reactions added algebraically, to get the resultant reactions as shown in Fig. 145.

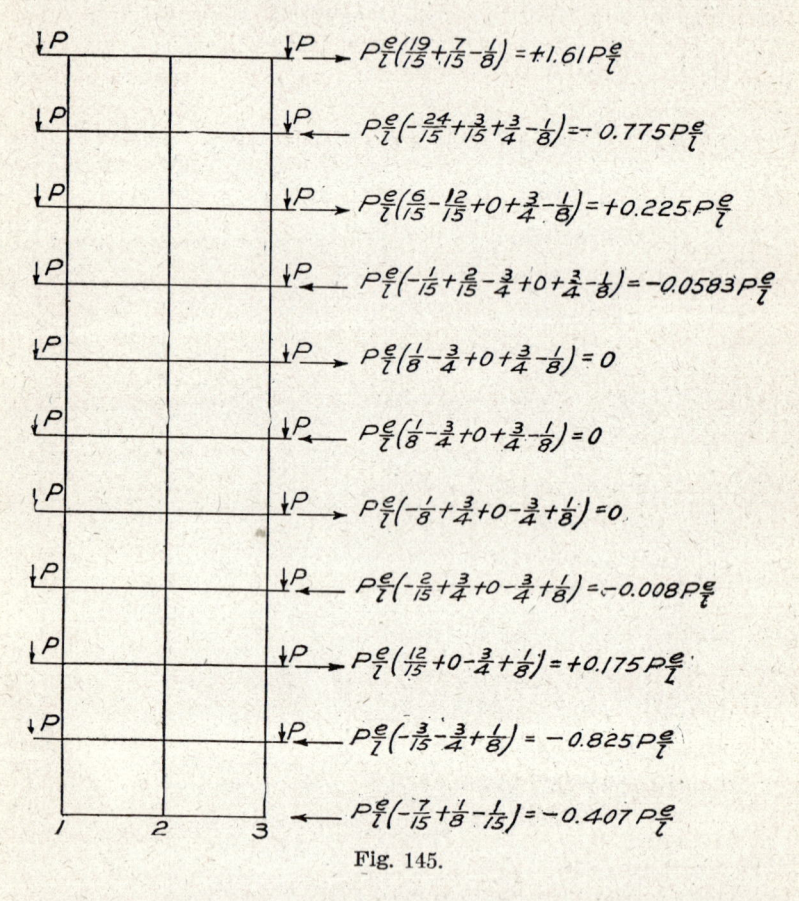

$$P\tfrac{e}{l}\left(\tfrac{19}{15}+\tfrac{7}{15}-\tfrac{1}{8}\right)=+1.61 P\tfrac{e}{l}$$

$$P\tfrac{e}{l}\left(-\tfrac{24}{15}+\tfrac{3}{15}+\tfrac{3}{4}-\tfrac{1}{8}\right)=-0.775 P\tfrac{e}{l}$$

$$P\tfrac{e}{l}\left(\tfrac{6}{15}-\tfrac{12}{15}+0+\tfrac{3}{4}-\tfrac{1}{8}\right)=+0.225 P\tfrac{e}{l}$$

$$P\tfrac{e}{l}\left(-\tfrac{1}{15}+\tfrac{2}{15}-\tfrac{3}{4}+0+\tfrac{3}{4}-\tfrac{1}{8}\right)=-0.0583 P\tfrac{e}{l}$$

$$P\tfrac{e}{l}\left(\tfrac{1}{8}-\tfrac{3}{4}+0+\tfrac{3}{4}-\tfrac{1}{8}\right)=0$$

$$P\tfrac{e}{l}\left(\tfrac{1}{8}-\tfrac{3}{4}+0+\tfrac{3}{4}-\tfrac{1}{8}\right)=0$$

$$P\tfrac{e}{l}\left(-\tfrac{1}{8}+\tfrac{3}{4}+0-\tfrac{3}{4}+\tfrac{1}{8}\right)=0$$

$$P\tfrac{e}{l}\left(-\tfrac{2}{15}+\tfrac{3}{4}+0-\tfrac{3}{4}+\tfrac{1}{8}\right)=-0.008 P\tfrac{e}{l}$$

$$P\tfrac{e}{l}\left(\tfrac{12}{15}+0-\tfrac{3}{4}+\tfrac{1}{8}\right)=+0.175 P\tfrac{e}{l}$$

$$P\tfrac{e}{l}\left(-\tfrac{3}{15}-\tfrac{3}{4}+\tfrac{1}{8}\right)=-0.825 P\tfrac{e}{l}$$

$$P\tfrac{e}{l}\left(-\tfrac{7}{15}+\tfrac{1}{8}-\tfrac{1}{15}\right)=-0.407 P\tfrac{e}{l}$$

Fig. 145.

In this very simple case, the loads and eccentricities are taken equal throughout, and the transverse members between columns are assumed to be rigid. In practice, such columns do not have a constant moment of inertia as here assumed, nor are the connections of the horizontal members pivoted. If, for example, the loads on column 3 were concentric while those on column 1 were eccentric, the problem would be statically indeterminate, and the reactions would depend on the stiffness of the columns.

The moments are a maximum at the ends of the segments, and have opposite signs above and below the points of division. The maximum moment is Pe at the top of the column. The moment at the bottom of the upper segment is $Pe - 1.61 P \dfrac{e}{l} l = -0.61 Pe$. At the top of the second segment the moment is $-0.61 Pe + Pe = +0.39\, Pe$. At the intermediate points (three stories or more from the top or bottom), the moment is $\pm \tfrac{1}{2} Pe$. This is the resultant of the opposite kinds of bending produced in any particular story by the various loads.

In high office buildings, each story is usually treated as an independent column—or rather as a block—for eccentric loads, and the moment is taken equal to Pe. These columns are usually so short that their bending, compared with the eccentricity which may be somewhat indefinite, is negligible. To get an idea of how much this bending is, consider an $8'' \times \tfrac{1}{4}''$ Z-bar column having a length of 14 ft. and carrying a load of 25,000 lbs. with an eccentricity of 6 inches. Assuming pivoted ends, equation (50) is applicable provided l is taken as half the length.

$$y_{max} = 6 \left[\sec\left(\frac{84}{2.46} \sqrt{\frac{25000}{11.3 \times 29000000}} \right) - 1 \right]$$

$= (\sec\, 17.09° - 1) = 6\,(1.046 - 1) = 0.276$ inches.

If the entire load on the column is eccentric, the bending will, of course, be much greater.[1]

115. Combinations of Buckling and Bending. When a column is subjected to a transverse load in addition to the longitudinal load, the bending due to the transverse force has more influence upon the buckling stress than that due to the longitudinal force P. The lever arm of P is due to a combination of the action of both loads. In practice, such a column is sometimes treated as a block in which the unit stress in the extreme fibre is

$$s = \frac{P}{A} + \frac{Mv_1}{I}$$

and is allowed to be as large as the working stress in tension. Of course s should not exceed the working stress given by a column

---

[1] For stresses in columns due to transverse forces, see *Wind Stresses in the Steel Frames of Office Buildings*, by W. M. Wilson and G. A. Maney, Engineering Experiment Station, University of Illinois, Bulletin No. 80.

Stresses in Tall Buildings, by Cyrus A. Melick, Bulletin No. 8, College of Engineering, Ohio State University.

formula because the accidental eccentricities, etc., may conspire to make M greater than that calculated from the deflection given by the formulas below. In practice M is usually taken as dependent upon the transverse load only, but to be exact both loads must be considered as acting simultaneously. The law of superposition is not accurate enough in some cases. Fig. 146 shows a common case for which

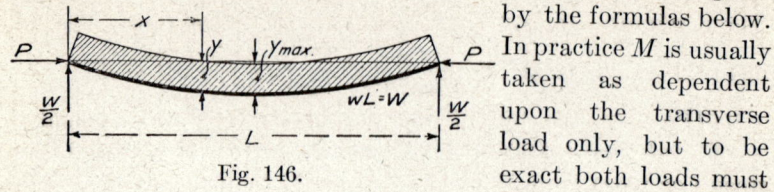

$$M_x = \tfrac{1}{2} W_x - \tfrac{1}{2} wx^2 + Py$$

Fig. 146.

The equation of the elastic line is

$$EI\frac{d^2y}{dx^2} = -M_x = \tfrac{1}{2}wx^2 - \tfrac{1}{2}wLx - Py$$

$$\theta y = \frac{w}{P}\left(\tfrac{1}{2}\theta x^2 - \tfrac{1}{2}\theta Lx - \frac{1}{\theta}\right) + C_1 \sin\theta x + C_2 \cos\theta x \qquad [1]$$

$$\theta = \sqrt{\frac{P}{EI}}$$

when $x=0$, $y=0$, hence

$$C_2 = \frac{w}{\theta P}$$

when $x=L$, $y=0$, hence

$$C_1 = \frac{w(1-\cos\theta L)}{\theta P \sin\theta L} = \frac{w}{\theta P}\tan\tfrac{1}{2}\theta L$$

Substituting the values of C_1 and C_2

$$\theta y = \frac{w}{\theta P}(\tfrac{1}{2}\theta^2 x^2 - \tfrac{1}{2}\theta^2 Lx - 1 + \cos\theta x + \tan\tfrac{1}{2}\theta L \sin\theta x)$$

When $x = \tfrac{1}{2}L$

$$\theta y_{max} = \frac{w}{\theta P}(\tfrac{1}{8}\theta^2 L^2 - \tfrac{1}{4}\theta^2 L^2 - 1 + \cos\tfrac{1}{2}\theta L + \tan\tfrac{1}{2}\theta L \sin\tfrac{1}{2}\theta L)$$

$$y_{max} = \frac{w}{\theta^2 P}(\sec\tfrac{1}{2}\theta L - 1 - \tfrac{1}{8}\theta^2 L^2) \qquad (63)$$

The equation for y_{max} may be put into a simpler form by developing $\sec \tfrac{1}{2}\theta L$ into a series in accordance with the formula

$$\sec x = 1 + \frac{x^2}{2} + \frac{5 x^4}{24} + \frac{61 x^6}{720} + \ldots \text{ etc}$$

---

[1] For the formula of integration see Johnson's "*Differential Equations,*" Art. 82, or Boyd's "*Differential Equations,*" Arts. 33 and 41.

Art. 115. COMBINATIONS OF BUCKLING AND BENDING. 199

Terms higher than those given are negligible in practical examples. Now

$$y_{max} = \frac{w}{\theta^2 P}\left(\tfrac{1}{8}\theta^2 L^2 - \tfrac{1}{8}\theta^2 L^2 + \frac{5\,\theta^4 L^4}{24\times 16} + \frac{61\,\theta^6 L^6}{720\times 6}\right)$$

$$= \frac{5\,w\,L^4}{384\,P}\left(\theta^2 + \frac{12\,\theta^4\,L^2}{120}\right) = \frac{5\,WL^3\theta^2}{384\,P}\left(1 + \frac{\theta^2 L^2}{10}\right)$$

$$= \frac{5\,W L^3}{384\,EI}(1 + \tfrac{1}{10}\theta^2 L^2) \text{ nearly}$$

$$= \frac{5\,W L^3}{384\,EI}\left(1 + \tfrac{1}{10}\frac{P L^2}{EI}\right) \tag{64}$$

It will be noted that the first term of this expression for the maximum deflection is equal to the deflection when the transverse load only is acting, and the second term is the additional deflection due to the addition of P. The second term is usually small compared with the first, and may be neglected in order to simplify the practical applications of the equation. A further simplification may be made by substituting $\tfrac{1}{8}WL = M_t =$ maximum moment due to transverse load.

$$y_{max} = \frac{5 M_t L^2}{48\,EI} \text{ approximately} \tag{65}$$

$$s_{max} = \frac{P}{A} + (M_t + P y_{max})\frac{v_1}{I} \text{ approx.}$$

Substituting the value of y_{max}

$$s_{max} = \frac{P}{A} + M_t\frac{v_1}{I}\left(1 + \frac{5\,P L^2}{48\,EI}\right) \text{ approx.} \tag{66}$$

The law of super-position of stresses holds when the last term is negligible.

Equation (66) is best solved by trial. A numerical example will illustrate the application of the above equations and the effect of the approximations.

Assume a column of 2 channels 15 in.$\times$33 lbs.$\times$360 in. long; $w = 12\tfrac{1}{2}$ lbs. per inch; $I = 625$; $A = 19.8$ sq. in. $E = 30{,}000{,}000$. $P = 180{,}000$ lbs. $W = 4{,}500$ lbs.

$$M_t = \tfrac{1}{8} WL = \tfrac{1}{8}\,4{,}500\times 360 = 202{,}500 \text{ in. lbs.}$$

$$\theta = \sqrt{\frac{P}{EI}} = \sqrt{\frac{180{,}000}{30{,}000{,}000\times 625}} = 0.0031$$

$\theta^2 = 0.0000096$

$\tfrac{1}{2}\theta L = 0.0031\times 180 = 0.558 = 32.°0$

$$\frac{P L^2}{EI} = \frac{180{,}000\times 360\times 360}{30{,}000{,}000\times 625} = 1.245$$

From equation (63)
$$y_{max} = \frac{12.5}{0.0000096 \times 180,000}\left(1.1792 - 1 - \frac{0.558 \times 0.558}{2}\right)$$
$$= \frac{12.5 \times 0.0235}{0.0000096 \times 180,000} = 0.17 \text{ inches}$$

From equation (64)
$$y_{max} = \frac{5 \times 4500 \times 360 \times 360 \times 360}{384 \times 30,000,000 \times 625}(1 + 0.1245) = 0.1645 \text{ in.}$$

From equation (65)
$$y_{max} = \frac{5 \times 202.500 \times 360 \times 360}{48 \times 30,000,000 \times 625} = 0.146 \text{ in.}$$

Equations (63) and (64) give practically the same result, while equation (65) give a close approximation.

From equation (66)
$$s_{max} = \frac{180,000}{19.8} + 202.500\frac{7.5}{625}\left(1 + \frac{5 \times 1.245}{48}\right)$$
$$= 9100 + 2750 = 11,850 \text{ lbs. per sq. in.}$$

Whether or not this is excessive depends upon the column formula used.

The case illustrated in Fig. 147 is of common occurrence in practice.

$$M_x = P_t\frac{l_2}{L}x + Py$$

$$M_{x'} = P_t\frac{l_1}{L}x + Py_1$$

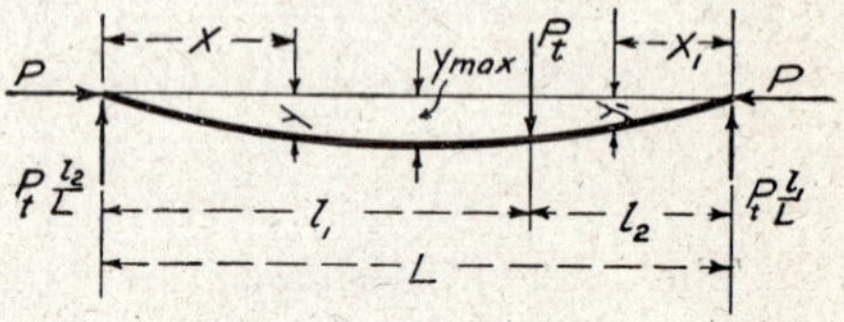

Fig. 147.

Considering first the longer segment and proceeding as in the case of Fig. 146.

$$EI\frac{d^2y}{dx^2} = -P_t\frac{l_2}{L}x - Py$$

$$y = C_1 \sin\theta x + C_2 \cos\theta x - \frac{P_t l_2}{PL}x$$

since $y = 0$ when $x = 0$, $C_2 = 0$ and the equation of the elastic line becomes

$$y = C_1 \sin\theta x - \frac{P_t l_2}{LP}x \qquad (a)$$

Similarly

$$y_1 = C'_1 \sin\theta x_1 - \frac{P_t l_1}{LP}x_1 \qquad (a_1)$$

Art. 115·COMBINATIONS OF BUCKLING AND BENDING. 201

To evaluate C_1 and C_1' we have the conditions $y=y_1$, when $x=l_1$, and $x_1=l_2$, and $\dfrac{dy}{dx}=\dfrac{dy_1}{dx_1}$ when $x=l_1$ and $x_1=l_2$.

Differentiating equations (a) and (a_1), imposing the conditions, eliminating, and reducing

$$C_1 = \frac{P_t}{\theta P} \frac{\sin l_2 \theta}{\sin(l_1\theta + l_2\theta)} \quad (b)$$

Substituting this value in equation (a), differentiating and putting $\dfrac{dy}{dx}=0$, that value of x may be found which will make $y=y_{max}$. The resulting equation is, however, too complicated for practical use. Only a slight error will be committed if it is assumed that the maximum deflection occurs at the same point that it does when the longitudinal load is not acting; and to be on the safe side, the maximum moment from transverse load may also be taken as coming at this point. Under these assumptions,

and
$$M_{max} = P_t \frac{l_2}{L} l_1 + P y_{max} \quad (67)$$

$$y = y_{max} \text{ when } x = l_1 \sqrt{\tfrac{1}{3} + \tfrac{2}{3}\frac{l_2}{l_1}} = x'$$

From (a) and (b)

$$y_{max} = \frac{P_t}{P}\left(\frac{\sin l_2\theta \sin \theta x'}{\theta \sin(l_1\theta + l_2\theta)} - \frac{l_2}{L}x'\right) \quad (68)$$

As in the case of Fig. 146, it will usually be found accurate enough to neglect that part of the deflection due to P, in which case

$$y_{max} = P_t \frac{l_1 l_2 x'}{6 EIL}\left(2 l_2 + l_1 - \frac{x'^2}{l_1}\right) \text{ approx.} \quad (69)$$

There is, however, not much difference in the ease with which equations (68) and (69) are applied.

When P_t is in the middle $l_1 = l_2 = \tfrac{1}{2}L = x'$ and equation (68) becomes,

$$y_{max} = \frac{P_t}{2 P\theta}(\tan\tfrac{1}{2}\theta L - \tfrac{1}{2}\theta L) \quad (70)$$

An equation similar to equation (64) may be gotten if $\tan \tfrac{1}{2}\theta L$ is developed according to the formula

$$\tan x = x + \tfrac{1}{3}x^3 + \tfrac{2}{15}x^5 + \ldots \text{etc.}$$

powers higher than the fifth being negligible in ordinary cases. Equation (70) becomes

$$y_{max} = \frac{P_t \theta^2 L^3}{48 P}(1 + \tfrac{1}{10}\theta^2 L^2)$$

Substituting the value of θ

$$y_{max} = \frac{P_tL^3}{48\,EI}\left(1 + \frac{1}{10}\frac{P L^2}{EI}\right) \qquad (71)$$

This equation is similar to equation (64), the first term being the deflection due to the transverse load acting alone.

If the second term in the parenthesis be neglected and $\frac{1}{4}P_tL = M_t =$ maximum moment due to transverse load, be introduced

$$y_{max} = \frac{M_tL^2}{12\,EI} \text{ approximately} \qquad (72)$$

and

$$s_{max} = \frac{P}{A} + M_t\frac{v_1}{I}\left(1 + \frac{P L^2}{12\,EI}\right) \text{ approx.} \qquad (73)$$

If the *ends* are *fixed*, the deflection will be much smaller, and values of y_{max} corresponding to the approximate values given above are sufficiently accurate. For this case equation (66) for uniform load becomes,

$$s_{max} = \frac{P}{A} + \tfrac{1}{24}WL\left(1 + \frac{P L^2}{16\,EI}\right)\frac{v_1}{I} \text{ at the middle} \qquad (74)$$

$$s_{max} = \frac{P}{A} + \tfrac{1}{12}WL\frac{v_1}{I} \text{ at the ends} \qquad (75)$$

Equation (73) for a single load at the middle becomes

$$s_{max} = \frac{P}{A} + M_t\frac{v_1}{I}\left(1 + \frac{PL^2}{24\,EI}\right) \text{ at the middle} \qquad (76)$$

$$s_{max} = \frac{P}{A} + M_t\frac{v_1}{I} \text{ at the ends} \qquad (77)$$

If but *one end* is *fixed* and the other free to turn, the approximate formula corresponding with equation (66) for uniform load is

$$s_{max} = \frac{P}{A} + \tfrac{9}{128}WL\left(1 + \frac{PL^2}{13\,EI}\right)\frac{v_1}{I} \text{ at } y_{max} \qquad (78)$$

$$s_{max} = \frac{P}{A} + \tfrac{1}{8}WL\frac{v_1}{I} \text{ at the fixed end} \qquad (79)$$

Equation (73) for a single load at the middle becomes

$$s_{max} = \frac{P}{A} + \tfrac{5}{32}PL\left(1 + \frac{PL^2}{16.7\,EI}\right)\frac{v_1}{I} \text{ at } y_{max} \qquad (80)$$

$$s_{max} = \frac{P}{A} + \tfrac{3}{16}P_tL\frac{v_1}{I} \text{ at the fixed end} \qquad (81)$$

Art. 115 COMBINATIONS OF BUCKLING AND BENDING.

If the longitudinal forces are *eccentric*, the moment is increased or decreased; the eccentricity is added to or subtracted from the maximum deflection as given in the above equations.

The column load is often made eccentric in order to neutralize the maximum bending moment due to the transverse load. Thus in the case of Fig. 146, it would only be necessary to move the forces P downward so that

$$Pe = \tfrac{1}{8}WL$$

the column then being treated as if it carried a concentric load P. On account of the moment Pe being constant throughout the whole length of the column, and the moment from the uniform load decreasing toward the ends, the column would bend in two segments, and a small excess of Pe over $\tfrac{1}{8}WL$ would cause the column to go over into single flexure—the weakest condition. It would be better to make the moment zero at about $\tfrac{1}{3}L$ from the ends so that the column would have two points of contra-flexure and be bent into three segments, but the end conditions are usually too uncertain to make this assumption safe.

If the ends are *partly fixed*, as they always are in practice, it may be impossible to counterbalance the center moment, because it may not be practical to have an eccentricity large enough to turn the ends sufficiently; besides, as the center moment decreases, the end moments increase. It might be a question of equalizing the end and center moments (see equations (74) and (75)), but the uncertainty of the end conditions would render the problem indeterminate.[1]

---

[1] See article by Prof. J. E. Boyd, in Eng. News, Vol. 57, page 404.

QUESTIONS AND PROBLEMS. CHAPTER IX.

1. A block 15 inches square is subjected to a load of 90,000 lbs., the resultant of which lies 2 inches from the center, on a line through the center parallel to one side. Find the maximum and minimum stresses.

2. In problem 1 where should the load be placed in order to have a tensile stress of 100 lbs. per sq. in. on one side? What is the maximum compressive stress in this case? At what points is the stress zero?

3. A pier 2 ft. square and 6 ft. high is subjected to a direct load of 180,000 lbs. at the center and a horizontal force at the top. What is the greatest value of this horizontal force in order that no part of the pier shall be in tension? With this force acting, what is the maximum compressive stress in the pier?

4. A cast iron block 4 in. square has its resultant load at the middle. Compare its strength with that of a block 4 in.$\times$6 in. with the load 2 in. from a 4 in. face.

5. A solid steel rod 2 in. in diameter and 5 ft. long is subjected to a compressive stress of 50,000 lbs. 0.1 in. from the center, the ends being pivoted. Find the deflection at the center and the maximum unit stress.

6. A 6 in.$\times$4 in.$\times$½ in. angle 5 ft. long is used as a column with pin ends. Find the total safe load concentrically placed, by Euler's formula, with a factor of safety of 5.
Calculate the safe load of a similar angle 10 ft. long.
Compare these results with the values obtained from Rankine's formula, with constants as given in the "Cambria" handbook.

7. Find the safe load with a factor of safety of 5, on a latticed column made of two 10 in. 20 lb. channels 6 in. back to back, toes turned out, ends fixed, and length 20 ft.

8. Find the safe load on a 12 in. 40 lb. I beam, 16 ft. long medium steel used as a column, by Rankine's formula, using the constants of the Philadelphia building laws. Solve the same by the Straight Line formula of the New York building laws. (See "Cambria.")

9. Find the safe load on a cast iron column 10 ft. long, 8 in. outside diameter, 6½ in. inside diameter, by the New York laws and the Philadelphia laws.

10. Find the safe load on a 10 in. round yellow pine column, 12 ft. long with flat ends by the New York formula.

11. What is the diameter of a solid medium steel rod 5 ft.

long, with pivoted ends, which is to carry a concentric load of 24,000 lbs.? Solve by the Philadelphia laws.

12. Select an I beam for a column 12 ft. long, pin ends, with a factor of safety of 5, using Rankine's formula with "Cambria" constants.

13. A 4 in.×4 in. wooden strut, 10 ft. long, lies in a horizontal position and carries a load of 20 lbs. per ft. of length, and is subjected to a direct compression along its axis of 1200 lbs. Find the deflection at the center and the maximum unit stress. E=1,200,000.

14. A horizontal compression member with pin ends consists of two 10 in. 20 lb. channels and two 12 in.×½ in. plates. The length is 30 ft. and the webs of the channels are vertical. The direct compression is 80,000 lbs. and there is a concentrated load of 4000 lbs. at the middle. Find the deflection and maximum unit stress.

CHAPTER X.

ROOF TRUSSES.

116. Roof Construction. Where trusses are used to support the roofs of buildings they are usually spaced from 10 to 20 ft. apart and receive their load from beams called *purlins*, which rest directly on the top chords of the trusses. The roof covering is carried by the purlins.

The trusses may either rest on walls or on columns at the sides of the building. When the trusses are supported on masonry walls, provision for the expansion and contraction of the trusses due to temperature changes must be made. Otherwise these changes would either crack the walls or produce excessive temperature stresses in the trusses. When the trusses are supported on columns they are usually fastened rigidly to the tops of the columns, and the movements due to temperature changes are taken up by the elasticity of the columns, producing bending stresses in them.

The loads from the roof are more or less uniformly distributed along the top chords or *rafters* of the roof trusses, and in calculating the stresses in the trusses are assumed to be concentrated at the upper panel points as shown in Figs. 50 and 53. This assumption gives the stresses with sufficient accuracy, but in designing the top chord or rafter the bending due to the purlins not coming exactly at the panel points must be taken into account. The rafter is usually subjected to both direct stress and bending stresses (115).

117. Truss Elements. The simplest truss is one made of three members in the form of a triangle as shown in Fig. 48, Art. 50.

Such a truss can not be deformed without changing the length of its members, that is, without inducing stresses in them. It is, therefore, a stable structure under loads if properly designed (2).

Fig. 148 shows a truss which may be deformed without changing the lengths of the sides of the rectangle *CDEF*, and is, therefore, not a stable structure unless the joints are so constructed as to offer sufficient resistance. In properly constructed trusses, it is assumed that the joints do not offer enough resist-

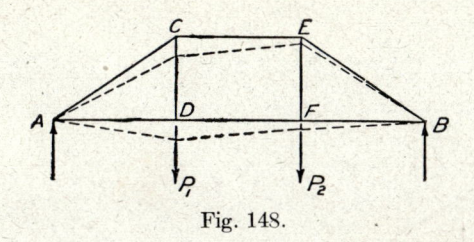

Fig. 148.

ance to the small changes of angles between members to affect the stresses in them.

If there were a diagonal member DE (in tension) or CF (in compression), the truss would be stable, because it would be composed of triangles. *Every truss, therefore, in order to be a stable structure, should be an assemblage of triangles.* Any deformation of such a truss will be accompanied by axial stresses, that is, direct tension and compression.

118. Types of Roof Trusses. Roof trusses may be made in a great variety of forms, varying with the character of the building, the clearance requirements and the materials of construction. Fig. 149 shows some common types used in mill building construction. The lower chords are usually horizontal. The number of panels depends upon the purlin spacing, the span length, and the loads.

For timber construction, the *Howe truss*, Fig. 149 (d), or the *quadrangular truss*, Fig. 149 (h), is best adapted. All of the members may be made of timber except the verticals, which are made of steel rods with screw ends, nuts, and washers.

The eight-panel *Fink truss*, Fig. 149 (f), is by far the commonest in use; it may be made into a sixteen-panel truss by subtrussing each panel.

The triangular truss, Fig. 149 (i), is commonly used for flat roofs.

Stresses in roof trusses are usually gotten graphically, but since, for a given pitch of roof, all roof trusses of a certain type are similar figures, whatever the span may be, the stresses will be proportional to the panel loads. A table of stresses due to one-pound panel loads will, therefore, answer for all spans of

208   TYPES OF ROOF TRUSSES.   Art. 118.

the same type and pitch by simply multiplying them by the panel load. Such tables will be found in many structural handbooks.

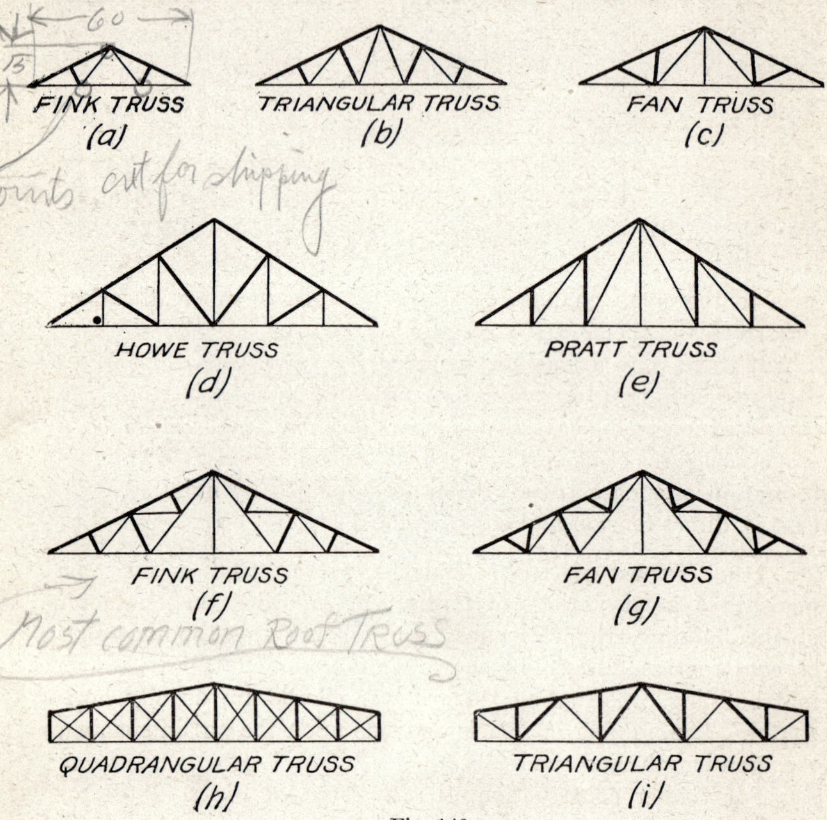

FINK TRUSS (a)
TRIANGULAR TRUSS (b)
FAN TRUSS (c)
HOWE TRUSS (d)
PRATT TRUSS (e)
FINK TRUSS (f)
FAN TRUSS (g)
QUADRANGULAR TRUSS (h)
TRIANGULAR TRUSS (i)

Fig. 149.

A few of the more unusual types of roof trusses are shown in Fig. 150. *Three-hinged arches* are frequently used for exposition buildings, auditoriums, drill halls, etc., where it is desirable to have a large floor space unobstructed by columns. The *scissors truss* is used for buildings with steep roofs where the trusses are exposed on the interior, such as churches. Here the trusses are usually made of timber except the vertical rod in the middle. The *cantilever trusses* are used for grand stand roofs and sometimes for freight houses where the cantilever portion covers the loading platform.

The *saw-tooth roof* was invented especially for the weaving

Art. 118. TYPES OF ROOF TRUSSES. 209

sheds of the New England mills, but has come to be used extensively for shops of all kinds. The steep sides of the trusses are placed to face the north, and this side of the roof is made of glass. The slope of the steep side is such that the direct rays of the sun will not strike the glass. This gives a very light interior for the building without the objection of direct sunlight. If there is objection to having columns in the building at points m and n, a top chord member opq (shown dotted)

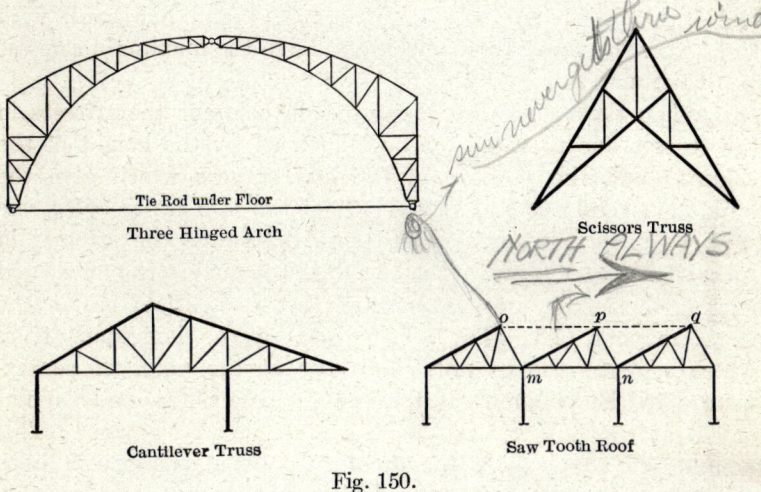

Fig. 150.

Three Hinged Arch — Tie Rod under Floor
Scissors Truss
Cantilever Truss
Saw Tooth Roof

may be put in. This top chord member will be exposed above the roof.

119. Stresses in Roof Trusses. Great refinement is not necessary in calculating the stresses in roof trusses, as the loads which they have to carry cannot be accurately determined. The stresses should usually be calculated for the following conditions of loading:

  I. Dead Load.
 II. Snow Load on the Whole Roof.
III. Snow Load on Half the Roof.
 IV. Live Load (if any).
  V. Wind from the Right.
 VI. Wind from the Left.

The *dead load* includes the weight of the structure itself with the roof covering and all fixed loads. *live load* would be the weight of a traveling crane inside the building and supported by the roof trusses, or any movable loads which might come on the trusses.

In adding the stresses found from the above loadings it must be borne in mind that the maximum wind and snow could not be acting on the same side of the roof at the same time. The wind would blow the snow off.

For the common types of trusses shown in Fig. 149, when supported with one end free to move longitudinally, it will be found that the combination of dead load and live load, with snow over the whole roof, will usually give the maximum stresses in all the members.

When the trusses are supported on columns the stresses in the trusses due to wind will be influenced by the height of the columns and the position of the knee braces which give the building lateral stability. Fig. 151 shows two types of trusses supported by columns. In order to determine the stresses in these trusses graphically, the imaginary members shown dotted outside the columns are added and the stresses laid out in the usual manner (54). The lower point of the imaginary truss which replaces the column should be at the point of contraflexure in the column. If the columns are considered as pin-ended at the bottom, this point will be at the bottom. This assumption would give the greatest possible stresses in both the trusses and the columns. The replacing of the columns by the imaginary members will not affect the stresses in the truss. The stresses in the columns must be analyzed algebraically (115). (See Chapter XIV.)

The stresses will now be determined for the truss shown in Fig. 151 (*a*) with the data given in Fig. 152. The stress

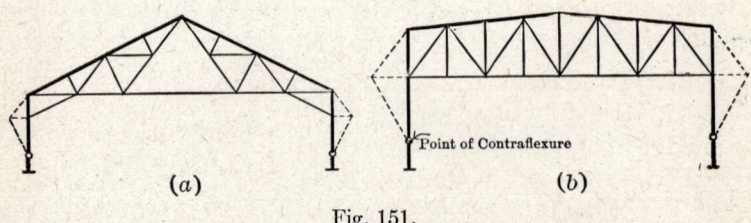

Fig. 151.

diagrams for dead load and for full snow load are exactly similar to that shown in Fig. 53. One diagram will answer for both of these, the stresses being proportional to the panel loads. The

Art. 110. STRESSES IN ROOF TRUSSES. 211

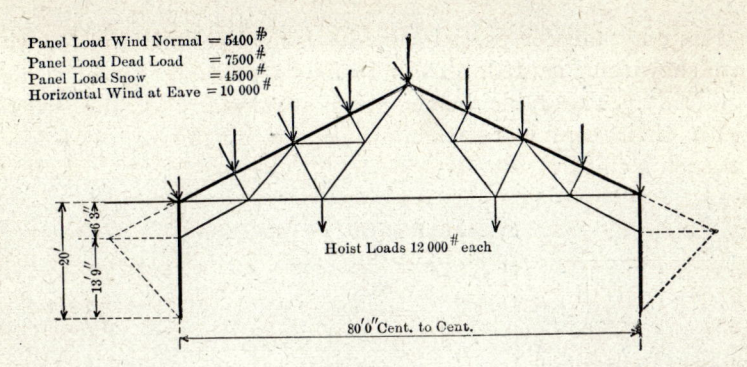

Panel Load Wind Normal = 5400 #
Panel Load Dead Load = 7500 #
Panel Load Snow = 4500 #
Horizontal Wind at Eave = 10 000 #

Hoist Loads 12 000 # each

Fig. 152.

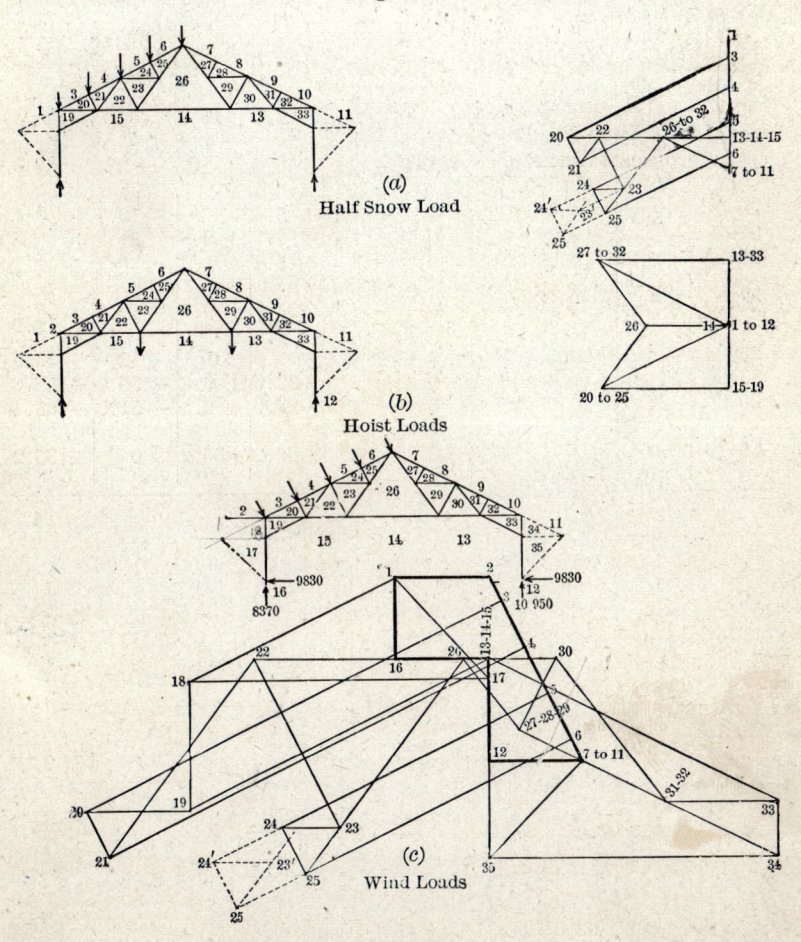

(a) Half Snow Load

(b) Hoist Loads

(c) Wind Loads

Fig. 153.

stress diagrams for partial snow load, for live load and for wind are shown in Fig. 153. The reactions are usually obtained algebraically. The table below gives a summary of the stresses with their combinations, showing the maximum total stress in each member.

SUMMARY OF STRESSES.

Member.	Dead Load.	Full Snow.	Live Load.	Snow. R. Half.	Snow. L. Half.	Wind. Left.	Wind. Right.	DL+LL +Snow	DL+LL +S+W
3–20	+58.7	+35.2	+26.8	+10.0	+25.2	+48.5	−10.7	+120.7	+144.0
4–21	+55.4	+33.2	+26.8	+10.0	+23.2	+48.5	−10.7	+115.4	+140.7
5–24	+52.0	+31.2	+26.8	+10.0	+21.2	+29.8	+ 6.9	+110.0	+118.6
6–25	+48.6	+29.2	+26.8	+10.0	+19.2	+29.8	+ 6.9	+104.6	+115.2
19–20	−52.5	−31.5	−24.0	− 9.0	−22.5	−11.7	−12.1	−108.0	−111.1
15–22	−45.0	−27.0	−24.0	− 9.0	−18.0	−24.2	+ 7.6	− 96.0	−102.2
14–26	−30.0	−18.0	−15.0	− 9.0	− 9.0	− 2.2	− 2.2	− 63.0	− 56.2
20–21	+ 6.7	+ 4.0	0	0	+ 4.0	+ 5.4	0	+ 10.7	+ 12.1
22–23	+13.3	+ 8.0	0	0	+ 8.0	+19.7	− 8.8	+ 21.3	+ 33.0
24–25	+ 6.7	+ 4.0	0	0	+ 4.0	+ 5.4	0	+ 10.7	+ 12.1
21–22	− 7.5	− 4.5	0	0	− 4.5	−25.7	+19.7	− 12.0	− 33.2 / + 12.2
23–24	− 7.5	− 4.5	0	0	− 4.5	− 6.0	0	− 12.0	− 13.5
23–26	−15.0	− 9.0	−15.0	0	− 9.0	−22.0	+ 9.8	− 39.0	− 52.0
25–26	−22.5	−13.5	−15.0	0	−13.5	−27.9	+ 9.8	− 51.0	− 65.4
15–19	0	0	0	0	0	−35.2	+35.2	0	± 35.2

QUESTIONS AND PROBLEMS. CHAPTER X.

1. What is a truss element? What is a truss?

2. What assumption with regard to the joints of a truss is made in calculating the stresses?

3. Make a sketch of some roof truss in your vicinity, showing the manner of attaching the purlins and the points of application of the loads to the truss. Are there any live loads carried by the truss? Are the roof loads applied at the panel points?

4. Consult Kidder's "Architects and Builders' Pocket-Book," and Ketchum's "Structural Engineer's Handbook," for examples of roof trusses and roof construction.

5. What are purlins? Rafters? Kneebraces?

6. In what way do the stresses in a rafter usually differ from those in the other members of a roof truss? In a knee brace?

7. What types of trusses are commonly used for steel mill buildings? For drill halls? For churches? For timber construction? For flat roofs? For shops where columns are not objectionable?

8. How may the saw-tooth roof be modified to eliminate intermediate columns?

9. How are the stresses in roof trusses usually determined?

10. For what different loadings are the stresses in roof trusses calculated? What combinations of these loadings are possible?

11. How is lateral stability secured when the trusses are supported on columns?

12. Determine the stresses in the truss of Fig. 151 (*b*) for the following data:

Span 60 ft. Depth at center, 12 ft. Depth at eaves, 8 ft. Height to bottom chord, 20 ft. Dead load panel load, 10000 lbs. Snow load panel load 5000 lbs. Horizontal wind load at eaves, 12000 lbs.

CHAPTER XI.

BRIDGE TRUSSES.

120. Construction. Bridge trusses differ from roof trusses in form and in the character of the loads which they have to carry. In the past, in America, the principal consideration in selecting types of bridge trusses has been economy in first cost. Little attention was given to the æsthetic side of the question. But recently more thought has been given to this subject, especially for bridges in the more thickly populated districts of our country. Frequently, a structure of pleasing outline and proportion can be constructed which will cost no more than some ungainly structure which will forever be an eyesore.

The primary loads on bridge trusses are moving loads, and these cause the stresses in certain members to reverse and render certain forms of truss desirable for the usual materials of construction.

The loads on bridge trusses are carried to the panel points by the floor joists or stringers, so that in all except a few old types now out of date, no loads are appiled to the trusses between the panel points. In the truss of Fig. 148, unequal loads at D and F are produced in connection with the dead load when the live load covers a part of the span. As shown, a diagonal member DE would be in tension, but if the load P_2 were greater than P_1, a diagonal member CF would be in tension.

Members made of eyebars or rods have practically no stiffness and can not, therefore, carry any compressive stress. If such members are used for the above diagonals, there will be two in the panel; one acts when P_1 is the greater load, and the other when P_2 is the greater. Both diagonals can not be in action at the same time and, therefore, the truss is always an assemblage of triangles. If both diagonals were made stiff members so that

Art. 120.   CONSTRUCTION.   215

they could carry compression, one could not change in length without affecting the other, and the stresses would be statically indeterminate (42).

Fig. 154 shows a simple truss supported at both ends. The top chord is in compression just as the top flange of a girder,

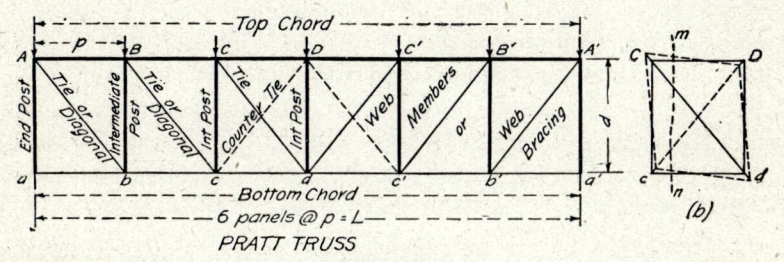

Fig. 154.

similarly supported, is in compression. In like manner does the bottom chord compare with the bottom flange of a girder. The web members resist the shear by direct tension and compression, the diagonal members being all tension members and the vertical members being in compression. The chord members can resist no part of the vertical shear since they have no vertical components. If one or both chords were inclined, they would carry a part of the shear. The chords resist all of the bending moment.

Panels are the longitudinal divisions of a truss, formed by the web members.

Panel points are the centers of the joints where the web members are attached to the chords.

A *panel length* is the distance between panel points usually measured horizontally.

Chord Members are the upper and lower members of a truss.

A *main tie* is a web member in tension under full load. For a certain position of the live load its stress may reduce to zero.

A *counter tie* is a diagonal web member in tension under certain *partial* loads only. Counter ties are not necessary in trusses carrying dead loads only. If, in Fig. 154, a continuous live load moves across the bridge from right to left, it tends to distort the rectangle $CDdc$ so as to produce tension in the main tie, and there will be no stress in the counter tie. But if the live load moves from the left to the right, the distortion will be in the opposite direction until the head of the live load passes a certain point in the bridge. This distortion and that due to the dead load are of opposite kind and may neutralize each other; in which case there will be no shear in the panel, and no diagonal member will be required. If the live load is great enough, compared with the dead load, the distortion will become such as to produce tension in the counter tie. As the live load moves to the right, the stress in the tie decreases and becomes zero; then the stress in the counter tie increases, reaches a maximum and decreases to zero; then the stress in the tie increases until the left end of the live load stands somewhere in the panel in question.

No counter ties are required in those panels where there is no possibility of a reversal of stress, or where the live load negative shear is always less than the dead load positive shear.

A *counter brace* is a diagonal web member capable of taking compression and subject to alternating stresses of tension and compression (as cD Fig. 167), or subject only to compression under partial loading (as the dotted diagonals in Fig. 160). If in Fig. 154 the counter tie were omitted and Cd were made a compression member, it would be a counter brace, and its stress would reverse during the passage of the live load. If the counter brace happens to be so attached that it can take no tension, as is the case in a Howe Truss (Fig. 160), it gets stress only under certain partial loads just as a counter tie does, but the stress is of opposite kind.

It is the custom to use counter ties in some types of trusses, and counter braces in others. In some types, counter ties can not be used.

Counter ties are made adjustable in length so that an *initial stress* may be put into them. The initial stress in the counter tie produces the same initial stress in the main tie, as is evident if the distortion of the panel is considered. Stresses will also be induced in the posts and chords of the panel, but no other members of the truss will be effected. These stresses, whose magnetude are usually much in doubt, may usually be neglected as the following consideration will show. Their purpose is to prevent shock when the live load passes over the structure and the stresses change from one diagonal to the other in a panel.

Fig. 154 (*b*) represents the panel $CDdc$. When the counter tie cD is shortened, the tendency is to deform the panel as shown by the dotted lines. This deformation is resisted by the main tie and consequently a tensile stress is set up in it. Take a section mn

through the panel, and if there are no other stresses in the diagonals than the initial stresses, from Σ vertical Components$=0$ we have:

The Vert. Comp. of the initial stress in $cD=$

The Vert. Comp. of the initial stress in Cd; therefore as the inclinations of the members are equal, the initial stresses in them are equal.

Now suppose that a load is put on the bridge in such a position that it would produce a tensile stress in cD. This stress would elongate cD which would cause the dotted parallelogram to approach its original shape of zero stress and thus relieve the initial stress in Cd.

Let the initial stress in the diagonals be represented by T. From Hooke's Law (11) that stress is proportional to deformation, it will require a *total* stress of $2T$ in cD to cause the parallelogram to resume its original rectangular shape. But when the figure is a rectangle, the stress in Cd is zero and, taking the section mn again and Σ Vert. Comp.$=0$.

Vert. Comp. of stress in $cD=$ shear in the panel.

Therefore when the shear in the panel is sufficient to produce a tensile stress in cD equal to twice the initial stress, the initial stress in Cd is reduced to zero and all the initial stresses disappear. Any further increase of stress in cD will further elongate that diagonal, and consequently buckle the diagonal Cd, as neither of the diagonals are capable of taking compression. If the stress in cD, due to the load, is less than $2T$, by Hooke's Law, one half is taken up in relieving stress in Cd and the other half is added to the initial stress in cD.

A *post* or *brace* is a web member in compression when the bridge is fully loaded. When the chords are not parallel, there may be tension in some of the intermediate posts and a reversal of stress when the live load comes on. Such reversals are undesirable.

121. Classification of Trusses. Trusses may be classified in many different ways. So far as supports are concerned, they may be classified just as solid beams are classified (66). The material of which they are made is usually structural steel. Sometimes they are made of timber or a combination of timber and iron. Otherwise they may be classified as follows:

    As to uses.
        Bridge trusses.
        Roof trusses.
        Cranes.
    As to connections at the joints.
        Pin-connected trusses.
        Riveted trusses.
    As to chords.
        Trusses with parallel chords.
        Trusses with inclined chords.
    As to web bracing.
        Trusses with triangular web bracing.
        Trusses with quadrangular web bracing.
        Trusses with sub-trussed web bracing.
        Trusses with sub-divided web bracing.
        Trusses with multiple systems of web bracing.
        Trusses with combined systems of web bracing.

When a bridge truss is deep enough to permit overhead bracing between trusses, it is called a *high truss*. A *low truss* is not deep enough to permit overhead bracing and is often called a *pony truss*. (Figs. 165 and 166.)

When the trusses of a bridge support the floor near the lower chord, the bridge is a *through bridge*; if the floor is supported near the upper chord, it is a *deck bridge*; and if between the chords, it is a *half-deck bridge*.

Figs. 155 to 174 show bridge trusses of various types. These are explained below in detail. In these figures, heavy lines denote compression members; light lines, tension members; heavy dotted lines, counter braces; and light dotted lines, counter ties.

Any type of truss may, in general, be modified so as to be supported at the top or bottom chord, and may carry loads at both chords.

122. Bridge Trusses Now Out of Date. Some notable wooden bridges were built in this country late in the eighteenth and early in the nineteenth century. The building of iron bridges began in 1840, the compression members being of cast iron and the tension members of wrought iron. About 1863 the

Art. 122. BRIDGE TRUSSES NOW OUT OF DATE. 219

first bridge having all members of wrought iron was built, and cast iron was gradually abandoned. About 1870 steel began to be used, and wrought iron went out of use about 1890.[1]

The early bridge builders were very successful in view of the fact that they knew nothing about stresses in trusses. To Mr. Squire Whipple belongs the credit of having first analyzed the stresses in a truss. In a small book which is published at Utica, New York, in 1847, he gave the correct analysis of bridge stresses and the details of design for a Wipple truss bridge (Fig. 159). In this design, pin connections were first introduced. Mr. Whipple not only gave, in his small book, much sound theory and good practice, but built many bridges of the Whipple and bow-string types.

The following are the most important of the older types of trusses; for others, and for an account of the evolution of the modern truss, reference should be made to the works cited in the foot note below.

BOLLMAN TRUSS
Fig. 155.

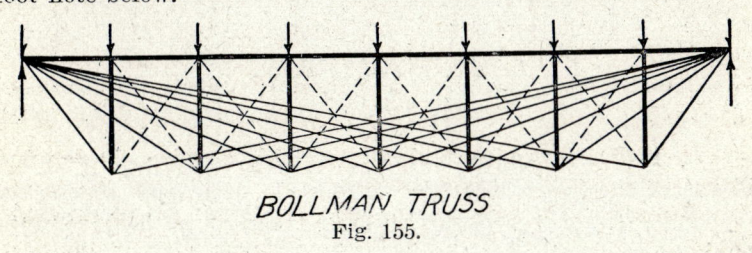

Fig. 155 shows the *Bollman truss*, which was patented about 1850 and introduced as an "iron suspension truss bridge." Each

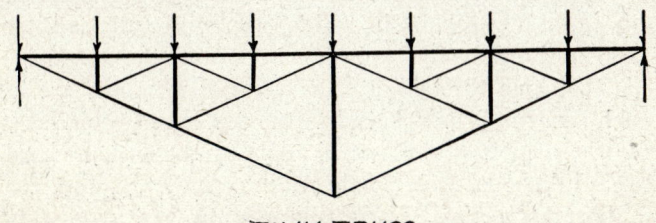

FINK TRUSS
Fig. 156.

---

[1] For historical data concerning American bridge building, see a paper by C. C. Schneider, Pres. Am. Soc. C. E., in the Engineering Record, Vol. LI, p. 707. Also see paper by Theo. Cooper, M. Am. Soc. C. E., in Trans. Am. Soc. C. E., Vol. XXI, p. 1; Johnson's *Modern Framed Structures* Chapt. I, and Merriman and Jacoby's *Roofs and Bridges*, Part I, Chapter V, sixth Edition.

panel load is separately suspended by ties running to the supports. There is no bottom chord and the diagonal members shown dotted take no calculable stress but serve to stiffen the truss.

The *Fink truss* was introduced about the same time as the Bollman. It was invented by Albert Fink, an assistant engineer on the Baltimore & Ohio Railroad. Fig. 156 shows the principle upon which this truss was built. The path of each panel load is easily followed; only the middle panel load is carried directly to the supports; parts of the other panel loads also go over the same path. For long spans, the truss was usually built so that about half of the posts were of the same length. The Fink truss necessarily had an even number of panels. The stresses may be easily calculated.

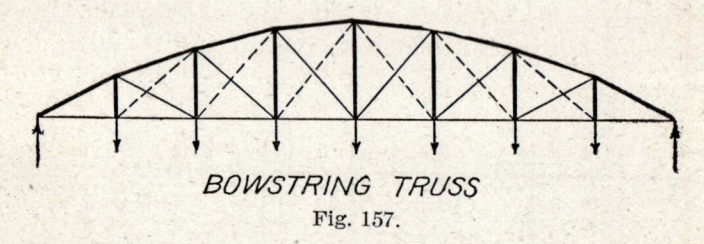

BOWSTRING TRUSS
Fig. 157.

In 1840 Mr. Squire Whipple built his first iron bridge and it was of the *bow-string type* (Fig. 157). He pointed out the economic advantages of this style of truss in the book referred to above. Since the bending moment decreases towards the ends, the chord stresses may be made constant by varying the depth in a certain way. The upper and end panel points were usually made to lie on a parabola, in which case, with full load, there is no stress in the diagonal web members, and the stress in each chord is the same throughout; the vertical members are in tension, each carrying a panel load to the top chord, which acts like an arch whose horizontal thrust is taken by the bottom chord. In this case all diagonal web members are counter ties and, for partial loading, the verticals are in compression.

If the upper joints lie above a parabola through the ends, the counter ties will be as shown in Fig. 157; if they lie below, the ties and counter ties will have the reverse directions.

The stresses in a bowstring truss are easily calculated. Under full load, and with a parabolic truss, the upper chord resists all the shear in each panel. It is to be noted that the tie and counter tie, in a panel, do not have the same inclination.

Art. 122.   BRIDGE TRUSSES NOW OUT OF DATE.   221

Many bridges with bowstring trusses of short span were built. In modern bridges, the curved top chord is used only for long spans and only the intermediate panel points are located on the curve, the end posts being given a steeper inclination than in the bowstring truss.

A few *double-bowstring* or *lenticular trusses* have been built in this country. In this type, both the upper and lower panel points are on curves. A notable example is the Smithfield Street bridge over the Monongahela River at Pittsburgh, consisting of two spans of 360 feet each.

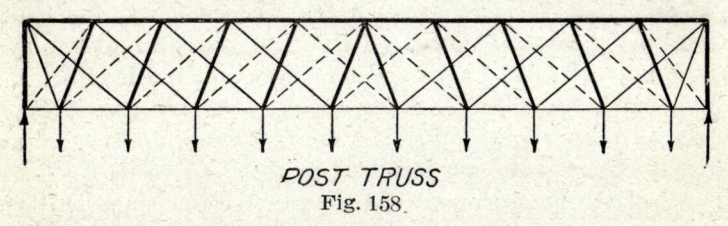

POST TRUSS
Fig. 158.

Mr. S. S. Post invented a bridge in which the trusses were of the style shown in Fig. 158. In 1865 he built the first iron bridge of this type, the top chord being of cast iron.

The *Post truss* has a double system of web bracing. The braces have a horizontal projection of one half panel length, and the main ties (except the end ones) of a panel and a half. It was built with a counter tie in each panel. The stresses are statically indeterminate. For full load, the two systems may be assumed to act independently, but for partial loads, the counter ties on one side of the middle act as a single system, while the main ties on the other side act as a double system.

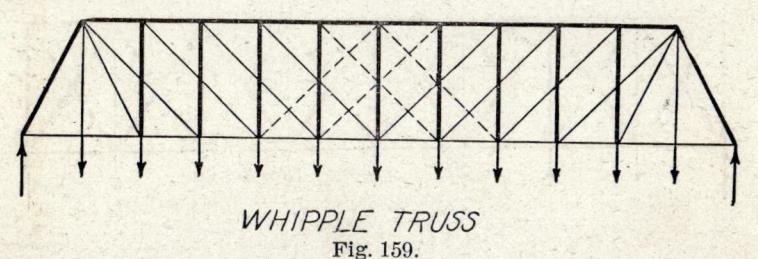

WHIPPLE TRUSS
Fig. 159.

In 1852-3 Mr. Squire Whipple built the first *Whipple-truss* bridge on the Rensselaer and Saratoga Railroad. It was replaced in 1883 because it was designed for a much smaller load than it was then carrying.

The Whipple truss (Fig. 159) is called a *double intersection* truss because it has two systems of web bracing. It is a combination of two Pratt trusses (Fig. 161) with common chords. The object was to avoid long panels and the consequent expensive floor system, and at the same time, to have an economic inclination for the diagonal web members. It was used for long spans and many examples of it are still to be seen, particularly in highway bridges. It was displaced by the Baltimore type of truss. See Figs. 163 and 164.

The stresses are statically indeterminate, but it is the practice to assume that the two systems act independently, the chord stresses being added together (134). The division into two systems is not the same for partial loading as for full loading, and certain ambiguities arise. Since about 1890 very few Whipple trusses have been built. The simpler trusses, whose stresses are statically determinate, are preferred by most engineers.

All of the preceding trusses were of the pin-connected type although, usually, there were some joints with special details. The eyebar was not introduced until 1861.

123. Modern Bridge Trusses. The *Howe truss* was patented by William Howe in 1840. This truss has been used extensively, particularly in the first construction of railways. It is still being used in sections of the country where timber is cheap and economy in first cost is important. Many Howe truss bridges have been replaced by steel bridges.

In the Howe truss the diagonal members are in compression and the vertical members in tension. (See Fig. 160.) All members except the vertical tension members are made of timber. The

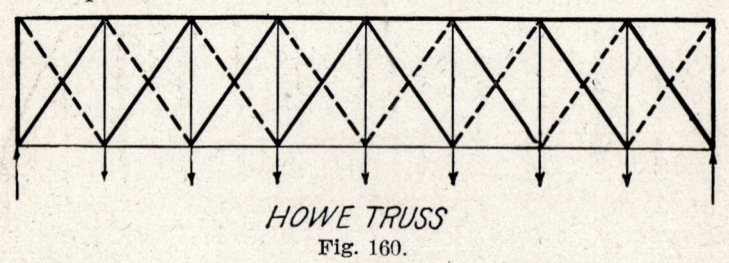

HOWE TRUSS
Fig. 160.

vertical tension members are wrought iron rods with screw ends; their use, with cast iron angle blocks at the joints, against which the diagonal members abut, permits simple and satisfactory details with the minimum amount of metal. The main diagonals are made of two sticks of timber between which the counter braces pass. The chords are made of uniform section throughout the length of the bridge. The panels are short and the loaded chord is made deeper than the other chord, because it carries the floor and acts as a beam in addition to taking the direct stress. Counter braces are used in each panel.

The Howe truss bridge is sometimes called a combination bridge, but this designation belongs more properly to those bridges in which all tension members are made of iron or steel.[1]

The *Pratt truss,* which is shown with inclined end posts in Fig. 161 and with vertical end posts in Fig. 154, was patented

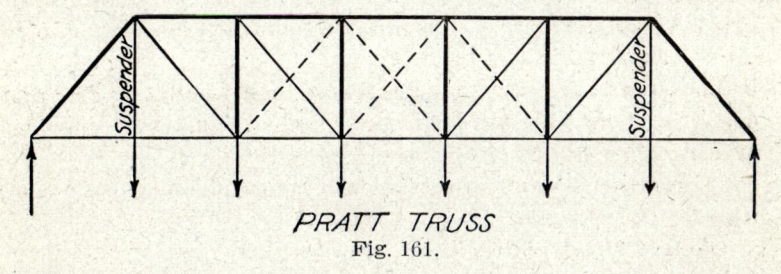

PRATT TRUSS
Fig. 161.

in 1844. It differs from the Howe truss in that the main diagonal members have an opposite inclination and are, therefore, in tension while the vertical members (except the suspenders) are in compression. At first, only the ties were made of iron, and it was not popular on account of requiring more of this expensive material than the Howe truss. The compression members are shorter than in the Howe truss and, therefore, require less material, but this was unimportant until iron bridges were introduced. On account of its simplicity, the Pratt truss has become by far the commonest type of bridge truss in this country. Its characteristic is diagonal tension and vertical compression members.

As the stress in the top chord increases toward the middle, and since it is made of the same outer dimensions in each panel, it becomes difficult, in *long spans,* for several practical reasons, to avoid an excess of material in the end panels, unless the depth of the truss varies, so as to make the stresses in the panels more nearly equal. Fig. 162 shows a form often used and is commonly called a *camel-back* truss. The appearance is much enhanced if all the joints of the top chord are put on a regular curve.

---

[1] For details of modern Howe truss bridges, see Johnson's *Modern Framed Structures,* Chapter XXIII.

The web bracing may be of either the Warren or the Pratt type.

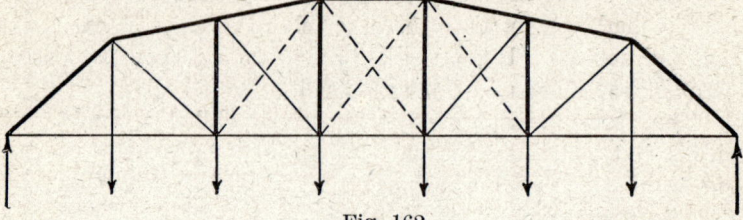

Fig. 162.

As the span increases, economic construction requires the depth of the truss to increase. The panel length must also increase if an economical inclination of the diagonal members is to be had; but there is a limit also to the panel length. This difficulty was avoided in the Whipple truss by running the diagonals over two panels. The same object is accomplished by putting a sub-truss in each panel of a Pratt truss to carry every other panel load to the main truss.

This forms the *Baltimore truss* which was introduced in 1871. (Fig. 163.) It is a sub-trussed Pratt truss in which the stresses are statically determinate.

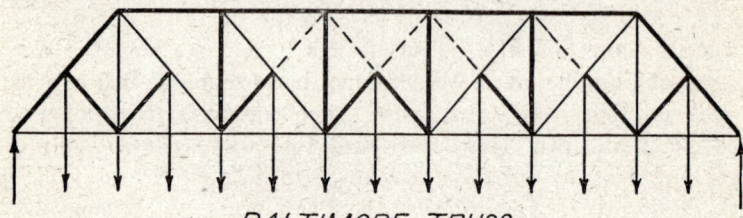

BALTIMORE TRUSS
Fig. 163.

As in the case of the Pratt truss, it is economical to have a curved upper chord for very long spans as shown in Fig. 164, and then it is called the *Pettit truss*.

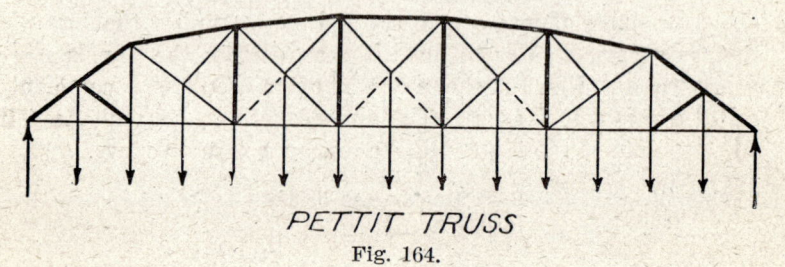

PETTIT TRUSS
Fig. 164.

In either case the sub-trussing may be of the style shown in Fig. 163 or in Fig. 164, and other members may be introduced simply to hold the compression members at the middle.

The two panels at each end are sometimes made as in Fig. 162 in order that the end posts may not have such a flat inclination; this makes a combination of Pratt and Baltimore web bracing.

For short-span highway bridges, the Pratt truss is often modified as shown in Fig. 165. This truss is frequently made with end posts having an inclination of 45 degrees; when the end panels of the top chord are half as long as the intermediate panels, it is called a *half-hip truss*.

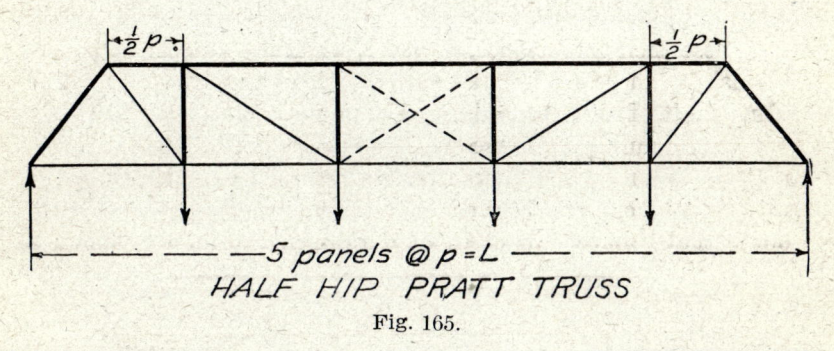

HALF HIP PRATT TRUSS
Fig. 165.

Fig. 165 shows a *triangular* or *Warren truss*. The use of this style of triangular truss is now confined mostly to small highway

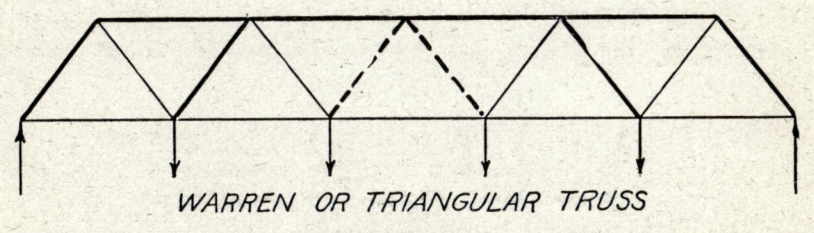

WARREN OR TRIANGULAR TRUSS
Fig. 166.

bridges with floor beams attached below the bottom chord. For longer spans, the *sub-divided Warren truss*, as shown in Fig. 167, is used, and the floor beams are attached to the vertical members above the bottom chord. The suspender evidently carries a single panel load. The other vertical members carry no stress above the floor-beams except that part of the dead load which acts at the upper joints.

SUB-DIVIDED WARREN TRUSS
Fig. 167.

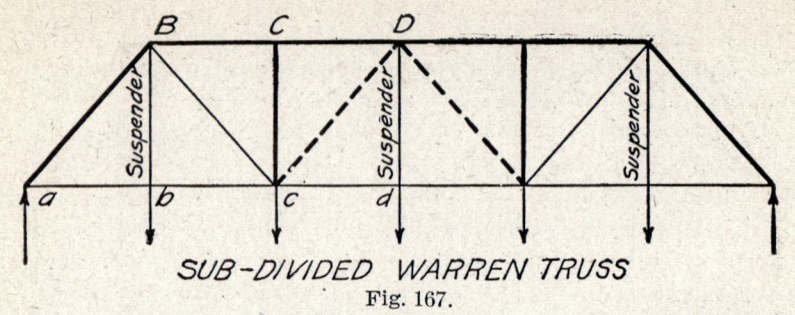

In the Warren truss the compression members of the web are longer than in the Pratt truss, and some of them are subject to alternating stresses of tension and compression. These disadvantages lose their importance, however, when the number of panels is small, as there are but few such members (see Fig. 167). The usual limit of span for this style of truss is about 150 feet.

While multiple intersection trusses are not in general favor, multiple intersection Warren trusses are used on several lines of railways on account of the severe treatment they will stand, without actual collapse, in cases of derailment. Fig. 168 shows a

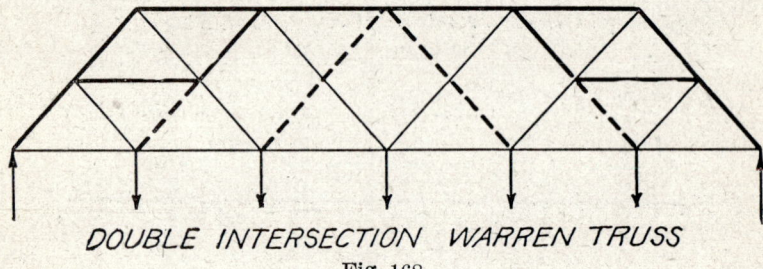

DOUBLE INTERSECTION WARREN TRUSS
Fig. 168.

double intersection Warren truss; this is sometimes sub-trussed by inserting short suspenders from the intersections of the diagonals to the lower chord. The stresses are calculated upon the assumption that the two systems act independently (135.)

Fig. 169 shows a combination of four trusses with the necessary modifications at the ends to allow inclined end posts. The four systems are assumed to act independently.

The term "*lattice girder*" is commonly applied to either the single or multiple intersection Warren truss when the connections are riveted; but it would be more appropriate to designate trusses, with more than two systems of web bracing, as lattice trusses. In such trusses—when the web members are connected

Art. 123.   MODERN BRIDGE TRUSSES.   227

QUADRUPLE INTERSECTION WARREN TRUSS

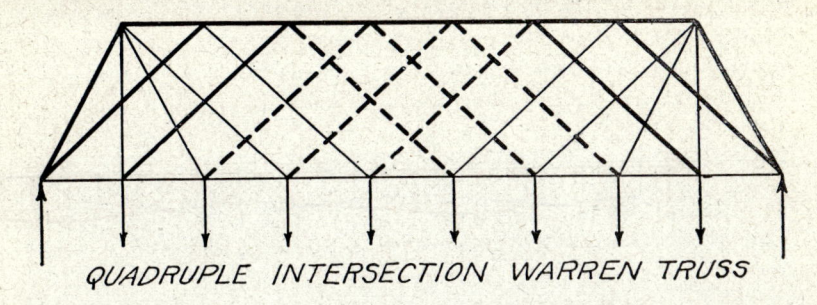

Fig. 169.

together at their intersections—it is usually assumed that the web members, cut by any cross section, take equal amounts of the shear.

The *Town lattice truss* bridge was patented in 1820 and was built entirely of wood. Bridges of this type are still to be seen in this country.

Very few Warren trusses are built with *pin connections*, and few Pratt trusses with *riveted connections*. Riveted Pratt trusses are used for low trusses in which the number of panels exceeds from six to eight. Baltimore and Pettit trusses are nearly always built with pin connections. In general, pin connections are used in bridges of long span in which the dead load is large compared with the live load, and riveted connections in bridges of short span.

124. Special Types of Bridge Trusses. The *cantilever truss* is used in bridges of long span, and particularly for those which it is not practical to erect on falsework. Bridges of this type are combinations of simple trusses supported at their ends and of cantilever trusses, and these may have any style of web bracing. Fig. 170 shows a common arrangement for a deck structure. The shore spans are usually erected on falsework and the rest of the bridge is built out from the two ends (by means of over-hanging travelers) in two cantilevers to meet at the middle of the suspended span. The members of the lower chord, shown dotted, are so made that the stress in them may be relieved. The final arrangement is such that the suspended span DE is freely supported by the cantilever arms CD and EF.

The bridge is, of course, made symmetrical when possible. Two other arrangements of spans are indicated diagramatically n Fig. 170. A fixed panel may take the place of a fixed span when conditions demand. There may be either an anchor span or a simple span at the end of the bridge, but it is usually not wise to have a cantilever arm at the end, since it must be

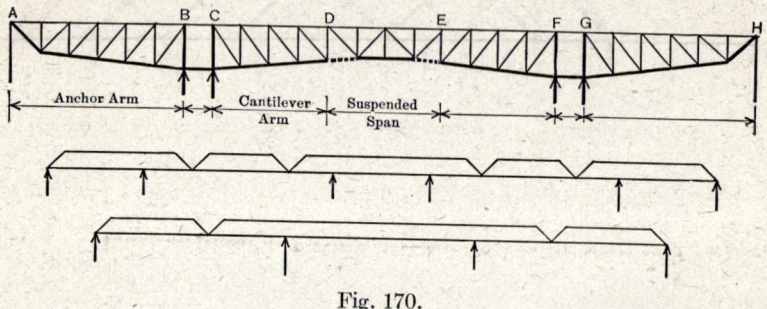

Fig. 170.

free to deflect upward and downward and this may interfere with the traffic.

The cantilever bridge now being built over the St. Lawrence River near Quebec, Canada, will have a channel span of 1800 ft., which will be the longest span in the world. The suspended span of this bridge is 640 ft. long and when completed will be one of the longest simple spans yet built. The Municipal Bridge

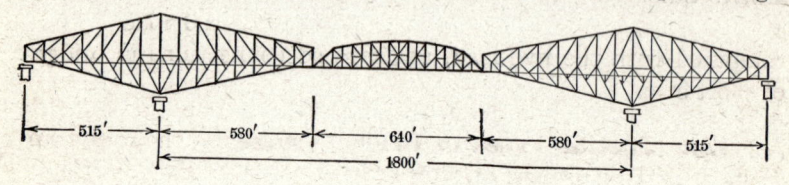

Fig. 171. The Quebec Bridge.

over the Mississippi River at St. Louis contains simple trusses with a span of 668 ft., and the bridge over the Ohio River at Metropolis, Ill., for the C. B. & Q. R. R., which is now under construction, will contain a simple span of 723 ft. All of these long simple spans have trusses of the Pettit type. Fig. 171 shows the outline of the trusses of the Quebec bridge. The web bracing of the cantilever and anchor arms is called the "K" type. It is statically determinate.

The cantilever bridge over the Firth of Forth, in Scotland, has two spans of 1710 ft. each; these are the longest now in existence.

Art. 124.   SPECIAL TYPES OF BRIDGE TRUSSES.   229

The Wabash Railroad bridge over the Monongahela River, at Pittsburgh, is a cantilever bridge having a channel span of 812 ft.

The longest span of the cantilever bridge at Memphis, Tenn., is 790 ft. There are numerous other examples of this type of construction in this country.

Many different styles of *swing-bridge trusses* have been built; the type now in common use is shown in Fig. 172. In long spans, some of the panels may be sub-trussed. The form is that of two simple spans hung from a central tower. When the draw is open, the truss is simply a double cantilever. When the draw is closed and the ends are raised so that there will be no stress in the top chord at the tower, the truss consists of two simple spans. For any intermediate end conditions, the

SWING BRIDGE TRUSS
Fig. 172.

truss is continuous over four supports. It is evident that there will be many members subject to reversals of stress.

This style of truss is usually made partially continuous by putting bracing in the tower panel so light that it carries practically no shear.

In place of the tower a single post is used for short spans, making the truss a two-span continuous truss.

The stresses in continuous trusses are statically indeterminate, but the assumption that the moment of inertia of the truss is constant (97) is usually made in calculating the stresses in swing bridges. This assumption of course is not strictly true.

Swing bridge trusses are very seldom built with pin connections at all joints, but are either riveted or partly riveted and partly pin-connected.

Arches differ from the trusses described above in that they have inclined reactions for vertical loads (Fig. 40). The abutments must be capable of resisting a horizontal thrust or else the feet of the arch must be held by a tie between them (Fig. 150 (a)).

Figs. 173 and 174 show three-hinged arches; there is a hinge at each support and one at the crown. The arch of Fig. 173 is called a *spandrel-braced arch*; the bottom chord may be conceived to be an arch which is braced by the trussing. If

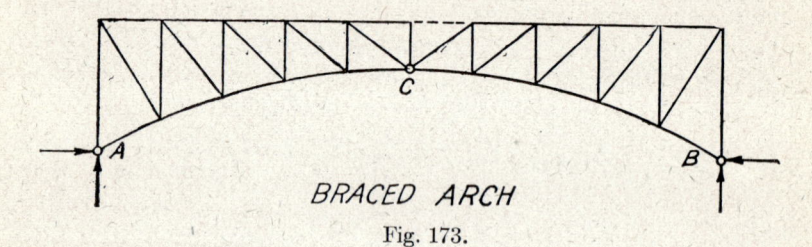

BRACED ARCH

Fig. 173.

the arch is parabolic there will be no stress in the top chord or diagonal members, provided there is a full and symmetrical load; the trussing is stressed under partial load. In Fig. 174, the arch consists of two trusses set up against each other, the loads being applied, through posts, at the upper joints. Arches

THREE HINGED ARCH

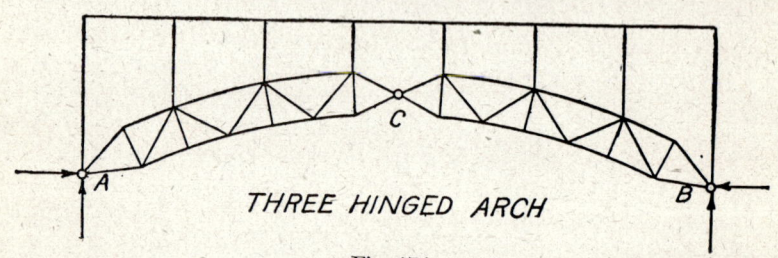

Fig. 174.

of this kind are of many different styles, and plate girders are often used in place of the trusses.

Arches are also built without hinges and with only two hinges, but for these the reactions are statically indeterminate. Stresses in arches with hinges are calculated upon the assumption that there is no friction at the hinges. The reactions and stresses for a three-hinged arch, being statically determinate, their determination offers no difficulties to one familiar with the application of the laws of equilibrium (46).

Art. 124.   SPECIAL TYPES OF BRIDGE TRUSSES.   231

The three-hinged arch is so built that the crown is free to move up and down with changes in temperature. In the other kinds, changes of temperature induce stresses in the arch.

The trusses used in *suspension bridges* are simply stiffening trusses, suspended from the cables, and prevent excessive deflections of them. The cables themselves are sometimes trussed to stiffen them.

QUESTIONS AND PROBLEMS. CHAPTER XI.

1. Name two types of trusses that usually have two diagonals in at least some of the panels.

2. What causes a reversal of stress in some members of a truss? Can the stresses in any of the chord members of a truss simply supported at the ends ever reverse? In what kind of a truss may there be a reversal of stresses in the chords?

3. If the stress in a counter tie is 25000 lbs. when there is no initial stress, what will it be when the initial stress is 10000 lbs.? What when the initial stress is 15000 lbs.?

4. What types of trusses are best adapted to construction in wood?

5. Classify the trusses illustrated in the preceding chapter as to web bracing.

6. When was the first book on stresses in trusses published?

7. What was the development of bridge building as to materials used?

8. Why did each type of truss mentioned in Art. 122 go out of use?

9. What are the economic reasons for using trusses with curved chords for the longest spans only?

10. What types of trusses are commonly made with riveted connections and what with pin connections?

11. Does the cantilever bridge have any advantage over a series of simple spans so far as the substructure is concerned? For a series of equal spans; what is the advantage of the simple trusses over the cantilever trusses?

12. What kind of trusses are used in the Queensboro bridge over the East River in New York?

13. What traffic is provided for in the plans of the cantilever bridge over the St. Lawrence River near Quebec?

14. What are the two arch bridges over the Niagara River? What are the lengths of their spans? What the number of hinges?

CHAPTER XII.

STRESSES IN SIMPLE BRIDGE TRUSSES FROM UNIFORM LOADS.

125. Dead Loads for Bridges. The dead load consists of the weight of the structure itself. It is estimated by comparison with similar structures which have been built or from empirical formulas. The dead load is usually assumed to be uniformly distributed over the length of the bridge. In a simple bridge truss (one supported at its ends), the chord members increase in weight toward the middle, while the web members increase toward the ends. The weight of the floor and floor system is uniform longitudinally except the weight of the floor beams, which is concentrated at the panel points. The wind bracing increases in weight toward the ends. Thus it is seen that the assumption of uniform load for the dead load is not far wrong. The construction reduces the entire dead load to concentrated loads at the panel points of the trusses, and the assumption of its uniform distribution makes these panel loads equal when the panels are equal.

The dead load is estimated in two parts, the weight of the floor and the weight of the steel work. The *floor* as here considered does not include any of the supporting steel work. For ordinary *railroad bridges* it includes the rails, ties, guard-rails and their fastenings, and the *steel work* consists of the weight of the trusses, the floor system and the bracing between the trusses. The *floor system* consists of the stringers supporting the ties, and the floor beams supporting the stringers. The floor beams are usually riveted to the posts. For unusual constructions and for *highway bridges* the weight of the floor may be easily calculated.

The weight of all the steel work must be estimated from a similar bridge whose weight is known. For ordinary bridges of a given type and loading, an empirical formula of the form $w = aL + b$ is often used for estimating the weight of the steel work per foot of bridge. L is the span length and a and b are constants which vary with the style of bridge, the loading, the specifications, etc.

In *highway bridges*, the dead load consists of the floor and its support, the joists, the car tracks (if any), handrailing, and the *remainder* of the steel work. Ordinary country highway bridges have plank floors, the planks being laid transversely on longitudinal beams called joists, placed two to three feet apart. The joists rest on transverse beams called floor beams, which are suspended from the trusses at the panel points or riveted to the posts. City bridges frequently have paved floors, the paving being supported by the joists through the means of buckle plates, reinforced concrete slabs, brick or concrete arches, etc. The floor being designed first, its weight may be calculated. The weight of the floor beams, trusses and bracing is estimated from a similar bridge or by means of an empirical formula.

The *panel load* for dead load is equal to the uniform dead load per foot per truss multiplied by the panel length. In pony trusses (121) this may be considered as all applied at the lower or loaded chord panel points, but when horizontal bracing is used in the plane of both chords the dead load should be divided between them. It is sometimes assumed that two-thirds of the dead load acts at the "loaded chord" and one-third at the "unloaded chord."

After all the stresses are calculated and the design is finished, a careful estimate of the weight should be made from the design. If the total suspended weight differs materially from the dead load assumed in the original calculations, the stresses and the design should be revised.

126. Live Loads. For *railway bridges* the live load is usually specified as a series of wheel loads representing two locomotives, followed by a uniform train load (see Chapter XIII), but an "equivalent uniform live load" is sometimes used (142). For *highway bridges* both concentrated and uniform moving loads are usually specified.[1] The loads for which to design highway bridges are not nearly so definite as those for railway bridges. The floor system is usually designed for a road roller or traction engine and the trusses for a uniform moving load per foot. The

---

[1] See Cooper's *General Specifications for Steel Highway Bridges and Viaducts*.

loads are generally taken in strict accordance with some standard specification.

Uniform loads are taken of indefinite length, and as advancing from either end of the bridge until the whole bridge is covered. As in the case of the dead load, the construction converts the uniform load into panel loads concentrated at the panel points of the loaded chord.

127. General Considerations Regarding Stresses in Simple Trusses.
The methods of Chapters IV and V are adequate for the determination of stresses in any statically determinate truss (42), but it will be advisable to consider the common forms of trusses more in detail, and particularly with regard to live load and maximum stresses. No new methods are introduced, although the simplicity of some of the trusses may make old methods seem new.

The object is to find the maximum stress in each member and if a reversal of stress is possible, both the maximum tensile and maximum compressive stresses are to be found.[1] (28).

It is as simple a matter to find live load stresses as to find dead load stresses, but first the *proper position of the live load must be known,* which will produce the maximum stress in each member, and *for those members which are subject to a reversal of stress, two positions of the live load must be determined.*

With uniform loads, the maximum panel loads will be equal for a symmetrical truss having equal panel lengths, and the maximum stress in any member will be equal to that in the member which is symmetrically located with it, with regard to the center line of the truss; in other words, the maximum stresses will be the same on both sides of the center line. It follows that only half the stresses need be calculated. It is customary and convenient to assume that the live load advances from right to left and to find (in those members subject to a reversal of stress) the maximum stress of one kind to the left of the center line of the truss, and the maximum stresses of the opposite kind (counter stresses) to the right of the center. This procedure avoids turning the live load around so as to advance from left to right.

---

[1] A few specifications also require minimum stresses, and, in this case, it must be remembered that the dead load stress is not always the minimum stress; the stress in a main tie, for example, may be zero.

For a partial live load, there must necessarily be some partial panel loads; for, if the head of the uniform live load is at a panel point, the live load at that point is $\tfrac{1}{2}P$, and if it extends into the panel, the panel load ahead will be less than $\tfrac{1}{2}P$ and the one behind, less than P. It is an easy matter to let the head of the load extend into the panel a distance x, write an equation for the shear or moment whose maximum is desired, in terms of x, and then to find the derivative of the shear or moment with respect to x; placing this equal to zero, the value of x which will give the desired maximum is found.[1] This, however, is a useless refinement, as the actual loads are not uniform and the true stresses may vary greatly from those found by the use of the uniform live load. It is always assumed (and this assumption is on the safe side) that the live load is added a full panel load at a time. The partial panel load ahead is neglected. We have then to deal with full panel loads only, for both dead load and live load. The dead load, of course, always acts as a full load over the entire bridge, but when the live load is considered, it will be necessary to deal with partial loads as well as with full load.

It is sometimes convenient to calculate the stresses in a truss for unit panel loads. The stresses for any other panel load may then be gotten by proportion on the slide rule. In the same way trusses may be gotten for a similar truss of different dimensions, if all the angles between members are the same. This is apparent, if it is remembered that, for any particular loading, the stress diagrams made for different panel loads will be similar figures.

In trusses with *parallel* chords, it is more convenient to write the stresses first, for the unit panel loads, in terms of functions of the angle of inclination of the diagonal members with the vertical, because these may be written by inspection and errors are less liable to occur. Thus if the stress in a diagonal member is $4\tfrac{1}{2} P \sec \theta$, $4\tfrac{1}{2}$ is called the coefficient of stress for this particular member, while $P \sec \theta$ is the same for all diagonals.

The algebraic methods of getting stresses are usually preferred, particularly for trusses with parallel chords. If a stress is determined by considering some joint, that joint should be chosen at which the determination is the simplest. When the

---

[1] See Johnson's *Modern Framed Structures*, Ninth Edition, Part I, Art. 82.

Art. 127. STRESSES IN SIMPLE TRUSSES. 237

method of sections is simpler than the other method, for any particular stress, it should be used. Involved numerical work should be avoided in order to reduce the probability of error (40).

Some general principles will be deduced which will determine positions of live load for maximum stresses in *certain* simple trusses; but it should be remembered that the simplest way of finding maximum live load stresses, and one which is applicable to any case, is to calculate all stresses for each panel load separately and then to make combinations of stresses from such panel loads as may reasonably be supposed to act at the same time. If certain panel loads produce compressive stresses in a member, and all of the others produce tensile stresses, the sum of the former gives the maximum compressive stress and the sum of the latter the maximum tensile stress. The following

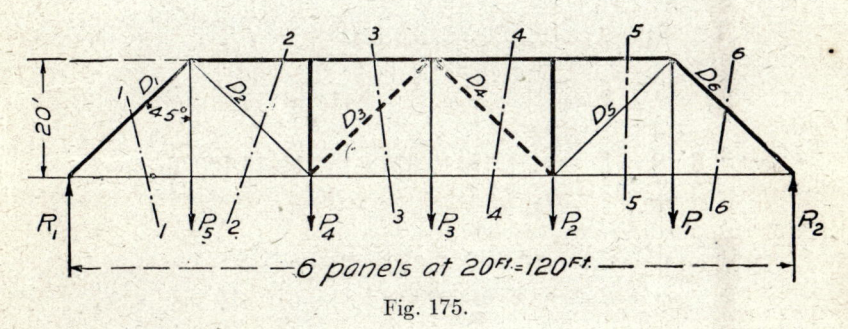

Fig. 175.

example applied to the web members of the truss of Fig. 175 will illustrate this.

The stresses are to be found for a dead load of 300 lbs. and a live load of 800 lbs. per lineal foot of truss.

Dead load panel load $= 300 \times 20 = $ 6000 lbs.
Live load panel load $= 800 \times 20 = 16000$ lbs.

The dead load is, of course, a full load, there being **five panel loads of 6000 lbs. each**, which, for the sake of simplicity, **are assumed to act, all at the lower joints.**

Dead load stresses.

$$R_1 = R_2 = 2\tfrac{1}{2} \times 6{,}000 = 15{,}000 \text{ lbs.}$$

Sect. 1-1. $D_1 = R_1$ sec. $45°$. $D_1 = 15{,}000 \times 1.414 = 21{,}200$ lbs.
Sect. 2-2. $D_2 = (R_1 - P_5)$ sec. $45°$. $D_2 = 9{,}000 \times 1.414 = 12{,}700$ lbs.
Sect. 3-3. $D_3 = (R_1 - P_5 - P_4)$ sec. $45°$.

$$D_3 = 3{,}000 \times 1.414 = 4{,}200 \text{ lbs.}$$

Since the shear acts upward on the left of each section, D_1

and D_3 must be in compression and D_2 in tension. On account of the symmetry, $D_1=D_6$, $D_2=D_5$, $D_3=D_4$.

Live load stresses. If P_1, P_2, and P_3 are considered separately, the stresses due to P_4 and P_5 may be gotten by inspection because each load is equal to 16,000 lbs., and P_5, for example, will produce the same stress in D_2 as P_1 produces in D_5.

Stresses for $P_1 = 16{,}000$ lbs.

$R_1 = \frac{1}{6}$ of $16{,}000 = 2{,}670$ lbs. $R_2 = \frac{5}{6}$ of $16{,}000 = 13{,}330$ lbs.

Sect. 1-1. $D_1 = R_1 \sec 45° = 2670 \times 1.414 = 3780$ lbs.

$+D_1 = -D_2 = +D_3 = -D_4 = +D_5$ since the shear that each must carry is the same and since the shear is up in each panel, the signs alternate as the directions of the diagonals alternate.

Sect. 6-6. $D_6 = R_2 \sec 45° = 13{,}330 \times 1.414 = 18{,}850$ lbs.

Stresses for $P_2 = 16{,}000$ lbs.

Sect. 1-1. $R_1 = \frac{2}{6}$ of $16{,}000 = 5{,}330$ lbs.

$R_2 = \frac{4}{6}$ of $16{,}000 = 10{,}670$ lbs.

$D_1 = R_1 \sec 45° = 5{,}330 \times 1.414 = 7{,}550$ lbs.

$+D_1 = -D_2 = +D_3 = -D_4$

Sect. 6-6. $D_6 = R_2 \sec 45° = 10{,}670 \times 1.414 = 15{,}100$ lbs.

$+D_6 = -D_5$

Stresses for $P_3 = 16{,}000$ lbs.

$R_1 = \frac{1}{2}$ of $16{,}000 = 8{,}000 = R_2$.

$D_1 = R_1 \sec 45° = 8{,}000 \times 1.414 = 11{,}310$ lbs.

$+D_1 = +D_6 = -D_2 = -D_5 = +D_3 = +D_4$.

For P_3 the stresses are symmetrical.

		D_1	D_2	D_3	D_4	D_5	D_6
D. L.		+21.2	−12.7	+ 4.2	+ 4.2	−12.7	+21.2
L. L.	P_1	+ 3.8	− 3.8	+ 3.8	− 3.8	+ 3.8	+18.9
	P_2	+ 7.6	− 7.6	+ 7.6	− 7.6	−15.1	+15.1
	P_3	+11.3	−11.3	+11.3	+11.3	−11.3	+11.3
	P_4	+15.1	−15.1	− 7.6	+ 7.6	− 7.6	+ 7.6
	P_5	+18.9	+ 3.8	− 3.8	+ 3.8	− 3.8	+ 3.8
Max.		+77.9	−50.5	+26.9 − 7.2	+26.9 − 7.2	−50.5	+77.9

Collecting the above results in the table on p. 238, carefully noting the signs, the resultant maximum stresses are found: they are symmetrical. The stresses for D_1 are all compressive. The stress in D_2 is tensile except for load P_5; the maximum tensile stress in D_2 occurs when the live load extends from the right support into the panel of D_2. There can be no compressive stress in D_2 because P_5 is the only load producing compression and its stress is less than the dead load tensile stress; the minimum stress is $-12.7 + 3.8 = -8.9$. The maximum compressive stress in D_3 occurs when the live load extends from the right support into the panel of D_3, and the maximum tensile stress for the complementary loading. In the second case the live loads P_4 and P_5 produce $7.6 + 3.8 = 11.4$ tension; the dead load compression being less than this, the resultant is $11.4 - 4.2 = 7.2$ tension. D_3 is a *counterbrace*.

Since the stresses in D_2 and D_5 are the same and likewise in D_3 and D_4, the stresses of one kind may be found on the right of the center and those of the other kind on the left. According to the above table, P_5 should act for a maximum compression or a minimum tension in D_2; P_5 and P_4 should act for a maximum tension in D_3; P_1, P_2, and P_3 should act for a maximum compression in D_3; P_1, P_2, P_3, and P_4 should act for a maximum tension in D_2; and all loads should act for a maximum in D_1. The general rule, for position of live load, is quite similar to that for a solid beam (102).

128. Position of Live Load for Maximum Chord Stresses. Any load on a truss, *supported at its two ends*, will bend it downward, thus producing positive bending moment at any section. It follows that, *in order to have a maximum bending moment at any joint of a truss, as much load as possible should be on—there should be a full load, for live load*. This rule is the same as for a solid beam (102). Now since the stress in any chord member is a maximum when the moment at a *joint* is a maximum, there must be a full load for any chord stress.

If the truss bends downward it is apparent that the top chord must be in compression and the bottom chord in tension. If in the example of the previous article, the chord stresses had been calculated, it would have been found that each panel load produces stress of the same kind in each chord.

Of course, the above rule can not be applied to continuous trusses, cantilever trusses, and trusses with inclined reactions like the three-hinged arch.

240   LIVE LOAD FOR MAXIMUM CHORD STRESSES. Art. 128.

The above rule may also be deduced by the following simple analysis. In Fig. 176 (a) consider the chord member U_3. Taking the section 3-3, the center of moments will be at d. Consider the

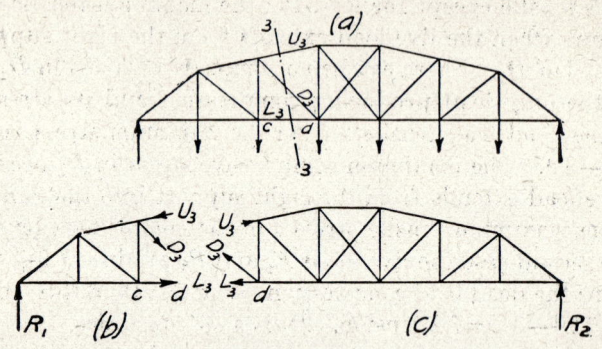

Fig. 176.

part to the left of the section as in Fig. 176 (b), and let R_1 be the reaction due to any load on the right of the panel cd. Since there are no loads on the part under consideration, and since the moments of D_3 and L_3 are each zero, the moment of R_1 about d must equal the moment of U_3 about d. Since the former is clockwise, the latter must be anti-clockwise, that is, U_3 acts in the direction shown which makes it compression.

In like manner let R_2 be the reaction for any load on the left of the panel cd and it will be the only external force acting on the part to the right of the section as shown in Fig. 176 (c). Since the moment of R_2 about d is counter-clockwise, that of U_3 must be clockwise and U_3 must act in the direction shown which makes it compression again. It follows that any and all loads produce compression in U_3, and for a maximum all should act, that is, there should be a full live load. This is true no matter how much shear the chord carries. There can be no reversal of chord stresses and the live and dead load stresses are of the same sign. since both are calculated for full load they are proportional to the loads, and live load *chord* stresses may be taken from the dead load stresses by means of the slide rule.

It has been shown that there are vertical and horizontal shearing stresses, and bending stresses in a solid beam; that the vertical shearing stresses resist the shear, the bending stresses resist the bending moment, and the horizontal shearing stresses produce the increment of the bending moment (75). In a Pratt

Art. 128. LIVE LOAD FOR MAXIMUM CHORD STRESSES. 241

truss (see Fig. 58, Art. 59), the vertical component of the diagonal in a panel corresponds with the vertical shearing stresses of the solid beam; the horizontal component corresponds with the horizontal shearing stresses; the increments of chord stress toward the center, produced by the diagonals at the joints, correspond with the increments of the bending stress; and the chord stresses correspond with the resultants of the bending stresses. In Fig. 58, section rs, $U_1=L_2=33{,}300$ lbs. is the couple which forms the moment of resistance.

In a truss with inclined chords, the horizontal components form the moment of resistance. In Fig. 177, the section 3-3, through C, (considering the part on the right) cuts off the forces U_2, V_2, and L_3. Considering the horizontal and vertical components of U_2, and taking center of moments at c, so that the moment of V as well as of V_2 and L_3 shall be zero,

$$Hd = M_c$$

M_c being the sum of the moments of external forces about c. But it is also true that

$$L_3 d = M_c = M_c$$

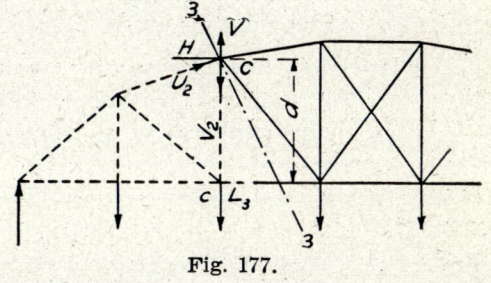

Fig. 177.

It follows that $H = L_3$ and this is the couple which forms the moment of resistance.

Now since the horizontal componet of a chord stress is a bending stress, and since the moment is always positive, the chord stress itself must always be *either* compressive or tensile. It follows that the vertical component of a chord stress, which resists a part of the shear, must always be of the same sign even though the shear may reverse.

129. Position of Live Load for Maximum Web Stresses. Let the shear in any panel of a truss be first considered. For maximum shear in a panel, the same principle applies for determining the position of the live load as for determining the maximum shear at any cross section of a solid beam, but in a truss both the positive and negative shears must be investigated (102). The greater of these is usually called the *positive shear*, and the lesser, the *negative shear* in the panel.

If, in Fig. 178, panel 4-5 is considered, the maximum shear in it will occur when there are no loads to the left of panel 4-5, and when all the loads on the right act. If R_1 is the reaction for loads 1, 2, 3, and 4, then $R_1 + \tfrac{6}{7} P$ is the reaction when load 6 is added. In the first case,

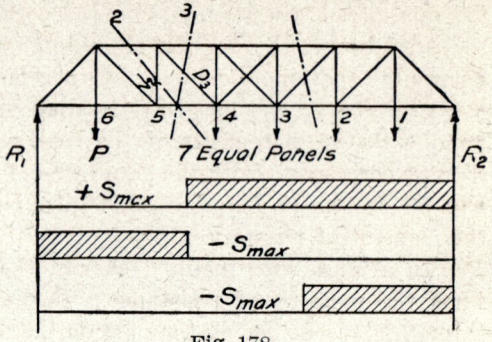

Fig. 178.

Shear in panel 4-5 $= R_1$

In the second case,

Shear in panel 4-5 $= R_1 + \tfrac{6}{7} P - P = R_1 - \tfrac{1}{7} P$

A load on the left increases the reaction less than it decreases the shear; the result is a decrease of shear. If the load be all on the left of the panel the shear is evidently of opposite kind (consider R_2) and the same reasoning applies. Fig. 178 shows, diagrammatically, the positions of the loads for both maxima. In symmetrical trusses, it is customary to consider the panel 2-3 in place of 4-5 for maximum negative shear (127); the shear is the same for both. The positive shear is found on the left and the negative shear on the right of the center of the truss. The above conclusions are confirmed by the results of the stresses given in Art. 127.

For maximum positive shear in any panel of a truss, the live load should extend from that panel to the farther support, and for maximum negative shear to the nearer support. The live load shear in a panel may reverse but the dead load shear is always positive. *Whether or not there will be a resultant reversal of shear depends upon the relative amounts of the live load and dead load.*

When there is a reversal of shear in a panel, there will be a reversal of stress in the web members of that panel (V_2 and D_3, Fig. 178) if the chords are parallel, for then the web member alone must resist the shear (sections 2-2 and 3-3). *When the chords are not parallel, the web member does not carry all of the*

Art. 129. LIVE LOAD FOR MAXIMUM WEB STRESSES. 243

shear; neither does its stress necessarily reverse when the shear reverses. In Fig. 179

$$S_2 = R_1 - P = U_2 \cos \theta_2' - D_2 \cos \theta_2$$

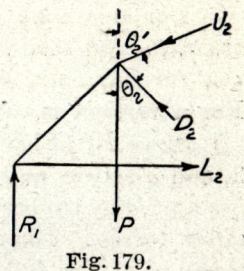

U_2 can not reverse; its sign, in the equation, will always be plus. Should D_2 be in tension, its sign will be plus and the shear, S_2, will be positive. When D_2 is in compression, however, S_2 may be positive or negative, according as $U_2 \cos \theta_2'$ is greater or less than $D_2 \cos \theta_2$; the stress in D_2 may be reversed without reversing the shear or vica-versa. Evidently, when the chords are inclined, the maximum stresses in a web member do not depend upon the shear in such a way that the above rule for positions of live load may be confidently applied. It will now be shown that *this rule does give the positions for maximum web stresses also, with certain exceptions.*

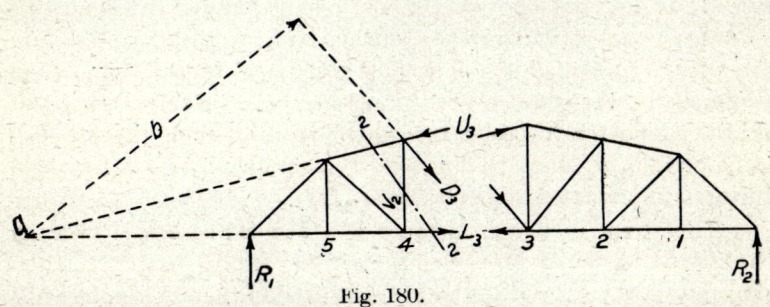

Fig. 179.

Fig. 180.

The maximum stress in D_3 occurs when the moment about a (Fig. 180) is a maximum, because

$$D_3 b = M_a \text{ of external forces.}$$

Considering the part to the left of the section, and no loads on this part, R_1 is the only external force. The moment of R_1 about a is anti-clockwise, and therefore that of D_3 must be clockwise. *D_3 is in tension for any load to the right of the section.* Considering the part to the right and loads to the left of the section only, R_2 is the only external force. The moment of R_2 about a is anti-clockwise and therefore that of D_3 must be clockwise. *D_3 is in compression for any load to the left of the section.* A similar analysis for V_2 will show that V_2 is in compression for any load on the right of the section 2-2, and in tension for any load on the left.

For maximum stress of one kind in any web member of a truss, the live load should extend from its panel to one support, and for maximum stress of the other kind, to the other support. For a vertical member, the panel is determined by the section.

Since D_3 (Fig. 180) has its maximum tension with loads 1, 2, and 3 acting, and its maximum compression with loads 4 and 5 acting, the algebraic sum of these stresses will be the full load stress for D_3. This will be a check on the stresses in D_3 if the stress in D_3 for full load is determined; and this may easily be done, because the ratio of live load stress to dead load stress is equal to the ratio of live load to dead load.

If a load on the right of a panel produces stress of one kind, and a load on the left stress of the opposite kind, there must be some position of a load in the panel which will produce zero stress. In Fig. 180, for example, a load in the panel 3-4 may be so located that it will produce such panel loads at 3 and 4 that the tension produced by one will be just equal to the compression produced by the other. There must also be a certain position of a load which will produce zero shear in the panel. These positions are easily found and are convenient in placing a live load for *actual* maximum stress or shear (127).

The stress in a web member will also be zero for loads on the left of its panel (for example) if the chords cut by the section intersect on the right-hand reaction, for then the moment of the external force is zero. A case of this kind is illustrated in the roof truss of Fig. 51, Art. 54; there is no stress in any web member of the right-hand half. A section through any web member cuts off but one external force (R_2) on the right and it passes through the center of moments, E.

When there are loads on both sides of the cutting section, the web stress is zero, evidently, when the chords cut intersect on the resultant of all external forces on one side of the section. A graphic method of getting the location of this resultant is given in Art. 61; its position may, however, be more quickly determined algebraically. The moment of the resultant about the point of application of the reaction must equal the sum of the moments of the loads on one side of the section about the same point.

If the center of moments of a web member lies between the supports, that is, if the chords cut by a section through it inter-

Art. 129. LIVE LOAD FOR MAXIMUM WEB STRESSES.   245

sect between the supports, its stress will not reverse and it will be a maximum for full live load. For appearance sake, simple

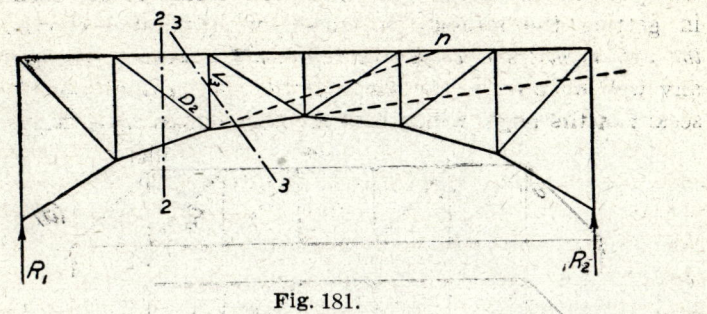

Fig. 181.

trusses are occasionally made as shown in Fig. 181. Rollers are placed under one end of the truss so that the reactions will be vertical. Considering D_2, its center of moments is at n. For loads on the right of section 2-2, R_1 is the only external force acting on the left-hand part of the truss; to balance its moment about n, D_2 must be in tension. For loads on the left of the section, R_2 is the only external force acting on the right-hand part; to balance its moment about n, D_2 must be in tension. Hence D_2 is in tension for any load and its maximum stress occurs with full load.

Similar reasoning will show that V_3 is in tension for loads on the left of section 3-3, and in compression for loads on the right; its center of moments lies beyond the supports.

In this truss, then, some of the web members will not suffer a reversal of stress, and their maximum stresses occur for full load, while the others follow the regular rule for maximum shear in a panel. Since the chords are always a maximum for full load, the general principle may be laid down that, *when the center of moments for a member lies between the supports*, its stress is a *maximum for full load*.

A roof truss with curved lower chord, and one arm of a swing bridge with curved upper chord, when treated as a simple span, are other cases in which the center of moments for a web member may come between the supports.

Another exception to the rule will be found in Art. 137 for maximum tension in the posts of a truss having a curved chord and counter ties.

246 STRESSES IN PRATT TRUSS BY COEFFICIENTS. Art. 130.

130. Stresses in a Pratt Truss by Coefficients. As was pointed out in Art. 127, it is convenient to use coefficients in getting the stresses in trusses with parallel chords. *For the web members a coefficient represents a shear.* The stress in any web member is the shear at the section multiplied by the secant of the angle which that member makes with the vertical.

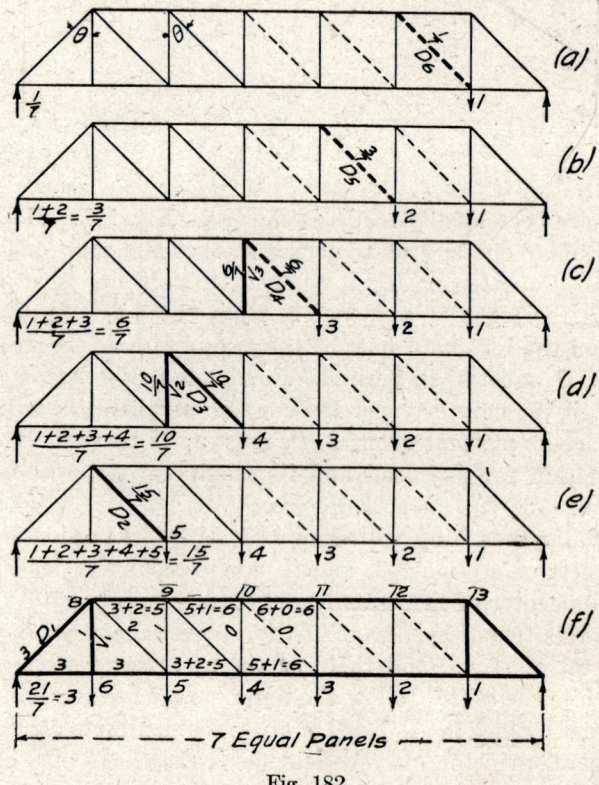

Fig. 182.

If the *member is vertical*, its secant is one. The *chord stresses* may be obtained by horizontal resolutions at the joints. Evidently the vertical members have no horizontal components, so *the stress in any chord is made up of the sum of the horizontal components of the diagonals* between that chord and the end of the truss. Therefore, the chord coefficients will be multiplied by $\sec\theta \times \sin\theta$ or $\tan\theta$, where θ is the angle of the diagonal with the vertical.

Art. 130. STRESSES IN PRATT TRUSS BY COEFFICIENTS. 247

All vertical stresses = coefficient $\times P$.
All diagonal stresses = coefficient $\times P \sec \theta$.
All chord stresses = coefficient $\times P \sec \theta \sin \theta$.
  = coefficient $\times P \tan \theta$.

It is necessary to keep the coefficients for dead load and live load in the web members separate, as the panel loads are different. It is also necessary to keep clearly in mind what loading will produce a maximum *live* load stress in any particular member as determined by the rules of Arts. 128 and 129. This is shown in Fig. 182, in which the member having maximum stresses for a particular loading are shown in heavy lines. The counter-tie live load stresses are determined on the right of the center line and the main tie stresses on the left. Since the

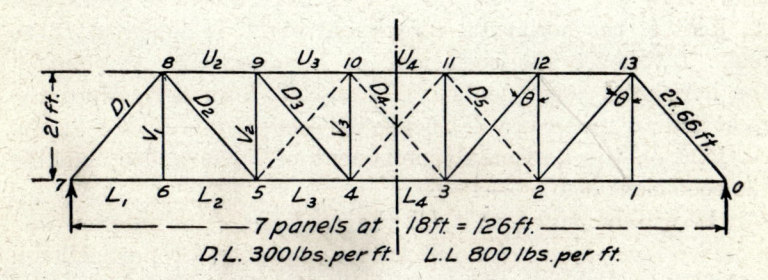

Fig. 183.

verticals are always in compression they are determined on the left—they have no counter stresses. The stress in a suspender is a maximum whenever there is a full panel load at its lower end. According to the rule, it requires a full load to produce a maximum stress in the end diagonals.

Fig. 183 gives the dimensions of a truss similar to that shown in Fig. 182. Its stresses will now be calculated by the method of coefficients.

In Fig. 183, the diagonal length is $\sqrt{21^2 + 18^2} = 27.66$ ft.

$$\text{Sec. } \theta = \frac{27.66}{21} \qquad \text{Tan. } \theta = \frac{18}{21}$$

D. L. P. = $300 \times 18 = 5,400$ lbs.   L. L. P. = $800 \times 18 = 14,400$ lbs.

D. L. P. sec $\theta = 5,400 \dfrac{27.66}{21} = 7120$ lbs.

$L.\ L.\ P.\ \sec\theta = 14{,}400\ \dfrac{27.66}{21} = 19000\text{ lbs.}$

$D.\ L.\ P.\ \tan\theta = 5{,}400\ \dfrac{18}{21} = 4630\text{ lbs.}$

$L.\ L.\ P.\ \tan\theta = 14{,}400\ \dfrac{18}{21}\ 12340\text{ lbs.}$

Fig. 182 shows the left-hand reactions for the various cases which it is necessary to consider; having these the shears in the different panels are easily gotten. The coefficients on the web members are these shears for unit panel loads. In Fig. 182 (*f*) $R_1 = 3$, and the shear in panel 4-5 is $3-2=1$, which, by the method of sections, determines D_3. At joint 7, L_1 must be equal to the horizontal component of D_1, hence its coefficient is 3. At joint 6, $L_2 = L_1$, hence they have the same coefficient. At joint 5, the horizontal component of D_2 is added to L_2 to make L_3, hence the coefficient of $L_3 = 3+2 = 5$. At joint 8, the horizontal components of D_1 and D_2 both act toward the right and are resisted by U_2, hence the coefficient of U_2 is $3+2=5$. At joint 9, the horizontal component of D_3 is added, making the coefficient of U_3, $5+1=6$.

It will be noted that all the coefficients for interior web members are smaller for full load than those for partial load. Likewise would the coefficients for the chord members be smaller for any partial load than for full load. Since the dead load is a full load, the coefficients of Fig. 182 (*f*) may be used for dead load coefficients, with the exception of the vertical posts as noted later.

The diagonal members (except the end posts), the suspenders, and the lower chord are always in tension; the posts and top chord are always in compression. The dead load shear in the middle panel is zero and therefore there can be only live load stress in D_4. The dead load shear in panel 4-5 is $+1 \times 5400 = +5400$ lbs.; the maximum live load negative shear is, from Fig. 182 (*b*), $-\tfrac{3}{7} \times 14{,}400 = -6170$ lbs.; the resultant shear is $-6170 + 5400 = -770$ lbs., and therefore a counter-tie will be required in this panel. The dead load shear in panel 5-6 is $+2 \times 5400 = +10{,}800$ lbs.; the maximum negative live load shear is, from Fig. 182 (*a*), $-\tfrac{1}{7} \times 14{,}400 = -2060$ lbs.; the resultant is positive and therefore no counter-tie will be required in this panel.

Art. 130. STRESSES IN PRATT TRUSS BY COEFFICIENTS. 249

Diagonal Stresses.

$$D_1 = 3P \sec\theta = 3 \times 7,120 = +21,360 \text{ D. L.}$$
$$ = 3P \sec\theta = 3 \times 19,000 = +57,000 \text{ L. L.}$$
$$ \overline{+78,360} \text{ Total.}$$

$$D_2 = 2P \sec\theta = 2 \times 7,120 = -14,240 \text{ D. L.}$$
$$ = \tfrac{15}{7}P \sec\theta = \tfrac{15}{7} \times 19,000 = -40,700 \text{ L. L.}$$
$$\phantom{D_2 = \tfrac{15}{7}P \sec\theta = \tfrac{15}{7} \times 19,000 =} \overline{-54,940} \text{ Total.}$$

$$D_6 = \tfrac{1}{7}P \sec\theta = \tfrac{1}{7} \times 19,000 = -2,720 \text{ L. L.} \qquad \text{No reversal.}$$

$$D_3 = P \sec\theta = 7,120 = -7,120 \text{ D. L.}$$
$$ = \tfrac{10}{7}P \sec\theta = \tfrac{10}{7} \times 19,000 = -27,140 \text{ L. L.}$$
$$\phantom{D_3 = \tfrac{10}{7}P \sec\theta = \tfrac{10}{7} \times 19,000} \overline{-34,260} \text{ Total.}$$

$$D_5 = \tfrac{3}{7}P \sec\theta = \tfrac{3}{7} \times 19,000 = -8,140 \text{ L. L.}$$
$$\text{Dead load same as } D_3 = +7,120 \text{ D. L.}$$
$$\phantom{\text{Dead load same as } D_3 xxxx} \overline{-1,020} \text{ Total.} \quad \text{Reverses.}$$

$$D_4 = \tfrac{6}{7}P \sec\theta = \tfrac{6}{7} \times 19,000 = -16,300 \text{ L. L. and total.}$$

The counter stress D_5 is the same as the resultant shear in its panel multiplied by $\sec\theta$. If there were no counter tie, D_3 would be a counter-brace and V_2 would also be in tension.

The *dead load* is divided between the upper and lower panel points. It is usually considered that *one-half the weight of the trusses and bracing is delivered at each chord and that all of the weight of the floor system is delivered at the loaded chord*. If q equals the proportion of the *total dead load panel* load which is delivered at the *unloaded chord*, the dead load coefficients for the verticals will be as follows:

$$\text{D. L. Coefficient for } V_1 = 1 - q.$$

$$\text{D. L. Coefficient for } V_2 = 1 + q.$$

$$\text{D. L. Coefficient for } V_3 = q.$$

Assuming q in this case to be $\tfrac{1}{3}$, the following are the stresses in the verticals:

$$V_1 = \tfrac{2}{3} \times 5,400 = -3,600 \text{ D. L.}$$
$$ = 1 \times 14,400 = -14,400 \text{ L. L.}$$
$$ \overline{-18,000} \text{ Total.}$$

250 STRESSES IN PRATT TRUSS BY COEFFICIENTS. Art. 130.

$$V_2 = 1\tfrac{1}{3} \times 5{,}400 = +\ 7{,}200 \text{ D. L.}$$
$$= \tfrac{10}{7} \times 14{,}400 = +20{,}600 \text{ L. L.}$$
$$\overline{+27{,}800 \text{ Total.}}$$

$$V_3 = \tfrac{1}{3} \times 5{,}400 = +\ 1{,}800 \text{ D. L.}$$
$$= \tfrac{6}{7} \times 14{,}400 = +12{,}300 \text{ L. L.}$$
$$\overline{+14{,}100 \text{ Total.}}$$

Chord Stresses.

$$L_1 = L_2 = 3P \tan \theta = 3 \times 4{,}630 = -13{,}890 \text{ D. L.}$$
$$= 3P \tan \theta = 3 \times 12{,}340 = -37{,}020 \text{ L. L.}$$
$$\overline{-50{,}910 \text{ Total.}}$$

$$-L_3 = +U_2 = 5P \tan \theta = 5 \times 4{,}630 = 23{,}150 \text{ D. L.}$$
$$= 5P \tan \theta = 5 \times 12{,}340 = 61{,}700 \text{ L. L.}$$
$$\overline{84{,}850 \text{ Total.}}$$

$$-L_4 = +U_3 = +U_4 = 6P \tan \theta = 6 \times 4{,}630 = 27{,}780 \text{ D. L.}$$
$$= 6P \tan \theta = 6 \times 12{,}340 = 74{,}040 \text{ L. L.}$$
$$\overline{101{,}820 \text{ Total.}}$$

If it is not required to keep the dead and live load chord stresses separate, the total may be gotten by one operation.

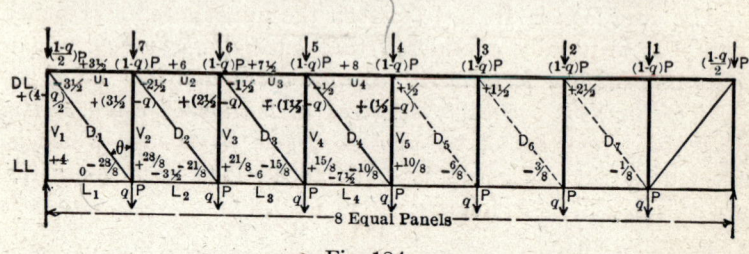

Fig. 184.

A truss diagram with stresses marked on the members is called a stress diagram. Sometimes only the total stresses are given and sometimes both dead load and live load stresses. The *character* of each stress *must* be indicated.

When the total stress is to be an equivalent static stress, the live load stress must be kept separate from the dead load stress until the impact stress has been added, as this is usually a certain percentage of the live load stress. (88.) (5.)

Fig. 184 shows a *Deck Pratt* truss with the coefficients

Art. 130. STRESSES IN PRATT TRUSS BY COEFFICIENTS. 251

written on the members. The *dead load* panel concentrations are indicated at the upper and lower panel points. The *live load* is all applied at the upper panel points. The coefficients for dead load on the web members are given near the upper ends and those for live load near the lower ends. The diagonals are shown in one direction only to avoid confusion. The main tie stresses are figured on the left half and the counters on the right.

There are two conditions affecting the stress in the middle vertical V_5. When the counter D_5 is acting as shown,

$$V_5 = (\tfrac{1}{2} - q)\, D.\,L. + \tfrac{10}{8}\, L.\,L.,$$

but when the bridge is symmetrically loaded with a live load at joint 4, the counter D_5 will not be in action and

$$V_5 = (1 - q)\, D.\,L. + 1\, L.\,L.$$

Both of these stresses must be calculated to see which is the larger.

131. Stresses in a Simple Warren Truss. Fig. 185 shows a simple Warren truss. The upper joints are vertically

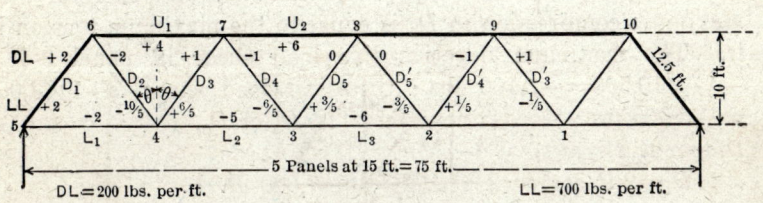

Fig. 185.

opposite the middle of the lower panels, which gives all of the diagonals the same angle of inclination.

The coefficients for the web members are obtained in a manner exactly similar to that shown in Fig. 182. The coefficients for dead load are shown near the top of the member and for live load near the bottom. In this case all of the dead load is considered as acting at the lower panel points, as the truss is not deep enough for overhead bracing. The coefficients for the chord members are obtained by resolving horizontally at the joints as in the case of the Pratt truss.

It is evident that the lower chord is in tension, and the upper chord and end posts in compression. Since there are two diagonals in each panel, a section may be taken through either, and its vertical component must be equal to the shear in the panel. Since all diagonals have the same inclination, the *stresses in the two diagonals of a panel must be equal*, for a particular loading; but since they are inclined in opposite directions, *their stresses will be of opposite kind*. For full load, D_1 is in compression; D_2 is in tension; D_3 is in compression; D_4 is in tension; D_5 is in compression. Those near the middle of the truss may reverse under partial live load.

The diagonal length $= \sqrt{7.2^2 + 10^2} = 12.5$ ft.

$$Sec.\ \theta = \frac{12.5}{10} \qquad Tan.\ \theta = \frac{7\ 5}{10}$$

D. L. P. $= 200 \times 15 = 3{,}000$ lbs. L. L. P. $= 700 \times 15 = 10{,}500$ lbs.
D. L. P. sec $\theta = 3{,}000 \times 1.25 = 3{,}750$ lbs.
L. L. P. sec $\theta = 10{,}500 \times 1.25 = 13{,}125$ lbs.
D. L. P. tan $\theta = 3{,}000 \times 0.75 = 2{,}250$ lbs.
L. L. P. tan $\theta = 10{,}500 \times 0.75 = 7{,}875$ lbs.

The dead load shear in the middle panel is zero and, therefore, there is no dead load stress in D_5. The maximum plus and minus shears in the middle panel are the same and, therefore, the maximum compression in D_5 is equal to the maximum tension in it. The maximum negative live load shear in panel 3-4 is $-\frac{1}{5} \times 10{,}500 = -2{,}100$ lbs.; the dead load shear is $+1 \times 3{,}000 = +3{,}000$ lbs.; there is no reversal in D_4 or D_3.

Diagonal Stresses.

$D_1 = 2P$ sec $\theta = 2 \times\ 3{,}750 = +\ 7{,}500$ D. L.
$ =$ do $= 2 \times 13{,}125 = +26{,}250$ L. L.
$\phantom{D_1 =\ \text{do}\ = 2 \times 13{,}125 =\ }\overline{+33{,}750}$ Total.

D_2 same as D_1 but sign is $-$

$+D_3 = -D_4 =\ P$ sec $\theta = 1 \times\ 3{,}750 =\ 3{,}750$ D. L.
$ = \tfrac{6}{5}P$ sec $\theta = \tfrac{6}{5} \times 13{,}125 = 15{,}750$ L. L.
$\phantom{+D_3 =\ \ = \tfrac{6}{5}P\ \text{sec}\ \theta = \tfrac{6}{5} \times 13{,}125 = }\overline{19{,}500}$ Total.

$ = \tfrac{1}{5}P$ sec $\theta = \tfrac{1}{5} \times 13{,}125 = 2{,}625$ L. L.

and as stated above there is no reversal.

$D_5 = \tfrac{3}{5}P$ sec $\theta = \tfrac{3}{5} \times 13{,}125 = 7{,}875$ L. L. and Total.

If one-third of the dead load be taken at each upper joint and two-thirds at each lower joint, the dead load coefficients of D_1, D_3 and D_5 will be increased by one-sixth and of D_2 and D_4,

Art. 131.   STRESSES IN A SIMPLE WARREN TRUSS.   253

decreased by one-sixth, as may readily be shown by taking successive sections.

Chord Stresses.

$L_1 = 2P \tan \theta = 2 \times 2{,}250 = -\ 4{,}500$ D. L.
$\ \ = \ \ $ do $\ = 2 \times 7{,}875 = -15{,}750$ L. L.
$\qquad\qquad\qquad\qquad\quad\overline{-20{,}250}$ Total.

$U_1 = 4P \tan \theta = 4 \times 2{,}250 = +\ 9{,}000$ D. L.
$\ \ = \ \ $ do $\ = 4 \times 7{,}875 = +31{,}500$ L. L.
$\qquad\qquad\qquad\qquad\quad\overline{+40{,}500}$ Total.

$L_2 = 5P \tan \theta = 5 \times 2{,}250 = -11{,}250$ D. L.
$\ \ = \ \ $ do $\ = 5 \times 7{,}875 = -39{,}375$ L. L.
$\qquad\qquad\qquad\qquad\quad\overline{-50{,}625}$ Total.

$-L_3 = +U_2 = 6P \tan \theta = 6 \times 2{,}250 = 13{,}500$ D. L.
$\ \ = \ \ $ do $\ = 6 \times 7{,}875 = 47{,}250$ L. L.
$\qquad\qquad\qquad\qquad\quad\overline{60{,}750}$ Total.

As a check, taking the total panel load 13,500,

$$M_8 = 0 \text{ or } 2\tfrac{1}{2} \times 15 \times R_1 - 13{,}500\ (1\tfrac{1}{2} + \tfrac{1}{2})\ 15 = 10\ L_3.$$

$$L_3 = \tfrac{1}{10}(2\tfrac{1}{2} \times 15 \times 27{,}000 - 27{,}000 \times 15) = 60{,}750 \text{ lbs.}$$

It should be noted that the horizontal components of the diagonal stresses *all* act toward the right at the upper joints and toward the left at the lower joints; hence the chord coefficients are gotten by the addition, at each joint, of all the diagonal coefficients.

132. Stresses in a Subdivided Warren Truss. Fig. 186 shows a subdivided Warren truss of eight panels. This

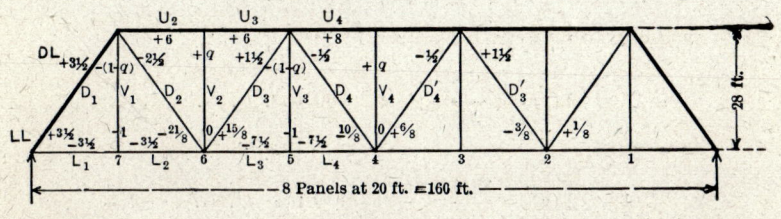

Fig. 186.

is a very common type for riveted bridges up to 200 ft. span. The coefficients are given on the truss diagram and are obtained

254   STRESSES IN A SUBDIVIDED WARREN TRUSS.   Art. 132.

in a manner exactly similar to those for the Pratt truss of Art. 130. The stresses will be figured for the following data:

$$\begin{aligned}\text{Weight of trusses and bracing} &= 1200 \text{ lbs. per ft. of bridge}\\ \text{Weight of floor system} &= 1000 \text{ lbs. per ft. of bridge}\\ \text{Total dead load} &= 2200 \text{ lbs. per ft. of bridge}\\ \text{Live load} &= 4000 \text{ lbs. per ft. of bridge}\end{aligned}$$

From these data the following values are found:

$$\text{Dead load panel load} = \frac{2200}{2} \times 20 = 22{,}000 \text{ lbs.}$$

$$\text{Live load panel load} = \frac{4000}{2} \times 20 = 40{,}000 \text{ lbs.}$$

$$q = \frac{\tfrac{1}{2} \times 1200}{2200} = \frac{3}{11}.$$

Diagonal length = 34.4 ft.

$$\text{Sec } \theta = \frac{34.4}{28} \qquad \text{tan } \theta = \frac{20}{28}.$$

Diagonal Stresses.

$$D_1 = 3\tfrac{1}{2} \times 22{,}000 \times \frac{34.4}{28} = +\ 94{,}600 \text{ lbs. } D.\,L.$$

$$ = 3\tfrac{1}{2} \times 40{,}000 \times \frac{34.4}{28} = +172{,}000 \text{ lbs. } L.\,L.$$

$$\phantom{D_1 = 3\tfrac{1}{2} \times 40{,}000 \times \frac{34.4}{28} =}\ +266{,}600 \text{ lbs. Total.}$$

$$D_2 = 2\tfrac{1}{2} \times 22{,}000 \times \frac{34.4}{28} = -\ 67{,}600 \text{ lbs. } D.\,L.$$

$$ = \tfrac{21}{8} \times 40{,}000 \times \frac{34.4}{28} = -129{,}000 \text{ lbs. } L.\,L.$$

$$\phantom{D_2 = \tfrac{21}{8} \times 40{,}000 \times \frac{34.4}{28} =}\ -196{,}600 \text{ lbs. Total.}$$

$$D_3 = 1\tfrac{1}{2} \times 22{,}000 \times \frac{34.4}{28} = +\ 40{,}500 \text{ lbs. } D.\,L.$$

$$ = \tfrac{15}{8} \times 40{,}000 \times \frac{34.4}{28} = +\ 92{,}100 \text{ lbs. } L.\,L.$$

$$\phantom{D_3 = \tfrac{15}{8} \times 40{,}000 \times \frac{34.4}{28} =}\ +132{,}600 \text{ lbs. Total.}$$

$$D_4 = \tfrac{1}{2} \times 22{,}000 \times \frac{34.4}{28} = -\ 13{,}500 \text{ lbs. } D.\,L.$$

$$ = \tfrac{10}{8} \times 40{,}000 \times \frac{34.4}{28} = -\ 61{,}400 \text{ lbs. } L.\,L.$$

$$\phantom{D_4 = \tfrac{10}{8} \times 40{,}000 \times \frac{34.4}{28} =}\ -\ 74{,}900 \text{ lbs. Total.}$$

Art. 132. STRESSES IN A SUBDIVIDED WARREN TRUSS. 255

$$D'_4 = \tfrac{1}{2} \times 22{,}000 \times \tfrac{34.4}{28} = -13{,}500 \text{ lbs. } D.\,L.$$

$$ = \tfrac{6}{8} \times 40{,}000 \times \tfrac{34.4}{28} = +36{,}900 \text{ lbs. } L.\,L.$$

$$\phantom{D'_4 = \tfrac{6}{8} \times 40{,}000 \times \tfrac{34.4}{28} =\ } +23{,}400 \text{ lbs. Total reversal.}$$

$$D'_3 = 1\tfrac{1}{2} \times 22{,}000 \times \tfrac{34.4}{28} = +40{,}500 \text{ lbs. } D.\,L.$$

$$ = \tfrac{3}{8} \times 40{,}000 \times \tfrac{34.4}{28} = -18{,}500 \text{ lbs. } L.\,L.$$

$$\text{No reversal.}$$

Verticals.

$$V_1 = V_3 = \tfrac{8}{11} \times 22{,}000 = -16{,}000 \text{ lbs. } D.\,L.$$

$$ = 1 \times 40{,}000 = -40{,}000 \text{ lbs. } L.\,L.$$

$$\phantom{V_1 = V_3 = 1 \times 40{,}000 =\ } -56{,}000 \text{ lbs. Total.}$$

$$V_2 = V_4 = \tfrac{3}{11} \times 22{,}000 = +6{,}000 \text{ lbs. } D.\,L. \text{ Total.}$$

Chord Stresses.

$$U_2 = U_3 = 6 \times 22{,}000 \times \tfrac{20}{28} = +94{,}300 \text{ lbs. } D.\,L.$$

$$ = 6 \times 40{,}000 \times \tfrac{20}{28} = +171{,}400 \text{ lbs. } L.\,L.$$

$$\phantom{U_2 = U_3 = 6 \times 40{,}000 \times \tfrac{20}{28} =\ } +265{,}700 \text{ lbs. Total.}$$

$$U_4 = 8 \times 22{,}000 \times \tfrac{20}{28} = +125{,}700 \text{ lbs. } D.\,L.$$

$$ = 8 \times 40{,}000 \times \tfrac{20}{28} = +228{,}600 \text{ lbs. } L.\,L.$$

$$\phantom{U_4 = 8 \times 40{,}000 \times \tfrac{20}{28} =\ } +354{,}300 \text{ lbs. Total.}$$

$$L_1 = L_2 = 3\tfrac{1}{2} \times 22{,}000 \times \tfrac{20}{28} = -55{,}000 \text{ lbs. } D.\,L.$$

$$ = 3\tfrac{1}{2} \times 40{,}000 \times \tfrac{20}{28} = -100{,}000 \text{ lbs. } L.\,L.$$

$$\phantom{L_1 = L_2 = 3\tfrac{1}{2} \times 40{,}000 \times \tfrac{20}{28} =\ } -155{,}000 \text{ lbs. Total.}$$

$$L_3 = L_4 = 7\tfrac{1}{2} \times 22{,}000 \times \tfrac{20}{28} = -117{,}800 \text{ lbs. } D.\,L.$$

$$ = 7\tfrac{1}{2} \times 40{,}000 \times \tfrac{20}{28} = -214{,}300 \text{ lbs. } L.\,L.$$

$$\phantom{L_3 = L_4 = 7\tfrac{1}{2} \times 40{,}000 \times \tfrac{20}{28} =\ } -332{,}100 \text{ lbs. Total.}$$

133. Stresses in a Half-hip Truss. The end panels of a half-hip truss (Fig. 187) are like those of a Warren truss

256   STRESSES IN A HALF-HIP TRUSS.   Art. 133.

and the balance of the truss is like a Pratt. The coefficients for the *web members* are gotten in the same manner as for a Pratt and a Warren. It must be remembered that the *secant* for the end diagonals is *different* from that for the intermediates.

For the *chord stresses* the horizontal components are added as in the preceding cases, but it must be remembered that the *tangent* for the intermediate diagonals is *double* that of the end diagonals, so that in adding the coefficients for the intermediate diagonals they must be *doubled*; thus at joint 6, the coefficient for U_2 is $4 + 2 \times 1 = 6$. The tangent of the *end diagonals* is then used in connection with all the chord coefficients.

If the slope of the end diagonals is not exactly half that of the intermediate ones, the chord coefficients will have to be written in two parts, as $4P \tan \theta + 1P \tan \theta'$ for U_2.

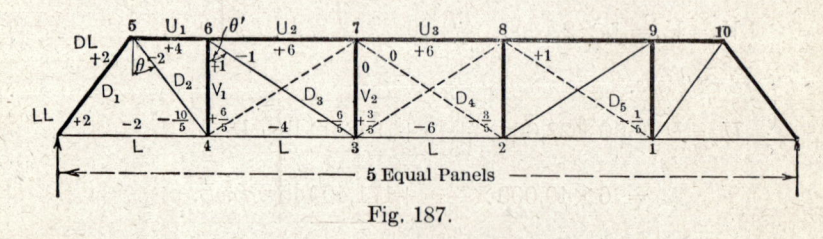

Fig. 187.

Fig. 187 gives the coefficients for dead and live load, assuming all of the dead load as acting at the lower chord.

134. Stresses in a Whipple Truss.

The Whipple truss is statically indeterminate (42), but it is usually assumed that the two trusses into which it may be separated act independently in transmitting the stresses (122). This assumption is not true, as may readily be seen by considering a single load at any point. Suppose a load is acting at joint 5, Fig. 188 (*a*). According to the above assumption this would produce stresses in the truss of Fig. 188 (*b*), but no stress in the truss of Fig. 188 (*c*) except in the chords and end posts. But truss (*b*) cannot deflect without causing deflection in truss (*c*) also. Therefore, the load at joint 5 produces stresses in truss (*c*) as well as truss (*b*). (8.)

According to the usual assumption the truss is separated into two parts, Fig. 188 (*b*) and (*c*), and the coefficients written; then those for the members common to both trusses are added and put on the original diagram, Fig. 188 (*a*). Each truss is assumed to carry alternate panel loads.

Art. 134.   STRESSES IN A WHIPPLE TRUSS.   257

Here, as in the half-hip truss, the slope of the end diagonals is only half that of the intermediate ones and this must be remembered in writing the chord coefficients and in using them.

The center post is similar to the center post of the Pratt truss with an even number of panels (Fig. 184); it has two con-

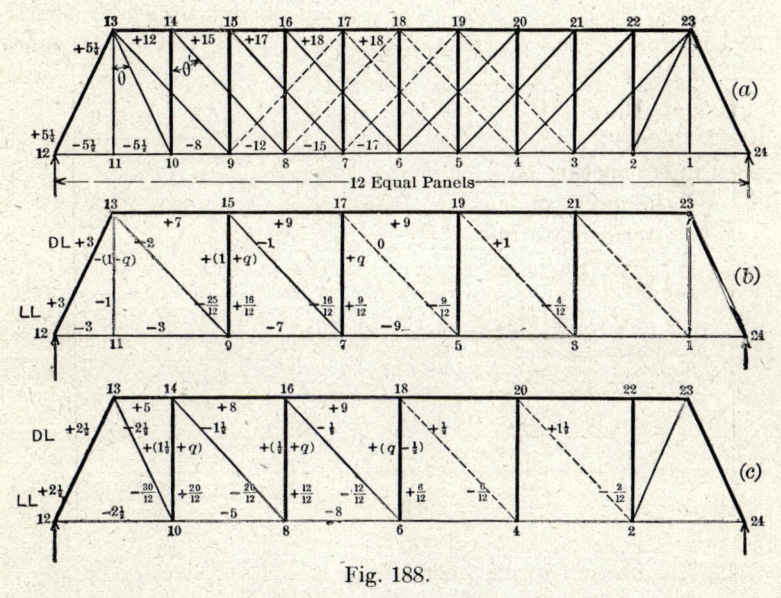

Fig. 188.

ditions affecting the stress. When the counter is acting as shown

$$V_6 = (q - \tfrac{1}{2}) D.\,L. + \tfrac{6}{12} L.\,L.,$$

but when the bridge is symmetrically loaded, the counter will not be in action, and

$$V_6 = +q\, D.\,L.$$

The first case will usually govern in a through bridge.

135. Stress Coefficients for a Double-intersection Warren Truss. The double-intersection truss of Fig. 189 (a) is treated as a deck structure. Whether or not there are joints at the intersections of the web members, the stresses are statically indeterminate according to equation (8), Art. 42. Upon the usual assumption of two independent trusses as shown in Figs. 189 (b) and (c), the stresses are statically determinate and the final stresses in the chords are equal to the sums of the stresses in these two trusses.

As the stresses obtained in this manner are only approximate, it is useless to complicate the problem by separating the dead load into the portions carried at the two chords, although this may be done if desired. In what follows all of the loads will be considered as applied at the upper chord.

The case of full load will be considered first. Trusses b and c are unsymmetrical about their centers, but if the reac-

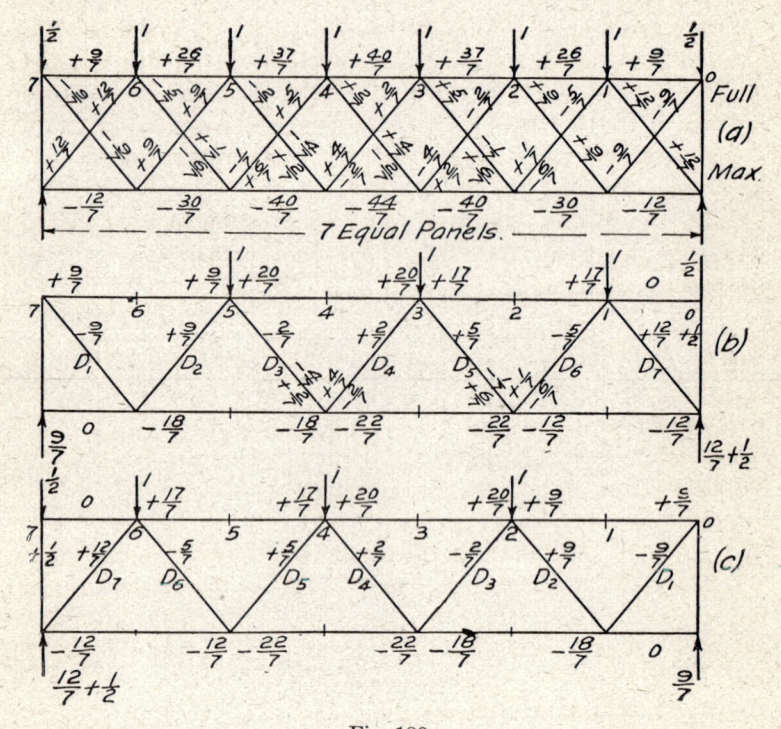

Fig. 189.

tions are first gotten and then the diagonal coefficients, with their proper signs, the chord coefficients are easily determined. One end load will be assumed to act on truss b and the other on truss c.

Fig. 189 (b). $R_1 = \dfrac{1+3+5}{7} = \dfrac{9}{7} =$ shear in panels 6-7 and 5-6.

Fig. 189 (c). $R_1 = \dfrac{2+4+6}{7} = \dfrac{12}{7} =$ shear in panel 6-7.

Evidently, R_2 for the first truss is the same as R_1 for the

Art. 135. DOUBLE-INTERSECTION WARREN TRUSS.

second, and R_2 for the second, the same as R_1 for the first. The sum of the reactions is equal to the total load.

Fig. 189 (b). Shear in panels 4-5 and 3-4 $= \frac{9}{7} - \frac{7}{7} = \frac{2}{7}$ up

Shear in panels 2-3 and 1-2 $= \frac{2}{7} - \frac{7}{7} = \frac{5}{7}$ down

Shear in panel 0-1 $= \frac{5}{7} + \frac{7}{7}$ down.

The same results will be obtained, of course, by starting at the right hand end. The shear reverses at 3. In order to determine the character of the stress it is only necessary to consider the direction of the shear in a panel, and the kind of distortion it tends to produce in the diagonal.

For similar members, the coefficients of truss c are the same as of truss b.

In Fig. 189 (b), chord 5-7 is in compression to resist D_1 and its coefficient is $\frac{9}{7}$. At 5, the top chord 5-6 and both diagonals act toward the right and, therefore, the coefficient for 3-5 is

$$\frac{9}{7} + \frac{9}{7} + \frac{2}{7} = \frac{20}{7}$$

At 3, one diagonal acts toward the right and the other (D_5) toward the left; the coefficient for 1-3 is $\frac{20}{7} + \frac{2}{7} - \frac{5}{7} = \frac{17}{7}$. At 1, both diagonals act toward the left; the coefficient for 0-1 is $\frac{17}{7} - \frac{5}{7} - \frac{12}{7} = 0$ as is apparent at joint o. These coefficients may be checked by starting at the right-hand end and proceeding in a similar manner. It is somewhat easier to work from both ends, up to the point where the shear changes.

The coefficients for truss c may be taken off of truss b. Adding the chord coefficients, the final chord coefficients are gotten as shown in Fig. 189 (a), or they may be gotten directly on Fig. 189 (a), from the diagonal coefficients.

The live load coefficients for the diagonals are independent for each truss, but are the same in the two trusses for members with the same subscript. For the end panels (D_1, D_2, and D_7) the full load coefficients are the maximum also. For the other panels the diagonal coefficients are easily found if the proper partial load is considered, and are given at the lower ends of D_3 to D_6 in Fig. 189 (b).

Having all the coefficients it is a simple matter to calculate the stresses (131).[1]

---

[1] It is possible to have a multiple-intersection truss that is statically determinate. Some of these are, however, collapsible or unstable. A discussion of such trusses may be found in a paper by Mr. G. N. Linday, in the Journal of the Western Society of Engineers, Vol. VIII, p. 272; also in Mueller-Breslan's Graphische Statik, Vol. I.

136. Stresses in a Baltimore Truss. Fig. 190 shows three ways in which *sub-trussing* may be put in. Heavy lines indicate compression members and light lines tension members. By horizontal and vertical resolutions at the junction of the diagonals the stress in the *sub-diagonal* may be found in any case. The stress in the *sub-vertical*, V_s, is evidently equal

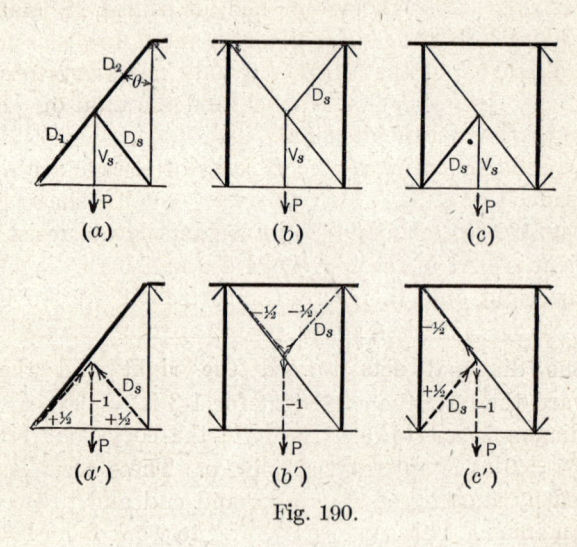

Fig. 190.

to the load at its lower extremity—unity. Assuming compression in each of the three diagonals in Fig. 190 (*a*), we get,

$$D_1 \sin \theta - D_2 \sin \theta - D_s \sin \theta = 0,$$

$$D_1 \cos \theta - D_2 \cos \theta + D_s \cos \theta = P.$$

Dividing the first equation by $\sin \theta$ and the second by $\cos \theta$ and subtracting, we get

$$2D_s = P \sec \theta \quad \text{or} \quad D_s = \tfrac{1}{2} P \sec \theta.$$

Thus we get the coefficient for D_s to be $\tfrac{1}{2}$. By a similar process the coefficient for D_s may be shown to be $\tfrac{1}{2}$ in any case where the inclinations of the diagonals are equal and the loads vertical. Figs. 190 (*a'*), (*b'*) and (*c'*) show diagrammatically the paths of the stresses from the sub-panel loads.

Fig. 191 shows a Baltimore truss of sixteen panels with the sub-diagonals in tension. The top chord is usually supported at the sub-panel points by vertical struts V_s', as this reduces

Art. 136.   STRESSES IN A BALTIMORE TRUSS.   261

the effective length of the top chord as a column (113), and also reduces the bending moment due to its own weight (115). The *dead load* coefficients shown in Fig. 191 are obtained as follows.

It is evident that panel load 15 is equally divided at 17, and is carried downward to the right and the left. The half panel load carried to the right is added to load 14, making the coefficient of V_1, $(1\frac{1}{2}-q)$.

The shear in panel 14-15 is $7\frac{1}{2}-1=6\frac{1}{2}$, and it is resisted by the algebraic sum of the vertical components of the diagonals in the panel which is $7-\frac{1}{2}=6\frac{1}{2}$.

Since D_3, D_5, and D_7 are the only diagonals in action in their respective panels, their coefficients are the shears in these panels, namely $7\frac{1}{2}-2=5\frac{1}{2}$, $7\frac{1}{2}-4=3\frac{1}{2}$, and $7\frac{1}{2}-6=1\frac{1}{2}$. Writing

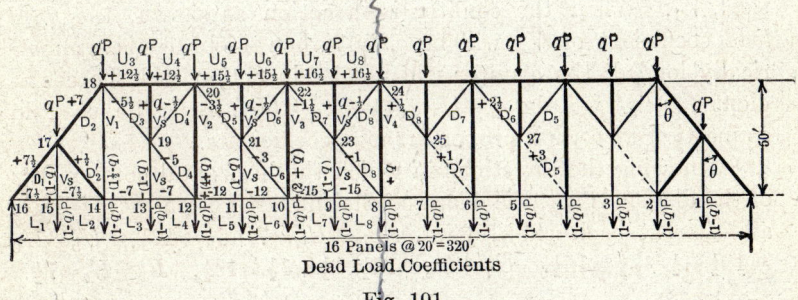

Fig. 191.

the horizontal and vertical resolution equations at joints 19, 21, or 23, as was done in Fig. 190, it is found that the sub-panel loads coming to these points are divided and carried upward so that the coefficient of each sub-diagonal is $\frac{1}{2}$.

Now the coefficients for the diagonals in those panels having two diagonals may be gotten, for we know that the upper one carries a half panel load. The shear in panel 12-13 is $7\frac{1}{2}-3=4\frac{1}{2}$, and is resisted by the algebraic sum of the vertical components of D'_4 and D_4. Since these act in opposite directions, and that of D'_4 is $\frac{1}{2}$, that of D_4 must be 5. Looking at it in another way, it is known that one-half the load at 13 is carried by D'_4; then the shear carried by D_4 is $7\frac{1}{2}-2\frac{1}{2}=5$. In a similar manner, the shear resisted by D_6 is $7\frac{1}{2}-4\frac{1}{2}=3$, and by D_8 is $7\frac{1}{2}-6\frac{1}{2}=1$.

The same results may be obtained by taking resolutions at joints 19, 21, and 23.

Sub-diagonal D'_8 in connection with D'_7 forms the counter of panel 8-10 or 6-8. When these are in action, D_7 becomes the sub-diagonal and D_8 goes out of action. The dead load coefficients to be used in connection with the live load to find the stresses in the counters, are given on the right half of Fig. 191. D'_8 and D'_6 may get their maximum stress as a sub-diagonal or as a counter, depending upon the relation of the dead load to the live load. Both stresses must be calculated to find out which is the greater.

The coefficient for a *post* may be gotten by taking a section through it and a sub-diagonal, or by adding the diagonal coefficients at the upper joint to the load applied at the point. As in the case of the Pratt truss with an even number of panels, there are two conditions affecting the stress in the middle vertical, V_4. When the counter is in action as shown, the *dead load* coefficient of V_4 will be q, but when the bridge is symmetrically loaded, the counter will not be in action and the coefficient for V_4 will be $\frac{1}{2}+\frac{1}{2}+q=1+q$. These must be used in connection with their proper *live load* coefficients.

Knowing the directions in which the horizontal components of the diagonals act, the chord coefficients are gotten by algebraic addition at each chord joint. $U_3=U_4=7+5\frac{1}{2}=12\frac{1}{2}$. $U_5=U_6=12\frac{1}{2}-\frac{1}{2}+3\frac{1}{2}=15\frac{1}{2}$. $U_7=U_8=15\frac{1}{2}-\frac{1}{2}+1\frac{1}{2}=16\frac{1}{2}$. $L_1=L_2=7\frac{1}{2}$. $L_3=L_4=7\frac{1}{2}-\frac{1}{2}=7$. $L_5=L_6=7+5=12$. $L_7=L_8=12+3=15$.

As a *check*, with a section through U_7, D_7, and L_7, $M_{22}=0$ or $50L_7 = 7\frac{1}{2} \times 6 \times 20 - 1(1+2+3+4+5)20$.

$$L_7 = \frac{45 \times 20 - 15 \times 20}{50} = \frac{30 \times 20}{50} = 15 \times \tfrac{40}{50} = 15 \, tan \, \theta.$$

$M_8 = 0$, or

$50U_7 = 7\frac{1}{2} \times 8 \times 20 - 1(2+3+4+5+6+7)20$.

$$U_7 = \frac{60 \times 20 - 27 \times 20}{50} = \frac{33 \times 20}{50} = 16\frac{1}{2} \times \tfrac{40}{50} = 16\frac{1}{2} \, tan \, \theta.$$

The *live load* coefficients for the *counter ties* (maximum negative shears) are gotten on the right of the center line just as for a Pratt truss. This is evident for those panels having but one diagonal. (The main tie is not in action when the counter tie is.) In the other panels the stress in the upper member is also zero for live load unless the *sub-panel* load is on; but when the sub-panel load acts, the shear carried by the counter tie is de-

Art. 136.   STRESSES IN A BALTIMORE TRUSS.   263

creased by half of this panel load, and increased by the increase in R_1, which is always less than one-half a panel load. Thus for panel 6-7, with loads 1-6 inclusive acting, the shear is $\frac{21}{16}$ with load 7 added; the coefficient for D'_7 is $\frac{28}{16} - \frac{8}{16} = \frac{20}{16}$. In short, the loading for maximum negative shear follows our adopted rule (129).

In combining the dead and live load stresses in the counter ties to find the resultant maximum, it must be remembered that the total shear in a panel is resisted by the algebraic sum of the vertical components of the diagonals *acting* in the panel. In panel 7-8, the diagonal D_8' is the only one acting for the partial loading (1 to 7 inclusive), and therefore D_8' resists the entire resultant shear in the panel, just as for diagonals D_3, D_5 and D_7. In panel 6-7, D_7' is not the only diagonal acting, as the dead load panel load at 7 is divided between the two diagonals just as shown for the left half of the truss, and therefore D_7 will always carry at least ½ panel load of dead load. This makes the resultant stress in $D_7' = [\ \frac{21}{16}\ L.L.P.L. + (7½ - 9 + ½) DLPL]\ sec\ \theta = [\frac{21}{16}\ L.L.P.L - D.L.P.L.]\ sec\ \theta$.

For maximum *positive shear* (to the left of the center), the coefficients in the panels having but one diagonal are the same as for a Pratt truss. For D_5, for example, loads 1 to 11 inclusive should act; the left hand reaction is $\frac{66}{16}$ and this is the coefficient.

In the panels having two diagonal members, the coefficient for the main diagonal may be greater when the sub-panel ahead is on than when the loading follows the rule for maximum shear in the panel. Trying both loadings and remembering that the upper diagonal carries one-half of the *sub-panel load only*,

For D_8, loads 1 to 8. Shear $= \dfrac{1+2+3+4+5+6+7+8}{16} = \dfrac{36}{16}$

"   "   1 to 9.   Shear $= \dfrac{36+9}{16} - \dfrac{1}{2} = \dfrac{45-8}{16} = \dfrac{37}{16}$

For D_6, loads 1 to 10. Shear $= \dfrac{45+10}{16} = \dfrac{55}{16}$

"   "   1 to 11. Shear $= \dfrac{55+11}{16} - \dfrac{1}{2} = \dfrac{66-8}{16} = \dfrac{58}{16}$

For D_4, loads 1 to 12. Shear $= \dfrac{66+12}{16} = \dfrac{78}{16}$

"   "   1 to 13. Shear $= \dfrac{78+13}{16} - \dfrac{1}{2} = \dfrac{91-8}{16} = \dfrac{83}{16}$

For D_2, loads 1 to 14. Shear $= \dfrac{91+14}{16} = \dfrac{105}{16}$

"   "   1 to 15. Shear $= \dfrac{105+15}{16} - \dfrac{1}{2} = \dfrac{120-8}{16} = \dfrac{112}{16}$

An inspection of these figures shows that, for *this style* of web bracing, *the maximum stress in the main diagonal of a panel having two diagonal members, occurs when the sub-panel load ahead of the panel is on.* It will be noted also that the shear carried by these diagonals is always decreased by a half panel load, when the sub-panel load acts, while it is always increased more than this; the smallest increase above is $\frac{9}{16}$ for the first panel load to the left of the center.

Taking a section through a post and sub-diagonal, remembering that there is no stress in the sub-diagonal when the sub-panel load is not on, and that it carries a half panel load when the sub-panel load is on, we have

For V_4, loads 1 to 7, at joint 24, $\frac{28}{16}+0 = \frac{28}{16}$
"   "   1 to 9, $\frac{45}{16}-1\frac{1}{2}=\frac{21}{16}$
For V_3, loads 1 to 9, at joint 22, $\frac{45}{16}+0 = \frac{45}{16}$
"   "   1 to 11, $\frac{66}{16}-1\frac{1}{2}=\frac{42}{16}$
For V_2, loads 1 to 11, at joint 20, $\frac{66}{16}+0 = \frac{66}{16}$
"   "   1 to 13, $\frac{91}{16}-1\frac{1}{2}=\frac{67}{16}$

For the posts, the regular rule for loading applies in getting maximum stress, *except for the post V_2,* in which the stress will be slightly larger if two more panel loads are added than the rule requires. All of the post coefficients will be larger than those given above if it is assumed reasonable to have a discontinuous load; if loads 1 to 11 inclusive, except load 10, acted, for example, the coefficient for V_3 would be $\frac{48}{16}$.

For the position of live load (loads 1 to 7) which gives a maximum stress in V_4, (the center post) the acting members of the truss are as shown in Fig. 191, and the total stress in V_4 is equal to the sum of the vertical components of the diagonals meeting at joint 24, plus whatever load is applied at joint 24, or

$V_4 = [\frac{28}{16}L.L.P.L. - \frac{1}{2}D.L.P.L.] + [\frac{1}{2}D.L.P.L.] + [qD.L.P.L.]$
$= \frac{28}{16}L.L.P.L. + qD.L.P.L.$

For a symmetrical loading with live loads at joints 7, 8, and 9,

$V_4 = (1+q)D.L.P.L. + 1L.L.P.L.$

Art. 136.   STRESSES IN A BALTIMORE TRUSS.   265

The one of these two values which is the greater is the one to be used. It depends upon the relation of the live load to the dead load.

The live load coefficients are shown in Fig. 192. Having

Live Load Coefficients

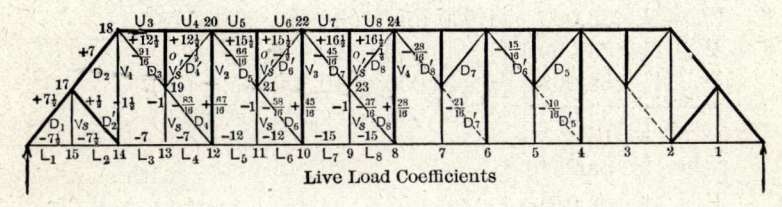

Fig. 192.

all of the coefficients, it is a simple matter to find the stresses. The following loads will be used in figuring the stresses:

Weight of trusses and bracing = 2200 lbs. per ft. of bridge.
Weight of floor system   = 1100 lbs. per ft. of bridge.

Total dead load   = 3300 lbs. per ft. of bridge.
Live load   = 4000 lbs. per ft. of bridge.

From these we get the following constants:

$$\text{Dead load panel load} = \frac{3300}{2} \times 20 = 33{,}000 \text{ lbs.}$$

$$\text{Live load panel load} = \frac{4000}{2} \times 20 = 40{,}000 \text{ lbs.}$$

$$q = \frac{\frac{1}{2} \times 2200}{3300} = \frac{1}{3}.$$

Diagonal length = 64.03 ft.

$$\sec \theta = \frac{64}{50}. \qquad \tan \theta = \frac{40}{50} = 0.8.$$

$D_1 = (7\frac{1}{2} \times 33{,}000 + 7\frac{1}{2} \times 40{,}000) \sec \theta = 700{,}800$ lbs.   (+)
$D_2 = (7 \times 33{,}000 + 7 \times 40{,}000) \sec \theta = 654{,}000$ lbs.   (+)
$D'_2 = (\frac{1}{2} \times 33{,}000 + \frac{1}{2} \times 40{,}000) \sec \theta = 46{,}700$ lbs.   (+)
$D_3 = (5\frac{1}{2} \times 33{,}000 + \frac{91}{16} \times 40{,}000) \sec \theta = 523{,}500$ lbs.   (−)
$D_4 = (5 \times 33{,}000 + \frac{83}{16} \times 40{,}000) \sec \theta = 476{,}800$ lbs.   (−)
$D_5 = (3\frac{1}{2} \times 33{,}000 + \frac{66}{16} \times 40{,}000) \sec \theta = 359{,}000$ lbs.   (−)
$D_6 = (3 \times 33{,}000 + \frac{58}{16} \times 40{,}000) \sec \theta = 312{,}300$ lbs.   (−)
$D_7 = (1\frac{1}{2} \times 33{,}000 + \frac{45}{16} \times 40{,}000) \sec \theta = 207{,}400$ lbs.   (−)
$D_8 = (1 \times 33{,}000 + \frac{37}{16} \times 40{,}000) \sec \theta = 160{,}600$ lbs.   (−)
$D'_4 = D'_6 = D'_8 = (\frac{1}{2} \times 33{,}000 + \frac{1}{2} \times 40{,}000) \sec \theta = 46{,}700$ lbs. (−)

$D'_8 = (\frac{28}{16} \times 40{,}000 - \frac{1}{2} \times 33{,}000) \sec\theta = 68{,}500$ lbs. $(-)$

as counter, max.

$D'_7 = (\frac{21}{16} \times 40{,}000 - 1 \times 33{,}000) \sec\theta = 25{,}000$ lbs. $(-)$

$D'_6 = (\frac{15}{16} \times 40{,}000 - 2\frac{1}{2} \times 33{,}000) \sec\theta =$ no reversal as counter.

$V_s = \frac{2}{3} \times 33{,}000 + 40{,}000 = 62{,}000$ lbs. $(-)$

$V'_s = \frac{1}{3} \times 33{,}000 = 11{,}000$ lbs. $(+)$

$V_1 = 1\frac{1}{6} \times 33{,}000 + 1\frac{1}{2} \times 40{,}000 = 98{,}500$ lbs. $(-)$

$V_2 = 4\frac{1}{3} \times 33{,}000 + \frac{67}{16} \times 40{,}000 = 310{,}500$ lbs. $(+)$

$V_3 = 2\frac{1}{3} \times 33{,}000 + \frac{45}{16} \times 40{,}000 = 189{,}500$ lbs. $(+)$

$V_4 = \frac{1}{3} \times 33{,}000 + \frac{28}{16} \times 40{,}000 = 81{,}000$ lbs. $(+)$

with counter.

$V_4 = 1\frac{1}{3} \times 33{,}000 + 1 \times 40{,}000 = 84{,}000$ lbs. $(+)$

symmetrical load, max.

$U_3 = U_4 = 12\frac{1}{2}(33{,}000 + 40{,}000) \tan\theta = 730{,}000$ lbs. $(+)$

$U_5 = U_6 = 15\frac{1}{2}(33{,}000 + 40{,}000) \tan\theta = 905{,}200$ lbs. $(+)$

$U_7 = U_8 = 16\frac{1}{2}(33{,}000 + 40{,}000) \tan\theta = 963{,}600$ lbs. $(+)$

$L_1 = L_2 = 7\frac{1}{2}(33{,}000 + 40{,}000) \tan\theta = 438{,}000$ lbs. $(-)$

$L_3 = L_4 = 7\phantom{\frac{1}{2}}(33{,}000 + 40{,}000) \tan\theta = 408{,}800$ lbs. $(-)$

$L_5 = L_6 = 12\phantom{\frac{1}{2}}(33{,}000 + 40{,}000) \tan\theta = 700{,}800$ lbs. $(-)$

$L_7 = L_8 = 15\phantom{\frac{1}{2}}(33{,}000 + 40{,}000) \tan\theta = 876{,}000$ lbs. $(-)$

Fig. 193 shows a Baltimore truss of 14 panels with sub-diagonals all compression members; the other diagonals (except-

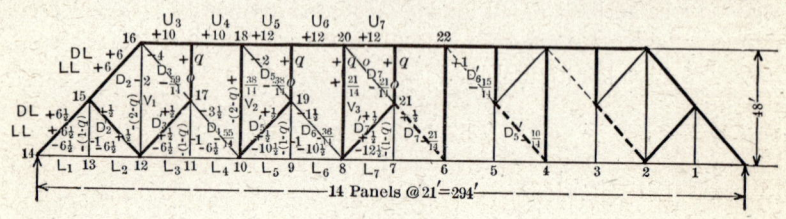

Fig. 193.

ing end posts) are tension members. The sub-panel loads are carried to the main truss as shown in Fig. 190 (c).

The coefficients for *dead load* will be gotten first. For the diagonals in the panels having but one diagonal, the coefficient is equal to the shear in the panel; for the other diagonals, the algebraic sum of their vertical components must equal the shear in the panel. Panel 12-13 is similar to the second panel in Fig. 191. The shear in panel 11-12 is $6\frac{1}{2} - 2 = 4\frac{1}{2}$; since D'_3 carries a half panel load of shear, D_3 must carry 4, because both vertical components act downward. The shear in panel 7-8 is $\frac{1}{2}$ and this is resisted by D'_7, making the coefficient D_7 zero.

Art. 136.   STRESSES IN A BALTIMORE TRUSS.   267

At joint 12, the horizontal components of D'_3 and D'_2 balance each other; the coefficient of L_3 must, therefore, be the same as for L_2. At joint 10, $L_5 = 6\frac{1}{2} + 3\frac{1}{2} + \frac{1}{2} = 10\frac{1}{2}$. At joint 8, $L_7 = 10\frac{1}{2} + 1\frac{1}{2} + \frac{1}{2} = 12\frac{1}{2}$. At joint 16, $U_3 = 6 + 4 = 10$. At joint 18, $U_5 = 10 + 2 = 12$. At joint 20, $U_7 = 12 + 0 = 12$.

As a check $M_8 = 0$, section through U_7, D'_7, and L_7.

$$48 U_7 = 6\frac{1}{2} \times 6 \times 21 - (1 + 2 + 3 + 4 + 5)21.$$

$$U_7 = \frac{(39-15)21}{48} = 12 \times \tfrac{42}{48} = 12 \tan \theta.$$

For the same section $M_{22} = 0$.

$$48 L_7 = 6\frac{1}{2} \times 8 \times 21 - (2 + 3 + 4 + 5 + 6 + 7)21.$$

$$L_7 = \frac{(52-27)21}{48} = 12\frac{1}{2} \times \tfrac{42}{48} = 12\frac{1}{2} \tan \theta.$$

At joint 12, one-half of each of the loads 11 and 13 is added to load 12, making $V_1 = 2 - q$.

The coefficients for the posts are evident by considering joints 18 and 20.

The *live load* coefficients are gotten as for a Pratt truss, except that in the panels with two diagonals, the sub-diagonal carries a half panel load of shear, and, that, as was shown for the truss of Fig. 192, D_2 *requires a full load.*

A question might arise as to the middle panel 6-7-8. The compression sub-diagonal cannot hang slack and, under full load it is a question whether D'_7 or D_7 is acting as the sub-diagonal; but under partial loading for maximum counter stress the distortion of the panel (120) throws the upper half of the diagonal, from joint 21 to 22, out of action (being a tension member) and the coefficients are as given in Fig. 193. This form of sub-trussing is often used for riveted bridges.

The maximum shear in panel 7-8 is $\tfrac{28}{14}$, of which D'_7 carries $\tfrac{7}{14}$, and D_7, $\tfrac{21}{14}$. The maximum shear in panel 9-10 is $\tfrac{45}{14}$, of which D'_5 carries $\tfrac{7}{14}$ and D_5, $\tfrac{38}{14}$. In like manner the coefficient for D_3 is $\tfrac{66}{14} - \tfrac{7}{14} = \tfrac{59}{14}$.

As the calculation of stresses is now a simple matter, only a few will be given.

Dead Load.

      Trusses and bracing = 1600 lbs. per ft. of bridge.
      Floor system   = 2000 lbs. per ft. of bridge.

          Total   = 3600 lbs. per ft. of bridge.

Live Load = 2000 lbs. per ft. of bridge.
Dead load panel load = $\frac{1}{2} \times 3600 \times 21 = 37,800$ lbs.
Live load panel load = $\frac{1}{2} \times 2000 \times 21 = 21,000$ lbs.

$$q = \frac{\frac{1}{2} \times 1600}{3600} = \frac{2}{9}.$$

Diagonal length = 63.8 ft.

$$sec\ \theta = \frac{63.9}{48}. \qquad tan\ \theta = \frac{42}{48}.$$

$D'_6 = (\frac{15}{14} \times 21,000 - 1 \times 37,800)\ sec\ \theta$ = no reversal. Therefore, D'_6 is not required and only panel 6-7-8 needs counters.

$D_7 = \frac{21}{14} \times 21,000\ sec\ \theta = 41,900$ lbs. $(-)$

$D'_7 = (\frac{1}{2} \times 21,000 + \frac{1}{2} \times 37,800)\ sec\ \theta = 39,100$ lbs. $(+)$
Max. comp.

$D'_7 = (\frac{21}{14} \times 21,000 - \frac{1}{2} \times 37,800\ sec\ \theta = 16,800$ lbs. $(-)$.
Max. tens.

$V_1 = (2 \times 21,000 + 1\frac{7}{9} \times 37,800) = 109,200$ lbs. $(-)$
$V_2 = (\frac{38}{14} \times 21,000 + 2\frac{2}{9} \times 37,800) = 141,000$ lbs. $(+)$

137. Stresses in a Camel-back Truss. For trusses with inclined chords, as in Figs. 162 and 164, coefficients of stress cannot be written by inspection as in trusses with parallel chords. The simplest way is to get the stresses directly by the method of sections, using the moment equation. The calculation of the lever arms for the upper chords and diagonals is somewhat laborious and should be checked by scaling from an accurate diagram to avoid large errors.

The end and middle panels of Fig. 194 are quite similar to those considered in Art. 130. Since D'_4 is zero under full load, it is evident, at joint 10, that V_3 will be in tension to resist the vertical component of U_3. At joint 9 there are four vertical components, but it will be found that V_2 will also be in tension under certain loads—the posts are subject to reversals of stress.

As was pointed out in Art. 129, no reversal of shear in a panel does not necessarily mean that a counter tie is not required, or that there is no reversal of stress in the diagonal. Nor will the compressive stress in a diagonal, when the counter tie is not present, be equal to the tensile stress in the counter tie, because their inclinations are different; their horizontal components are equal, however, for the same loading.

This fact furnishes a ready means of finding a counter stress

Art. 137.   STRESSES IN A CAMEL-BACK TRUSS.   269

after it has been found that the main diagonal stress reverses. To prove that it is true, consider D_3 for example, Fig. 194. Taking a section through U_3, D_3, and L_3, the algebraic sum

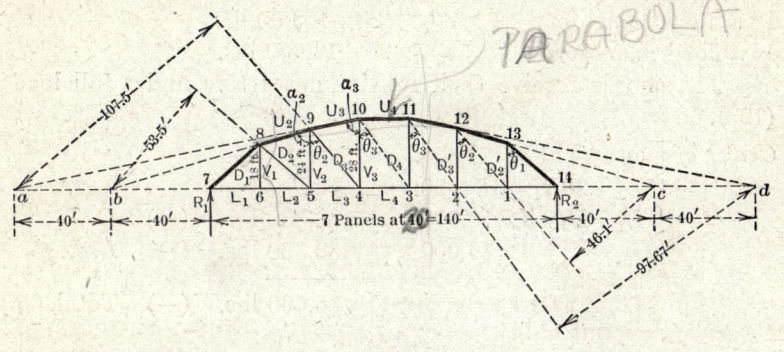

Fig. 194.

of the horizontal components of the stresses cut must equal zero, because all external forces are vertical.

$$U_3 \sin \alpha_3 = D_3 \sin \theta_3 + L_3.$$

Substituting the values of U_3 and L_3 in terms of the moments at 4 and 9, for whatever loading may be under consideration,

$$D_3 \sin \theta_3 = \frac{M_4 \sin \alpha_3}{28 \sin \alpha_3} - \frac{M_9}{24} = \frac{M_4}{28} - \frac{M_9}{24}.$$

In a similar manner, if D_3 is omitted and the counter tie, D'_3 inserted in this panel,

$$D'_3 \sin \theta'_3 = -\left(\frac{M_{10}}{28} - \frac{M_5}{24}\right) = -\left(\frac{M_4}{28} - \frac{M_9}{24}\right).$$

This proves that if a tensile diagonal is used in a panel of a truss with inclined chords and vertical posts, the horizontal component of its stress is the same as the horizontal component of the stress in the compressive diagonal would be if it were used.

The stresses will now be calculated for the *camel-back Pratt* truss of Fig. 194, for the following data:

Dead Load,
Trusses and bracing = 600 lbs. per ft. of bridge.
Floor system   = 400 lbs. per ft. of bridge.

Total   = 1000 lbs. per ft. of bridge.

$$q = \frac{\frac{1}{2} \times 600}{1000} = 0.3.$$

Live load = 1600 lbs. per foot of bridge,
Dead load panel load = $\frac{1}{2} \times 1000 \times 20 = 10{,}000$ lbs.
Live load panel load = $\frac{1}{2} \times 1600 \times 20 = 16{,}000$ lbs.

The chords receive their maximum stresses under full load (128).

Center of moments at 8,
$$18L_1 = 20R_1 = 3P \times 20.$$
$$L_1 = L_2 = 3 \times 10{,}000 \times \tfrac{20}{18} = 33{,}330 \text{ lbs.} \quad (-) \quad D.\,L.$$
$$= 3 \times 16{,}000 \times \tfrac{20}{18} = 53{,}330 \text{ lbs.} \quad (-) \quad L.\,L.$$
$$\overline{}$$
$$86{,}660 \text{ lbs.} \quad (-) \quad \text{Total.}$$

Center of moments at 9.
$$24L_3 = 40R_1 - 20P = 3P \times 40 - P \times 20 = 100P.$$
$$L_3 = \frac{100 \times 10{,}000}{24} = 41{,}600 \text{ lbs.} \quad (-) \quad D.\,L.$$
$$= \frac{100 \times 16{,}000}{24} = 66{,}670 \text{ lbs.} \quad (-) \quad L.\,L.$$
$$\overline{}$$
$$108{,}330 \text{ lbs.} \quad (-) \quad \text{Total.}$$

Center of moments at 10;
$$28L_4 = 60R_1 - (20 + 40)P = 120P.$$
$$L_4 = \frac{120 \times 10{,}000}{28} = 42{,}860 \text{ lbs.} \quad (-) \quad D.\,L.$$
$$= \frac{120 \times 16{,}000}{28} = 68{,}570 \text{ lbs.} \quad (-) \quad L.\,L.$$
$$\overline{}$$
$$111{,}430 \text{ lbs.} \quad (-) \quad \text{Total.}$$

For the top chords the lever arms must be calculated This may be done by similar triangles, thus,
Center of moments at 5,
$$\frac{\text{Arm of } U_2}{20} = \frac{24}{\text{Length of } U_2}. \quad \text{Arm of } U_2 = 23.0 \text{ ft.}$$
$$23U_2 = 40R_1 - 20P = 100P.$$
$$U_2 = \frac{100 \times 10{,}000}{23} = 43{,}480 \text{ lbs.} \quad (+) \quad D.\,L.$$
$$= \frac{100 \times 16{,}000}{23} = 69{,}560 \text{ lbs.} \quad (+) \quad L.\,L.$$
$$\overline{}$$
$$113{,}040 \text{ lbs.} \quad (+) \quad \text{Total.}$$

Art. 137.   STRESSES IN A CAMEL-BACK TRUSS.   271

Center of moments at 4,
$$\text{Arm of } U_3 = \frac{20 \times 28}{20.4} = 27.45 \text{ ft.}$$
$$27.45 U_3 = 60 R_1 - (20+40)P = 120P,$$
$$U_3 = \frac{120 \times 10{,}000}{27.45} = 43{,}710 \text{ lbs.} \quad (+) \quad D.L.$$
$$= \frac{120 \times 16{,}000}{27.45} = 69{,}940 \text{ lbs.} \quad (+) \quad L.L.$$
$$\overline{}$$
$$113{,}650 \text{ lbs.} \quad (+) \quad \text{Total.}$$

Center of moments at 3,
$$\text{Arm of } U_4 = 28 \text{ ft.}$$
$$28 U_4 = 80 R_1 - (20+40+60)P = 120P.$$
$$U_4 = \frac{120 \times 10{,}000}{28} = 42{,}860 \text{ lbs.} \quad (+) \quad D.L.$$
$$= \frac{120 \times 16{,}000}{28} = 68{,}570 \text{ lbs.} \quad (+) \quad L.L.$$
$$\overline{}$$
$$111{,}430 \text{ lbs.} \quad (+) \quad \text{Total.}$$

If the *main diagonals* are to be tension members, they will have the same direction of inclination as in a Pratt truss, as shown in Fig. 194. The position of the loads for maximum stresses in the diagonals will follow the regular rule as shown in Art. 129.

For the *end post* the maximum stress will occur under full load. Taking vertical resolutions at joint 7,
$$D_1 \cos \theta_1 = R_1 = 3P.$$
$$D_1 = 3 \times 10{,}000 \times \frac{26.9}{18} = 44{,}830 \text{ lbs.} \quad (+) \quad D.L.$$
$$= 3 \times 16{,}000 \times \frac{26.9}{18} = 71{,}730 \text{ lbs.} \quad (+) \quad L.L.$$
$$\overline{}$$
$$116{,}560 \text{ lbs.} \quad (+) \quad \text{Total.}$$

For D_2, with a section through U_2, D_2, and L_2, and a center of moments at b, the lever arm may be found by similar triangles.

$$\frac{\text{Arm of } D_2}{18} = \frac{80}{\text{Length of } D_2} \quad \text{Arm of } D_2 = 53.5 \text{ ft.}$$

$$53.5 D_2 = 40 R_1 - 60P = 60P, \text{ for dead load.}$$
$$= 40 R_1 = 40 \times \tfrac{15}{7} P, \text{ for live load.}$$

$$D_2 = \frac{60 \times 10{,}000}{53.5} = 11{,}210 \text{ lbs. } (-) \quad D.\,L.$$

$$= \frac{40 \times 34{,}290}{53.5} = 25{,}630 \text{ lbs. } \quad (-) \quad L.\,L.$$

$$\overline{36{,}840 \text{ lbs. } (-) \quad \text{Total.}}$$

Center of moments at a,

$$\frac{\text{Arm of } D_3}{24} = \frac{140}{\text{Length of } D_3} \quad \text{Arm of } D_3 = 107.5 \text{ ft.}$$

$$107.5 D_3 = 80R_1 - (100 + 120)P = 20P, \text{ for dead load.}$$
$$= 80R_1 = 80 \times \tfrac{10}{7} P, \text{ for live load.}$$

$$D_3 = \frac{20 \times 10{,}000}{107.5} = 1{,}860 \text{ lbs. } (-) \quad D.\,L.$$

$$= \frac{80 \times 22{,}860}{107.5} = 17{,}010 \text{ lbs. } (-) \quad L.\,L.$$

$$\overline{18{,}870 \text{ lbs. } (-) \quad \text{Total.}}$$

D_4 is best obtained from the shear in the panel, as the chords are horizontal.

$D_4 = 0$ for dead load.
$$= \tfrac{6}{7} \times 16{,}000 \sec \theta_3 = 16{,}850 \text{ lbs. } (-) \quad L.\,L., \text{ Total.}$$

Center of moments at d,

$$\frac{\text{Arm of } D'_3}{28} = \frac{120}{\text{Length of } D'_3} \quad \text{Arm of } D'_3 = 97.67 \text{ ft.}$$

$$97.67 D'_3 = 80R_2 - (100 + 120)P = 20P, \text{ for dead load.}$$
$$= 220R_1 = 220 \times \tfrac{3}{7} P, \text{ for live load (considering part to the left of the section).}$$

$$D'_3 = \frac{20 \times 10{,}000}{97.67} = 2{,}050 \text{ lbs. } (+) \quad D.\,L.$$

$$= \frac{220 \times 6{,}860}{97.67} = 15{,}450 \text{ lbs. } (-) \quad L.\,L.$$

$$\overline{13{,}400 \text{ lbs. } (-) \quad \text{Total.}}$$

Center of moments at c,

$$\frac{\text{Arm of } D'_2}{24} = \frac{60}{\text{Length of } D'_2} \quad \text{Arm of } D'_2 = 46.1 \text{ ft.}$$

$$46.1 D'_2 = 40R_2 - 60P = 60P, \text{ for dead load.}$$
$$= 180R_1 = 180 \times \tfrac{1}{7} P, \text{ for live load.}$$

$$D'_2 = \frac{60 \times 10{,}000}{46.1} = 13{,}010 \text{ lbs. } (+) \quad D.\,L.$$

$$= \frac{180 \times 2{,}290}{46.1} = 8{,}920 \text{ lbs. } (-) \quad L.\,L.$$

No reversal.

Art. 137.   STRESSES IN A CAMEL-BACK TRUSS.   273

Counters are required in the three middle panels only.

Another method of getting the stresses in the diagonals is to consider the horizontal components at the lower joints. This will require the calculation of the live load stresses in the lower chords for the position of the live load giving a maximum stress in each diagonal; for instance, at joint 5,

$$D_2 \sin \theta_1 = L_3 - L_2.$$

For a maximum stress in D_3, loads 1 to 5 inclusive must be on the truss, giving a reaction $R_1 = \tfrac{15}{7}P$.

$$L_2 = R_1 \times \tfrac{20}{18} = \tfrac{15}{7} \times 16{,}000 \times \tfrac{20}{18} = 38{,}100 \text{ lbs.} \quad (-)$$
$$L_3 = R_1 \times \tfrac{40}{24} = \tfrac{15}{7} \times 16{,}000 \times \tfrac{40}{24} = 57{,}140 \text{ lbs.} \quad (-)$$
$$D_2 \sin \theta_1 = 57{,}140 - 38{,}100 = 19{,}040 \text{ lbs.}$$
$$D_2 = 19{,}040 \times \frac{26.9}{20} = 25{,}620 \text{ lbs. } L.L.,$$

which corresponds with the value found by the moment equation.

As stated in the beginning of this article, the *vertical posts* are subject to reversals of stress and each kind of stress must be calculated.

V_1 is a *suspender* and gets whatever load is applied at joint 6.

$$\begin{aligned}V_1 = (1-q)P &= 0.7 \times 10{,}000 = 7{,}000 \text{ lbs.} \quad (-) \quad D.L.\\ = 1P &\phantom{= 0.7 \times 10{,}000} = 16{,}000 \text{ lbs.} \quad (-) \quad L.L.\end{aligned}$$
$$\overline{}$$
$$23{,}000 \text{ lbs.} \quad (-) \quad \text{Total.}$$

For *maximum compression in the posts*, the position of the loads follows the regular rule, as was proven in Art. 129.

Center of moments at b,

$$80V_2 = 40R_1 - 60P - 80(1-q)P = 4P \text{ for dead load.}$$
$$= 40R_1 = 40 \times \frac{10}{7} \times P \text{ for live load.}$$

$$V_2 = \tfrac{4}{80} \times 10{,}000 = 500 \text{ lbs.} \quad (+) \quad D.L.$$
$$= \tfrac{5}{7} \times 16{,}000 = 11{,}430 \text{ lbs.} \quad (+) \quad L.L.$$
$$\overline{}$$
$$11{,}930 \text{ lbs.} \quad (+) \quad \text{Total compression.}$$

Center of moments at a,
$$140V_3 = 80R_1 - (100+120)P - 140(1-q)P = -78P \text{ for dead load.}$$
$$= 80R_1 = 80 \times \frac{6}{7} \times P \text{ for live load.}$$

$$V_3 = -\frac{78}{140} \times 10{,}000 = -5{,}570 \text{ lbs.} \quad (-) \quad D. L.$$
$$= \frac{24}{49} \times 16{,}000 = +7{,}830 \text{ lbs.} \quad (+) \quad L. L.$$
$$\overline{\quad 2{,}260 \text{ lbs.} \quad (+) \quad \text{Total compression.}}$$

To find the maximum tension in V_2, the rule for position of the live load cannot be applied because it is possible to have three different trusses with different combinations of counters and main ties in action, depending upon the position of the live load. If the main ties were capable of resisting compression as well as tension and counters were not used, the regular rule would apply. The tension in the post is produced by the upward component of the stresses in the top chords. This is lessened by the downward component of the stress in any diagonal acting at the top of the post. Therefore, *a maximum tension in a post will occur with as much load as possible on the bridge* (to produce compression in the top chords) *with no stress, or as little stress as possible in the diagonals connecting at the top of the post.*[1]

Considering V_2, we know that with loads 6 and 5 on, diagonal D_3 is not in action. The problem is to find how much more load may be added without bringing this diagonal into action. We can write an equation for the total stress in D_3 with loads 6 and 5 on the bridge and enough more loads to make $D_3 = 0$. This will give us the position of the loads for maximum tension in the post.

Center of moments at a,
$$107.5D_3 = 80R_1 - (100+120)(D. L. + L. L.) = 0.$$
Solving this
$$R_1 = \frac{220}{80} \times (D. L. + L. L.) = 71{,}500 \text{ lbs. total when } D_3 = 0.$$
$$DLR_1 = 3P \qquad\qquad = 30{,}000 \text{ lbs.}$$
$$\overline{\qquad\qquad R_1 = 41{,}500 \text{ lbs. } L. L. \text{ when } = D_3 = 0.}$$

---
[1] For an extensive discussion of this problem see Mueller-Breslau's *Graphische Statik*, Vol. I.

Art. 137.   STRESSES IN A CAMEL-BACK TRUSS.   275

If this value of R_1 comes out less than the value of R_1 for loads 5 and 6 alone, use the greater value. This would show that D_3 could not reverse.

With this value of R_1 the live load stress in V_2 may be obtained without actually finding the exact position of the live load which produces the stress. We know that loads 5 and 6 are on, plus some more which are beyond the section, and do not enter into our moment equation.

Center of moments at b,

$80V_2 = 40R_1 - (60+80)P = 40 \times 41{,}500 - 140 \times 16{,}000.$
$V_2 = 7{,}250$ lbs. $(-)$ *L. L.*
$D.\,L. = 500$ lbs. $(+)$ From former calculation.

$6{,}750$ lbs. $(-)$ Total tension.

The case of V_3 is much simpler. It is evident that the maximum tension occurs under full load as $D_4 = 0$ for a full load. Therefore, with a center of moments at a,

$140V_3 = 80R_1 - (100+120+140)P = -120P$ for live load.

$$V_3 = -\frac{120 \times 16{,}000}{140} = 13{,}710 \text{ lbs.} \quad (-) \quad L.\,L.$$

Dead load $= 5{,}570$ lbs. $(-)$

$\phantom{\text{Dead load} = \,}19{,}280$ lbs. $(-)$ Total tension.

A *graphic method* for finding all the maximum stresses, except the tension in the posts, which requires but two stress diagrams, is often used for trusses with inclined chords. This is illustrated in Fig. 195.

Fig. 195 (b) is drawn for panel loads of unity, distributed between the upper and lower joints in the same proportion as the dead load. If the stresses scaled from this diagram be multiplied by the dead load panel load, the dead load stresses in *all* the members will be obtained, and if the scaled stresses for the chords and end post be multiplied by the live load panel load, the live load stresses in these members will be obtained, as these get their maxima under full load. For this purpose only the stresses in the members on the left of the center of the truss should be scaled, as they are the ones in action for full load.

Fig. 195 (c) is drawn for a load at joint 1 only, such that

the left-hand reaction will be unity. For any other value of the reaction, the stress diagram will be a similar figure for all members from the left end of the truss to the point where the first load is met. As there are no loads between any web member and the left end of the truss when that member gets its maximum stress, this diagram may be used to find the maximum live load stresses in the web members, by multiplying the scaled stresses by the left-hand live load reaction for each position of

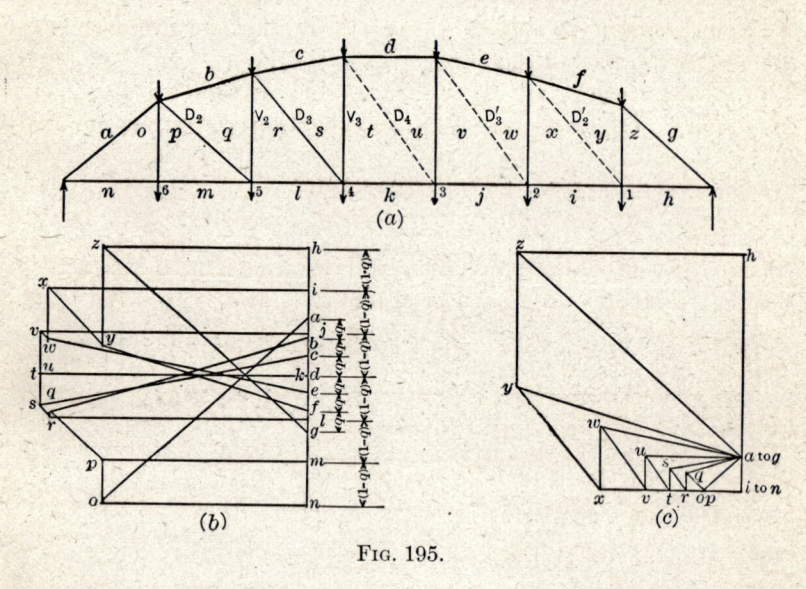

FIG. 195.

the load. These correspond to the live load coefficients in a truss with parallel chords.

For D'_2 Load 1 on $R_1 = \frac{1}{7} \times L.L.P.L.$

D'_3 Loads 1 and 2 on $R_1 = \frac{3}{7} \times L.L.P.L.$

D_4 and V_3 Loads 1, 2, and 3 on $R_1 = \frac{6}{7} \times L.L.P.L.$

D_3 and V_2 Loads 1, 2, 3, and 4 on $R_1 = \frac{10}{7} \times L.L.P.L.$

D_2 Loads 1, 2, 3, 4, and 5 on $R_1 = \frac{15}{7} \times L.L.P.L.$

Art. 138.   STRESSES IN A PETTIT TRUSS.   277

These, in connection with the dead load stresses, give all of the stresses with the exception of the tension in the posts.

138. Stresses in a Pettit Truss. For long span bridges the Pettit is by far the most common form of truss. The analysis of the stresses offers no particular difficulties which have not already been explained in connection with the Baltimore and camel-back Pratt. Fig. 196 shows a Pettit truss with the sub-diagonals in tension. The two end diagonals extend over only one panel in this case; in some cases they are run over two panels, as in the Baltimore.

It is evident that, as the inclinations of the two diagonals in a panel differ, the vertical component of the stress in the

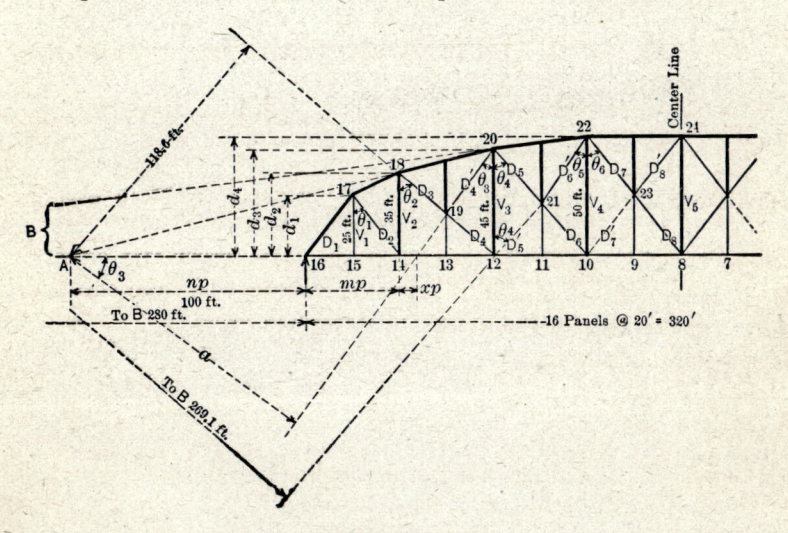

FIG. 196.

sub-diagonal no longer equals a half panel load. Its value may be found by vertical and horizontal resolutions, as was done in the case of the Baltimore truss (136), or by a moment equation. In Fig. 196 consider the forces acting at joint 19. Let $d_3 =$ depth of truss at V_3, $l =$ length of D'_4 and $p =$ panel length, then with a center of moments at 12,

$$D'_4 \times d_3 \sin \theta_3 = Pp. \qquad \sin \theta_3 = \frac{p}{l}. \qquad D'_4 = \frac{l}{d_3} P \ldots \ldots (a)$$

If the chords are parallel as in a Baltimore truss, $\dfrac{l}{d_3} = \frac{1}{2} \sec \theta$, and the sub-diagonal takes a half of a panel load as is proven in Art. 136.

The position of the live load for maximum stress in a diagonal where there is but one in action in the panel, as D_3 and D_5, follows the regular rule of loading to the section. Where the section cuts a sub-diagonal as well as the member whose stress is desired, the moment of the stress in the sub-diagonal enters into the equation of stress. Again referring to the double panel 12-14,

$$a = (n+m+x)p \cos\theta_3. \quad x = \frac{d_3-d_2}{d_3-\frac{1}{2}d_2}. \quad \cos\theta_3 = \frac{d_3-\frac{1}{2}d_2}{l}.$$

$$D'_4 a = \frac{l}{d_3}\left(n+m+\frac{d_3-d_2}{d_3-\frac{1}{2}d_2}\right)\frac{d_3-\frac{1}{2}d_2}{l}pP = \left[(n+m+1)p - \frac{(n+m+2)d_2}{2d_3}p\right]P.$$

$$n+m+2 = \frac{2d_3}{d_3-d_2}. \qquad n+m+1 = \frac{d_3+d_2}{d_3-d_2}.$$

$$D'_4 a = \frac{d_3}{d_3-d_2}pP \quad \dots \dots \dots \dots \dots \dots (b)$$

This equation will be useful in getting the stresses in the balance of the diagonals and in the vertical posts.

As with the Baltimore truss, in some cases the stress in the lower half of a main diagonal is greater when the sub-panel load ahead is on. This may be determined by trial.

For D_4, the increase in the reaction due to the addition of the sub-panel load at 13 is $\frac{13}{16}P$. The change in the stress in D_4 due to this load is

$$\frac{\frac{13}{16}Pnp - (n+m+1)pP + D'_4 a}{\text{arm of } D_4} = \frac{\left(\frac{13}{16}n - \frac{d_2}{d_3-d_2}\right)pP}{\text{arm of } D_4}.$$

If $\dfrac{d_2}{d_3-d_2}$ is greater than $\dfrac{13}{16}n$ the loading follows the regular rule, for maximum stress in D_4.

The same process is necessary with regard to the main verticals. For V_3, the regular rule would require loading up to joint 11 for maximum compression; if two more loads be added the increase in the reaction is $\frac{25}{16}P$. The change in the stress in V_3 due to this addition is

$$\frac{\frac{25}{16}Pnp - (n+m+1)pP - (n+m+2)pP + D'_4 a}{(n+m+2)p} = \frac{\frac{25}{16}n - \frac{2d_3+d_2}{d_3-d_2}}{n+m+2}P.$$

Art. 138.   STRESSES IN A PETTIT TRUSS.   279

If $\frac{2d_3+d_2}{d_3-d_2}$ is greater than $\frac{25}{16}n$, the loading follows the regular rule, for maximum compression in V_3.

For trusses with inclined chords, the loading for *compression in the posts* usually follows the regular rule.

Tension in the posts. On account of the action of the sub-diagonals, the *tension* in the main posts will seldom be very large. In general there are two possible positions which must be tested. For V_3 the load may extend from the left end up to joint 14, so that the sub-diagonal at the top of V_3 will have no live load stress, or it may extend beyond joint 12, thus reducing the tension in D_5 to a minimum.

A few of the stresses will now be calculated to illustrate the methods. The following loads will be assumed:

Weight of trusses and bracing = 2200 lbs. per ft.
Weight of floor system   = 1100 lbs. per ft.

Total dead load   = 3300 lbs. of ft. of bridge.
Live load   = 4000 lbs. per ft. of bridge.

From these the following constants are obtained:

Dead load panel load = 33,000 lbs.
Live load panel load = 40,000 lbs.

$$q = \frac{\frac{1}{2} \times 2200}{3300} = \frac{1}{3}.$$

Diagonal D_3. Loading from *right* to joint 13.
Center of moments at A, Arm of $D_3 = 118.6$ ft.
$118.6 D_3 = 7\frac{1}{2} P \times 100 - P(120+140) = 490P$ for dead load.

$$= \frac{91}{16} P \times 100 \text{ for live load.}$$

$$D_3 = \frac{490 \times 33{,}000}{118.6} = 136{,}300 \text{ lbs.} \quad (-) \quad D.\,L.$$

$$= \frac{9100 \times 40{,}000}{16 \times 118.6} = 191{,}800 \text{ lbs.} \quad (-) \quad L.\,L.$$

$$328{,}100 \text{ lbs.} \quad (-) \text{ Total.}$$

Diagonal D_4. Applying the criterion developed for the position of the live load:

$$\frac{d_2}{d_3-d_2} = \frac{35}{10} = 3.5. \qquad \frac{13}{16}n = \frac{13 \times 5}{16} = 4\frac{1}{16}.$$

The second term is greater; therefore the loading extends to joint 13.

Center of moments at A, Arm of $D_4 = 118.6$ ft.

$118.6 D_4 = 7\tfrac{1}{2} P \times 100 - P(120 + 140 + 160) + D'_4 a = 420 P$. D. L.

$= \dfrac{91}{16} P \times 100 - P \times 160 + D'_1 a = \dfrac{7980}{16} P$ for live load.

$D_4 = \dfrac{420 \times 33{,}000}{118.6} = 116{,}800$ lbs. $(-)$ D. L.

$= \dfrac{7980 \times 40{,}000}{16 \times 118.6} = 168{,}200$ lbs. $(-)$ L. L.

$ 285{,}000$ lbs. $(-)$ Total.

Sub-diagonal $D'_4 = \dfrac{34}{45} \times 33{,}000 = 24{,}900$ lbs. $(-)$ D. L.

$ = \dfrac{34}{45} \times 40{,}000 = 30{,}200$ lbs. $(-)$ L. L.

$ 55{,}100$ lbs. $(-)$ Total.

Counter D'_5. Loading from *left* to joint 12.
Center of moments at B, Arm of $D'_5 = 269.1$ ft.
D_6 is not in action and D_5 acts as a sub-diagonal.
$269.1 D'_5 = 7\tfrac{1}{2} P \times 280 - P(300 + 320 + 340 + 360) - D_5 \times 299$.

$D_5 = \dfrac{30.1}{45} \times P$.

$269.1 D'_5 = 580 P$, for dead load.

$269.1 D'_5 = \dfrac{10}{16} P \times 600 = 375 P$, for live load.

$D'_5 = \dfrac{580 \times 33{,}000}{269.1} = 71{,}100$ lbs. $(+)$ D. L.

$ = \dfrac{375 \times 40{,}000}{269.1} = 55{,}700$ lbs. $(-)$ L. L.

 No reversal.

Post V_3, applying the criterion developed for the position of the load for maximum compression:

$$\dfrac{2d_3 + d_2}{d_3 - d_2} = \dfrac{125}{10}. \qquad \dfrac{25}{16} n = \dfrac{125}{16}.$$

The first term is greater; therefore the loading follows the regular rule.

Art. 138. STRESSES IN A PETTIT TRUSS. 281

Center of moments at A.

$$180V_3 = 7\tfrac{1}{2}P \times 100 - P(120 + 140 + 160) - (1-q)P \times 180 + D'_4 a$$
$$= 300P, \text{ for dead load,}$$
$$= \frac{66}{16}P \times 100, \text{ for live load.}$$

$$V_3 = \frac{300 \times 33{,}000}{180} = 55{,}000 \text{ lbs.} \quad (+) \quad D.\,L.$$

$$= \frac{6600 \times 40{,}000}{180 \times 16} = 91{,}700 \text{ lbs.} \quad (+) \quad L.\,L.$$

$$\underline{}$$
$$146{,}700 \text{ lbs.} \quad (+) \text{ Total.}$$

Tension in V_3. As D'_5 cannot come into action in this case (see above) the position of the live load will be either 14 and 15, or 12, 13, 14, and 15.

Loads 12, 13, 14, and 15 on:

$$180V_3 = \frac{10}{16}P \times 420 - D'_4 a = 172.5P. \quad L.\,L. \text{ tension.}$$

Loads 14 and 15 on:

$$180V_3 = \frac{3}{16} \times 420 = 78.75P. \quad L.\,L. \text{ tension.}$$

The first case gives the greater tension, so,

$$V_3 = \frac{172.5 \times 40{,}000}{180} = 38{,}300 \text{ lbs.} \quad (-) \quad L.\,L.$$

Dead load from above = 55,000 lbs. (+)
$$\underline{}$$

No reversal.

139. Skew Bridges. When for any reason the supports for a bridge cannot be made perpendicular to the center line of the bridge, the bridge is said to be *skewed*. This is illustrated in Fig. 197.

The span is usually divided into equal panel lengths *along the center line of the bridge*, and the inclinations of the end posts are made equal. This causes the end suspenders to be inclined and the end panels of the trusses to be unequal.

The floor beams are usually placed normal to the trusses. This is done because the connections are more easily made and the construction is cheaper.

The inclinations of the end posts are usually made the same, as this will make the portal bracing lie in a plane, otherwise the portal would lie in a warped surface. Warped portals are expensive to construct, difficult to connect and are not as efficient as bracing in a plane.

The weight of the trusses and bracing is usually assumed to be equally divided among the panel points, but the weight of the floor system is proportional to the area of the floor tributary to the panel points. This will not make a great deal of

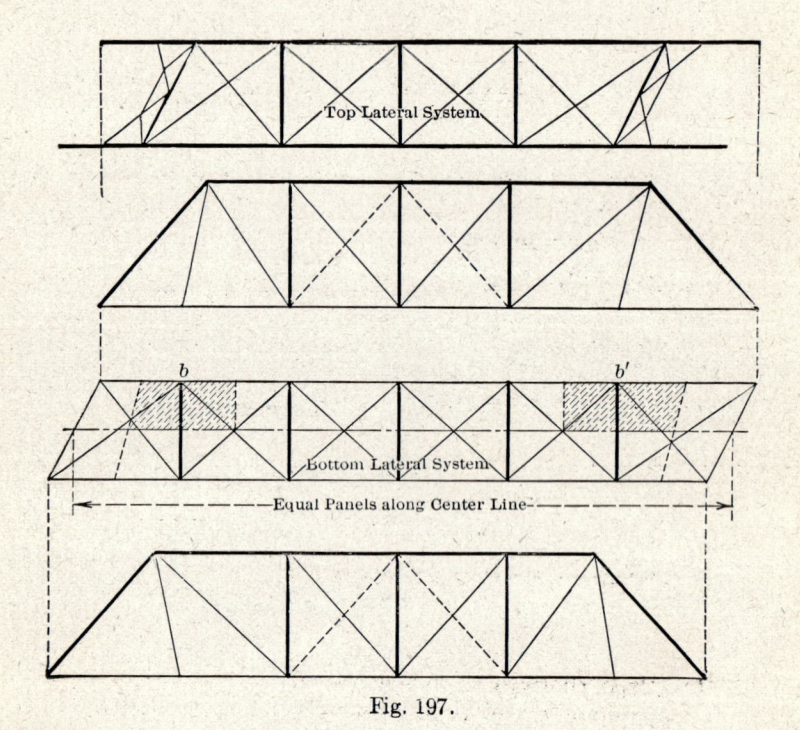

Fig. 197.

difference in the *dead load* panel loads of single track railroad bridges, but in *highway bridges* where the entire floor is covered with a heavy flooring there may be a considerable difference in the panel loads.

In single track railroad bridges the *live load* is usually assumed to be applied on the center line of the bridge. This makes the live load panel loads all equal, if the panels are equal on the center line. In double track bridges, and in highway bridges where the live load is usually specified in pounds per square foot of roadway, the end panel loads will be unequal. The shaded areas in Fig. 197 indicate the parts of the floor tributary to the panel points b and b'.

The inclinations of the diagonals, the panel lengths, and the panel loads all being irregular, the method of coefficients cannot be used, but the stresses must be calculated from the moments and shears directly.

1. How do the weights of the various parts of a bridge vary from the supports to the center?

2. How is the dead load estimated in a railroad bridge?

3. How are the panel loads of dead load assumed to act?

4. How much variation is usually allowed between the assumed dead load and the final estimated weight?

5. Make sketches of some bridge in your vicinity, showing the manner of supporting the floor covering, the joists and the floor beams. Make an estimate of the weight of the floor per panel, and of the steel work.

6. What stresses are required in a bridge design?

7. When a partial live load is on the bridge, how is the partial panel load at the head treated?

8. What is the relation of the stresses in two trusses similar to Fig. 167, if the span and height of one are 120 ft. and 24 ft., and of the other are 105 ft. and 21 ft., respectively, if the panel loads are 24,000 lbs. in each case?

9. In Fig. 167, what position of the live load will give a maximum stress in *BC*? What will the maximum stress in *BC* be if the span is 120 ft., height 24 ft., dead load 400 lbs. per lin. ft., live load 600 lbs. per lin. ft. of truss?

10. In the case of Problem 9, what will be the position of the live load for a maximum tension in *Bc*?

11. Where must the center of moments for a member lie in order for its stress to be a maximum for full load?

12. What is represented by a coefficient of stress?

13. Write the dead and live load coefficients on a Howe truss of 9 panels, all loads assumed to act at the upper chord.

14. Write the dead and live load coefficients on a deck sub-divided Warren truss of 8 panels; one third of the dead load assumed to act at the lower chord and two thirds at the upper.

15. Write the dead and live load coefficients on a deck Baltimore truss of fourteen panels with vertical end posts.

16. What is the condition for maximum tension in V_2, Fig. 194? In V_3?

17. Make sketches illustrating the four different trusses possible with different loadings, as affecting V_2 in Fig. 194.

CHAPTER XIII.

STRESSES IN RAILWAY BRIDGES FROM WHEEL LOADS.

140. Kinds of Stress. The *live load* on railway bridges produces stress in various ways.

1st. Vertical static stresses due to the weight of the locomotive and train in any position.

2nd. Vibratory stresses due to various causes, generally included under the term "Impact."

3rd. Horizontal static stresses due to the centrifugal force of the train, if the track is on a curve.

4th. Longitudinal static stresses due to the momentum of the train, and friction on the rails when the brakes are applied.

The vibratory stresses cannot be calculated, but are provided for in a more or less arbitrary way by taking a certain percentage (varying with different specifications) of the static live load stress as "impact stress," or by using small working stresses (28). No account, however, is usually taken (except in the general design of the bridge) of vibratory stresses which do not act vertically. Horizontal vibratory stresses also occur even when the track is *not* on a curve, when the wind is *not* blowing and when the brakes are *not* applied. Stresses in bridges having curved track will be treated in Art. 176. The stresses produced by the friction between the rails and the wheels is of particular importance in viaducts (steel trestles).

141. Loading. The live load on a railway bridge *all* consists of wheel loads, but nearly all railway bridge specifications require it to be assumed to consist of two consolidation engines *followed* by a *uniformly distributed* load representing the train.[1] The weights on the wheels and their distances apart may represent the actual engine in use which will produce the maximum effect on the bridges, but they usually represent typical engines supposed to be heavy enough to provide for future increase of weight.

Such a typical loading is shown in Fig. 198, which is Class $E40$ of Cooper's "General Specifications for Steel Railroad Bridges." In Cooper's loadings the class number is the same as

---

[1] The Specifications of the Pennsylvania Lines West of Pittsburg give a uniform load combined with a single concentrated load. Some specifications also give a special load on two axles 6 ft. to 8 ft. apart which governs for short spans.

286　　　　　　　　LOADING.　　　　　　　　Art. 141.

the load on a pair of driving wheels in thousands of pounds, and ten times that of the uniform load per foot. The other classes given in the specification are $E27$, $E30$, $E35$ and $E50$, but any

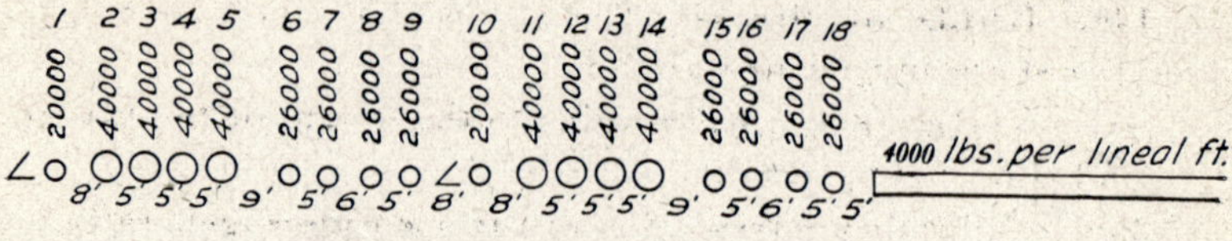

Cooper's Class E 40 Loading

Fig. 198.

intermediate class may be made by taking the loads in proportion to the class numbers. Since the spacing of the wheels is the same for all classes, and since the loads on corresponding wheels are in direct proportion to the class numbers, any stress due to the $E50$ loading, for example, is to that due to the $E40$ loading as 50 is to 40.

The $E40$ to $E60$ loadings are those oftenest used for steam railways. One locomotive (engine and tender) of the $E40$ loading weighs 142 tons and covers a distance of 56 ft.; this is an average load of about 5000 lbs. per foot, while that of the drivers alone is much greater. For spans somewhat less than the length of two locomotives, the loading giving maximum stresses consists entirely of wheel loads because these give a much greater load than the uniform load following. The average weight of locomotive now specified by a number of the principal railway systems is over 200 tons.[1]

142. Equivalent Loadings. On account of the laboriousness of calculating stresses from wheel loads as usually specified, many "equivalent loads" have been proposed, the idea being to substitute a simpler load which would give practically the same stresses as the wheel loads, or at least none that would be markedly smaller. Engineers are pretty well agreed that an equivalent load will give abundantly accurate results.[2] In order to approximate closely to the stresses given by the specified wheel loads, a number of different uniform loads are used for each

---

[1] For a comparison of different specifications see article by the author in *Eng. News*, Vol. 50, page 444.

[2] For a thorough discussion of this subject see *Trans. Am. Soc. C. E.*, Vol. 42, p. 189. Also *Eng. News*. Also Johnson's "Modern Framed Structures," Chapter VI.

bridge. Thus, a uniform load is used which will give the same maximum moment in the stringer as the specified wheel loads; another which will give the same maximum shear in the stringer, another that will give the same maximum floor beam concentration (and stress in the hip vertical); and another that will give the same maximum moment or end shear in the truss. A through plate girder is treated like a truss and a deck plate girder like a stringer. This method of equivalent uniform loads gives exact results then, so far as the maximum moments and shears in stringers, girders, and floor beams are concerned. In trusses, it gives results which are approximate except for the maximum moment or maximum end shear. This method necessitates the determination of equivalent uniform loads for different spans, for shears and moments, for each typical loading (only one set is needed for all Cooper Loadings). Having determined them for any particular loading for spans varying by suitable intervals, a table may be made or a diagram plotted for use in determining the equivalent uniform loads for any span lengths. This reduces the calculations to that for uniform load entirely and with results which, for ordinary bridges, may be accepted with full confidence.[1]

Some engineers calculate stresses from wheel loads and some use equivalent loads. One who is in the habit of calculating stresses from wheel loads can do so with facility, but never with the certainty and never in so short a time as from the simpler load. In most cases the uniform load should be used as a check if the stresses are calculated from wheel loads.

In order to be able to calculate equivalent uniform loads, we shall consider briefly methods of finding maximum moments and shears from a series of concentrated loads. From the moments we obtain the chord stresses and from the shears the web stresses.

143. Preliminary Considerations in the Calculation of Stresses from Wheel Loads.
The problem is to find the *position* of the loads that will give the greatest possible moment or shear at any point of a bridge. Having the proper position of the loads, it is a simple matter to calculate the moment or shear. (Chapters III to VI).

The maximum stress in any member may be found by trial

---

[1] For comparison of results by different methods, with those by wheel loads, see Trans. Am. Soc. C. E., Vol. 42, pp. 206 and 215. Also *Eng. News*, Also Johnson's "Modern Framed Structures," Part I, p. 246 (9th Edition). Also Du Bois's "Stresses in Framed Structures."

that is, by assuming a number of positions, calculating the stress for each position, and then comparing the results. This is indeed, *in some cases*, the quickest as well as the simplest way of arriving at the result, because the usual engine loadings are rather simple systems of concentrated loads. Certain simple criteria will, however, be developed whose employment will, in most cases, save time and enable us to determine if a certain assumed position will, or will not, give a maximum.

It will be noted that, in general, it is not only a question of finding the position of *a definite set of wheels on the span*, but of finding *what set of wheels must be on the span*. *This can only be done by trial*. To determine what set of wheels to try in any particular case certain fundamental principles will help.

1. *To find the maximum shear at any section of a solid beam, there should be as much load as possible between the section and the further support, and its center of gravity should be as near the section as possible.* There may be some load on the opposite side of the section, as is explained in Art. 151.

2. *To find the maximum shear in any panel of a truss, there should be as much load as possible between a support and the nearest panel point of the panel in question, and its center of gravity should be as near to this point as possible.* There will usually be some load in the panel as shown in Art. 147. Loading the longer segment gives the maximum positive shear and loading the shorter segment gives the maximum negative shear.

3. *To find the maximum moment at any point of a beam (includes truss) there should be as much load as possible on the span, and its center of gravity should be as near the center of moments as possible.*

These principles are applied roughly, of course, that is by

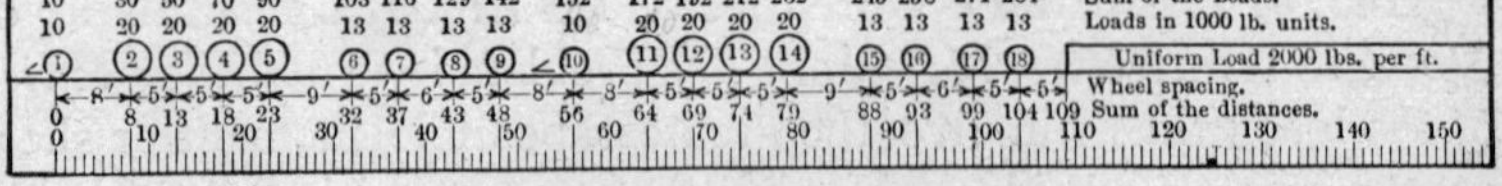

COOPER'S E40 LOADING FOR ONE RAIL.
Fig. 199.

inspection. A diagram of the loads should be made to scale on a piece of good paper or on tracing linen, as shown in Fig. 199. By moving this "loading strip" along a diagram of the beam or truss drawn to the same scale, and keeping in mind the

Art. 144. POSITION OF LOAD FOR MAXIMUM MOMENT. 289

above principles, the different positions to try will be limited to but a few when the following facts are taken into consideration.

If a moment diagram be made for a series of wheel loads on a beam, as in Fig. 118, it is evident that the *maximum moment comes under a wheel.* Of all the possible positions, therefore, which a series of loads may have, it is only necessary to try those in which *some wheel comes at the center of moments,* if this is possible, because the maximum moment at this point is wanted.

Likewise for shear, by principle (1) above, the shear increases as the loads move up to the section in question, and suddenly decreases as a load passes the section, therefore, *the shear is a maximum with a load at the section.* This is illustrated in Fig. 118.

By principle (2) above, the shear increases as the loads move toward the nearest panel point and decreases as a load passes this point, therefore (as in the case of a solid beam) *there must be a load at a panel point for a maximum shear in the panel ahead.*

The above principles are not perfectly general because they assume that chord stresses are gotten from moments and web stresses from shears.

144. Position of Load for Maximum Moment at Any Point of a Truss or Girder. In order to develop a criterion for the position of the typical loading that will give a maximum moment about any point, let us take some point of the truss shown in Fig. 200, as point 6 for instance. We have,

$$R_1 = G_1 \frac{L - a_1 - x}{L} + G_2 \frac{L - a_2 - x}{L} + G_3 \frac{L - a_3 - x}{L}$$

$$M_6 = R_1 a - G_1(a - a_1 - x) - G_2 \frac{p - (a_2 + x - np)}{p} c$$

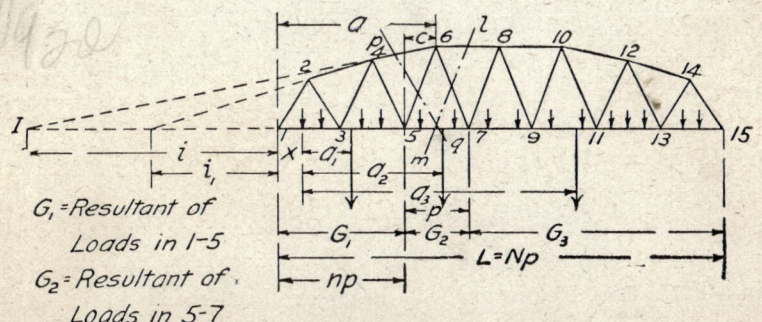

G_1 = Resultant of Loads in 1-5
G_2 = Resultant of Loads in 5-7
G_3 = Resultant of Loads in 7-15
G = Resultant of all Loads on the span

Fig. 200.

Substituting in the last equation for R_1 and differentiating we have for a maximum,

$$\frac{dM_6}{dx} = 0 = -\frac{G_1+G_2+G_3}{L}a + G_1 + G_2 \times \frac{c}{p}$$

$$\text{or}\quad \frac{G}{L} = \frac{G_1+G_2\times\frac{c}{p}}{a} \quad\ldots\ldots\ldots\ldots (82)$$

This then is the condition for maximum moment at point 6. With nothing but concentrated loads on the span, it will, in general, be impossible to satisfy this condition unless there is a load at 7 or 5, part of which may be counted with G_2 and part with G_3 or G_1. When all of the load at 7 is counted with G_2, $\dfrac{G_1+G_2\frac{c}{p}}{a} > \dfrac{G}{L}$

and when all of it is counted with G_3, $\dfrac{G_1+G_2\frac{c}{p}}{a} < \dfrac{G}{L}$ provided this particular position gives a maximum moment at 6. It is evident that so long as equation (82) holds true, a change in x, that is, a movement of the loads, so that one will come at 7, will not change the moment M_6. This will not be true if the movement causes any loads to pass 1, 5, 7, or 15, in which case G, G_1 or G_2 may change. G will change if there is any uniform load on the span, but in any case, the change in the moment M_6 will be slight as it will be due to a *small movement*. Hence we may always test by equation (82) with a load at 7 or 5, unless the uniform load reaches 7 or 5. With the type of loads usually specified, the uniform load would not reach 7 or 5.

Equation (82) is used, therefore, to find what loads of those on the span (with one at 7 or 5) will give a maximum moment at 6. Since *several different loadings may each give a maximum*, the moments must be calculated to see which is the greatest of these. With a little practice, it will not be necessary to test every possible loading by equation (82).

When $c = \frac{1}{2}p$ as in a Warren truss, equation (82) becomes

$$\frac{G}{L} = \frac{G_1 + \frac{1}{2}G_2}{a} \quad\ldots\ldots\ldots\ldots (83)$$

When $c = p$ or *when alternate web members are vertical* (as in a Pratt truss) equation (82) becomes

$$\frac{G}{L} = \frac{G_1+G_2}{a} \quad\text{or}\quad \frac{G}{N} = \frac{G_1+G_2}{n} \quad\ldots\ldots\ldots\ldots (84)$$

Art. 145. MAXIMUM MOMENT IN DECK PLATE GIRDER. 291

That is, *the total load per foot on the span must equal the load per foot to the left of the point at which the maximum moment is desired.* In other words, if P be the load at the point, $\dfrac{G_1+G_2+P}{a}$ must be greater than $\dfrac{G}{L}$ and $\dfrac{G_1+G_2}{a}$ must be less than $\dfrac{G}{L}$.

Equation (84) applies at any point of a truss having a single system of web bracing with alternate members vertical, whether the chords are inclined or parallel. *It also applies to any point of a girder or beam,* G_1+G_2 *being the load to the left of the section.*

145. Maximum Moment in a Deck Plate Girder. For a truss, moments are always wanted at the panel points, but in a deck plate girder carrying concentrated loads, the *maximum moment* is wanted and the center of moments must be found. While this occurs near the center of the span, the maximum moment at the *center* is materially different from the maximum moment in the girder. (101).

The problem is to find under which load and for what position of the loads the maximum moment occurs. In Fig. 201 let

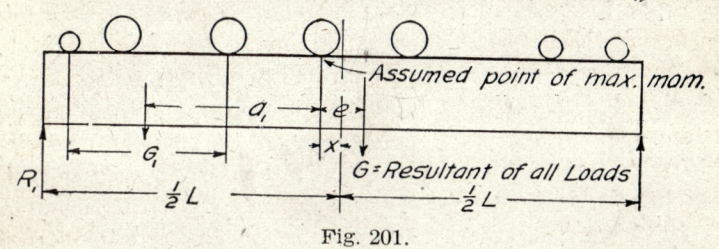

Fig. 201.

the load at which the maximum moment occurs be at a distance x from the center of the girder. e is the distance of this load from the center of gravity of all the loads on the span.

$$R_1 = \frac{G}{L}(\tfrac{1}{2}L+x-e)$$

$$M_{max} = R_1(\tfrac{1}{2}L-x) - G_1 a_1 = \frac{G}{L}(\tfrac{1}{2}L+x-e)(\tfrac{1}{2}L-x) - G_1 a$$

For a maximum $\dfrac{d\,M_{max}}{d\,x} = 0 = \dfrac{G}{L}(e-2x)$

Therefore for a maximum $\qquad e=2x \dots\dots\dots\dots (85)$

That is, *the load at which the maximum moment in the girder occurs, must be as far on one side of the center of the girder as*

LIMITING SPANS. Art. 146.

the center of gravity of the total load is on the other side of the center (101). In this case the load near the center becomes the point about which the maximum moment is desired, and various positions must be tested by equation (84) which becomes

$$\frac{G}{L} = \frac{G_1}{\frac{1}{2}L - x}$$

If the center of gravity of the total load is not easily located (x being therefore unknown) we must calculate the location of the center of gravity and determine if it is possible to have the assumed loading on the span and still satisfy equation (85). Then if P be the load near the center, placed $\frac{1}{2}e$ from the center, the loading will give a maximum moment at P if

$$\frac{G_1 + P}{\frac{1}{2}L \mp \frac{1}{2}e} > \frac{G}{L} \quad \text{and} \quad \frac{G_1}{\frac{1}{2}L \mp \frac{1}{2}e} < \frac{G}{L} \dots\dots\dots\dots(86)$$

The nearest wheel to the center of gravity does not always govern.

146. Limits of Span for which a Particular Series of Wheel Loads will give a Maximum Moment. It is evident that for a girder of less than about 80 ft. span, the maximum moment will occur when the drivers of one engine are near the middle of the span, and the smaller loads come on at both ends as the span increases, until both tenders are also on. If a certain number of wheels, say 5, give a maximum moment in a given span length, and 6 in another span length, there must be an intermediate length for which both give the same moment. In Fig. 202 for a maximum moment under wheel 4, the center of the span is 0.57 ft. to the left of the wheel, and in Fig. 203 it is 0.235 ft. to the right. In each case we can find R_1 and $M_{\max}$ in terms of L.

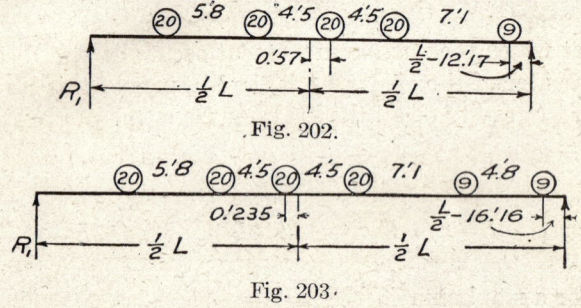

Fig. 202.

Fig. 203.

Putting the maximum moments equal to each other and solving for L we get the maximum span on which the loading of Fig. 202 governs, and minimum span on which that of Fig. 203 governs. Of course we must test by equation (86) in order to make sure

Handwritten annotations at top: SHEAR CRITERION = $\frac{G}{L} = \frac{G_2}{P}$ / Parallel Chords $i - \alpha$

Art. 147. CRITERION FOR MAXIMUM WEB STRESSES. 293

that no other loading will give a greater maximum. For example, it may be a question whether adding a load at the left, or right of those shown in Fig. 202 will give a greater moment in a span longer than the limiting span for the 5 loads. It will usually be found that the maximum moment occurs when the 3rd or 2nd driver is near the center.

147. Position of Load for Maximum Web Stresses in a Truss. The general case is a truss with one or both chords inclined. Since in this case the web does not carry all the shear, we resort to the moment equation to get the stresses in the web members.

Let us consider the diagonal 5-6 of Fig. 200. Taking the section pq the center of moments will be at I, and the stress in 5-6 will be a maximum when the moment about I is a maximum.

$$R_1 = \frac{L-(a+x)}{L}G_1 + \frac{L-(a_2+x)}{L}G_2 + \frac{L-(a_3+x)}{L}G_3$$

$$M_I = R_1 i - G_1(a_1+x+i) - G_2 \frac{p-(a_2+x-a+c)}{p}(a-c+i)$$

Substituting for R_1 and differentiating we have, when M_I is a maximum

$$\frac{dM_I}{dx} = 0 = -\frac{G_1+G_2+G_3}{L}i - G_1 + G_2\frac{(a-c+i)}{p}$$

or $\quad \dfrac{G}{L} = G_2 \dfrac{\frac{a-c}{i}+1}{p} - \dfrac{G_1}{i}$ ......(87) *(handwritten: CAMEL BACK — ISN'T USED MUCH)*

Equation (87) may be written in a form more convenient in application thus

$$\frac{G}{N} = G_2\left(\frac{a-c}{i}+1\right) - G_1\frac{p}{i} \dots\dots\dots\dots(88)$$

G_1 is usually 0 and some load near the head of the train, as wheel 2, 3 or 4 at the right hand end of the panel in question (the load extending to the right) will usually give a maximum. In general there must be a load at 7 to satisfy (88) so that when it is counted with G_2 the second member of equation (88) will be greater than $\dfrac{G}{N}$ and when it is counted with G_3 it will be less than $\dfrac{G}{N}$. If equation (88) is satisfied without a load at 7, the moment about I will not be changed if the loads are moved so that one will come at 7 unless some loads come on or go off the span. Even in the latter case, the effect upon the shear in 5-7, and therefore upon the stress in 5-6, will be slight. *Hence we may always test for positions giving maximum stress in a web member of any panel* (by equation (88)) *with a load at the right hand panel point of the panel.*

148. Particular Cases of the Application of the Criterion for Maximum Web Stresses. Equation (88) applies to any simple truss with a single system of web-bracing. In Fig. 200;

When $c=0$, 5-6 is vertical and we have *Pratt* bracing.

When $c=p$, 6-7 is vertical and we have *Howe* bracing.

When $c=\frac{1}{2}p$, we have the *Warren* type of bracing.

When the *chords* are *parallel* $i=\infty$ and equation (88) becomes

$$\frac{G}{N}=G_2 \quad (89)$$

In this case the chords carry no shear and therefore equation (89) is the *criterion for maximum shear in any panel.*[1] It will be noted that for parallel chords the criterion for maximum web stresses is independent of G_1. Equation (89) applies, in Fig. 200, to 6-7, because 6-8 is horizontal.

When i equals some multiple of a panel length, equation (88) is simplified.

149. Maximum Shear in a Pratt Truss. This is a particular case under equations (88) and (89). The criterion for maximum shear then, in any panel, is $\frac{G}{N}=G_2$. In general, this equa-

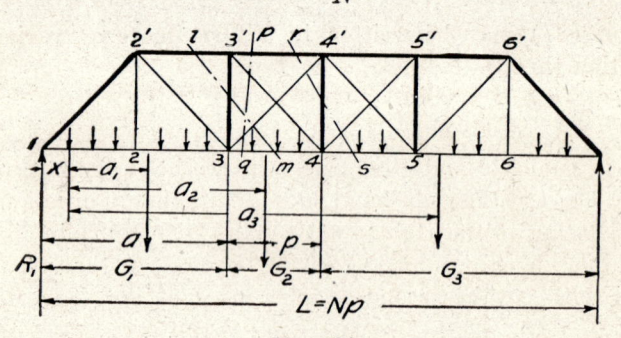

Fig. 204.

tion is satisfied, as shown for (88), when there is a load P at the

---

[1] Equation (89) may easily be derived independently of equation (88).

Art. 149.   MAXIMUM SHEAR IN A PRATT TRUSS.   295

right hand end of the panel in question, and when $G_2 < \frac{G}{N}$ and $G_2 + P > \frac{G}{N}$. In words, *the total average load per panel must equal the load in the panel in which the shear is wanted.*

It should be remembered that for maximum shear in panel 3-4, for instance, Fig. 204, a load near the head of the train (a driver) should generally be at 4, so that as much load as possible is concentrated at 4 and to the right of 4. A trial of 2 or 3 wheels at 4 by equation (89) will generally be sufficient.

For all web members the center of moments is at an infinite distance, but the section changes. For 3'-4 the section is pq and the panel in question is 3-4; for 3'-3, the section is lm, and the panel also 3-4; for 4'-4, the section is rs, and the panel is 4-5. The position of the loads for a maximum stress in 3'-4 and 3'-3 is just the same.

150. Fields of Shear in a Truss. From equation (89) we have $G = NG_2$. If P be the load at *any* panel point, G varies between NG_2 and $N(G_2+P)$ for maximum shear in the panel to the left of the point where P is located. Then P governs for all panel points for which the position of the load is such that the total load on the bridge lies between NG_2 and $N(G_2+P)$. The points on the diagram of loads at which G is *equal* to these two limits, may easily be found. Since the right end of the bridge must lie between these limits, when the load moves so that the end of the bridge passes from one of these limits to the other, the load P passes the panel points at which it governs for maximum shear. This range of P is called its *field of shear*. In this way we are saved the labor of testing a number of wheels at *each* panel point.

151. Position of Load for Maximum Shear in a Girder or Beam. Let it be required to find the maximum shear at any point C in the beam of Fig. 205. It is evident that the maximum shear at C occurs when R_1 is a maximum, so long as there are no loads

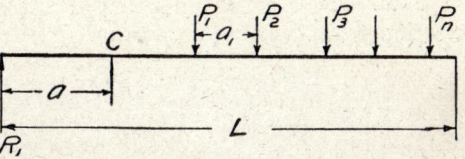

Fig. 205.

to the left of C. Loads coming on from the right and moving to the left increase R_1 until P_1 reaches C, when the shear at C is *a* maximum. As soon as P_1 passes C, the shear is suddenly decreased by P_1. Now as the loads move to the left the shear is again increased (because R_1 is increased and the shear=R_1-P_1) until P_2 reaches C, when it is again a maximum. This may be a larger or smaller maximum than the first, depending upon the relation between P_1 and the other loads, and upon a_1. When all the loads move a distance a_1, R_1 increases $\Sigma P \dfrac{a_1}{L}$. If this increase is greater than P_1, P_2 at C gives a greater maximum shear at C than P_1 at the same point. This is the criterion for finding which of *two* consecutive wheels at a point will give the greater shear. It will be found that the first or second wheel of the first engine at C will usually give the maximum shear at C. It is sometimes a very simple matter to calculate the shear for several possible positions without testing by the criterion. It should be remembered that for maximum shear at C, we should have as much weight near C and to the right of it as possible and no load to the left of it, unless such load will decrease the shear less than the movement to this position will increase R_1. If when P_2 is at C, P_1 has passed off the span, there has been a sudden increase of shear at C, which may have been still further increased by loads coming on at the right.

The *maximum shear in the beam* occurs of course at the end.

152. Maximum Floor Beam Concentration and Stress in the Hip Vertical.
Let Fig. 206, represent loads in two panels. It is required to find the criterion for maximum load on the floor beam at B, or maximum R_2.

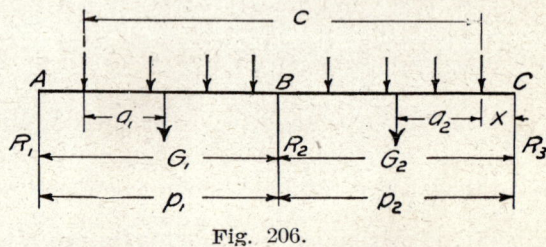

Fig. 206.

ABC is not a continuous beam, but two consecutive panels of stringers.

$$R_2 = \dfrac{c_2+x}{p_2}G_2 + \dfrac{p_1-(c+x-r_2-a_1)}{p_1}G_1,$$

for maximum R_2, $\dfrac{dR_2}{dx}=0=\dfrac{G_2}{p_2}-\dfrac{G_1}{p_1}$ or $\dfrac{G_1}{p_1}=\dfrac{G_2}{p_2}$ . . . . (90)

when the panel lengths are equal $G_1 = G_2$ . . . . (91)

Art. 152.   MAXIMUM FLOOR BEAM CONCENTRATION.   297

That is, *the loads in the two panels must be equal for a maximum load on the floor beam between them*. With concentrated loads this will, in general, require a load at the floor beam so that part of it may be considered in one panel and part in the other.

The criterion of equation (90) is the same as for maximum moment at B for a span of length p_1+p_2, as may be seen if (90) is taken by composition. We will have $\dfrac{G_1}{p_1} = \dfrac{G_2}{p_2} = \dfrac{G_1+G_2}{p_1+p_2} = \dfrac{G}{p_1+p_2}$, that is, the average load per foot on either panel must equal the average load per foot on the two panels. This is the same as the criterion of equation (84) in which G_1+G_2 corresponds to G_1 and a to p_1.

There may be several different loadings which will satisfy the criterion for maximum floor beam concentration. Having determined the positions it is a simple matter to calculate the concentrations. It is sometimes convenient to calculate the floor beam concentration from the maximum moment at the middle of a span equal to $2p$, since the position of the loads is the same in both cases. If the panels are equal, $G_1 = G_2$ and

$$R_2 = \frac{G_1}{p}(a_2+2p-c+a_1). \quad M_B = R_1 p - G_1(c+x-p-a_1).$$

For span $=2p$ $R_1 = \dfrac{G_1}{2p}(c+x-a_1+a_2+x)$. Substituting we have

$$M_B = \frac{G_1}{2}(c+x-a_1+a_2+x) - G_1(c+x-p-a_1).$$

$$= \frac{G_1}{2}(a_2+2p-c+a_1).$$

It is evident that if the maximum moment at B as given by the last equation is multiplied by $\dfrac{2}{p}$ we get the maximum floor beam concentration R_2.[1]

153. Stresses in a Pratt Truss from Wheel Loads.

Fig. 207 shows a single track Pratt truss railroad bridge of seven panels. We will assume the following loads:

Weight of trusses and bracing = 1650 lbs. per ft. of bridge.
Weight of floor system   = 1000 lbs. per ft. of bridge.

Total dead load   = 2650 lbs. per ft. of bridge.

[1] A method of calculating bridge stresses from wheel loads, embodying this principle, together with a complete table for Cooper's $E50$ loading, is given in *Eng. News*, Vol. 55, page 695.

$$q = \frac{\frac{1}{2} \times 1650}{2650} = 0.31.$$

Live load, Cooper's *E*40 loading.
The dead load coefficients are shown in Fig. 207.

For the live load stresses in the chords it will be necessary to get the maximum moments at joints 4, 5, and 6. For joint 6, using the loading strip with the principles enumerated in Art. 143 in mind, it is seen that one of the drivers of the first engine will probably give the maximum moment. The criterion, equa-

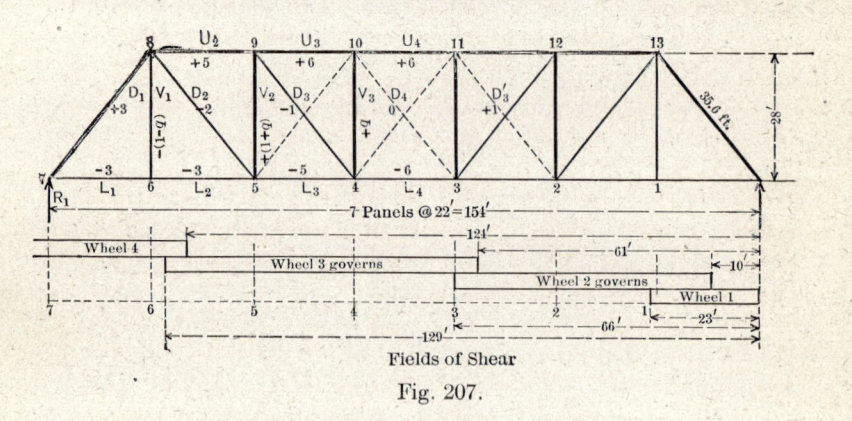

Fig. 207.

tion (84), may be simplified in application somewhat by dividing both sides by the panel length, making it read

$$\frac{G}{N} \begin{cases} > \dfrac{G_1 + G_2}{n} \\ < \dfrac{G_1 + G_2 + P}{n} \end{cases}$$

Using this criterion for joint 6, we get the following results: For joint 6, the panel in question is 6-7, $N=7$ and $n=1$.

Wheel 2 at joint 6, 31 ft. of uniform load on:

$$\frac{G}{N} = \frac{346}{7} = 49\tfrac{3}{7}. \qquad \frac{G_1+G_2}{n} = 10. \qquad \frac{G_1+G_2+P}{n} = 30.$$

As the first term does not fall between the limits of the other two, the criterion is *not* satisfied.

Art. 153. STRESSES IN A PRATT TRUSS FROM WHEEL LOADS.

Wheel 3 at joint 6, 36 ft. of uniform load on:

$$\frac{G}{N}=\frac{356}{7}=50\tfrac{6}{7}. \qquad \frac{G_1+G_2}{n}=30. \qquad \frac{G_1+G_2+P}{n}=50.$$

This does *not* satisfy the criterion.

Wheel 4 at joint 6, 41 ft. of uniform load on:

$$\frac{G}{N}=\frac{366}{7}=52\tfrac{2}{7}. \qquad \frac{G_1+G_2}{n}=50. \qquad \frac{G_1+G_2+P}{n}=70.$$

This *satisfies* the criterion, as 52 is greater than 50 and less than 70.

Wheel 5 at joint 6, 46 ft. of uniform load on and wheel 1 off:

$$\frac{G}{N}=\frac{366}{7}=52\tfrac{2}{7}. \qquad \frac{G_1+G_2}{n}=60. \qquad \frac{G_1+G_2+P}{n}=80.$$

This does *not* satisfy the criterion.

It will perhaps be found that some of the wheels of the second engine will satisfy the criterion for this joint, but the stresses given by them will be less than that for wheel 4, because there will be so much less load on the bridge.

By the same process it is found that wheels 6, 7, 11, and 12 will satisfy the criterion for joint 5, and wheels 10 and 11 for joint 4.

The maximum moment at joint 6 occurs with wheel 4 at that point. Taking moments about the right-hand reaction, we get, in 1000-pound units:

$$R_1 = \frac{29689}{154} = 192.8.$$

$$M_6 = R_1 \times 22 - (10\times 18 + 20\times 10 + 20\times 5) = 4241.3 - 480 = 3761.3$$

$$M_6 = M_8 = L_1 \times 28$$

$$L_1 = L_2 = \frac{3761.3}{28} = 134.3 \quad (-)\ L.\ L.$$

$$= 3 \times 29.15 \times \frac{22}{28} = 68.7 \quad (-)\ D.\ L.$$

$$\phantom{=3 \times 29.15 \times \frac{22}{28} =\ } \overline{203.0} \quad (-)\ \text{Total.}$$

Similarly for joint 5,
Wheel 6 at joint 5, $M_5 = 6024.3$.
Wheel 7 at joint 5, $M_5 = 6016.4$.
Wheel 11 at joint 5, $M_5 = 5751.7$.
Wheel 12 at joint 5, $M_5 = 5768.9$.

$$M_5 = M_9 = L_3 \times 28 = U_2 \times 28,$$

$$-L_3 = U_2 = \frac{6024.3}{28} = 215.2 \quad (+) \ L.\ L.$$

$$= 5 \times 29.15 \times \frac{22}{28} = 114.5 \quad (+) \ D.\ L.$$

$$\phantom{= 5 \times 29.15 \times \frac{22}{28} = } 329.7 \quad (+) \ \text{Total.}$$

For joint 4,
Wheel 10 at joint 4, $M_4 = 7166.1$
Wheel 11 at joint 4, $M_4 = 7191.3$

$$M_4 = U_3 \times 28$$

$$U_3 = \frac{7191.3}{28} = 256.8 \quad (+) \ L.\ L.$$

$$= 6 \times 29.15 \times \frac{22}{28} = 137.4 \quad (+) \ D.\ L.$$

$$\phantom{= 6 \times 29.15 \times \frac{22}{28} = } 394.2 \quad (+) \ \text{Total.}$$

If the shear in panel 3-4 were zero or such as to produce tension in diagonal 10-3, the stress in L_4 would be the same as that just found for U_3; but for this position of the load the shear in the panel is negative and 4-11 is in action. This will make the tension in L_4 slightly less than the compression in U_3. The maximum stresses in the members U_3, U_4, and L_4 are usually assumed to be equal.

The stresses in the web members are obtained from the shears. The shear criterion, equation (89) is best applied by finding the fields of shear (150). The shear criterion may be written thus:

$$G \begin{cases} > NG_2 \\ < N(G_2 + P). \end{cases}$$

Any wheel will satisfy this criterion at any point so long as the total load on the bridge lies between these two limits, with the load entering from the right.

Wheel 1 governs from $G = 7 \times 0$ until $G = 7 \times 10 = 70$, or from the time it (wheel 1) enters the bridge until wheel 5 is ready to come on. As soon as wheel 5 enters G becomes 90, and the criterion is not satisfied for wheel 1.

Wheel 2 governs from $G = 7 \times 10 = 70$ until $G = 7 \times 30 = 210$, or from the time wheel 4 enters the bridge until wheel 13 is ready to enter.

Art. 153. STRESSES IN A PRATT TRUSS FROM WHEEL LOADS. 301

Wheel 3 governs from $G=7\times30=210$ until $G=7\times50=350$, or from wheel 13 at the end of the bridge until 33 ft. of uniform load is on.

Wheel 4 governs from $G=7\times50=350$ until $G=7\times70=490$, or from 33 ft. of uniform load on until 103 ft. of uniform load is on. This more than covers the 154 ft. of our span.

These fields of shear are shown plotted in Fig. 207. The maximum shear in any panel will occur when the wheel in whose field of shear the right-hand panel point of the panel falls, is at that point. Occasionally a panel point will fall in the part where two fields of shear overlap. In that case both wheels must be used to find which will give the greater shear.

The maximum stress in D_1 occurs with wheel 4 at joint 6. This is the same position of the load that was found to give a maximum stress in L_1 and L_2, as it should be, because the stress in L_1 is the horizontal component of the stress in D_1.

With *wheel 4 at joint 6*, $R_1=192.8$ from the calculation for L_1. The portion of the load in panel 6-7 which is carried by the stringers to joint 7 is obtained by moments about 6.

$$R_7 = \frac{10\times18+20\times10+20\times5}{22} = \frac{480}{22} = 21.8.$$

Shear in panel 6-7 $=192.8-21.8=171.0$.

$$D_1 = 171.0 \times \frac{35.6}{28} = 217.4 \quad (+)\ L.\ L.$$

$$= 3 \times 29.15 \times \frac{35.6}{28} = 111.2 \quad (+)\ D.\ L.$$

$$\phantom{=3\times29.15\times\frac{35.6}{28}=}\ 328.6 \quad (+)\ \text{Total.}$$

Wheel 3 at joint 5, 14 ft. of uniform load on:

$$R_1 = \frac{20536}{154} = 133.4$$

$$R_6 = \frac{230}{22} = 10.4$$

$$\text{Shear} = 123.0$$

$$D_2 = 123.0 \times \frac{35.6}{28} = 156.4 \quad (-)\ L.\ L.$$

$$= 2 \times 29.15 \times \frac{35.6}{28} = 74.1 \quad (-)\ D.\ L.$$

$$\phantom{=2\times29.15\times\frac{35.6}{28}=}\ 130.5 \quad (-)\ \text{Total.}$$

Wheel 3 at joint 4, wheel 17, 2 ft. from end of span.

$$R_1 = \frac{14131}{154} = 91.8$$

$$R_5 = \frac{230}{22} = 10.4$$

$$\text{Shear} = 81.4$$

$$D_3 = 81.4 \times \frac{35.6}{28} = 103.5 \quad (-)\ L.\ L.$$

$$= 1 \times 29.15 \times \frac{35.6}{28} = 37.1 \quad (-)\ D.\ L.$$

$$140.6 \quad (-)\ \text{Total.}$$

Wheel 3 at joint 3, wheel 14 at end of bridge,

$$R_1 = \frac{8728}{154} = 56.67$$

$$R_4 = \frac{230}{22} = 10.45$$

$$\text{Shear} = 46.22$$

Wheel 2 also satisfies the criterion at joint 3.

$$R_1 = \frac{7668}{154} = 49.79$$

$$R_4 = \frac{80}{22} = 3.64$$

$$\text{Shear} = 46.15$$

Wheel 3 gives a slightly greater shear.

$$D_4 = 46.22 \times \frac{35.6}{28} = 58.8 \quad (-)\ L.\ L.\ \text{Total.}$$

Wheel 2 at joint 2, wheel 9, 4 ft. from the end of the bridge.

$$R_1 = \frac{4064}{154} = 26.4$$

$$R_3 = \frac{80}{22} = 3.6$$

$$\text{Shear} = 22.8$$

$$D'_3 = 22.8 \times \frac{35.6}{28} = 29.0 \quad (-)\ L.\ L.$$

$$= 1 \times 29.15 \times \frac{35.6}{28} = 37.1 \quad (+)\ D.\ L.$$

No reversal.

Art. 153. STRESSES IN A PRATT TRUSS FROM WHEEL LOADS. 303

Post V_2. Wheel 3 at joint 4,

$$\begin{aligned}
V_2 = \text{shear} &= 81.4 \quad (+) \; L.\,L. \\
= 1.31 \times 29.15 &= \underline{38.2} \quad (+) \; D.\,L. \\
& 119.6 \quad (+) \; \text{Total.}
\end{aligned}$$

Post V_3. Wheel 3 at joint 3,

$$\begin{aligned}
V_3 = \text{shear} &= 46.2 \quad (+) \; L.\,L. \\
= 0.31 \times 29.15 &= \underline{9.0} \quad (+) \; D.\,L. \\
& 55.2 \quad (+) \; \text{Total.}
\end{aligned}$$

For the hip-vertical, V_1, we must apply the criterion for maximum floor beam concentration, equation (91), Art. 152.

$$G_1 = G_2.$$

By inspection it is evident that wheel 12 or 13 at joint 6 will give a maximum load at that point.

Wheel 12 at joint 6, $\quad G_1 = 43, \quad P = 20, \quad G_2 = 53.$

If P be counted with G_1 it makes the first panel load the greater, and if it be counted with G_2 it makes the second panel load the greater, therefore it satisfies the criterion.

Wheel 13 at joint 6, $\quad G_1 = 50, \quad P = 20, \quad G_2 = 46.$

By the same reasoning this also satisfies the criterion.

Wheel 11 at joint 6, $\quad G_1 = 36, \quad P = 20, \quad G_2 = 60.$

This does *not* satisfy the criterion.

Wheel 14 at joint 6, $\quad G_1 = 60, \quad P = 20, \quad G_2 = 39.$

This does *not* satisfy the criterion.

With wheel 12 at joint 6, the portions of the load in the two adjacent panels going to the floor beam 6, are found by moments at joints 5 and 7.

Panel 6-7 $\quad R_6 = \dfrac{13 \times 1 + 10 \times 9 + 20 \times 17}{22} = 20.14$

Panel 5-6 $\quad R_6 = \dfrac{13 \times 3 + 20 \times 12 + 20 \times 17 + 20 \times 22}{22} = 48.14$

$$V_1 = 68.28 \; (-) \; L.\,L.$$

Wheel 13 at joint 6,

Panel 6-7 $R_6 = \dfrac{10 \times 4 + 20 \times 12 + 20 \times 17}{22} = 28.14$

Panel 5-6 $R_6 = \dfrac{13 \times 3 + 13 \times 8 + 20 \times 17 + 20 \times 22}{22} = 41.95$

$$V_1 = 70.09 \; (-) \; L.L. \text{ Max.}$$
$$0.69 \times 29.15 = 20.11 \; (-) \; D.L.$$
$$\overline{90.20 \; (-) \; \text{Total.}}$$

For the purpose of comparing the results obtained by the use of an equivalent uniform load (142) with the wheel load stresses, the stresses have been calculated for a uniform load which will give the same shear in the end panel as the wheel loads, and tabulated below.[1]

COMPARISON OF LIVE LOAD STRESSES.

Member.	Wheel Load Stress.	Equiv. Uniform Load Stress.
D_1	217.4	217.4
D_2	156.4	155.2
D_3	103.5	103.5
D_4	58.8	62.1
D'_3	29.0	31.0
V_1	70.1	57.0
V_2	81.4	81.4
V_3	46.2	48.8
$L_1 = L_2$	134.3	134.3
$-L_3 = U_2$	215.2	223.8
$-L_4 = U_3 = U_4$	256.8	268.6

With the exception of the hip-vertical, for which the wheel load stress should always be calculated, the equivalent uniform load gives results which are within about $4\tfrac{1}{2}\%$ of the wheel load stress in the worst case, and which are all on the side of safety.

---

[1] Curves showing the equivalent loads for Cooper's loadings are given in Johnson's " Modern Framed Structures," Ninth Edition, Part I, page 251, and in Morris's " Designing and Detailing of Simple Steel Structures," page 118.

Use Balt. for spans of 240' + over the use of table [Jamif. Rd.] curves is advised.

Art. 154.   STRESSES IN TRUSSES WITH SUB-PANELS.   305

154. Maximum Stresses in Trusses with Sub-panels. In Fig. 208 let us consider the members in the double panel 5-7. When the top chord 5'–7' is a maximum and when the diagonal 6'–7 is a maximum there is no stress in the counter 6'–7'. When the counter 6'–7' is a maximum, there is no stress in the diagonal 6'–7. Hence the position of the loads for maximum stresses in these members, cut by the section lm, can be determined by the previous methods. The counter 6'–7' is determined as 9'–10'.

The maximum stresses in 6-6' and 6'-5 result from a maximum load at 6, but 6'-5 may also take *tension* when acting with the counter 6'-7'. When 5-7' is stressed, 6'-7 is not in action. If 6'-7 is not in action, the only stress in 6'-5' comes from 6'-6, but a stress in 6'-6 tends to produce compression in 6'-5, hence for max-

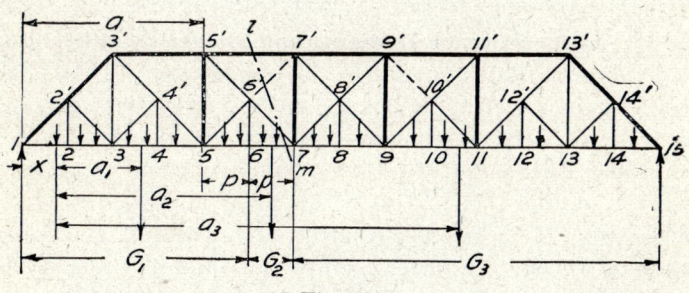

Fig. 208.

imum *tension* in 6'-5, 5'-7 and 6'-6 may be considered removed, and the stress in 5-7' is found as for a single diagonal in a panel (5-7) equal to $2p$. It must be remembered, however, that the maximum in 6'-7' comes when the panel 6-7 is considered, as given above. (136.)

When 5'-6' is a maximum, 6'-7' is not in action. Now we may consider any load at 6 as carried to 5 and 7, and that that part of it carried to 7 is taken through 7-5' as though it had been brought to 7 by the stringer. Hence *for a maximum in* 5'-6', we may disregard 6-6' and 5-6' if we call the panel length 5-7=$2p$. Then we have the ordinary case of a single diagonal in a panel.

For 5-5' we may do as for 5'-6', since they get their maximum stresses from the same loading.

For 5-7 the center of moments is at 5'. This case is evidently unusual because a load at 6 will *increase* the moment about 5′, while others to the left of the section *decrease* it.

$$M_{5'} = R_1 a - G_1\Big[a-(a_1+x)\Big] + G_2\Big[a+2p-(a_2+x)\Big]\frac{p}{p}$$

$$R_1 = G_1 + G_2 + G_3 - \Big[G_1\frac{a_1+x}{L} + G_2\frac{a_2+x}{L} + G_3\frac{a_3+x}{L}\Big]$$

Substituting this value of R_1 in the moment equation, we have then when $M_{5'}$ is a maximum.

$$\frac{dM_{5'}}{dx} = 0 = -\frac{G_1+G_2+G_3}{L}a + G_1 - G_2 \text{ or } \frac{G}{L} = \frac{G_1-G_2}{a} \dots (92)$$

Equation (92) is the criterion for a maximum moment at any point of the top chord. To satisfy this equation, *a load will*, in general, *have to stand at* 6 so that a part of it may be considered with G_1 and the remainder with G_2. Having determined the maximum moment at 5′ the stress in 5-7 is easily obtained.

155. Calculation of Moments and Shears by Wheel Loads.

It is evident from the preceding discussions that, in the calculations involved in getting maximum stresses in girders and trusses, it is necessary often to know the distance of any wheel from any other wheel, the center of gravity of any number of wheels, the left reaction, and the sum of the loads for any number of loads, and the sum of the moments, about any wheel of a number of preceding wheels. In order to save time and avoid mistakes as much as possible, tables are made and carefully checked, showing the total distances of each wheel from the first wheel, the total weight at any wheel, of all the preceding wheels, and the sum of the moments at any wheel of all the preceding wheels.

Such a set of tables, which has been found of convenient arrangement, is given below (pages 307–310). The tables are made up for one rail of Cooper's $E40$ loading.

A diagram might be made showing the position of the center of gravity for any possible combination of loads. This would reduce the number of forces on a span to two or three for the determination of moments, shears and reactions. With a table, however, these are determined by dealing with the individual wheel loads.

Another method of determining the moment at any point of a truss or the shear in any panel, is to calculate the *panel concentrations*, from the proper position of the loads and from these, the resulting moments and shears. This may be done

Art. 155. CALCULATION OF MOMENTS AND SHEARS.

TABLE A

Gives the sum of the moments of the loads to the right of the wheel under which the ○ appears, about this wheel., e.g., 5360 is the sum of the moments of wheels 9 to 15 inclusive about wheel 8.

No. 1	No. 2	No. 3	No. 4	No. 5	No. 6	No. 7	No. 8	No. 9	No. 10	No. 11	No. 12	No. 13	No. 14	No. 15	No. 16	No. 17	No. 18
	160	420	780	1240	1656	2137	2696	3320	3880	5160	6540	8020	9600	10,744	11,953	13,240	14,592
○		100	300	600	912	1289	1744	2264	2744	3864	5084	6404	7824	8,864	9,969	11,152	12,400
	○		100	300	547	859	1249	1704	2134	3154	4174	5494	6814	7,789	8,829	9,947	11,130
		○		100	282	529	854	1244	1624	2544	3564	4684	5904	6,814	7,789	8,842	9,960
			○		117	299	559	884	1214	2034	2954	3974	5094	5,939	6,849	7,837	8,890
				○		65	208	416	656	1296	2036	2876	3816	4,544	5,337	6,208	7,144
					○		78	221	411	951	1591	2331	3171	3,834	4,562	5,368	6,239
						○		65	195	615	1135	1755	2475	3,060	3,710	4,438	5,231
							○		80	400	820	1340	1960	2,480	3,065	3,728	4,456
								○		160	420	780	1240	1,656	2,137	2,696	3,320
									○		100	300	600	912	1,289	1,744	2,264
										○		100	300	547	859	1,249	1,704
											○		100	282	529	854	1,244
												○		117	299	559	884
													○		65	208	416
														○		78	221
															○		65
																○	

CALCULATION OF MOMENTS AND SHEARS   Art. 155.

TABLE B

Gives the sum of any number of consecutive wheel loads; e.g., the sum of the loads 8 to 15 inclusive is found at the intersection of line 8 and column 15 = 129.

	No. 1	No. 2	No. 3	No. 4	No. 5	No. 6	No. 7	No. 8	No. 9	No. 10	No. 11	No. 12	No. 13	No. 14	No. 15	No. 16	No. 17	No. 18	
No. 1	10	30	50	70	90	103	116	129	142	152	172	192	212	232	245	258	271	284	No. 1
No. 2		20	40	60	80	93	106	119	132	142	162	182	202	222	235	248	261	274	No. 2
No. 3			20	40	60	73	93	99	112	122	142	162	182	202	215	228	241	254	No. 3
No. 4				20	40	53	66	79	92	102	122	142	162	182	195	208	221	234	No. 4
No. 5					20	33	46	59	72	82	102	122	142	162	175	188	201	214	No. 5
No. 6						13	26	39	52	62	82	102	122	142	155	168	181	194	No. 6
No. 7							13	26	39	49	69	89	109	129	142	155	168	181	No. 7
No. 8								13	26	36	56	76	96	116	129	142	155	168	No. 8
No. 9									13	23	43	63	83	103	116	129	142	155	No. 9
No. 10										10	30	50	70	90	103	116	129	142	No. 10
No. 11											20	40	60	80	93	106	119	132	No. 11
No. 12												20	40	60	73	86	99	112	No. 12
No. 13													20	40	53	66	79	92	No. 13
No. 14														20	33	46	59	72	No. 14
No. 15															13	26	39	52	No. 15
No. 16																13	26	39	No. 16
No. 17																	13	26	No. 17
No. 18																		13	No. 18

Art. 155. CALCULATION OF MOMENTS AND SHEARS.   309

TABLE C

Gives the sum of the moments of the loads to the left of the wheel under which the ○ appears, about this wheel; e.g., 2745 is the sum of the moments of wheels 8 to 14 inclusive about wheel 15.

No. 1	No. 2	No. 3	No. 4	No. 5	No. 6	No. 7	No. 8	No. 9	No. 10	No. 11	No. 12	No. 13	No. 14	No. 15	No. 16	No. 17	No. 18
16,364	15,274	13,254	11,334	9514	7794	6793	5857	4999	4206	3676	2776	1976	1276	676	403	195	65
14,944	13,904	11,984	10,164	8444	6824	5888	5017	4224	3496	3016	2216	1516	916	416	208	65	○
13,589	12,599	10,779	9,059	7439	5919	5048	4242	3514	2851	2421	1721	1121	621	221	78	○	
12,041	11,111	9,411	7,811	6311	4911	4118	3390	2740	2155	1785	1205	725	345	65	○		
10,816	9,936	8,336	6,836	5436	4136	3408	2745	2160	1640	1320	840	460	180	○			
8,728	7,938	6,518	5,198	3978	2858	2247	1701	1233	830	600	300	100	○				
7,668	6,928	5,608	4,388	3268	2248	1702	1221	818	480	300	100	○					
6,708	6,018	4,798	3,678	2658	1738	1257	841	503	230	100	○						
5,848	5,208	4,088	3,068	2148	1328	912	561	288	80	○							
4,632	4,072	3,112	2,252	1492	832	520	273	104	○								
3,496	3,016	2,216	1,516	916	416	208	65	○									
2,851	2,421	1,721	1,121	621	221	78	○										
2,155	1,785	1,205	725	345	65	○											
1,640	1,320	840	460	180	○												
830	600	300	100	○													
480	300	100	○														
230	100	○															
80	○																

TABLE GIVING THE SUM OF THE MOMENTS OF ALL LOADS

The second line gives the sum of the moments of all loads to the left of the points indicated in the first line. The lower nine lines give the sum of the moments about these same points plus 1 to 9 feet.

Wheel.	No. 3	No. 4	No. 5	No. 6	No. 7	No. 8	No. 9	No. 10	No. 11	No. 12	No. 13	No. 14	No. 15	No. 16	No. 17	No. 18	
	230	480	830	1640	2155	2851	3496	4632	5848	6708	7668	8,728	10,816	12,041	13,589	14,944	
1 ft...	280	550	920	1743	2271	2980	3638	4784	6020	6900	7880	8,960	11,061	12,299	13,860	15,228	1 ft.
2 ft...	330	620	1010	1846	2387	3109	3780	4936	6192	7092	8092	9,192	11,306	12,557	14,131	15,512	2 ft.
3 ft...	380	690	1100	1949	2503	3238	3922	5088	6364	7284	8304	9,424	11,551	12,815	14,402	15,796	3 ft.
4 ft...	430	760	1190	2052	2619	3367	4064	5240	6536	7476	8516	9,656	11,796	13,073	14,673	16,080	4 ft.
5 ft...			1280		2735		4206	5392				9,888		13,331			5 ft.
6 ft...			1370				4348	5544				10,120					6 ft.
7 ft...			1460				4490	5696				10,352					7 ft.
8 ft...			1550									10,584					8 ft.
9 ft...																	9 ft.

UNIFORM LOAD

0 Ft.	10 Ft.	20 Ft.	30 Ft.	40 Ft.	50 Ft.	60 Ft.	70 Ft.	80 Ft.	90 Ft.	100 Ft.	110 Ft.	
16,364	19,304	22,444	25,784	29,324	33,064	37,004	41,144	45,484	50,024	54,764	59,704	1 ft.
16,649	19,609	22,769	26,129	29,689	33,449	37,409	41,569	45,929	50,489	55,249	60,209	2 ft.
16,936	19,916	23,096	26,476	30,056	33,836	37,816	41,996	46,376	50,956	55,736	60,716	3 ft.
17,225	20,225	23,425	26,825	30,425	34,225	38,225	42,425	46,825	51,425	56,225	61,225	4 ft.
17,516	20,536	23,756	27,176	30,796	34,616	38,636	42,856	47,276	51,896	56,716	61,736	5 ft.
17,809	20,849	24,089	27,529	31,169	35,009	39,049	43,289	47,729	52,369	57,209	62,249	6 ft.
18,104	21,164	24,424	27,884	31,544	35,404	39,464	43,724	48,184	52,844	57,704	62,764	7 ft.
18,401	21,481	24,761	28,241	31,921	35,801	39,881	44,161	48,641	53,321	58,201	63,321	8 ft.
18,700	21,800	25,100	28,600	32,300	36,200	40,300	44,600	49,100	53,800	58,700	63,800	9 ft.
19,001	22,121	25,441	28,961	32,681	36,601	40,721	45,041	49,561	54,281	59,201	64,321	

from the moment table by means of the following equation.[1]

$$P_n = \frac{M_{n+1} - 2M_n + M_{n-1}}{p} \quad \ldots\ldots\ldots\ldots (93)$$

in which P_n = concentration at the nth panel point.
  p = panel length.
  M_n = sum of the moments about the nth panel point of all the loads to the left of this point.
  M_{n+1} = sum of the moments about the $(n+1)$th panel point of all the loads to the left of this point.
  M_{n-1} = sum of the moments about the $(n-1)$th panel point of all the loads to the left of this point.

156. Equivalent Uniform Loads. For stringers and deck plate girders, the determination of an "equivalent uniform load" practically amounts to determining by the preceding methods the *maximum* moment and shear for each span and then calculating the uniform loads per foot which will produce equal maximum moments and shears.

The equivalent uniform load for trusses is usually based upon the maximum moment at the center of the span, or upon the maximum shear in the end panel of the truss. The former gives chord stresses that are a few per cent too large for trusses with an odd number of panels, and in all trusses gives shears which are a little too small. The end shear loading gives chord stresses which are too large, and in the case of long spans the error may be considerable.

For multiple intersection trusses, draw spans, arches and cantilever trusses, the criteria for position of wheel loads to produce maximum stresses are complicated. Methods for obtaining equivalent uniform loads for these are usually more or less approximate.

Panel lengths for multiple intersection trusses should be so chosen that there will be a reasonable distribution of the loads to the several systems of web bracing. For example, if there are two systems of webbing, and the distance center to center of driving wheel bases is 56 ft., the panel length should not be 28 ft. but preferably about 19 ft.

---

[1] For demonstration see Johnson's "Modern Framed Structures," Art. 101, page 87. (5th Edition.)

157. Graphical Methods.[1] For finding the position of the loads for maximum moments and shears, the graphical method is elegant, rapid and accurate. The application of the criteria are nearly always made graphically. The stresses are usually calculated from the actual wheel loads by the use of moment tables. We shall consider the special case of a truss in which the top chord joints are vertically over those of the bottom chord. Fig. 209 is a diagram of Cooper's class $E40$ Loading (see Fig. 198), laid out so that the ordinate at any point is equal to the sum of the loads to the left of that point, that is, the heights of the steps are equal to the wheel loads by scale.

To find the position of the loads for *maximum moment* at D we use equation (84), which requires that the load per foot on the whole span be equal to the load per foot to the left of D. Now the load on the span is represented by $FH-EG$ and on AD by $NM-EG$ or $NK-EG$, depending on whether load 11 is counted with the load on AD or DB. We must have then, if a maximum moment occurs when wheel 11 is at D,

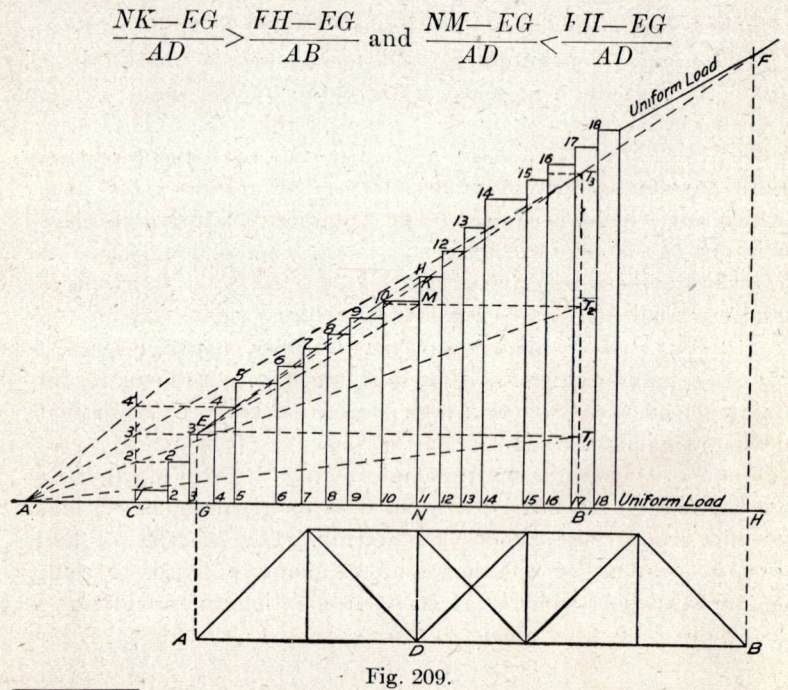

$$\frac{NK-EG}{AD} > \frac{FH-EG}{AB} \text{ and } \frac{NM-EG}{AD} < \frac{FH-EG}{AD}$$

Fig. 209.

---

[1] For a more extended discussion of graphical methods, see Johnson's "Modern Framed Structures," Ninth edition, Part I, page 218.

These three fractions are the slopes of the lines EK, EM, and EF, and since the slope of EF is greater than that of EM, and less than that of EK, wheel 11 at D will give a maximum moment.

Therefore, *when a thread stretched between the points where verticals from the ends of the span cut the "load line," intersects the "step" over the load at the point where a maximum moment is wanted, this position will give one of the maximum moments at the point.*

Having found the proper position of the load, the moment at D may be found graphically by placing a diagram of the truss on an equilibrium polygon for the typical loading, which must be drawn to the proper scale. After drawing the closing line the moment may be scaled off.[1]

To find the position of the loads for maximum shear in a panel we have from equation (89) $\dfrac{G}{AB} = \dfrac{G_2}{p}$, G being the total load on the span, and G_2 the load in the panel in which the maximum shear is wanted. In Fig. 209 lay off $A'C'$ equal to one panel length, regardless of position for a maximum. Now if lines be drawn through 1, 2', 3', etc., from A', their slopes will equal $\dfrac{G_2}{p}$. Now if we make $A'B' = AB$, $B'T_1$, $B'T_2$, $B'T_3$, etc., will represent the total load which may be on the span in order that equation (89) may be satisfied, when wheels 1, 2, 3, &c, respectively, are at the right hand end of the panel in question. Projecting points T_1, T_2, T_3, &c on to the load line, we see that load 4 must be at B, the right hand end of the bridge, when load 1 is at the right hand end of the panel in question. That is, wheel 1 must be at the right hand end of all panels which it passes in going from B towards A, for maximum shears in those panels, until wheel 4 reaches B, or wheel 1 is said to govern for this distance. Likewise wheel 2 governs at all panel points which it passes when the load moves from wheel 4 at B to wheel 10 at B, and wheel 3 governs at all points which it passes when the load moves from wheel 10 at B to wheel 16 at B. The distances that the wheels move while they govern, are called their respective "*fields of shear,*" and it will be found that these fields overlap by distances equal to the distances between the successive wheels.

---

[1] A convenient form of equilibrium polygon and a description of this method may be found by looking up the reference given on page 312.

To find the *shear* graphically, take the necessary moments from the equilibrium polygon. The moment of the loads on the span, about B, divided by AB, will give the reaction at A. The moment of the loads in the panel, about the right hand end of the panel, divided by the panel length, will give the load at the left end of the panel.

For *stringers* and *deck plate girders* it is simplest to find, by trial, the position of the loads giving maximum shear at any point.

QUESTIONS AND PROBLEMS. CHAPTER XIII.

1. It what parts of structures are longitudinal forces important?

2. What is "impact" and how is it taken into account?

3. In a railroad bridge how are loads actually applied? How are they usually specified?

4. The stress in a main diagonal of a bridge, due to Cooper's $E40$ loading, is 420,000 lbs. What would be the live load stress in this diagonal if the loading were increased so that one engine and tender weighed 150 tons?

5. Find the maximum span for which the four drivers of Cooper's engine will give a maximum moment and the minimum span for which the four drivers and the first tender wheel will give a maximum.

6. Find the position of Cooper's Loading which will give a maximum stress in the top chord 2'-3', of Fig. 204. Span = 120 ft. Find the position for maximum shear in panel 2-3.

7. Prove equation (93).

8. Why should the panel lengths be about 19 ft. for a bridge having two systems of webbing, if Cooper's loading is used?

9. Find the equivalent uniform load for center moment, and for shear in the end panel, for the truss of Fig. 207, for Cooper's $E60$ loading.

CHAPTER XIV.

STRESSES IN BRIDGES FROM HORIZONTAL FORCES.

158. Wind Loads. The horizontal forces acting upon a bridge are those due to wind, and in the case of a railway bridge with the track on a curve, those due to centrifugal force. There are also stresses in the transverse bracing due to vibration and swaying of the live load, which cannot be accurately determined, and which are taken care of by increasing the assumed wind load and by stiffening the general design.

The maximum actual pressure of the wind from observations covering nine years at the site of the Forth Bridge,[1] was 41 lbs. per square foot on a small area of 1.5 sq. ft., and 27 lbs. per square foot on an area of 300 sq. ft. Other observations also show that the wind pressures on large areas never are so great as on small ones. This is probably due to the wind moving in gusts and eddies of comparatively limited extent.

Bridge specifications require the structure to be designed for winds loads of from 30 to 50 lbs. per sq. ft. of exposed surface. Many specifications do not state the wind load in pounds per square foot, but in pounds per linear foot of bridge. The exposed surface is usually taken as double the area of one truss as seen in elevation plus the vertical area of the floor system considered solid. The area of a plate girder bridge is taken at $1\frac{1}{3}$ to $1\frac{1}{2}$ times the area of the elevation.

The action of the wind on the train produces a moving wind pressure which is usually taken at 10 sq. ft. $\times$ 30 lbs. = 300 lbs. per lin. ft. of bridge. For highway bridges, on account of the smaller vibratory stresses, the specified live load wind is frequently reduced to half that used for railroad bridges. On account of the variable nature of the wind, some specifications require that both the dead load and live load wind pressures be treated as moving loads.[2]

---

[1] "The Forth Bridge," *Engineering*, Feb. 28, 1890.
[2] See American Railway Engineering Association Specifications for Steel Railway Bridges, Art. 10.

Art. 159.   LATERAL SYSTEMS.   317

159. Lateral Systems. The horizontal forces are taken care of by horizontal trusses between the main vertical trusses, the chords of the latter acting also as chords for the wind trusses. The horizontal trusses are spoken of as lateral systems, and in high truss bridges we have a " top lateral system " and a " bottom lateral system." At the " loaded chord " the floor beams are usually made to act as members of the lateral system.

We, therefore, have, in addition to stresses from dead and live load, wind stresses in floor beams, and in the chords of the main trusses. Pony truss bridges and through plate girder bridges have but one lateral system. Deck plate girder bridges may have one or two systems.

The usual practice is to use adjustable rods for the diagonal members of ordinary highway bridge lateral systems, and angles with riveted connections for city bridges and railway bridges. These are all *usually* considered as tension members and therefore two diagonals are used in each panel. An exception is the deck plate girder bridge, whose lateral systems are usually Warren trusses.

The lateral system at the "loaded chord" is assumed to carry all the live load, due to the wind blowing against a moving train or against vehicles moving across a bridge, as well as its proportion of the dead load. The other system is assumed to carry dead wind load only. In a bridge having but one lateral system, this is proportioned to take all the dead and live wind load.

160. Deck Plate Girder Lateral Systems. Fig. 210 shows the top lateral system of a deck plate girder bridge. Fre-

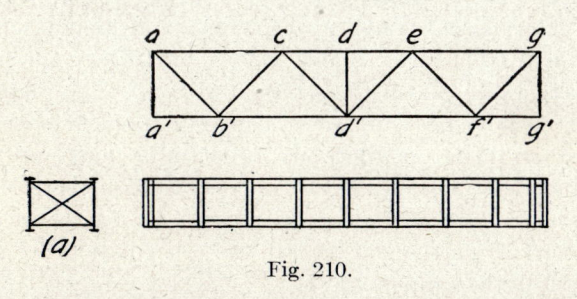

Fig. 210.

quently no bottom lateral system is used, in which case the wind loads from the bottom of the girder are transferred to the top by cross frames placed at intervals, usually not exceeding sixteen times the width of the girder flange.

If we assume the live load applied equally to the two girders (Fig. 210), dd' will carry a half panel of dead load wind, and a quarter panel of live load wind, ce being a panel length. dd is the top member of a cross frame. (Shown in Fig. 210 (a).) The intermediate frames are usually made heavier than would be necessary simply to take the wind stress. Similar cross-frames are also placed at aa' and gg'. These are figured to carry *all* the horizontal forces to the supports.

Since those diagonals which are in tension when the wind blows from one side are in compression when it blows from the other side, and, since it requires more material for a compression member than for a tension member, the diagonals are *all* proportioned for compression. Most specifications allow the chord stresses for wind to be neglected unless they exceed from 25% to 50% of the total live and dead load stresses from vertical loads.[1] The calculation of the stresses is a simple matter. (131.)

161. Through Plate Girder and Pony Truss Lateral Systems. For a Pony truss or through plate girder bridge, the laterals are usually calculated as tension members, even if they are made up of angles. Fig. 211 shows the lateral system of a railway bridge. It is figured as a simple Pratt truss— one system acting when the wind blows from one side, and the other when it blows from the other side.

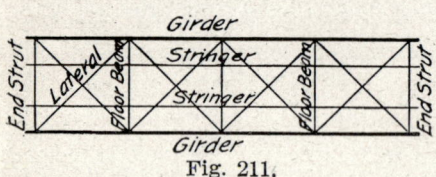

Fig. 211.

The laterals are riveted to the stringers at their intersections to keep them from rattling and saging, but this is not supposed to have any influence on the stresses in them. The plane of the laterals is usually near the lower flange of the floor beams. The wind stress in the latter, therefore, need not be taken into account as it reduces the tension already there. In case there is no end floor beam, the end strut is proportioned for ½ the component parallel to it, from the end lateral, the other half being assumed to go direct to the support.

162. Deck Bridge Lateral Systems. Fig. 212 shows a deck truss bridge with top and bottom lateral systems and sway brac-

---

[1] See Am. Ry. Eng. Assoc. Spec., 4th Edition, Art. 25.

Art. 162.   DECK BRIDGE LATERAL SYSTEMS.   319

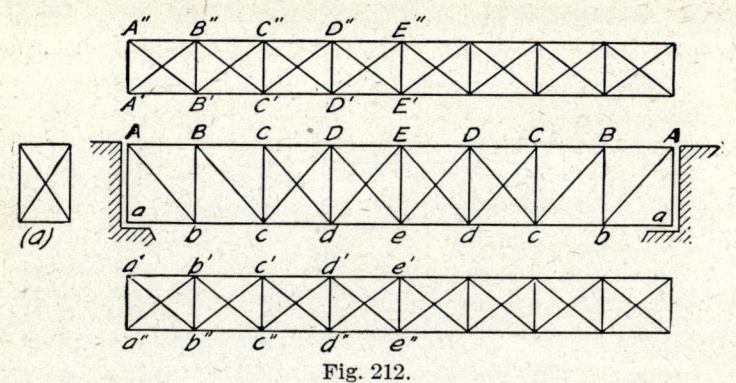

Fig. 212.

ing at the panel points. The bottom lateral system carries its part of the wind load directly to the supports. The reactions at the four shoes "a" are assumed to be equal. The top lateral system carries its load to the end sway frames at A, and these take it to the supports. In this case of an eight panel bridge, if there is no end floor beam at A and the stringers rest directly on the abutments, we shall have 4 panel loads of dead load and 3½ panel loads of live load wind going to the supports through the *end sway frames*. If there are end floor beams at A we will have 4 panel loads of each, dead and live wind load, going to the supports through the end sway frames. No stresses are calculated for the *intermediate sway bracing*, but it serves to prevent distortion of the cross section of the bridge due to loads on the bridge, not symmetrical with the center line between trusses and to the excess wind load at the top chord over that at the bottom chord.[1]

The lateral systems are simple Pratt trusses and the chord stresses must be taken into account if they exceed 25% to 50% of the total live and dead load stresses due to vertical load. There is no stress in *ab* from vertical loads, but it will be in compression from wind loads. There may be a reversal of stress in some of the other panels of the lower chord, especially if the span is long and the dead load comparatively small.

The stresses in the end sway frame are shown in Fig. 213.

P = one panel of wind load.

R = transverse component of end diagonal $A'B''$. (Fig. 212.)

---

[1] See Johnson's "Modern Framed Structures," Part I, Art. 191.

320   DECK BRIDGE LATERAL SYSTEM.   Art. 162.

In addition to the stress here shown in aa' it is assumed to get $\frac{1}{4}$ of the total wind load on the bottom lateral system. The horizontal reactions at a and a' are likewise increased.

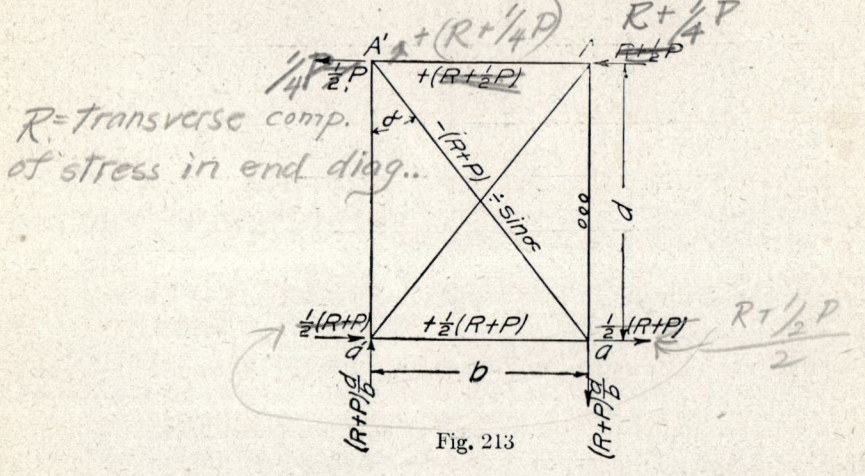

Fig. 213.

It is seen that a stress equal to $(R+P)\dfrac{d}{b}$ is *added* to the vertical load stress in the end post $A'a'$.

If the support is at the top chord as shown in Fig. 214, the end sway frame is inclined and carries the wind load from the lower lateral system to A. The stresses are obtained in exactly the same manner as given above for the vertical end frame. The horizontal components of the reactions at A and A' produce a uniform stress in the top chords, compression on one side or truss and tension on the other truss. These stresses *increase the wind chord stresses*. If the bridge in Fig. 212 was made with an inclined *end post aB*, the end sway frame, carrying the top lateral wind load, should be in its plane. In this case, as in that of Fig. 214, the horizontal components of the reactions would be taken up by a uniform stress in the chord.

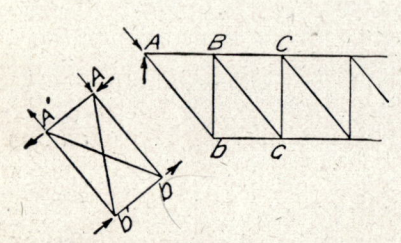

Fig. 214.

The wind on the train tends to overturn it as shown in Fig. 20, page 35. This increases the vertical load on the leeward truss and decreases it on the windward truss. The center

Art. 163.   THROUGH BRIDGE LATERAL SYSTEMS.   321

of moments should be taken at the panel point of the truss instead of at the rail, in figuring the increase of load on the truss. This will increase the lever arms a and b of Fig. 20. The increase of stress in the truss members due to wind is usually small with the exception of the chords; these receive stress both from the overturning moment of the wind on the train and from their action as chords of the lateral systems also.

The wind load also tends to overturn the bridge and sufficient anchorage must be provided at the shoes to take the difference between the upward pull of the wind and the downward reaction of the load acting at the same time.

163. Through Bridge Lateral Systems. In a through bridge with vertical or inclined end posts, the top lateral wind

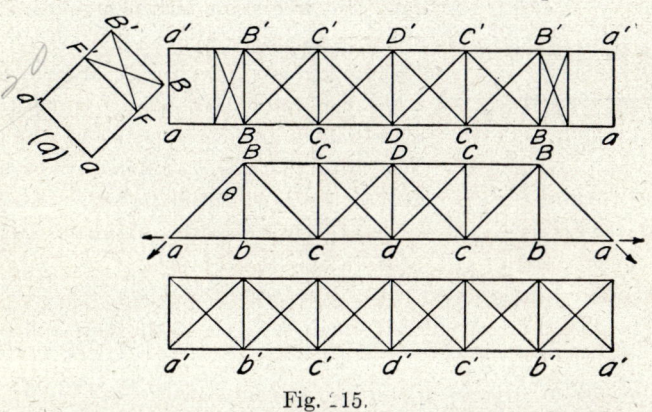

Fig. 215.

load is carried by the lateral system to the tops of the end posts and must be transferred through *portal bracing* and the end posts, to the supports. The end bracing cannot extend to the bottom of the posts as in a deck bridge, on account of clearance for traffic; therefore the end posts must act as beams and will be subjected to both bending and direct stresses. (115.)

There are transverse frames placed at the intermediate panel points also, to stiffen the bridge and reduce the vibration. These will transfer some of the top lateral load down to the bottom lateral system at each panel point. The amount of load so transferred will depend upon the relative stiffness of the two systems and of the portal bracing. It is frequently assumed that from one-third to one-half of the top lateral load is so transferred, the balance being carried to the portals.

The *top* and *bottom lateral systems* are figured exactly as in a *deck* bridge. (162.) Fig. 215 shows the lateral systems of a through bridge. Each portal gets a stress R equal to the transverse component of the end diagonal BC' or $B'C$, and half the wind loads on Ba, Bb, Bc, and BC, which may be called a panel load $= P$.

164. Portal Bracing. The stresses in the portal bracing depend upon the condition of the ends of the posts. In practice, one or both ends may be partially or wholly fixed, as far as elastic supports will permit fixity. (112.) The end conditions are due mainly to the *direct* stress in the post, which always exists to some extent. This direct stress is due to the dead and live loads on the structure, and to the wind.

End posts are nearly always made with two webs, each one of which transmits half of any direct stress in the post. This direct stress D offers a resistance to the turning of the end of the post equal to $\frac{1}{2}kD$. See Fig. 216. If $\frac{1}{2}kD$ is equal to or greater than the moment required to hold the end of the post in the line of its axis the ends may be considered fixed. (112.)

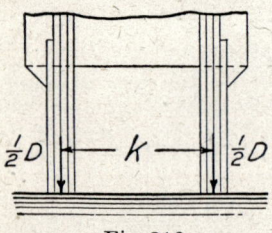

Fig. 216.

The maximum resultant of all stresses in the *post* will occur when the live load is on the bridge and the wind forces are acting. The maximum stresses in the *portal bracing* will occur, in general, when there is no live load on the bridge.

The problem of finding the exact stresses in the portal bracing is very complicated. The main factors which render it so are the following. (See Fig. 215 (a)).

1st. The condition of partial fixity of the posts at a and B.

2d. The distribution of the wind load reaction between the supports a and a'.

3d. The deflection of the point F compared with that of B.

4th. The stiffness of the connections at B and F.

The wind loads will cause the portal to deflect somewhat as shown in Fig. 217. This figure represents the general case in which the lengths of the posts are different. This could scarcely occur in a bridge, but might be met with in viaduct or elevated railway work, where the same analysis of stresses will hold good.

Art. 164. PORTAL BRACING. 323

If the location of the points of contraflexure in the posts are known, the stresses are very easily found.

In our analysis we will make the following assumptions, which are not strictly true, but which will give results abundantly accurate for all practical purposes.

1. The force acting at the top of the portal is equal to the reaction from the top lateral system plus one panel load.

2. Neglect the effect of the direct wind pressure on the side of the end post.

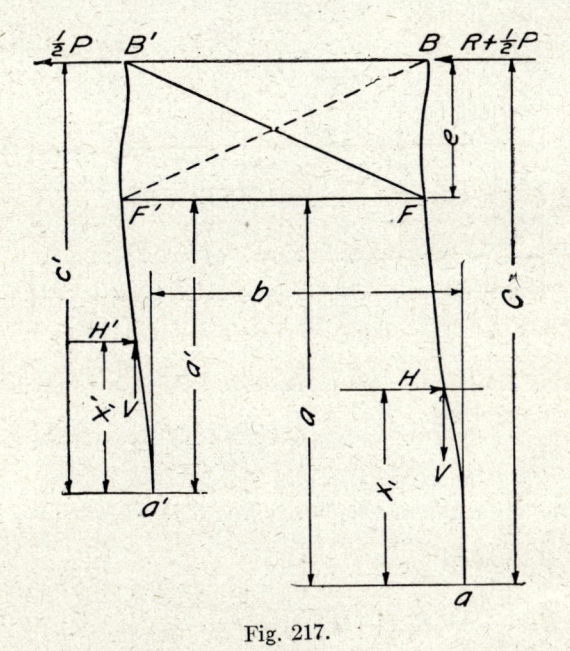

Fig. 217.

3. The longitudinal deformations of the members of the portal frame are neglected. This gives F and F' the same amount of deflection as B and B'.

4. The deflections of the posts are neglected in getting the lever arms of the vertical forces.

There will be three general cases to consider:

1. When the posts are fixed at both ends.
2. When the posts are partially fixed at the bottoms and fixed at the tops.
3. When the posts are partially fixed at both ends.

These will be considered separately.

165. General Case of Portal with Posts Fixed at Both Ends.

In Fig. 217 assume F to deflect as much as B, that is, the bracing to be rigid. So far as the post is concerned, we have the case of a beam fixed at both ends, a load at a distance a from one end and supports not on a level, as shown in Fig. 218.

Since there is no moment at the points of contraflexure (89) the reactions H, H', V, and V', Fig. 217, may be supposed, *when convenient*, to act at the points of contraflexure.

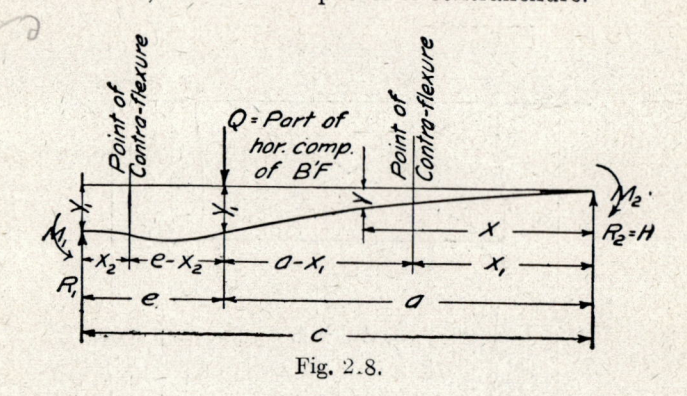

Fig. 2.8.

Taking moments about the point of contraflexure nearest a, Fig. 218, we have,

$$M_2 - R_2 x_1 = 0 \quad \text{or} \quad M_2 = R_2 x_1 \quad \quad \quad (94)$$

and for the equation of the elastic line (81) we have

$$M_{x<a} = EI\frac{d^2y}{dx^2} = R_2 x - M_2 \quad \quad \quad (95)$$

$$EI\frac{dy}{dx} = \tfrac{1}{2} R_2 x^2 - M_2 x + (C = 0) \quad \quad \quad (96)$$

$$EIy = \tfrac{1}{6} R_2 x^3 - \tfrac{1}{2} M_2 x^2 + (C' = 0) \quad \quad \quad (97)$$

Substituting for M_2 from (94) and making $x = a$

$$EIy_1 = \tfrac{1}{6} R_2 a^3 - \tfrac{1}{2} R_2 a^2 x_1 \quad \quad \quad (98)$$

$$y_1 = \frac{R_2 a^2}{2EI}\left(\tfrac{1}{3}a - x_1\right) \quad \quad \quad (99)$$

Similarly if the shear R_2' is in $a'\ F'$

$$y'_1 = \frac{R_2' a'^2}{2EI'}(\tfrac{1}{3}a' - x_1') \quad \quad \quad (100)$$

If FF' is rigid, $y_1 = y_1'$ and we have, after substituting for R_2 and R_2' their equivalents, H and H'.

Art. 165. PORTAL WITH POSTS FIXED AT ENDS.

$$\frac{y'_1}{y_1} = \frac{\dfrac{H'a'^2}{2EI'}(\tfrac{1}{3}a'-x'_1)}{\dfrac{Ha^2}{2EI}(\tfrac{1}{3}a-x_1)} = \frac{\dfrac{H'a'^2}{I'}(\tfrac{1}{3}a'-x'_1)}{\dfrac{Ha^2}{I}(\tfrac{1}{3}a-x_1)} = 1$$

multiplying both sides of the equation by $\dfrac{H}{H'}$,

$$\frac{H}{H'} = \frac{\dfrac{a'^2(\tfrac{1}{3}a'-x'_1)}{I'}}{\dfrac{a^2(\tfrac{1}{3}a-x_1)}{I}} = \frac{a'^2 I(\tfrac{1}{3}a'-x'_1)}{a^2 I'(\tfrac{1}{3}a-x)} \quad \ldots\ldots\ldots (101)$$

Now $H + H' = R + P \ \ldots\ldots\ldots\ldots\ldots\ldots\ldots (102)$

or $H' + \left(\dfrac{H}{H'}\right) H' = R + P$ or $H'\left(1 + \dfrac{H}{H'}\right) = R + P$ from which

$$H' = \frac{R+P}{\dfrac{a'^2 I(\tfrac{1}{3}a'-x'_1)}{a^2 I'(\tfrac{1}{3}a-x_1)} + 1} \quad \ldots\ldots\ldots\ldots\ldots\ldots (103)$$

If the posts have the same cross section $I = I'$ and they drop. If the supports are on a level $a = a'$ and (103) becomes

$$H' = \frac{R+P}{\dfrac{I\ (\tfrac{1}{3}a-x'_1)}{I'(\tfrac{1}{3}a-x_1)} + 1} \quad \ldots\ldots\ldots\ldots (104)$$

If $a = a'$ and $x_1 = x'_1$, (103) becomes

$$H' = \frac{R+P}{\dfrac{I}{I'}+1} = (R+P)\frac{I'}{I+I'} \quad \ldots\ldots\ldots\ldots (105)$$

In this case when $I = I'$ we have $H = H' = \tfrac{1}{2}(R+P) \ldots\ldots (106)$
This case is treated in Art. 169.

(102 and 103) determine H and H' when x_1 and x_1' are known. For the conditions given these depend upon the relation between c and a and c' and a'. The relation between c, a, and x_1 will now be found.

$$M_{x > a} = \frac{EI\, d^2 y}{dx^2} = R_2 x - M_2 - Q\ (x-a) \ldots\ldots\ldots\ldots (107)$$

This is the equation of the elastic line from F to B.

$$EI\frac{dy}{dx} = \tfrac{1}{2} R_2 x^2 - M_2 x - Q\ (\tfrac{1}{2} x^2 - ax) + C_1 \ \ldots\ldots (108)$$

The first members of equations (96) and (108) are equal when $x = a$. Hence $C_1 = -\tfrac{1}{2} Qa^2$.

PORTAL WITH POSTS FIXED AT ENDS. Art. 165.

$EIy = \frac{1}{6}R_2x^3 - \frac{1}{2}M_2x^2 - Q(\frac{1}{6}x^3 - \frac{1}{2}ax^2) - \frac{1}{2}Qa^2x + C_2$ ... (109)

$y = y_1$ when $x = a$ and when $x = c$

$EIy_1 = \frac{1}{6}R_2c^3 - \frac{1}{2}M_2c^2 - Q(\frac{1}{6}c^3 - \frac{1}{2}c^2a + \frac{1}{2}ca^2) + C_2$

$EIy_1 = \frac{1}{6}R_2a^3 - \frac{1}{2}M_2a^2 - Q(\frac{1}{6}a^3 - \frac{1}{2}a^3 + \frac{1}{2}a^3) + C_2$

Subtracting $0 = \frac{1}{6}R_2(c^3 - a^3) - \frac{1}{2}R_2x_1(c^2 - a^2) - Q(\frac{1}{6}c^3 - \frac{1}{6}a^3 - \frac{1}{2}c^2a + \frac{1}{2}a^2c)$

whence

$$\frac{R_2}{Q} = \frac{\frac{1}{6}(c^3 - 3ac^2 + 3a^2c - a^3)}{\frac{1}{6}(c^3 - a^3) - \frac{1}{2}x_1(c^2 - a^2)} = \frac{\frac{1}{6}(c-a)^3}{(c-a)[\frac{1}{6}(c^2 + ac + a^2) - \frac{1}{2}x_1(c+a)]}$$

$$= \frac{\frac{1}{6}(c-a)^2}{\frac{1}{6}(c^2 + ac + a^2) - \frac{1}{2}x_1(c+a)} \quad \ldots \ldots \ldots (110)$$

Also the equation of the elastic line from F to B is

$$M_{x>a} = EI\frac{d^2y}{dx^2} = R_1(c-x) - M_1 \ldots \ldots \ldots \ldots (111)$$

$$EI\frac{dy}{dx} = R_1(cx - \frac{1}{2}x^2) - M_1x + C_3 \ldots \ldots \ldots \ldots (112)$$

when $x = c, \frac{dy}{dx} = 0 = R_1(c^2 - \frac{1}{2}c^2) - M_1c + C_3$ and $C_3 = cM_1 - \frac{1}{2}R_1c^2$

$EIy = R_1(\frac{1}{2}cx^2 - \frac{1}{6}x^3) - \frac{1}{2}M_1x^2 - \frac{1}{2}R_1c^2x + cM_1x + C_4$ ... (113)

$y = y_1$ when $x = a$ and when $x = c$, whence

$EIy_1 = R_1(\frac{1}{2}ca^2 - \frac{1}{6}a^3) - \frac{1}{2}M_1a^2 - \frac{1}{2}R_1c^2a + M_1ac + C_4$.

$EIy_1 = R_1(\frac{1}{2}c^3 - \frac{1}{6}c^3) - \frac{1}{2}M_1c^2 - \frac{1}{2}R_1c^3 + M_1c^2 + C_4$.

$0 = R_1(\frac{1}{3}c^3 - \frac{1}{2}c^2a + \frac{1}{2}ca^2 - \frac{1}{6}a^3) - M_1(\frac{1}{2}a^2 - ac + \frac{1}{2}c^2)$

$$M_1 = R_1\frac{\frac{1}{6}(c-a)^3}{\frac{1}{2}(c-a)^2} = \frac{1}{3}R_1(c-a) = \frac{1}{3}R_1e \ldots \ldots \ldots (114)$$

$M_1 = R_1x_2$, therefore, $R_1x_2 = \frac{1}{3}R_1e$ and $x_2 = \frac{1}{3}e$ ... (115)

$M_{x_1} = 0 = R_1(c - x_1) - Q(a - x_1) - M_1$ ... (116)

$M_1 = \frac{1}{3}R_1e = \frac{1}{3}R_1(c-a)$ $R_1 = Q - R_2$. Hence

$0 = Q(c - x_1) - R_2(c - x_1) - Q(a - x_1) - \frac{1}{3}Q(c - a) + \frac{1}{3}R_2(c - a)$

From which $\dfrac{R_2}{Q} = \dfrac{a - x_1 - c + x_1 + \frac{1}{3}c - \frac{1}{3}a}{\frac{1}{3}c - \frac{1}{3}a - c + x_1} = \dfrac{\frac{2}{3}(a-c)}{x_1 - \frac{1}{3}(a+2c)}$ (117)

From (110) $= \dfrac{\frac{1}{6}(c-a)^2}{\frac{1}{6}(c^2 + ac + a^2) - \frac{1}{2}x_1(c+a)}$

Solving for x_1 we get ..... $x_1 = \dfrac{a(a+c)}{3a+c}$ .... (118)

IMPORTANT

When $c = 2a$ or $a = \frac{1}{2}c$, $x_1 = \frac{3}{5}a$ .... (119)

(x_1 would equal $\frac{1}{2}a$ if B did not deflect.)

When $c = a$ that is the portal is a single strut—a plate girder for example (see Art. 170) $x_1 = \frac{1}{2}a$ .... (120)

Art. 165. PORTAL WITH POSTS FIXED AT ENDS. 327

These would ordinarily be the limits for the relation between a and c, and x_1 would only vary from $0.6a$ to $0.5a$. Even if a were only $\tfrac{1}{3} c$ (which limit would very seldom be reached) x_1 would be only $0.67a$.

In order that the above equations may be applicable (see Art. 164) $\tfrac{1}{2}k_1 D \gtreqless M_1 \gtreqless \tfrac{1}{3}R_1(c-a) \gtreqless \tfrac{1}{2}H(a-x_1)$ .... (121)

(See Equations (114) and (116)).

$$\tfrac{1}{2}k_2 D \gtreqless M_2 \gtreqless R_2 x_1 \gtreqless H\frac{a(a+c)}{3a+c} \quad \ldots\ldots\ldots\ldots (122)$$

D may be a direct stress or a reaction. Special precautions must be taken in the construction if it is desired to have a *reaction* which will make the end of a column "fixed," since an exceedingly small change in the direction of the axis of the column will destroy this condition. In truss bridges we must depend upon the direct stress in the post to fix its ends.

D is made up of V, (Fig. 217) except at B, the dead load stress in the post, and in some cases, also the live load stress. (164.)

In Fig. 217 putting the forces H and V, and H' and V' at a and a' respectively, and taking moments of the external forces about the point of inflection in aF

$$V'b = (R+P)(c-x_1) + H'[x_1-(c-c')] + Hx_1 + M_1 + M_1' - M_2 - M_2'$$

$$V' = \frac{1}{b}[(R+P)(c-x_1) + H'(x_1-c+c') + Hx_1 + \tfrac{1}{3}R_1 e + \tfrac{1}{3}R_1' e - Hx_1 - H'x_1']$$

$$V' = \frac{1}{b}[(R+P)(c-x_1) - H'(c-c'+x_1'-x_1) + \tfrac{1}{3}R_1 e + \tfrac{1}{3}R_1' e] \quad (123)$$

or

$$V' = \frac{1}{b}[(R+P)(c-x_1) - H'(a-a'+x_1'-x_1) + \tfrac{1}{3}e(R_1+R_1')] \quad (124)$$

when $c=c'$, $V'=-V$, and

$$V' = -V = \frac{1}{b}[(R+P)(c-x_1) - H'(x_1'-x_1) + \tfrac{1}{3}e(R_1+R_1')] \quad (125)$$

when $c=c'$ and $x_1=x_1'$

$$V' = -V = \frac{1}{b}[(R+P)(c-x_1) + \tfrac{1}{3}e(R_1+R_1')] \ldots\ldots\ldots (126)$$

$$R_2 = H \ldots\ldots\ldots\ldots (127)$$

From equations (114) and (116) $R_1 = \dfrac{3H(a-x_1)}{2(c-a)}$ and from

Eq. (118) $R_1 = \dfrac{3Ha^2}{(c-a)(3a+c)}$ .... (128)

$Q = R_1 + R_2 = \frac{3}{2}H\dfrac{(a-x_1)}{(c-a)} + H = H\dfrac{2ac+c^2}{2ac+c^2-3a^2}$ .... (129)

Recapitulation:

Find x_1 from equation (118) and x_1' from a similar equation in a' and c'. Find H and H' from equations (103) and (102). Find R_1 from (128) and R_1' from a similar equation in H', a', and c'. Find V and V' from equations (124), (125) or (126).

Now *all* the *stresses* may be found.

At B Stress in $BB' = R + \frac{1}{2}P + R_1 = R + \frac{1}{2}P + \frac{3}{2}H\dfrac{a-x_1}{c-a}$ ... (130)

At B' Horiz. Comp. $B'F = BB' + \frac{1}{2}P + R_1' = R + P + R_1 + R_1'$ (131)

$\qquad\qquad = R + P + \frac{3}{2}H\dfrac{a-x_1}{c-a} + \frac{3}{2}H'\dfrac{a'-x_1'}{c-a}$ (132)

At F, Using equations (129) and (102)

$\qquad$ Horiz. Comp. $B'F = FF' + Q = FF' + \frac{3}{2}H\dfrac{a-x_1}{c-a} + H$

$FF' = R + P + \frac{3}{2}H\dfrac{a-x_1}{c-a} + \frac{3}{2}H'\dfrac{a'-x_1'}{c-a} - \frac{3}{2}H\dfrac{a-x_1}{c-a} - H$ ...(133)

$\qquad\qquad = H' + \frac{3}{2}H'\dfrac{a'-x_1'}{c-a} = H' + R_1'$ .... (134)

The maximum stress in $a'B'$ occurs at F' or a' and equals per. sq. in.

$\qquad \dfrac{DL + LL + V'}{A'} + \dfrac{H'(a'-x_1') \times \text{width of } a'B'}{2\,I'}$ .... (135)

or $\dfrac{DL + LL + V'}{A'} + \dfrac{H'x_1' \times \text{width of } a'B'}{2\,I'}$ .... (136)

whichever is the larger.

The maximum stress in aB occurs at F or a and equals per sq. in.

$\qquad \dfrac{DL + LL - V}{A} + \dfrac{H(a-x_1) \times \text{width of } aB}{2\,I}$ .... (137)

or $\dfrac{DL + LL - V}{A} + \dfrac{Hx_1 \times \text{width of } aB}{2\,I}$ .... (138)

whichever is the larger.

A = gross area of cross section.

DL = stress from Dead Load. LL = stress from Live Load.

V produces no stress in BF. V' produces a uniform stress in $a'B'$.

When the wind blows from the opposite direction the conditions in the posts are reversed. Both cases must therefore be considered in order to find the maximum stresses. The same is true of BB' and FF', the stresses in which will, in general, change, as can be seen from (130) and (134). The stress in BF' will be the same as in $B'F$. See Eq. (131).

The *connection* at B should be designed to take the stress in BB' and the vertical component of $B'F = V$, although these stresses do not act simultaneously. The connection at B' must take the horizontal component of $B'F$, an amount equal to the stress in BB' going to BB', and an amount equal to $\frac{1}{2}P + R_1'$ going to the post. The connection at F' takes the stress in FF' while at F, this much of the horizontal component of $B'F$ goes to FF' and the balance into the post. At F the vertical component of $B'F = V$ goes to the post.

166. General Case of Portal with Posts Fixed at Top and Partially Fixed at the Bottom. Assuming as in the previous case (see Fig. 217), that F deflects as much as B, the distribution of the load between H and H' may be found as follows:

For x greater than a (See Fig. 218).

$$EI\frac{d^2y}{dx^2} = M_2 - R_2 x + Q(x-a) \dots \dots \dots (139)$$

$$EI\frac{dy}{dx} = M_2 x - \tfrac{1}{2}R_2 x^2 + Q(\tfrac{1}{2}x^2 - ax) + C_1$$

$\frac{dy}{dx} = 0$ when $x = c$, whence $C_1 = \tfrac{1}{2}R_2 c^2 - M_2 c - Q(\tfrac{1}{2}c^2 - ac)$

$$EI\frac{dy}{dx} = M_2(x-c) - \tfrac{1}{2}R_2(x^2 - c^2) + Q(\tfrac{1}{2}x^2 - ax - \tfrac{1}{2}c^2 + ac) \quad (140)$$

For x less than a

$$EI\frac{d^2y}{dx^2} = M_2 - R_2 x \dots \dots \dots \dots \dots \dots (141)$$

$$EI\frac{dy}{dx} = M_2 x - \tfrac{1}{2}R_2 x^2 + C_2 \dots \dots \dots \dots \dots (142)$$

When $x = a$, $\frac{dy}{dx}$ from (140) $= \frac{dy}{dx}$ from (142).

$$M_2a - \tfrac{1}{2}R_2a^2 + C_2 = M_2(a-c) - \tfrac{1}{2}R_2(a^2-c^2) + Q(\tfrac{1}{2}a^2 - a^2 - \tfrac{1}{2}c^2 + ac)$$

$$C_2 = \tfrac{1}{2}R_2c^2 - M_2c - \tfrac{1}{2}Q(a-c)^2 \quad \ldots \ldots \ldots \ldots \ldots \ldots (143)$$

$$EIy = \tfrac{1}{2}M_2x^2 - \tfrac{1}{6}R_2x^3 + C_2x + (C_3 = 0) \quad \ldots \ldots \ldots \ldots (144)$$

C_2 is given by equation (143).

There is nothing in the derivation of equation (115) which will prevent its use in this case, in fact, the same relation may be derived from equation (140). We have then $x_2 = \tfrac{1}{3}e$ and taking moments about the upper point of inflection.

$$\tfrac{2}{3}Qe = R_2(a + \tfrac{2}{3}e) - M_2$$

$$M_2 = R_2x_1 \text{ and } M_2' = R_2'x_1' \quad \ldots \ldots \ldots \ldots \text{ (same as 94).} (145)$$

$$Q = R_2 \frac{c + \tfrac{1}{2}a - \tfrac{3}{2}x_1}{c - a} \quad \ldots \ldots \ldots \ldots \ldots \ldots \ldots \ldots \ldots \ldots (146)$$

Making $x = a$ and substituting (145) and (146) in **(144)**

$$EIy_1 = \tfrac{1}{2}R_2x_1a^2 - \tfrac{1}{6}R_2a^3 + \tfrac{1}{2}R_2ac^2 - R_2x_1ac - \tfrac{1}{2}Qa(a-c)^2$$

$$= R_2x_1(\tfrac{1}{2}a^2 - ac) + \tfrac{1}{2}R_2(ac^2 - \tfrac{1}{3}a^3) + \tfrac{1}{2}aR_2\frac{c + \tfrac{1}{2}a - \tfrac{3}{2}x_1}{a - c}(a-c)^2$$

$$= aR_2[\tfrac{1}{2}ax_1 - cx_1 + \tfrac{1}{2}c^2 - \tfrac{1}{6}a^2 + \tfrac{1}{2}ac + \tfrac{1}{4}a^2 - \tfrac{3}{4}ax_1 - \tfrac{1}{2}c^2 - \tfrac{1}{4}ac + \tfrac{3}{4}cx_1]$$

$$y_1 = \frac{aR_2}{EI}\left[-\tfrac{1}{4}ax_1 - \tfrac{1}{4}cx_1 + \tfrac{1}{12}a^2 + \tfrac{1}{4}ac \right]$$

$$= \frac{aR_2}{4EI}\left[a(\tfrac{1}{3}a + c) - x_1(a+c) \right] \ldots \ldots \ldots \ldots (147)$$

similarly

$$y_1' = \frac{a'R_2'}{4EI'}\left[a'(\tfrac{1}{3}a' + c') - x_1'(a'+c') \right] \ldots \ldots \ldots (148)$$

Now since $R_2 = H$, $R_2' = H'$, $H + H' = R + P$ and $y_1 = y_1' \ldots (149)$

$$\frac{y_1}{y_1'} = 1 = \frac{\frac{aH}{4EI}\left[a(\tfrac{1}{3}a+c) - x_1(a+c) \right]}{\frac{a'H'}{4EI'}\left[a'(\tfrac{1}{3}a'+c') - x_1'(a'+c') \right]}$$

$$\frac{H'}{H} = \frac{aI'[a(\tfrac{1}{3}a+c) - x_1(a+c)]}{a'I[a'(\tfrac{1}{3}a'+c') - x_1'(a'+c')]}$$

$$H' = \frac{R+P}{\frac{a'I[a'(\tfrac{1}{3}a'+c') - x_1'(a'+c')]}{aI'[a(\tfrac{1}{3}a+c) - x_1(a+c)]} + 1} \quad \ldots \ldots \ldots (150)$$

If $I = I'$ both drop out of the equation.

If the supports are on a level $a = a'$ and $c = c'$.

Art. 166.   PORTALS—POSTS PARTIALLY FIXED.

$$H' = \frac{R+P}{\dfrac{I \mid a(\tfrac{1}{3}a+c)-x_1'(a+c)\mid}{I'[a(\tfrac{1}{3}a+c)-x_1(a+c)]}+1} \quad \ldots\ldots\ldots (151)$$

If $a=a'$ and $x_1=x_1'$, $H' = \dfrac{R+P}{\dfrac{I}{I'}+1} = (R+P)\dfrac{I'}{I+I'}$ (152)

Equations (149) and (150) determine H and H' when x_1 and x_1' are known. These depend upon M_2 and M_2', which in turn depend on V. We must therefore solve by approximation. This can be more readily done if we transfer (150) as follows. From the derivation of (150) above,

$$\frac{H}{H^1} = \frac{a'I \mid a'(\tfrac{1}{3}a'+c')-x_1'(a'+c')\mid}{aI'[a(\tfrac{1}{3}a+c)-x_1(a+c)]} \quad \ldots\ldots\ldots\ldots (153)$$

For convenience let $m'=a'(\tfrac{1}{3}a'+c'), n'=(a'+c'), m=a(\tfrac{1}{3}a+c)$ and $n=(a+c)$, then $\dfrac{H}{H'} = \dfrac{a'I[m'-x_1'n']}{aI'[m-x_1n]}$

Now from (145) $x_1 = \dfrac{M_2}{H}$ and $x_1' = \dfrac{M_2'}{H}$ ... (same as 94). (154)

Then $aI'H(m-nx_1)=a'IH'(m'-n'x_1')$
$aI'Hm-aI'Hnx_1=a'IH'm'-a'IH'n'x_1'$

substituting from (154)
$aI'Hm-aI'nM_2=a'IH'm'-a'In'M_2'$

since $H=R+P-H'$
$aI'm(R+P)-aI'mH'-aI'nM_2=a'I(H'm'-n'M_2')$

$$H' = \frac{aI'[m(R+P)-nM_2]+a'In'M_2'}{a'Im'+aI'm}$$

$$H' = \frac{aI'[a(\tfrac{1}{3}a+c)(R+P)-(a+c)M_2]+a'I(a'+c')M_2'}{a'Ia'(\tfrac{1}{3}a'+c')+aI'(\tfrac{1}{3}a+c)a} \quad (155)$$

When $a=a'$, $c=c'$, $(m=m', n=n')$ and $I=I'$

$$H' = \tfrac{1}{2}[R+P+\frac{a+c}{a(\tfrac{1}{3}a+c)}(M_2'-M_2)]\ldots\ldots\ldots (156)$$

Get V and V' from equation (124) or (125).

$R_2=H$ and $R_2'=H'$ $\ldots\ldots\ldots\ldots\ldots\ldots\ldots\ldots (157)$

$R_1=\tfrac{3}{2}H\dfrac{a-x_1}{e}$ and $R_1'=\tfrac{3}{2}H'\dfrac{a'-x_1'}{e}\ldots\ldots (158)$

$Q=R_1+H$ and $Q'=R_1'+H'$ (See Eq. (129)) $\ldots$ (159)

To solve any particular problem, first find the approximate mean value of x_1 and x_1' by

$$\frac{\tfrac{1}{2}k_2 D}{\tfrac{1}{2}(R+P)} = x_m \text{ (for } a=a')$$

In this value of D, V is neglected. With this mean value, calling $H=H'$ in (158) find an approximate value of V from (124). The second term will become zero, but this will be a *close* approximation of V. With this value of V find D and D' and M_2 and M_2'. Substituting the latter in (155) or (156) we get H', and $H = R + P - H'$.

With these approximate values of H and H' we get from (154) and (158) values of x_1 and x_1', R_1 and R_1'. These in (124) give a new value of V. This should not differ much from the first approximation. Generally the effect of a change in V on H' can easily be seen without again going through the entire calculation.

167. General Case of Portal with Posts Partially Fixed at Both Ends.

In this case both x_1 and x_2 will be less than in the first case with both ends of the columns fixed.

The distribution of the load between H and H' may be found as follows:

When $x > a$,

$$EI\frac{d^2y}{dx^2} = R_1(c-x) - M_1 \quad\quad\quad (160)$$

$$EI\frac{dy}{dx} = R_1(cx - \tfrac{1}{2}x^2) - M_1 x + C_1 \quad\quad\quad (161)$$

$$EIy = R_1(\tfrac{1}{2}cx^2 - \tfrac{1}{6}x^3) - \tfrac{1}{2}M_1 x^2 + C_1 x + C_2 \quad\quad\quad (162)$$

When $x = a$ and $x = c$ in (162), $y = y_1$, and

$$C_1 = \tfrac{1}{2}M_1(c+a) - \tfrac{1}{3}R_1(c^2 + ac - \tfrac{1}{2}a^2) \quad\quad\quad (163)$$

When $x < a$,

$$EI\frac{d^2y}{dx^2} = M_2 - Hx \quad\quad\quad (164)$$

$$EI\frac{dy}{dx} = M_2 x - \tfrac{1}{2}Hx^2 + C_3 \quad\quad\quad (165)$$

$$EIy = \tfrac{1}{2}M_2 x^2 - \tfrac{1}{6}Hx^3 + C_3 x + (C_4 = 0) \quad\quad\quad (166)$$

When $x = 0$, $y = 0$, and $C_4 = 0$.

When $x = a$, $\dfrac{dy}{dx}$ from (165) $= \dfrac{dy}{dx}$ from (161)

$$C_3 = \tfrac{1}{2}Ha^2 - \tfrac{1}{3}R_1(c-a)^2 - M_2 a + \tfrac{1}{2}M_1(c-a) \quad\quad\quad (167)$$

Art. 167.   PORTALS—POSTS PARTIALLY FIXED.   333

When $x=a$ in (166), $y=y_1$,

$$EI y_1 = \tfrac{1}{3}Ha^3 - \tfrac{1}{2}M_2 a^2 - \tfrac{1}{3}R_1 a(c-a)^2 + \tfrac{1}{2}M_1 a(c-a) \ldots (168)$$

$$EI' y'_1 = \text{(same as (168) with the letters primed)} \ldots (169)$$

Σ Moments about $Q=0$ (Fig. 218).

$$R_1 = \frac{Ha + M_1 - M_2}{c-a} \ldots (170)$$

$$y_1 = y'_1 \text{ and } H = R + P - H' \ldots (171)$$

Combining (168) and (169), and substituting from (170) and (171),

$$H' = \frac{\frac{a}{I}[2(R+P)a(2a-c) - M_2(5a-2c) + M_1(c-a)] + \frac{a'}{I'}[M_2'(5a'-2c') - M_1'(c'-a')]}{\frac{2a^2}{I}(2a-c) + \frac{2a'^2}{I'}(2a'-c')} \quad (172)$$

When $a=a'$, $c=c'$, and $I=I'$,

$$H' = \tfrac{1}{2}(R+P) + \frac{(M_2' - M_2)(5a-2c) - (M_1' - M_1)(c-a)}{4a(2a-c)} \ldots (173)$$

Equation (123) becomes

$$V' = -V = \tfrac{1}{b}[(R+P)(c-x_1) - H'(a-a' + x_1' - x_1) + M_1 + M_1'] \ (174)$$

$$M_1 = \tfrac{1}{2}k_1 D_1 \text{ and } M_2 = \tfrac{1}{2}k_2 D_2 = H x_1 \ldots (175)$$

$$M_1' = \tfrac{1}{2}k_1' D_1' \text{ and } M_2' = \tfrac{1}{2}k_2' D_2' = H' x_1' \ldots (176)$$

It will be necessary to determine H and x_1 for two cases, one with the live load on the bridge and one with no live load acting.

$$D_1 = DL \text{ or } DL + LL \ldots (177)$$

$$D_1' = DL + V \text{ or } DL + LL + V = D_2' \ldots (178)$$

$$D_2 = DL - V \text{ or } DL + LL - V \ldots (179)$$

Since M_2' will be greater than M_2, x_1' will be greater than x_1. We can find a value which will be nearly a mean of the two by using equation (172) or (173) to find H' and neglecting V in equations (175) and (176). We have then:

$$\text{Approx. mean value of } x_1 \text{ and } x_1' = \frac{\tfrac{1}{2}k_2 D_2}{H} \ldots (180)$$

Since M_1 does not involve V it can be determined at once from (175). Guessing at a value of V, an approximate value of M_1' for use in (174) is obtained which may be revised as soon as V has been approximately determined. M_1' can be revised and again applied in (174), neglecting the second term, which is small. Now having a close approximation of V, we can find approximate values of D_2 and D_2', M_2 and M_2' from (179), (178), (175), and (176). From (172) or (173) we can find the corresponding value of H'. From (175) and (176) we find the first approximate values of x_1 and x_1'. Now a revised value of V can be found and applied to get as before new values of H', H, x_1, and x_1'. This process may be continued until the required degree of accuracy is attained.

The *stresses* for this case are found in exactly the same manner as for the first case, but the formulas in the recapitulation of Art. 165 have to be modified, because R_1 and Q are different. We have:

$$H(a-x_1) = R_1(e-x_2) \quad \quad (181)$$

and $R_1 x_2 = \tfrac{1}{2} k_1 D_1 = M_1$ . . . . (182)

from which $R_1 = \dfrac{1}{e}[H(a-x_1) + M_1]$ . . . . (183)

and $x_2 = \dfrac{M_1}{R_1}$ . . . . (184)

$Q = R_1 + H$ . . . . (185)

$BB' = R + \tfrac{1}{2}P + R_1 = R + \tfrac{1}{2}P + \dfrac{1}{e}[H(a-x_1) + M_1]$ . . . . (186)

Horiz. Comp. $B'F = R + P + R_1 + R_1' = R + P + \dfrac{1}{e}[H(a+x_1)$
$+ H'(a'+x_1') + M_1 + M_1']$ . . . . (187)

$FF' = H' + R_1' = H' + \dfrac{1}{e}[H'(a'-x_1') + M_1']$ . . . . (188)

The maximum stress in the posts may be gotten from equations (135) to (138) inclusive, remembering that H and H' are *not* the same as in (186), (187), and (188).

When the wind blows in the opposite direction the same remarks apply as in Art. 165.

168. Particular Cases of Stresses in Portal Bracing. We shall now apply the general formulas which have been developed, to the usual particular cases of construction of portals. The various cases will be distinguished by numbers followed by the letters *a*, *b*, and *c*. The letter *a* denotes that both ends of the posts are fixed; the letter *b* that the posts are fixed at their tops, and

Art. 169.   PORTAL WITH SIMPLE X BRACING   335

the letter c that both ends of the posts are only partially fixed. (The case of one or both ends *not fixed* cannot occur in practice.)

In all the cases which follow we take the supports on a level and assume the posts to be alike. Therefore
$$a'=a,\ c'=c,\ I'=I$$

It may happen, in any particular portal, that all three cases a, b, and c, occur, depending upon whether we are considering the windward or leeward post, or whether the posts are under dead load stress only or both dead and live loads are acting.

169. Case No. 1.   Simple X Bracing.

Case No. 1a.   *Portal with Posts Fixed Top and Bottom.*

In this case $x_1 = x_1'$ and

from equation (118) $x_1 = \dfrac{a(a+c)}{3a+c}$

from equation (106) $H = H' = \frac{1}{2}[R+P]$

from equation (128) $R_1 = \frac{3}{4}[R+P]\dfrac{a-x_1}{e} = R_1'$

From equation (126)
$$V = -V' = \frac{1}{b}[(R+P)(c-x_1) + \tfrac{2}{3}eR_1]$$
$$= \frac{1}{b}\left[(R+P)\left(c-x_1 + \frac{a-x_1}{2}\right)\right]$$
$$= \frac{1}{b}[(R+P)(c + \tfrac{1}{2}a - \tfrac{3}{2}x_1)]$$

from equation (130)
$$\text{Stress in } BB' = R + \tfrac{1}{2}P + \tfrac{3}{4}(R+P)\dfrac{a-x_1}{e}$$

from equation (132)
$$\text{Horiz. Comp. } B'F = (R+P)\left(1 + \dfrac{3(a-x_1)}{2e}\right)$$

from equation (134)
$$\text{Stress in } FF' = \tfrac{1}{2}(R+P)\left(1 + \dfrac{3(a-x_1)}{2e}\right)$$

from equation (136) Maximum stress *per sq. in.* in
$$a'B' = \dfrac{DL + LL + V'}{A} + \dfrac{\tfrac{1}{2}(R+P)x_1 \times width\ of\ a'B'}{2I}$$

From equation (138) Maximum stress *per sq. in.* in
$$aB = \dfrac{DL + LL - V}{A} + \dfrac{\tfrac{1}{2}(R+P)x_1 \times width\ of\ aB}{2I}$$

336   PORTAL WITH SIMPLE X BRACING.   Art. 169.

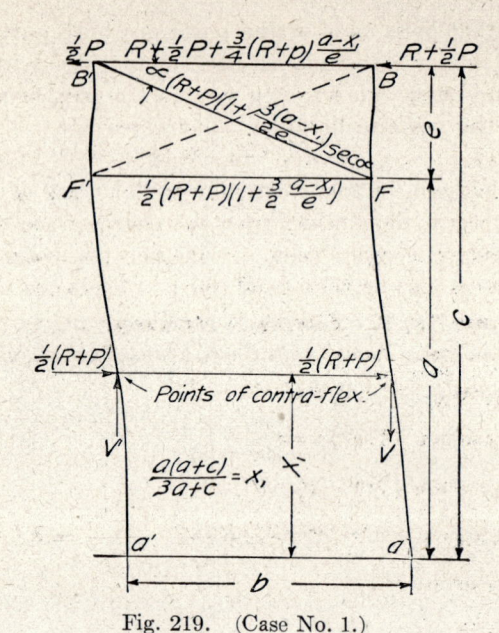

Fig. 219. (Case No. 1.)

(Stresses given are for Case No. 1a.)

The connection at B takes the stress in BB' and the vertical component of $B'F=V$, but these do not act simultaneously. When the wind is reversed, this connection takes the horizontal component of BF', an amount equal to the stress in BB' going to BB' and an amount equal to $\tfrac{1}{2}P + \tfrac{3}{4}(R+P)\dfrac{a-x_1}{e}$ going to the post.

The connection at F takes $\tfrac{1}{2}$ of the horizontal component of $B'F$ into FF' and the other half into the post. At the same time the vertical component of $B'F=V$ goes into the post.

If aB is inclined as shown in Fig. 215, the stress in the bottom chord of the truss from the top chord wind forces will be $\pm V \sin \theta$.

Case No. 1b. *Posts Fixed at the Top and Partially Fixed at the Bottom.* In order that a post may be fixed at the top we must have from equation (121) $\tfrac{1}{2}k_1 D = M_1 = \tfrac{1}{3}eR_1 = \tfrac{1}{2}H(a-x_1)$ taking $H = \tfrac{1}{2}(R+P)$, and $x_1 = \dfrac{a(a+c)}{3a+c}$ if equation (122) is also satisfied we have *Case No. 1a*.

Art. 169. PORTAL WITH SIMPLE X-BRACING. 337

In *case No. 1b* $x_1' > x_1$ and $H' > H$ (Fig. 217), although $a = a'$ and $c = c'$.

This case must be solved by approximation as indicated in Art. 166. Having thus found x_1, x_1', H, H', V and V' we find the stresses exactly as in *No. 1a*. This will be illustrated by an example.

Let us take a single track through railroad bridge of 8 panels at 24 ft., with a depth of 36.2 ft. and a width center to center of trusses of 16.5 ft., end posts inclined.

The dead load stress in the end post is 100,000 lbs. and the live load stress 212,000 lbs. The portal is connected so that in Fig. 219, $c = 43.5$ ft., $a = 31.5$ ft., $e = 12.0$ ft. C. to C. of bearings on top pin $= k_1 = 20$ in. C. to C. of bearings on bottom pin $= k_2 = 21$ in.

Wind Load per ft. $= 150$ lbs. on top chord. Wind Load per Panel $= P = 3,600$ lbs., $R = 2\frac{1}{2}P = 9,000$ lbs. $R + P = 12,600$ lbs.
Top: $\frac{1}{2}k_1 D = 10 \times 100,000 = 1,000,000$ in. lbs. $= D.\ L.$ Mom.
           $= 10 \times 212,000 = 2,120,000$ in. lbs. $= L.\ L.$ Mom.
           $\overline{3,120,000}$ in. lbs. $=$ Total.

This is at B. If the post is fixed at this point, it certainly will be at B' also.

Bottom: $\frac{1}{2}k_2 D = 10.5 \times 100,000 = 1,050,000$ in. lbs. $= D.\ L.$ Mom.
           $= 10.5 \times 212,000 = 2,230,000$ in. lbs. $= L.\ L.$ Mom.
           $\overline{3,280,000}$ in. lbs. $=$ Total.

From equation (121) $M_1 = \dfrac{12600}{4}(a - x_1)$,

$$x_1 = \frac{31.5(31.5 + 43.5)}{94.5 + 43.5} = 17.1$$

$M_1 = \dfrac{12600}{4}(31.5 - 17.1) = 45{,}300$ ft. lbs. $= 544{,}000$ in .lbs.

Since this is less than $\frac{1}{2}k_1 D$ above, the *tops* of the posts *are fixed*.

$M_2 = \frac{1}{2}(R + P)x_1 = 6{,}300 \times 17.1 \times 12 = 1{,}290{,}000$ in. lbs.

Since this is more than $\frac{1}{2}k_2 D$ under $D.\ L.$, not considering V which will make the difference still greater, the *bottom* of the post is *partially fixed* under dead load only. On account of the large margin it will evidently be *fixed* when the live load is on the bridge. We have then only the *former* case to consider here.

Neglecting V and calling $H = H'$, we get nearly a mean value of x_1 and x_1' from $\dfrac{\frac{1}{2}k_2 D}{\frac{1}{2}(R+P)} = \dfrac{1{,}050{,}000}{6300} = 167$ in. $= 13.9$ ft.

From (158), $R_1 = \frac{3}{2} H \dfrac{a - x_1}{e}$ Taking H as above

R_1 approx. $= \frac{3}{2} \times 6{,}300 \dfrac{31.5 - 13.9}{12} = 13{,}800 = R_1'$ approx.

From equation (125)

$$V = \dfrac{1}{b}\,[(R+P)(c-x_1) - H'(x_1' - x_1) + \tfrac{1}{3} e (R_1 + R_1')]$$

$$= \dfrac{1}{16.5}\,[12{,}600(43.5 - 13.9) + \tfrac{12}{3}\,27{,}600] = 29{,}300$$

1st Trial

$D = 100{,}000 - 29{,}300 = \ \ \ 70{,}700$ lbs.
$D' = 100{,}000 + 29{,}300 = 129{,}300$ lbs.
$M_2 = \ \ 70{,}700 \times 10.5 = \ \ \ 742{,}500$ in. lbs. $= \ \ 61{,}900$ ft. lbs.
$M_2' = 129{,}300 \times 10.5 = 1{,}358{,}000$ in. lbs. $= 113{,}200$ ft. lbs.

$\overline{M_2' - M_2} = 51{,}300$ ft. lbs.

From equation (156)

$H' = \frac{1}{2}(12{,}600 + \dfrac{31.5 + 43.5}{31.5(10.5 + 43.5)}\,51{,}300) = 7{,}430$

$H = 12{,}600 - 7{,}430 = 5{,}170$

$x_1 = \dfrac{61{,}900}{5170} = 12.0$ ft. $\quad x_1' = \dfrac{113{,}200}{7430} = 15.2$ ft.

2nd Trial

$R_1 = \frac{3}{2} \times 5{,}170\,\dfrac{31.5 - 12}{12} = 12{,}600$

$R_1' = \frac{3}{2} \times 7{,}430\,\dfrac{31.5 - 15.2}{12.0} = 15{,}100$

$V = \dfrac{1}{16.5}\,[12{,}600(43.5 - 12) - 7{,}430 \times 3.2 + \tfrac{12}{3} \times 27{,}700] = 29{,}300$

Since this is exactly what was used in the first trial we need not again calculate H and x_1.

In any case V will not vary much from the first approximate determination, and it is readily seen what effect a change in V will have upon M_2, M_2' and H'.

Now we have $x_1 = 12.0$ ft., $x_1' = 15.2$ ft., $H = 5{,}170$, $H' = 7{,}430$
$\qquad\qquad R_1 = 12{,}600$, $R_1' = 15{,}100$

Art. 169. PORTAL WITH SIMPLE X BRACING. 339

From equation (130)
    Stress in $BB' = 9{,}000 + 1{,}800 + 12{,}600 = 23{,}400$ lbs.
From equation (131)
    Horiz. Comp. $B'F = 23{,}400 + 1{,}800 + 15{,}100 = 40{,}300$ lbs.
From equation (134)
    Stress in $FF' = 7{,}430 + 15{,}100 = 22{,}530$ lbs.

The maximum stress in the posts occurs at a' but this comes under case *No. 1a*, as the live load must be on the bridge.

Case No. 1c. *Posts Partially Fixed Top and Bottom.* As in the previous case we first test by equation (121) and (122) to see whether or not either end of either post is fixed under any condition of loading. We solve by approximation in a manner exactly similar to the previous case, using equations of Art. 167. This will be illustrated by an example.

Let us consider a highway bridge of 150 ft. span with 9 panels at 16.67 ft. Depth = 22 ft. $b = 17.17$. $DL = 630$ lbs. per lin. ft. $LL = 1{,}600$ lbs. per lin. ft. End Posts inclined.

    DL Stress in End Post = 26,400 lbs.
    LL Stress in End Post = 66,800 lbs.
                              ─────────
                              93,200 lbs. Total.

$c = 28$ ft. $a = 20$ ft. $e = 8$ ft. $k_1 = 9$ in. $k_2 = 9\frac{1}{2}$ in.
$P = 150 \times 16\frac{2}{3} = 2{,}500$ lbs. $R + P = 16.67 \times 150 \times 4 = 10{,}000$ lbs.

Now let us test for fixity of the ends of the posts.
Assuming the ends fixed,

From equation (118) $x_1 = \dfrac{20(20+28)}{60+28} = \dfrac{20 \times 48}{88} = 10.9$ ft.

From equation (106) $H = H' = \tfrac{1}{2}(R+P) = 5{,}000$ lbs.

From equation (128) $R_1 = \tfrac{3}{2} \times 5{,}000 \dfrac{20-10.9}{8} = 8{,}500$ lbs. $= R_1'$

From equation (126) $V = \dfrac{1}{17.17}(10{,}000 \times 17.1 + \tfrac{8}{3} \times 17{,}000)$
                      $= 12{,}600$ lbs.

From equation (121) $M_1 = \tfrac{8}{3} \times 8{,}500 = 22{,}600$ ft. lbs.
                      $= 271{,}200$ in. lbs.

From equation (122) $M_2 = 5{,}000 \times 10.9 = 54{,}500$ ft. lbs.
                      $= 654{,}000$ in. lbs.

Top: $\tfrac{1}{2} k_1 D = 4.5 \times 93{,}200 = 420{,}000$ in. lbs. at B with LL on.
  or $= 4.5 \times 26{,}400 = 119{,}000$ in. lbs. at B with DL only.

½$k_1'D'$ = 4.5 × (93,200 + 12,600) = 476,000 in. lbs. at B' with LL. on.

or = 4.5 × (26,400 + 12,600) = 175,500 in. lbs. at B' with DL only.

These values are greater for live load stress and less for dead load only acting, in each post, than the value of M_1. Therefore the posts are *partially* fixed at the tops under dead load only.

Bottom: ½k_2L = 4.75 (93,200 − 12,600) = 383,000 in. lbs. at a
or   = 4.75 (26,400 − 12,600) = 65,500 in. lbs. at a
  ½$k_2'D'$ = 4.75 (93,200 + 12,600) = 502,000 in. lbs. at a'
or   = 4.75 (26,400 + 12,600) = 185,200 in. lbs. at a'

Since all of these are less than M_2, the bottom ends of the posts are not fully fixed under either condition. For maximum moment in the posts, this problem comes under case *No. 1b*. Here we shall consider the other case, that is, dead load only acting. We have from equation (174)

$$V = \frac{1}{b}[(R+P)(c-x_1) - H'(x_1'-x_1) + M_1 + M_1']$$

From equation (180) approx. mean value of x_1 and x_1'

$$= \frac{4.75 \times 26400}{5000} = 25 \text{ in.} = 2.1 \text{ ft.}$$

From equation (175)

$M_1 = 4.5 \times 26,400 = 119,000$ in. lbs. = 9,900 ft. lbs.

Before we can get M_1', we must know V.

For an approximate M_1' we will assume $V = 13,600$. (V will be larger than 12,600 determined from equation (126) because x_1 will be smaller.)

1st. Approx. $M_1' = 4.5(26,400 + 13,600) = 180,000$ in lbs.
  = 15,000 ft. lbs.

From equation (174)

1st. Approx. $V = \frac{1}{17.17}[10,000(28-2.1) + 9,900 + 15,000] = 16,700$

1st Trial:

$D = 26,400 - 16,700 = \quad 9,700$

Art. 169.   PORTAL WITH SIMPLE X BRACING.   341

$D' = 26{,}400 + 16{,}700 = 43{,}100$
$M_2 = 9{,}700 \times 4.75 = 46{,}000$ in. lbs. $= 3{,}830$ ft. lbs.
$M_2' = 43{,}100 \times 4.75 = 205{,}000$ in. lbs. $= 17{,}100$ ft. lbs.
$$13{,}270 = M_2' - M_2$$

From equation (173)

$$H' = \tfrac{1}{2} \times 10{,}000 + \frac{13{,}270 \times 44 - 5100 \times 8}{80 \times 12} = 5{,}560 \text{ lbs.}$$

$$H = 10{,}000 - 5{,}560 = 4{,}440 \text{ lbs.}$$

$$x_1 = \frac{3830}{4440} = 0.86 \text{ ft.}$$

$$x_1' = \frac{17100}{5560} = 3.07 \text{ ft.}$$

2d Trial:— $M_1 = 9{,}900$ as before.

$$M_1' = \frac{4.5}{12}(26{,}400 + 16{,}700) = 16{,}200 \text{ ft. lbs.}$$

From equation (174)

$$V = \frac{1}{17.17}[10{,}000(28 - 0.86) - 5{,}560(3.07 - 0.86) + 26{,}100]$$

$= 16{,}600$ lbs.
$D = 26{,}400 - 16{,}600 = 9{,}800$ lbs.
$D' = 26{,}400 + 16{,}600 = 43{,}000$ lbs.
$M_2 = 9{,}800 \times 4.75 = 46{,}500$ in. lbs. $= 3{,}880$ ft. lbs.
$M_2' = 43{,}000 \times 4.75 = 204{,}000$ in. lbs. $= 17{,}000$ ft. lbs.
$$13{,}120 = M_2' - M_2$$

$$H' = \tfrac{1}{2} \times 10{,}000 + \frac{13{,}120 \times 44 - 6300 \times 8}{80 \times 12} = 5{,}550 \text{ lbs.}$$

$$H = 10{,}000 \times 5{,}550 = 4{,}450 \text{ lbs.}$$

$$x_1 = \frac{3880}{4450} = 0.87 \text{ ft.}$$

$$x_1' = \frac{17000}{5550} = 3.06 \text{ ft.}$$

These values differing so little from those of the first trial shows that they are close enough for practical purposes.

From Eq. (183)

$$R_1 = \tfrac{1}{8}[4{,}450(20-0.87) + 9{,}900] = 11{,}880$$
$$R_1' = \tfrac{1}{8}[5{,}550(20-3.06) + 16{,}130] = 13{,}770$$

From Eq. (186)

Stress in $BB' = 8{,}750 + 11{,}880 = 20{,}630$ lbs.

From Eq. (187)

Horiz. Comp. $B'F = 10{,}000 + 11{,}880 + 13{,}770 = 35{,}650$ lbs.

From Eq. (188)

Stress in $FF' = 5{,}550 + 13{,}770 = 19{,}320$ lbs.

Maximum stress in the posts occurs at F', but this comes under case *No. 1b*.

For connections see remarks under Case No. *1a*.

170. Case No. 2. Plate Girder Portal.

Case No. 2a. *Posts Fixed Top and Bottom.* In this case $e = 0$ and $a = c$ and $\tfrac{1}{2}k_2 D \gtreqless \tfrac{1}{4}(R+P)a$.

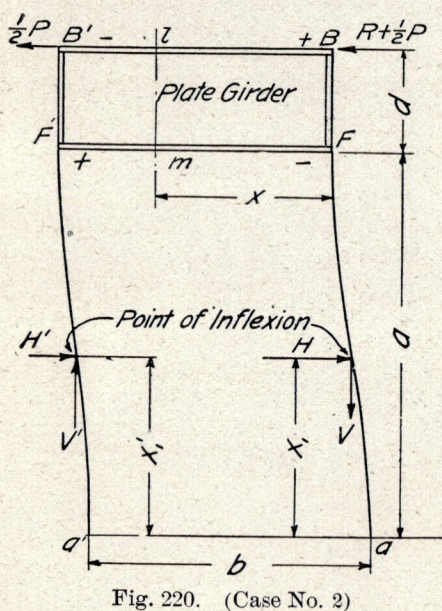

Fig. 220. (Case No. 2)

From equation (118)
$$x_1 = \tfrac{1}{2}a = x_1'$$
From equation (106)
$$H = H' = \tfrac{1}{2}(R+P)$$
From equation (122)
$$M_2 = \tfrac{1}{4}(R+P)a$$
From equation (126)
$$V = -V'$$
$$= \tfrac{1}{b}(R+P)(a+d-x_1)$$

Bending moment in the posts at a, a', F and $F' = \tfrac{1}{4}(R+P)a$.

The maximum stress in the posts is at F' and is found from equation (135).

To find the stresses in the girder take any section lm, with the center of moments at m.

$$BB'd - (R+\tfrac{1}{2}P)d - H(a-x_1) + Vx = 0.$$
$$BB'd = (R+\tfrac{1}{2}P)d + \tfrac{1}{4}(R+P)a - Vx.$$

$$BB' = R + \tfrac{1}{2}P + \tfrac{1}{4}(R+P)\frac{a}{d} - V\frac{x}{d} = \tfrac{1}{2}R + H\left(1 + \tfrac{1}{2}\frac{a}{d}\right) - V\frac{x}{d}$$

When $x=0$, $BB' = \tfrac{1}{2}R + H\left(1 + \tfrac{1}{2}\frac{a}{d}\right)$

When $x=\tfrac{1}{2}b$, $BB' = \tfrac{1}{2}R$.

When $x=b$, $BB' = \tfrac{1}{2}R - H\left(1 + \tfrac{1}{2}\frac{a}{d}\right)$

BB' has therefore a uniform compressive stress equal to $\tfrac{1}{2}R$ and a uniformly varying stress. The latter equals zero at the center, is compressive on the windward side and tensile on the leeward side.

With the center of moments at l

$$FF'd = H(\tfrac{1}{2}a + d) - Vx \qquad FF' = H\frac{(\tfrac{1}{2}a+d)}{d} - V\frac{x}{d}$$

When $x=0$, $FF' = H\left(1 + \tfrac{1}{2}\frac{a}{d}\right)$

When $x=\tfrac{1}{2}b$, $FF' = 0$.

When $x=b$, $FF' = -H\left(1 + \tfrac{1}{2}\frac{a}{d}\right)$.

FF' has therefore a uniformly varying stress from compression on the leeward side through zero at the center to tension on the windward side.

The difference in stress between BB' and FF' is $\tfrac{1}{2}R$.

The vertical shear in the web at any section is V.

The moment at the middle of the girder at any section $l_m = \tfrac{1}{2}(R + \tfrac{1}{2}P)d + \tfrac{1}{2}H(a+d) - Vx$.

For the connection BF the moment is $\tfrac{1}{2}(R + \tfrac{1}{2}P)d + \tfrac{1}{2}H(a+d)$, and the shear is V.

All stresses are reversed when the direction of the wind is reversed.

Case No. 2b. *Posts Fixed at the Top and Partially Fixed at the Bottom.* (See Fig. 220.) In this case from equations (121) and (122) $\tfrac{1}{2}k_1 D \gtreqless \tfrac{1}{8}(R+P)a$ and $\tfrac{1}{2}k_2 D < \tfrac{1}{4}(R+P)a$, but on account of the construction the posts may always be considered *fixed at the top*, so the latter condition is the only one that need be tested.

An approximate mean value of x_1 and x_1' is determined from the equation $x_m = \dfrac{\tfrac{1}{2}k_2 D}{\tfrac{1}{2}(R+P)}$. V is neglected in this value of D.

Approx. $V = \dfrac{1}{b}(R+P)(a+d-x_m)$

$D = DL(+LL) - V \qquad D' = DL(+LL) + V$
$M_2 = \tfrac{1}{2}k_2 D \qquad\qquad M_2' = \tfrac{1}{2}k_2 D'$

From equation (156) $H' = \tfrac{1}{2}[R+P+\dfrac{3}{2a}(M_2'-M_2)]$

$$H = R+P-H'$$

$$x_1 = \dfrac{M_2}{H} \qquad x_1' = \dfrac{M_2'}{H'}$$

$$V = \dfrac{1}{b}[(R+P)(a+d-x_1) - H'(x_1'-x_1)]$$

If this value of V is near enough to the value given above, we need not again determine H, H', x_1 and x_1'.

The bending in the posts at $a = Hx_1$, at $a' = H'x_1'$, at $F = H(a-x_1)$ and at $F' = H'(a-x_1')$.

The maximum stress in the posts will occur at a' or F'. Other stresses are gotten in a manner exactly similar to the previous case (No. 2 a).

$$BB' = R + \tfrac{1}{2}P + H\dfrac{a-x_1}{d} - V\dfrac{x}{d}$$

$$FF' = H\dfrac{a+d-x_1}{d} - V\dfrac{x}{d}$$

Shear in the girder web at any section $= V$.

The moment at the middle of the girder at any section $lm = \tfrac{1}{2}(R+\tfrac{1}{2}P)d + H(a-x_1+\tfrac{1}{2}d) - Vx$.

For the *connection BF*

the moment $= \tfrac{1}{2}(R+\tfrac{1}{2}P)d + H\left(a-x_1+\dfrac{d}{2}\right)$ and the shear $= V$.

All stresses are reversed when the direction of the wind is reversed.

Case No. 2c with the posts only *partially fixed* at both the top and bottom, can never occur because by the construction the tops of the posts are always fixed regardless of the direct stresses. Of course the connection BF must be properly designated.

171. Case No. 3. Latticed Portal.

Case No. 3a. *Posts Fixed Top and Bottom.* (See Fig. 221.) The stresses for this case are the same as for No. *2a* excepting, of course, that the stresses in BB' and FF', in place of varying uniformly, increase at intervals equal to the distance between connections of web members.

The shear at any section may be taken as equally distributed over the web members cut. The connection at F must take the

Art. 172.   KNEE BRACED PORTAL.   345

stress in FF' at F, and the stress in the web member connecting at F. In the connection at F' the stresses are of opposite kind. Similarly for connections at B and B'.

Intermediate connections between B and F must take their portion of the shear and must hold the post in line between B and F. When the wind reverses all wind stresses reverse.

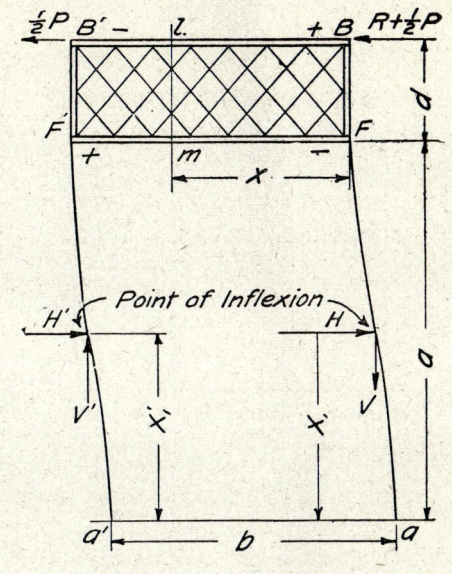

Case No. 3b. The stresses are found exactly as for case No. 2 b, and the remarks under No. 3a apply.

Fig. 221. (Case No. 3.)

Case No. 3c. Cannot occur. See remarks under Case No. 2c

172. Case No. 4. Knee Braced Portal. Case No. 4a. *Posts Fixed at Both Ends.* (See Fig. 222.) Whatever pieces are inserted simply for the sake of appearance, or to stiffen other members are not considered as taking any stress. A latticed portal in appearance, may be made of this, but only the members shown by full lines in Fig. 222 are calculated to take the stresses. The members shown by dotted lines simply serve to stiffen the knee braces at their middle.

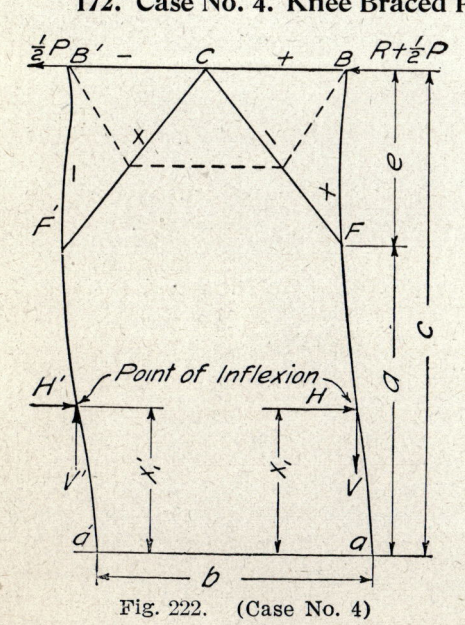

Fig. 222. (Case No. 4)

From equation (118) $x_1 = x_1' = \dfrac{a(a+c)}{3a+c}$

From equation (106) $H = H' = \tfrac{1}{2}(R+P)$

From equation (128) $R_1 = R_1' = \tfrac{3}{4}(R+P)\dfrac{a-x_1}{e}$

From equation (121) $\tfrac{1}{2}k_1 D \gtreqless M_1 \gtreqless \tfrac{1}{3}eR_1.$
From equation (122) $\tfrac{1}{2}k_2 D \gtreqless M_2 \gtreqless Hx_1.$

From equation (126) $V = -V' = \dfrac{1}{b}[(R+P)(c-x_1) + \tfrac{2}{3}eR_1].$

$$= \dfrac{1}{b}\left[(R+P)\left(c - x_1 + \dfrac{a-x_1}{2}\right)\right]$$

Stress in $BC = R + \tfrac{1}{2}P + R_1 = R + \tfrac{1}{2}P + \tfrac{3}{4}(R+P)\dfrac{a-x_1}{e}$

Stress in $CB' = \tfrac{1}{2}P + R_1' = \tfrac{1}{2}P + \tfrac{3}{4}(R+P)\dfrac{a-x_1}{e}$

Horiz. Comp. $CF = Q = R_1 + H =$ Horiz. Comp. $CF'.$
Stress in $BF = -B'F' = V -$ Vert. Comp. $CF = 0.$
Bending in the posts at a and $a' = \tfrac{1}{2}(R+P)x_1.$
Bending in the posts at F and $F' = \tfrac{1}{2}(R+P)(a-x_1).$
The maximum stress in the posts is at $a'.$

The connection at B takes the stress in BC and at B', the stress in $B'C.$

The connection at C transfers the Horiz. Comp. of CF and CF' to $BB'.$

When the direction of the wind is reversed the stresses are all reversed.

Case No. 4b. *Posts Fixed at the Top and Partially Fixed at the Bottom.*

$\tfrac{1}{2}k_1 D \gtreqless M_1 \gtreqless \tfrac{1}{3}eR_1$ and $\tfrac{1}{2}k_2 D < M_2 < Hx_1$

The approximate mean value of x_1 and x_1' is obtained from the equation $x_m = \dfrac{\tfrac{1}{2}k_2 D}{\tfrac{1}{2}(R+P)}$, neglecting V in D.

Approximate value of $R_1 = R_1' = \tfrac{3}{4}(R+P)\dfrac{a-x_m}{e}$

Approximate value of $V = \dfrac{1}{b}[(R+P)(c-x_m) + \tfrac{2}{3}eR_1]$

$D = DL(+LL) - V \qquad D' = DL(+LL) + V$
$M_2 = \tfrac{1}{2}k_2 D \qquad M_2' = \tfrac{1}{2}k_2 D'$

$H' = \tfrac{1}{2}[R + P + \dfrac{a+c}{a(\tfrac{1}{3}a+c)}(M_2' - M_2)], \qquad H = R + P - H',$

$x_1 = \dfrac{M_2}{H}$ and $x_1' = \dfrac{M_2'}{H'}$

Art. 173. LATTICED PORTAL FOR SHALLOW TRUSSES.

2nd Approximation.
$$R_1 = \tfrac{3}{2} H \frac{a-x_1}{e} \qquad R_1' = \tfrac{3}{2} H' \frac{a-x_1'}{e}$$

$$V = \frac{1}{b}[(R+P)(c-x_1) - H'(x_1'-x) + \tfrac{1}{3}e(R_1+R_1')]$$

Now find D, H, and x_1 as above. Having now R_1, R_1', H, H', x_1, x_1' and V, the stresses are found as in case *No. 4a*.

Case No. 4c. *Posts Partially Fixed at Both Ends.*
$\tfrac{1}{2}k_1 D < M_1 < \tfrac{1}{3}eR_1$ and $\tfrac{1}{2}k_2 D < M_2 < Hx_1$. In these two test equations the values of R_1, H and x_1 are the same as those given under Case *No. 4a*. The approximate mean value of x_1 and x_1' is
$$x_m = \frac{\tfrac{1}{2}k_2 D}{\tfrac{1}{2}(R+P)},$$
neglecting V in D.

$M_1 = \tfrac{1}{2}k_1 D$. Approx. $M_1' = \tfrac{1}{2}k_1(D + \text{approx.}\ V)$ from which

Approx. $V = \dfrac{1}{b}[(R+P)(c-x_m) + M_1 + M_1']$.

Now proceed as under case *No. 4b*, using however equation (183) for $R_1 = \dfrac{1}{e}[H(a-x_1)+M_1]$.

173. Case No. 5. Latticed Portal for Shallow Trusses.

Case No. 5a. *Posts Fixed at Both Ends.* The style of portal shown in Fig. 223 is used when the clearance line comes but little below the top of the end posts. The top flange EE' is supposed to be fastened to the top chords of the trusses. The posts may be either fixed or partially fixed at B and B' so, as far as they are concerned we may have any of the three general cases.

H, V, x_1, and M_1 may be gotten as for case *No. 4a*.

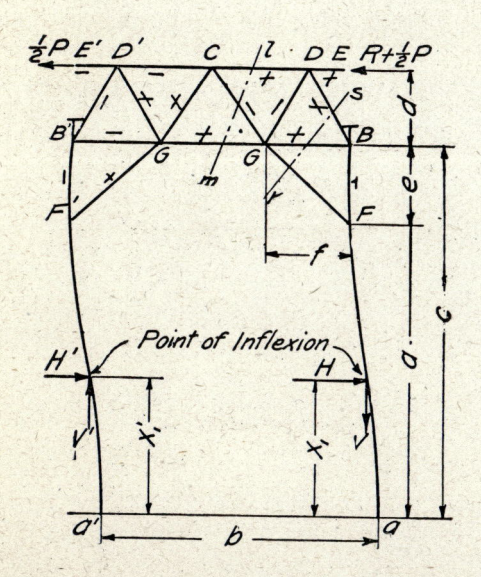

Fig. 223. (Case No. 5)

Taking the section lm with the center of moments at C,
$$GG'd + H(c+d-x_1) - V\frac{b}{2} + M_1 = 0.$$

$GG'd + \tfrac{1}{2}(R+P)(c+d-x_1) - \tfrac{1}{2}(R+P)(c-x_1) - M_1 + M_1 = 0.$
$GG' = \tfrac{1}{2}(R+P) = H.$

Taking the center of moments at G,

$$CD = H\frac{c-x_1}{d} - V\frac{f}{d} + \frac{M_1}{d} + R + \tfrac{1}{2}P = -CD'.$$

Vert. Comp. of $GC = V = -$Vert. Comp. of CG'.

Taking the section rs and the center of moments at B

Horiz. Comp. of $GF = H\dfrac{c-x_1}{e} + \dfrac{M_1}{e} = R_1 + H.$

$BF =$ Vert. Comp. of $GF - V = -B'F'.$
Vert. Comp. of $DB =$ Vert. Comp. of $DG = BF.$
$GB =$ Horiz. Comp. of $DB - R_1 = -G'B'.$
$DE = R + \tfrac{1}{2}P$ and $D'E' = \tfrac{1}{2}P.$

When the direction of the wind is reversed the stresses are reversed.

Case No. 5b. *Posts Fixed at the Top and Partially Fixed at the Bottom.* H, V, R_1, and x_1 are found exactly as under case *No. 4b*, and then the stresses are found as in the preceding case, *No. 5a*.

Case No. 5c. *Posts Partially Fixed at Both Ends.* The external forces are found in exactly the same manner as under case *No. 4c*, and then the stresses as in case *No. 5a*.

174. Case. No. 6. Plate Girder Portal, Knee Braced.

Case No. 6a. *Posts Fixed Top and Bottom.* In Fig. 224 if the plate girder $BEE'B'$ is rigidly connected to the post at EB, we may take the post as fixed at B in all cases, as with the *Case No. 2*, Art. 170. H, V, x_1 and R_1 may be gotten as for the case *No. 4a*,
$M_1 = \tfrac{1}{3}eR_1.$

With a section lm and a center of moments at G_1,

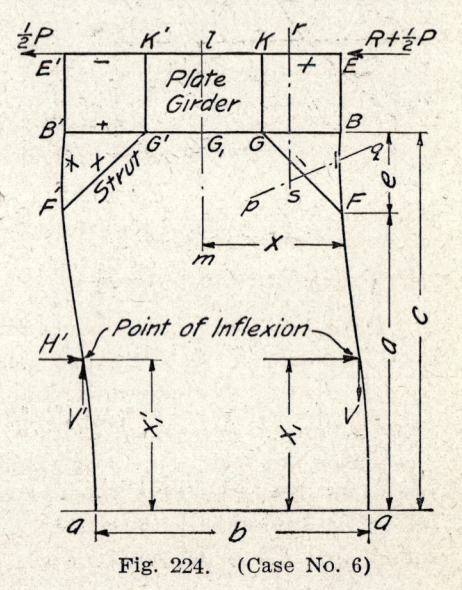

$KK' = H\dfrac{c-x_1}{d} - V\dfrac{x}{d} + \dfrac{M_1}{d} + R + \tfrac{1}{2}P.$

Fig. 224. (Case No. 6)

Art. 174.   PLATE GIRDER PORTAL KNEE BRACED.   349

With the center of moments at l

$$GG' = H\frac{c+d-x_1}{d} - V\frac{x}{d} + \frac{M_1}{d}$$

$$KK' - GG' = \tfrac{1}{2}R$$

Shear between GK and $G'K' = V$.

The stresses to the right of G in the girder are statically indeterminate. According to the above value of GG' the stress in the bottom flange increases as x decreases. We may assume that the increase from G to B is taken by GF, whence GB is constant and equal to the stress given above for GG' when $x = f$, therefore,

$$GB = H\frac{c+d-x_1}{d} - V\frac{f}{d} + \frac{M_1}{d} = -G'B'$$

Taking a section rs with a center of moments at E,

$$\text{Horiz. Comp. of } GF = H\frac{c+d-x_1}{d+e} + \frac{M_1}{d+e} - GB\frac{d}{d+e}$$

$$= V\frac{f}{d+e} = -\text{Horiz. Comp. of } G'F'.$$

Taking a section rs with a center of moments at B,

$$KE = H\frac{c-x_1}{d} + \frac{M_1}{d} + R + \tfrac{1}{2}P - \text{Horiz. Comp. } GF\frac{e}{d}$$

Taking a section pq at F,

$$BF = V - \text{Vert. Comp. of } GF = -B'F'.$$

$$= V - V\frac{e}{d+e} = V\frac{d}{d+e}$$

Connections at G and F should take care of both components of GF, the strut being either in tension or compression.

The connection at E should take the stress EK and at B the stress GB. In addition the connection between E and B should take a *shear* equal to $V\dfrac{d}{d+e}$

Case No. 6b. *Posts Fixed at Top and Partially Fixed at the Bottom.* H, V, x_1, and R_1 may be gotten as for the case No. *4b*. Then the stresses are found exactly as in the preceding case No. *6a*.

Case No. 6c. This case cannot occur under the supposition stated at the beginning of this article. Should EB not be continuous with the post, this case resolves itself into one similar to No. 5, which will be treated in Art. 175.

175. Case No. 7. Plate Girder Portal for Shallow Trusses. Case No. 7a. *Posts Fixed both Top and Bottom.* This case is exactly similar to *No. 5.*

There is a horizontal shear in the girder, equal to $R+P$ which is transmitted to B. This girder also takes a vertical shear and a bending moment. The *vertical shear* equals V between GK and $G'K'$ and equals the stress in BF between BE and GK.

The *moment* is a maximum at GK and $G'K'$ and equals $BF \times f$.

With a section lm and center of moments at B, Horiz. Comp. of GF

$$= H\frac{a-x_1+e}{e} + \frac{M_1}{e} = R_1 + H.$$

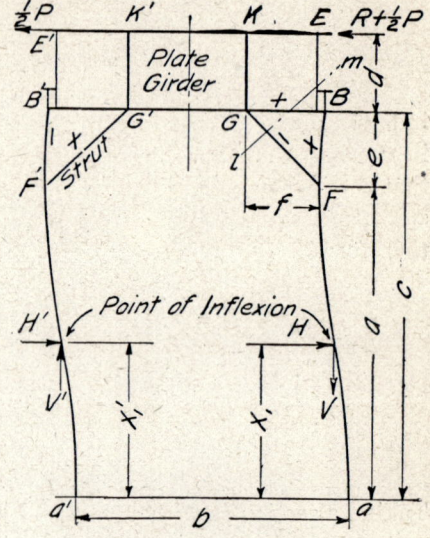

Fig. 225. (Case No. 7)

$BF=$ Vert. Comp. of $GF - V$.

H, V, M_1 and x_1 may be found as for case *No. 4a*.

Cases No. 7b and No. 7c are to be treated in a manner exactly similar to Cases *No. 5b* and *No. 5c*.

176. Stresses in Railway Bridges having Curved Track.[1]

The stresses in railway bridges having curved track, are different from those in bridges with straight track, on account of the resistance which must be offered by the track, in changing the direction of a moving train, on account of the center line of track deviating from the axis of the bridge, and on account of the displacement of the center of gravity of the train due to the superelevation of the outer rail.

We have then, affecting *live load stresses*, "centrifugal force," and "eccentricity."

The centrifugal force of a body of weight P moving in a circular path is $CP = \dfrac{PV^2}{gr} = \dfrac{PV^2}{32.2r}$ .... (189)

---

[1] For a complete discussion of this subject see Trans. Am. Soc. C. E., Vol. XXV, p. 459.

Art. 176.   STRESSES DUE TO CURVED TRACK.   351

If D_c be the degree of curve, $r = \dfrac{5730}{D_c}$[1], approximately for curves under 5°, from which

$$CP = \frac{PV^2 D_c}{32.2 \times 5730} \quad \ldots\ldots\ldots\ldots\ldots\ldots (190)$$

If the velocity of the train be taken at 50 mi. per hour = 73 ft. per sec., equation (190) becomes $CP = \dfrac{73 \times 73}{32.2 \times 5730} PD_c$, or $CP = 0.0288 PD_c$. In other words, the centrifugal force equals nearly 3% of the load for every degree of curvature. It is frequently specified 3% for all curves up to 5° and the additional, reduced to 1% for every degree over 5° on account of the slower speed on sharp curves.

To illustrate the method of calculating live load stresses in bridges having curved track, let us consider a 160 ft. span, single track, through bridge, of 8 panels at 20 ft. Let us suppose the track to be on a 5° curve, that the axis of the stringers corresponds with the axis of the bridge, and that the latter bisects the middle ordinate of the curve in the span length. Fig. 226 shows the eccentricity of the center line of track at the floor beams.

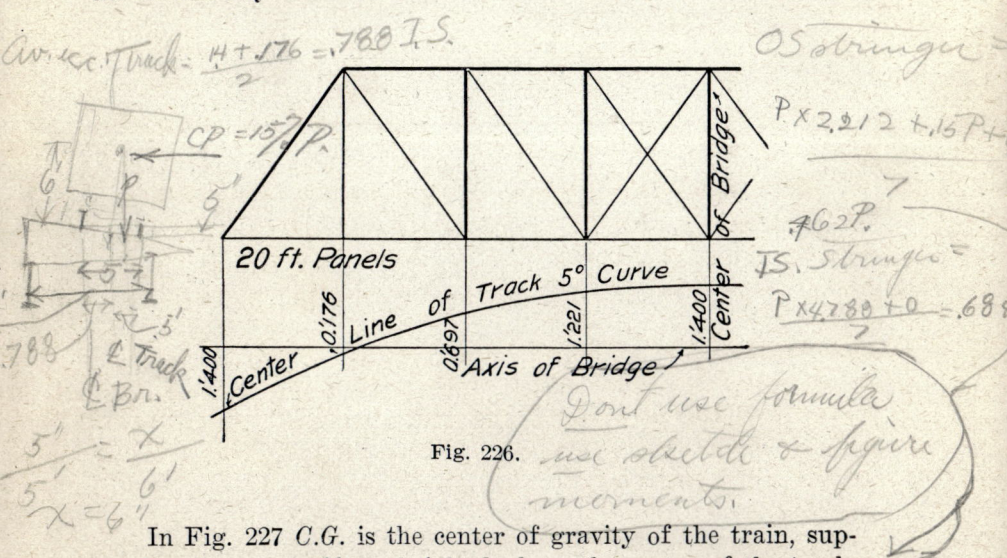

Fig. 226.

In Fig. 227 C.G. is the center of gravity of the train, supposed to be at a uniform height k above the center of the track.

---

[1] See Carhart's "Field Book for Civil Engineers," page 31, 32 & 33.

CP is the centrifugal force of the weight P, and e is the eccentricity of the center of gravity with respect to the axis of the bridge. e equals the eccentricity of the center line of track, plus or minus $k \tan \alpha$.

Let us assume in our example, $k = 6.0$ ft., superelevation of the outer rail $= 5$ in. $= 0.417$ ft., $f_1 = 6.833$ ft., $f = 10.3$ ft., $b_1 = 7.0$ ft., $b = 17.0$ ft., and the centrifugal force as 3% per degree of curvature.

Stringers. For the stringers the eccentricity of the center line of track is assumed to be the mean of the eccentricities at

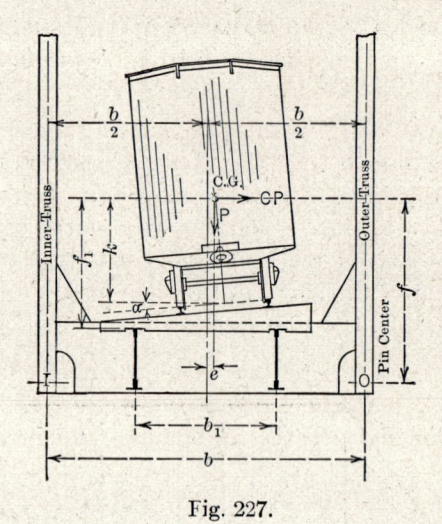

Fig. 227.

the ends of the panel and the load is applied at the top of the stringers. Taking moments about the outer stringer in Fig. 227, we get the load on the *inner stringer*,

$$V_1 = \frac{P(\tfrac{1}{2}b_1 - e) - CPf_1}{b_1}.$$

Taking moments about the inner stringer we get the load on the *outer stringer*,

$$V_1' = \frac{P(\tfrac{1}{2}b_1 + e) + CPf_1}{b_1}.$$

We see that the load on the inner stringer is a maximum when $CP = 0$, that is, when the train is standing still, and that the load on the outer stringer is a maximum when CP is a maximum, or when the train is moving at maximum speed.

The sign of e in these equations depends upon which side of the axis of the bridge the center of gravity falls. This is best determined by making a free-hand sketch in each case and putting the dimensions on it.

Taking the third panel, for example, the average eccentricity of the center line of track $=\dfrac{0.697=1.221}{2}=0.959$ ft. This is decreased by the tilting of the train due to the elevation of the outer rail, 0.5 ft., assuming 5 ft. between centers of rails. Therefore, $e=0.959-0.5=0.459$ ft.

Maximum load on inner stringer $=\dfrac{P(3.5-0.459)}{7.0}=\tfrac{1}{2}P\times 0.87,$

Maximum load on outer stringer $=\dfrac{P(3.5+0.459)+0.15P\times 6.833}{7.0}$
$=\tfrac{1}{2}P\times 1.42.$

That is, the maximum load on the inner stringer of this panel is 87%, and on the outer stringer 142% of what it would be if the track were straight.

The stresses are calculated as if the track were straight, and then they are multiplied by the coefficients obtained as above.

The maximum load on any outer stringer will occur in the panels nearest the middle of the span, and on any inner stringer will occur in the end panels. In this case the maximum load on any stringer will occur on the outer stringer of the panel next to the middle of the span, and will be 153% of what it would be for a straight track.

The stringers are usually made alike throughout the span. Sometimes they are off-set so as to have nearly the same eccentricity in all the panels. This increases the shop work and the cost per pound of the work, but may result in a saving in the total weight of the structure.

The top flanges of the stringers are subjected to transverse shear and bending. If the shear be supposed equally divided between the two stringers of a panel and if there is bracing between the top flanges as shown in Fig. 228, there will be a bending moment due to carrying the centrifugal force to the panel points, a, b, c, d, and e. There will be tension in ac and compression in bd. This action is a relief to the outer stringer flange, which will be greater if the bracing is put as shown in Fig. 229.

The shear is transmitted to the floor beam through the stringer connection, producing a horizontal shear and a moment on the rivets.

Laterals. In Fig. 227 the horizontal shear CP is resisted by one system of laterals, CP being a panel load. When the centrifugal force is large, it is advisable to make the laterals so as to act as two systems, half being taken by each. We have assumed in Fig. 227 that all of CP is taken up by the *lower* lateral system. In the reality posts will take a *small* portion to the top lateral system. The bottom laterals being below the pin center, their longitudinal components must be transmitted to the bottom chord by bending in the posts.

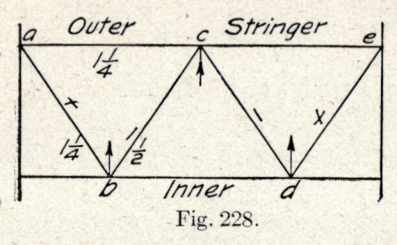

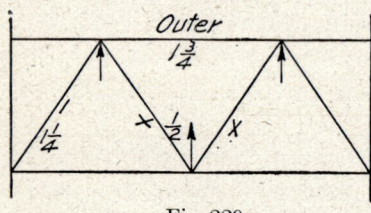

Fig. 228.

Fig. 229.

Since C is a constant for any particular bridge (unless it is on a compound curve), CP and P will be the same for each panel, if the live load is a uniform load. Otherwise the maximum shear and maximum moment at any point of the horizontal truss will occur for the same position of the load as for maximum shear and moment at that point in the vertical truss.

It is sufficiently accurate to use an equivalent uniform load in figuring the stresses in the laterals.

Floor Beams. The eccentricity of the center line of track for the floor beams is taken as the average of the eccentricites of the stringers of the two adjacent panels. The center of moments should be taken at the center line of the lower chord, as this is the assumed point of support of the floor beam.

Taking moments about 0 in Fig. 227, we have for the inside reaction,

$$V = \frac{P(\tfrac{1}{2}b - e) - CPf}{b}.$$

Taking moments about I, we have for the outside reaction,

$$V' = \frac{P(\tfrac{1}{2}b + e) + CPf}{b}.$$

Art. 176.   STRESSES DUE TO CURVED TRACK.   355

V, the reaction at the inner truss, is a maximum when the train is standing still and V' is a maximum when the train is running at maximum speed. The maximum V and V' do not occur at the same time. From these, the maximum moment and shear in the floor beam are obtained. As in the case of the stringers, the floor beams are usually all made alike.

In our example, taking the floor beam between the second and third panels, Fig. 226, we have

$$\text{Eccentricity of track} = \frac{1.221 + 2 \times 0.697 - 0.176}{4} = 0.61 \text{ ft.}$$

$e = 0.61 - 0.5 \text{(decrease due to elevation of outer rail)} = 0.11$ ft.

$$\text{Max. } V \text{ (inner truss)} = \frac{P(8.5 - 0.11)}{17} = \tfrac{1}{2} P \times .987.$$

$$\text{Max. } V' \text{ (outer truss)} = \frac{P(8.5 + 0.11) + 0.15 P \times 10.3}{17} = \tfrac{1}{2} P \times 1.195.$$

That is, the maximum reaction at the inner end of the beam is 98.7%, and at the outer end 119½% of what it would be if the track were straight.

The moment in the beam at the inner stringer is $V(\tfrac{1}{2}b - \tfrac{1}{2}b_1)$, and at the outer stringer is $V'(\tfrac{1}{2}b - \tfrac{1}{2}b_1)$. Use the larger.

Use V or V' for the live load, to find the number of rivets required in bearing on the beam web at the stringer connections, remembering that these rivets also take a horizontal shear of $\tfrac{1}{2}CP$ and a moment of $\tfrac{1}{4}CPd_s$ (d_s being the depth of the stringer) when the train is moving.

The compression in the bottom flange of the floor beam, as a member of the lateral system, tends to reduce the tension from direct load and, therefore, need not be considered.

Trusses. The panel loads for the trusses are equal to the respective floor beam reactions. These must be obtained for each panel point using P to represent the load on the track in each panel. These panel loads then may be used to get coefficients on the truss members, which may be divided by the ordinary coefficients for uniform load (130). This gives a percentage of the straight track stress for each member. The stresses may be calculated as if the track were straight, by the method of wheel loads or from equivalent uniform loads, and the stresses multiplied by their respective percentages.

356   STRESSES DUE TO CURVED TRACK.   Art. 176.

Figure 230 shows the straight track coefficients, curved track coefficients, and the percentages of the straight track stresses to use for the curved track stresses.

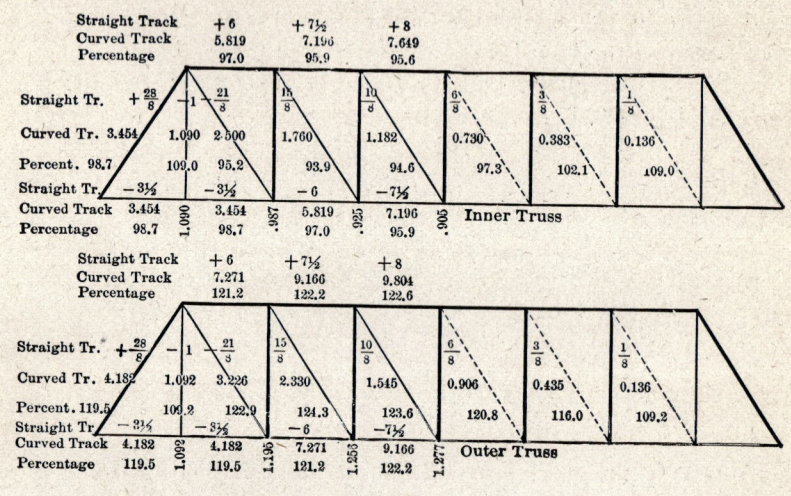

```
          Straight Track   +6      +7½     +8
          Curved Track    5.819   7.196   7.649
          Percentage      97.0    95.9    95.6

Straight Tr.  +28/8   −1    −21/3   −15/8   −10/8    6/8     3/8     1/8
Curved Tr.  3.454    1.090  2.500   1.760   1.182   0.730   0.383   0.136
Percent.    98.7   109.0   95.2    93.9    94.6    97.3   102.1   109.0
Straight Tr.        −3½    −3½     −6      −7½
Curved Track 3.454  3.454  5.819   7.196         Inner Truss
Percentage   98.7   98.7   97.0    95.9

          Straight Track   +6      +7½     +8
          Curved Track    7.271   9.166   9.804
          Percentage     121.2   122.2   122.6

Straight Tr.  +28/8   −1    −21/3   15/8    10/8    6/8     3/8     1/8
Curved Tr.  4.182   1.092  3.226   2.330   1.545   0.906   0.435   0.136
Percent.   119.5  109.2  122.9   124.3   123.6  120.8   116.0   109.2
Straight Tr.        −3½    −3½     −6      −7½
Curved Track 4.182  4.182  7.271   9.166         Outer Truss
Percentage  119.5  119.5  121.2   122.2
```

Fig. 230.

It is evident that the outer truss will have larger stresses than the inner, nevertheless, the trusses are *usually made alike*. The inner truss is made stronger than necessary. When the curve is sharp, it might be desirable, on account of economy, to move the track nearer the inner truss, thus equalizing the stresses in the trusses. This cannot be done in the bottom chord (of a through bridge) because this also belongs to the lateral system. The stresses in the top chords may be made equal. This will necessitate spreading the trusses in order to preserve the required clearance. On account of the slope of the end post in a through bridge, the clearance is calculated at some distance inside the ends of the bridge.

Moving the track nearer to the inner truss does not save material in the trusses, but it saves drafting and shop work by making the trusses alike (except the bottom chords). This is done in through bridges at the expense of extra material in the floor beams and lateral systems, and if the substructure is to be new, at considerable extra expense in it, because of the increased width.

Art. 176.   STRESSES DUE TO CURVED TRACK.   357

It will be noted that the wind may have the same or opposite effect, to that of the centrigufal force, in the lower chord, and that the *maximum compression* in the lower chord *due to centrifugal force*, does *not* occur when there is a maximum tension in this chord from vertical load.

358   QUESTIONS AND PROBLEMS. CHAPTER XIV.

1. If a tension chord stress due to vertical loads is 240,000 lbs., and the wind stress in the same chord member is 72,000 lbs., what unit stress must be used in determining the cross section according to the Specifications for Steel Railroad Bridges of the Am. Ry. Engineering Assoc. (4th Edition, see Secs. 15 and 25).

2. The bridge shown in Fig. 204 has a span of 120 ft., height 25 ft., distance cent. to cent. of trusses, 16 ft. The end post stresses are, Dead Load = 94,000 lbs., Live Load = 196,000 lbs. $k_1 = 14$ inches. $k_2 = 15$ inches. The end posts are alike. $l = 8$ ft. Wind Load = 150 lbs. per lin. ft. of top chord. Are the end posts fixed at either end? Find the stresses in the portal bracing if it is of the type shown in Fig. 217.

Find the maximum stress per sq. in. in the End Posts if $I = 1,790$, and the maximum width of the member is 21 inches.

3. Find the percentages of the load which will go to the stringers of the second panel of Fig. 226.

4. Find the percentages of load which will go to the hip verticals of Fig. 226.

5. Show why the maximum bottom chord stresses of the two trusses of a through bridge on a curve will not be equal, when the track is so placed that the maximum stresses in the top chords are equal.

INDEX.

	Art.	Page
Algebraic and Graphic Methods Compared	43	50
Method for Stresses	50	67
Solution of Stresses in a Truss	58	77
Angle θ How Measured	50	70
Any Number of Forces in Equilibrium	34	40
Application of the Equations of Equilibrium	40	45
Of the Laws of Equilibrium to the Structure as a Whole.... Chap. IV		55
Of the Laws of Equilibrium to a Part of a Structure, Chap. V		67
Of Loads	5	3
Arches	124	230
Reactions for Three-hinged	46	60
Arch Roof Trusses	118	209
Assumptions in Stresses in Girders	79	119
In the Theory of Flexure	68	94
Axes of Symmetry	73	105
Principal	73	105
Baltimore Truss	123	224
Stresses in	136	260
" "	154	305
Beam Continuous for Three Spans, Maximum Live Load Moment	107	170
Continuous for Three Spans, Maximum Live Load Shear	105	169
Continuous for Two Spans, Maximum Live Load Moment	106	169
Continuous for Two Spans, Maximum Live Load Shear	104	167
Defined	2	1
Deflection due to Shear	87	135
Deflection for Uniform Load	83	130
Deflection of a Cantilever	82	129
Deflection for any Number of Loads	85	132
Deflection for Concentrated Load	84	131
Deflection of, with Variable Cross-section	86	134
Moments and Shears	93	155
Moment in	57	77
Of Any Cross-section, Moment of Resistance	70	96
Of Rectangular Section, Bending Stresses	69	96
Principal Stresses in	76	112
" "	77	116
Point of Maximum Moment in	74	108

INDEX.

	Art.	Page
Beam, Relation between Moment and Shear in.	74	107
Shear in.	57	76
Stayed against Transverse Buckling.	68	95
" " "	70	98
Beams and Girders, Deflection of............Chap. VII		127
Loaded and Supported in Different Ways......Chap. VIII		144
Stresses in........................Chap. VI		91
Beams, Bending Stresses in.	68	92
Classification.	66	91
Combinations of Concentrated and Uniform Loads.	94	156
Continuous, General Equations.	97	160
" Moments and Shears.	96	158
" Practical Uses.	98	163
Live and Dead Loads on.	103	167
Live Loads on.	99	164
" "	100	164
" "	101	165
Moments and Shears in Cantilever.	92	154
Resilience of.	88	137
Shearing Stresses in.	75	108
Stresses in.	57	76
"	67	92
Stresses beyond the Elastic Limit.	80	121
Table of.	90	145
With Fixed Ends, Moments and Shears.	95	157
Bending and Buckling Combined.	115	197
Bending Moment and Shear, Relation between in a Beam.	74	107
Bending Moment in a Beam.	57	76
Bending Stress.	12	10
For a Beam of Rectangular Cross-section.	69	96
In Solid Beams, Theory of Flexure.	68	92
Blocks and Columns, Stresses in.............Chap. IX		175
Blocks, Eccentric Loads on.	109	175
Stresses in.	108	175
Bollman Truss.	122	219
Bow's Notation.	53	72
Bowstring Truss.	122	220
Box-girder Defined.	2	2
Bridge Construction.	120	214
Bridge Pier, Stresses in.	109	178
Bridges, Dead Loads.	125	233
Bridge Stresses from Uniform Loads..........Chap. XII		233
Bridge Trusses, Modern.	123	222
Bridge Trusses.........................Chap. XI		214
" " Now Out of Date.	122	218
" " Special.	124	227
Buckling and Bending, Combined.	115	197
Buckling of Compression Flange of a Beam.	68	95

INDEX.

	ART.	PAGE
Buckling of Compression Flange of a Beam	70	98
Buckling Stresses	12	10
" " in a Girder	79	118
Calculation of Moments and Shears from Wheel Loads	155	306
Camel Back Truss	123	224
Graphical Solution	137	276
Stresses in	137	268
Cantilever Beam, Deflection of	82	129
Moments and Shears in	92	154
Cantilever Bridges	124	228
Cantilever Roof Truss	118	209
Cantilever Truss, Stresses in	55	74
Center of Gravity	71	99
Center of Moments	30	36
Centrifugal Force	176	350
Chord Members Defined	120	215
Chord Stresses, Maximum Live Load	128	239
Circle, Moment of Inertia of	72	102
Circular Cross-section, Shearing Stresses	75	112
Classification of Beams	66	91
Of Trusses	121	217
Closing Line	37	43
Coefficients for a Baltimore Truss	136	260
For a Deck Pratt Truss	130	250
For a Double Intersection Warren Truss	135	257
For a Half Hip Truss	133	255
For a Pratt Truss	130	246
For a Simple Warren Truss	131	251
For a Sub-divided Warren Truss	132	253
For a Whipple Truss	134	256
Columns and Blocks, Stresses in	Chap. IX	175
Columns in Buildings, Eccentrically Loaded	114	193
Concentrically Loaded	111	182
Deflection of	110	179
Eccentrically Loaded	110	179
Effect of Variations of Length on Strength	112	186
End Conditions	112	184
Ends Fixed by Direct Stress	112	188
Column Formulas	113	189
Compared	113	191
Euler's	112	186
Rankine's	113	190
Straight Line	113	191
Columns in Towers	114	193
Combinations of Buckling and Bending	115	197
Of Uniform Dead and Live Load on a Beam	103	167
Comparison of Graphic and Algebraic Methods	43	50

INDEX.

	Art.	Page
Comparison of Live Load Stresses by Various Methods	153	304
Components of a Force	30	37
Compression Defined	7	5
And Bending Combined	115	197
Flanges Stayed	68	95
Compressive Stresses	12	10
Concentrated Load	4	3
Concentrated Loads on Blocks	108	175
Concentrated Moving Loads on Beams	100	164
" " "	101	165
Concurrent Forces	30	36
Continuous Beam of Three Spans, Maximum Live Load Moment	105	169
Of Three Spans, Maximum Live Load Shear	105	169
Of Two Spans, Maximum Live Load Moment	106	169
Of Two Spans, Maximum Live Load Shear	104	167
Practical Uses	98	163
Continuous Beams, General Equations	97	160
Moments and Shears	96	158
Continuous Moving Live Load on a Beam	102	166
Contra-flexure Points	89	140
Cooper's Loadings	141	285
Counter Brace Defined	120	216
Counters, Initial Stresses in	120	216
Counter Tie Defined	120	215
Couple	30	36
Crane, Stresses in	51	70
Cremona Diagrams	50	68
Criteria for Maximum Stresses Applied Graphically	157	312
Criterion for Maximum Moment	100	164
" " "	101	165
" " "	144	289
" " "	145	291
Criterion for Maximum Stress in Hip Vertical	152	296
For Maximum Web Stresses	147	293
" "	148	294
Cullmann's Method, Graphical Solution by Sections	60	80
Curved Chord Bridges	123	224
" "	137	268
" "	138	227
Curved Track Bridges	176	350
Dead Load	4	3
Distribution of	130	294
For Bridges	125	233
Variation of from Estimate	125	234
Deck Bridge	121	218
Lateral Systems	162	318
Deck Plate Girder, Maximum Moment	145	291

INDEX. 363

	Art.	Page
Deck Plate Girder, Lateral Systems	160	317
Deck Pratt Truss Stresses	130	250
Deflection Due to Compression and Bending	115	200
Of a Beam Due to Shear	87	135
" Due to a Concentrated Load	84	131
" Due to Any Number of Loads	85	132
" Due to Uniform Load	83	130
" Having Variable Cross-section	86	134
Of a Cantilever Beam	82	129
Of a Girder with Flange Plates	86	134
Of an Eccentrically Loaded Column	110	179
Of Beams and Girders .... Chap. VII		127
Of Beams, Table of	90	145
Deformation	9	6
Deformations beyond the Elastic Limit ...... Chap. II		22
Hardening Effect of Non-elastic	27	30
Non-elastic	20	22
Of Reinforced Concrete	11	8
Transverse	9	6
Within the Elastic Limit .... Chap. I		1
Derrick, Stresses in	62	84
Distributed Load	4	3
Distribution of Stress	13	10
Double Intersection Truss	122	222
" " "	123	226
" " Warren Truss Stresses	135	257
Ductility and Plasticity	22	23
Early Bridge Trusses	122	218
Eccentric Loads on Blocks	109	175
On Columns	110	179
Effective Depth of Girder	79	120
Elasticity and Stress	7	4
Modulus of	11	6
Elastic Limits	8	5
Natural	26	29
Shifting of	26	28
Elastic Line, Equation of	81	127
End Condition of Columns	112	184
Equilibrant	30	36
Equilibrium Described	29	35
Laws of	39	44
Laws of Applied to a Part of a Structure .... Chap. V		67
Laws of Applied to Structure as a Whole .... Chap. IV		55
Methods of Application of the Laws of	40	45
Of Any Number of Forces	34	40
Of Four Forces	33	39

INDEX.

	Art.	Page
Equilibrium of Two Forces	31	37
Of Three Forces	32	38
The Laws of...........................Chap. III		35
Which Equations to Use	41	47
Equivalent Loadings for Railway Bridges	142	286
" " "	156	311
Equivalent Static Stress	5	4
Equivalent Uniform Live Load	126	234
Estimates of Dead Load	125	233
Euler's Formula	112	186
External Forces	3	2
Factor of Safety	24	26
Fatigue	25	28
Of Iron and Steel	28	30
Fields of Shear in a Pratt Truss	153	298
In a Truss	150	295
Fink Roof Truss Stresses	56	75
Fink Truss	118	207
"	122	219
Fixed End Beams, Moments and Shears	95	157
Columns	112	184
Flange Defined	2	2
Of Girder	79	120
Stayed against Buckling	68	95
Flat End Columns	112	184
Flaws or Cracks, Effect on Strength of Beams	89	140
Flexure, Assumptions of the Theory of	68	94
Of Column	110	179
Theory of	68	92
Theory Applicable to what Materials	68	94
Floor Beam, Maximum Stresses	152	296
Stresses Due to Curved Track	176	354
Force Polygon	35	41
Triangle	32	38
Forces Acting on Structures	3	2
Components of	30	37
Concurrent	30	36
Co-planar	30	35
In Equilibrium:		
Two	31	37
Three	32	38
Four	33	39
Any Number	34	40
Line of Action of	30	35
Non-concurrent	32	38
"	34	39
Parallel or Nearly Parallel	37	42

	Art.	Page
Forces, Properties and Relations of	30	35
Forth Bridge	124	228
Girder Defined	2	1
Deflection of	Chap. VII	127
Forms of	70	97
Lateral Systems	160	317
" "	161	318
Position of Load for Maximum Moment	100	164
" " " "	101	165
" " " "	144	289
" " " "	145	291
" " " Shear	102	166
" " " "	151	295
Stresses in	Chap. VI	91
"	79	118
With Flange Plates, Deflection of	86	134
Girders and Beams Loaded and Supported in Different Ways	Chap. VIII	144
Graphic and Algebraic Methods Compared	43	50
Graphical Application of the Criteria	157	312
Solution, Method of Sections by Moments	61	82
Determination of Reactions	46	56
Methods, Rules to be Observed	44	51
Method of Sections for Uniform Load	64	87
Method, Stresses in a Camel Back Truss	137	275
Graphic Statics, Method of Lettering	53	72
Stresses by Sections, Culmann's Method	60	80
Gravity Axis	71	99
Half Deck Bridge	121	218
Half Hip Truss	123	225
Stresses in	133	255
Hardening Effects of Non-elastic Deformation	27	30
Hardness, Causes of in Iron and Steel	25	28
High Truss	121	218
Highway Bridge Dead Loads	125	234
Highway Bridge Live Loads	126	234
Hinge Defined	46	59
Hip Vertical Maximum Stresses	152	296
Hooke's Law	8	5
Horizontal Forces, Stresses in Bridges from	Chap. XIV	316
Horizontal Shearing Stresses	75	108
Howe Truss		89
"	118	207
"	123	222
How Shearing Stresses Occur	17	14

	Art.	Page
I Cross-section, Bearing Stresses	75	112
Impact	5	3
Effect of	88	139
Indeterminate Cases, Statically	42	49
Inertia, Moment of	72	101
Initial Stresses	13	11
In Counters	120	216
Intermediate Sway Bracing	162	319
Internal Forces	3	3
Kinds of Loads	4	3
Of Stress	12	9
Of Structures	2	1
"K" Type of Web Bracing	124	228
Lateral Stresses Due to Curved Track	176	354
Lateral Systems	159	317
For Deck Bridges	162	318
For Deck Plate Girder	160	317
For Pony Truss	161	318
For Through Bridge	163	321
For Through Plate Girder	161	318
Lattice Girder	123	226
Portal	172	345
Portal for Shallow Trusses	173	347
Launhardt Formula	28	32
Law of Lever	46	56
Laws of Equilibrium and their Application......Chap. III		35
Lenticular Truss	122	221
Lever Arm	30	36
Limits of Span for which a Series of Wheels Gives a Maximum Moment	146	292
Lines of Principal Stress	77	116
Live Load	4	3
"	126	234
Continuous on a Beam	102	166
Maximum Stresses in Chords	128	239
Maximum Stresses in Web Members	129	241
On Beams	99	164
"	100	164
"	101	165
Load, Dead	4	3
Loaded Chord	125	234
Loading Strip or Diagram	143	288
Loading for Railway Bridges	141	285
Loads, Concentrated	4	3
Distributed	4	3
Kinds of	4	3

INDEX. 367

	ART.	PAGE
Loads, Live	4	3
Manner of Application	5	3
Loads on Beams, Combinations of Dead and Live	103	167
On Blocks	108	175
On Roof Trusses	119	209
Low Truss	121	218
Main Tie	120	215
Manner of Application of Loads	5	3
Masonry, Tensile Stresses in	109	177
Materials of Construction	6	4
Maxwell Diagrams	50	68
Modern Bridge Trusses	123	222
Modulus of Elasticity	11	6
Of Rupture, in Cross Breaking	80	122
Shear	18	15
Moment	30	36
Moment and Shear Calculations from Wheel Loads	155	306
Diagrams	91	154
Relation between in a Beam	74	107
Moment Areas	65	88
Diagrams	63	87
" Table of for Beams	90	145
Due to Moving Live Loads on Beams	100	164
" " "	101	165
In a Beam, Point of Maximum	74	108
Maximum in a Continuous Beam of Two Spans	106	169
" " " Three Spans	107	170
Moment in Inertia	70	97
" "	72	101
Of Resistance, Beam of any Cross-section	70	96
" Beam of Rectangular Cross-section	69	96
" In a Beam	57	76
" Of Web of Girder	79	120
Position of Load for Maximum	100	164
" " "	101	165
" " "	128	239
" " "	144	289
" " "	145	291
Tables for Wheel Load Calculations	155	307
Moments and Shears in Cantilever Beams	92	154
Moments and Shears for a Simple Beam	93	155
For Beams Having Fixed Ends	95	157
For Continuous Beams	96	158
Moments, Center of	30	36
In Beams, Table of	90	145
Moving Uniform Load on a Beam	102	166
Multiple Intersection Trusses	123	227

368   INDEX.

	Art.	Page
Natural Elastic Limit	26	29
Neutral Axis	68	93
"	71	99
Non-elastic Deformation, Hardening Effects of	27	30
Properties of Iron and Steel	25	28
Stress and Deformation	20	22
Normal Stresses	14	12
Notation	Front.	
Oblique Loading	73	103
Panel Length	120	215
Loads	125	234
"	127	236
Panels Defined	120	215
Parallel Forces	37	42
Pettit Truss	123	224
Pettit Truss Stresses	138	277
Pier, Stresses in	109	178
Pivot End Columns	112	185
Plasticity	22	23
Plate Girder Defined	2	2
Lateral System, Deck	160	317
" " Through	161	318
Portal	170	342
Portal for Shallow Trusses	175	350
Portal Knee Braced	174	348
Poisson's Ratio	9	6
"	78	118
Pole	37	43
Pony Truss	121	218
Lateral Systems	161	318
Portal Bracing	164	322
Knee Braced	172	345
Latticed	171	344
" for Shallow Trusses	175	350
Plate Girder	170	342
" for Shallow Trusses	174	348
" with Knee Braces	174	347
Posts Fixed at Both Ends	165	324
Posts Fixed at Top, Partially Fixed at Bottom	166	329
Posts Partially Fixed at Both Ends	167	332
Simple X Bracing	169	335
Stresses in	168	334
Position of Load for Maximum Moment	100	164
" " " "	101	165
" " " "	128	239
" " " "	144	289

	Art.	Page
Position of Load for Maximum Moment	145	291
" " Web Stress	147	293
" " Stress Found Graphically	157	312
Post Truss	122	221
Pratt Truss	118	208
"	123	223
" Maximum Shear from Wheel Loads	149	294
" Stresses by Coefficients	130	246
Stresses from Wheel Loads	153	297
Principal Stresses	12	9
In a Beam	76	112
"	77	116
Problems and Questions on:		
Beams and Girders Loaded and Supported in Various Ways		172
Bridge Trusses		232
Columns and Blocks		204
Deflections of Beams and Girders		142
Laws of Equilibrium and Their Application		52
Reactions		65
Roof Trusses		213
Simple Stresses		89
Stresses and Deformations beyond the Elastic Limit		33
Stresses and Deformations within the Elastic Limit		18
Stresses from Horizontal Forces		358
Stresses from Wheel Loads		315
Stresses in Beams and Girders		123
Stresses in Simple Bridge Trusses from Uniform Load		284
Purlins Defined	116	206
Stresses	73	106
Quebec Bridge	124	228
Radius of Gyration	109	178
Rafters Defined	116	206
Railway Bridges, Dead Loads	125	233
Equivalent Loadings	142	286
" "	156	311
Having Curved Track	176	350
Live Loads	126	234
Loading	141	285
Stresses Due to Wheel Loads . . . . .Chap. XIII		285
Rankine's Formula	113	190
Reactions . . . . .Chap. IV		55
By String Polygon	47	61
For Any Number of Loads	47	60
For a Single Force	46	55
For a Three-hinged Arch	46	60
For Uniform Loads	48	63

INDEX.

	Art.	Page
Reactions, Reinforced Concrete Deformations	11	8
Resilience	19	16
Of Beams	88	137
Resultant	30	36
Location of	36	42
Of Bending and Shearing Stresses in a Beam, Principal Stresses	76	112
Polygon	28	44
Roof Construction	116	206
Purlin, Stresses in	73	106
Trusses	Chap. X	206
Roof Trusses, Loads on	119	209
On Columns	119	210
Types	118	207
Wind Load Stresses	54	73
Rupture Modulus	80	122
Saw-tooth Roof	118	209
Scissors Truss	118	208
Section Modulus	70	98
Shear and Bending Moment, Relation in a Beam	74	107
Shear and Moment Calculations from Wheel Loads	155	306
Diagrams	91	154
Shear, Deflection of a Beam Due to	87	135
Diagrams for Beams, Table of	90	145
Fields of in a Truss	150	295
Modulus	18	15
In a Beam	57	76
In a Continuous Beam of Two Spans	104	167
" " " Three Spans	105	169
In a Girder or Beam	102	166
" "	151	295
In a Pratt Truss from Wheel Loads	149	294
Shearing Stresses	12	9
"	15	12
"	17	14
In Solid Beams	75	108
Shears	16	13
Shears and Moments for a Simple Beam	93	155
Beams Having Fixed Ends	95	157
Cantilever Beams	92	154
Continuous Beams	96	158
Shears, Maximum Live Load in a Truss	129	242
Short Beams	76	113
"	87	137
Simple Beam Defined	2	1
Skew Bridges	139	281
Special Types of Bridge Trusses	124	227
Statically Indeterminate Cases	42	49

INDEX. 371

	Art.	Page
Statical Moment	70	97
Statics Defined	1	1
Steel, Properties in the Non-elastic State	25	28
Straight Line Formula	113	191
Strain, see Deformation	9	6
Strength of Materials Defined	1	1
Stress Calculation from Wheel Loads	143	287
Stress Defined	7	5
Stress Deformation Diagrams	21	22
Stress Diagrams	50	67
For Roof Trusses	119	211
Stress, Equivalent Static	5	4
Stresses	Chap. V	67
Stresses and Deformations beyond the Elastic Limit	Chap. II	22
Stresses and Deformations within the Elastic Limit	Chap. I	1
Stresses, Bending	12	10
Beyond the Elastic Limit in Beams	80	121
Buckling	12	10
Compression	12	10
In a Baltimore Truss	136	260
" "	154	305
Camel Back Truss	137	268
Cantilever Truss	55	74
Compound Fink Roof Truss	56	75
Crane	51	70
Derrick	62	84
Double Intersection Warren Truss	135	257
Half Hip Truss	133	255
Pettit Truss	138	277
Pratt Truss by Coefficients	130	246
Pratt Truss from Wheel Loads	153	297
Roof Truss for Wind Load	54	73
Simple Warren Truss	131	251
Sub-divided Warren Truss	132	253
Unsymmetrical Truss	52	71
Whipple Truss	134	256
Stresses in Beams and Girders	Chap. VI	91
Stresses in Beams, Resultant of Shearing and Bending	76	112
Stresses in Blocks and Columns	Chap. IX	175
In Bridges from Horizontal Forces	Chap. XIV	316
In Girders	79	118
Stresses, Initial	13	11
In Portal Bracing	164	322
" "	168	334
In Railway Bridges from Wheel Loads	Chap. XIII	285
" " Having Curved Track	176	350
In Roof Trusses	119	209
In Simple Bridge Trusses from Uniform Loads	Chap. XII	233

INDEX.

	ART.	PAGE
Stresses in Simplest Form of Truss	50	67
In Simple Trusses	127	235
In Solid Beams	57	76
" "	67	92
In Trusses, Algebraic Solution	58	77
In Trusses with Sub-panels from Wheel Loads	154	305
Maximum in Web Members from Wheel Loads	147	293
" " " "	148	294
Maximum Live Load in Chords	128	239
Maximum Live Load in Web Members	129	241
Normal	14	12
Principal	12	9
Shearing	12	9
"	15	12
"	17	14
Shearing in a Beam	75	108
Tensile	12	10
Tensile and Compressive	14	12
Torsional	12	10
Unit	10	6
Working	10	6
Stress Intensities	12	9
Kinds of	12	9
"	140	285
Non-elastic	20	22
Working, for Cases of Compound Stress	78	117
Stringer Stresses Due to Curved Track	176	352
String Polygon	37	42
As a Moment Diagram	63	87
For Reactions	47	61
Properties of	38	43
Sub-divided Warren Truss Stresses	132	253
Sub-trussing	136	260
"	154	305
Suspension Bridges	124	231
Sway Bracing	162	319
Swing Bridges	124	229
Table of Beams	Chap. VIII	144
Tensile and Compressive Stresses	14	12
Tensile Stresses	12	10
Tension Defined	7	5
Theorem of Three Moments	97	161
Theory of Flexure	64	86
Through Bridge	121	218
Lateral Systems	163	321
Through Plate Girder Lateral Systems	161	318
Tie Defined	120	215

INDEX.

	Art.	Page
Torsional Stress	12	10
Towers, Columns in	114	193
Town Lattice Truss	123	227
Transverse Deformation	9	6
Truss, Baltimore	123	224
Bollman	122	219
Bowstring	122	220
Camel Back	123	223
Defined	2	2
Double Intersection	122	222
" "	123	226
Elements	117	206
Trusses Classified	121	217
Modern Bridge	123	222
Special Types	124	227
Stresses in Simple	127	235
Swing Bridge	124	229
Truss, Fink	118	207
"	122	219
Half Hip	123	225
High	121	218
Howe	118	207
"	123	222
Lenticular	122	221
Low	121	218
Pettit	123	224
Pony	121	218
Post	122	221
Pratt	118	208
"	123	223
Scissors	118	208
Stresses in a Baltimore	136	260
" "	154	305
Camel Back	137	268
Double Intersection Warren	135	257
Half Hip	133	255
Pettit	138	277
Pratt	130	246
Simple Warren	131	251
Sub-divided Warren	132	253
Whipple	134	256
Warren	123	225
Whipple	122	221
Types of Roof Trusses	118	207
Ultimate Strength	21	23
" "	23	24
In Bending and Tension Compared	80	121

INDEX.

	ART.	PAGE
Ultimate Strength of Columns	111	183
Uniform Load, Reactions for	48	63
Stresses in Bridges from	Chap. XII	233
Unit Stresses	10	6
For Cases of Compound Stress	78	117
Unloaded Chord	125	234
Unsymmetrical Truss	52	71
Vibratory Stresses	5	4
Warren Truss	123	225
Stresses in	131	251
"	132	253
Web Members	120	215
Web, Moment of Resistance of	79	120
Web Stresses, Maximum from Wheel Loads	147	293
" " "	148	294
Maximum Live Load	129	241
Wheel Load Calculations	155	306
Position for Maximum Shear	151	295
Shear in a Pratt Truss	149	294
Stress Calculations	143	287
Stresses in a Pratt Truss	153	297
Stresses in Floor Beam and Hip Vertical	152	296
Stresses in Railway Bridges	Chap. XIII	285
Stresses in Web Members	147	293
" " "	148	294
Whipple, Squire	122	219
Whipple Truss	122	221
Stresses in	134	256
Wind Loads	158	316
Work Done in Deforming a Body, Resilience	19	16
Working Stresses	10	6
" "	24	27
For Cases of Compound Stresses	78	117
Young's Modulus	10	7

Size of section concrete — 8" diam
            steel section — 1" diam

—40°F
.0000067 CS
.0000055 CC

30,000,000
2,000,000

PORTAL BRACING 10/8/20

When $x > a$ $\quad EI\dfrac{d^2y}{dx^2} = -M_x = xH - M_2$

Mom Crib.

$\dfrac{G}{L} > \dfrac{G_1+G_2}{a}$

$< \dfrac{G_1+G_2+P}{a}$

$Wa + Wx + \dfrac{Wx^2}{2}$

Shear Crib.

→ vertil $G > NG_2$

$< N(G_2+P)$

$G_1 + P > G_2$ Hip Vert.
$G_1 < G_2 + P$

375
141
―――
375
1500
375
―――
52875

Bridges Began P 285